Contemporary Slavery

UBC Press gratefully acknowledges the financial support for their publishing program of the Government of Canada (through the Canada Book Fund), the Canada Council for the Arts, and the British Columbia Arts Council.

Originally published in Canada in 2017 by UBC Press, Vancouver, BC

First published in the United States of America in 2018 by Cornell University Press

Printed in the United States of America

Library of Congress Cataloging-in-Publication Data

Names: Bunting, Annie, 1964– editor. | Quirk, Joel, editor. | Container of (work): Allain, Jean, 1965– Contemporary slavery and its definition in law.

Title: Contemporary slavery : the rhetoric of global human rights campaigns / edited by Annie Bunting and Joel Quirk.

Description: Ithaca : Cornell University Press, 2018. | "Originally published in Canada in 2017 by UBC Press, Vancouver, BC"—Title page verso. | Includes bibliographical references and index.

Identifiers: LCCN 2017054633 (print) | LCCN 2017057131 (ebook) | ISBN 9781501718779 (epub/mobi) | ISBN 9781501718786 (pdf) | ISBN 9781501718762 | ISBN 9781501718762 (pbk. : alk. paper)

Subjects: LCSH: Slavery. | Human trafficking. | Human rights.

Classification: LCC HT867 (ebook) | LCC HT867 .C57 2018 (print) | DDC 306.3/62–dc23

LC record available at https://lccn.loc.gov/2017054633

Cornell University Press strives to use environmentally responsible suppliers and materials to the fullest extent possible in the publishing of its books. Such materials include vegetable-based, low-VOC inks and acid-free papers that are recycled, totally chlorine-free, or partly composed of nonwood fibers. For further information, visit our website at cornellpress.cornell.edu.

Contemporary Slavery

The Rhetoric of Global Human Rights Campaigns

EDITED BY ANNIE BUNTING
AND JOEL QUIRK

Cornell University Press
Ithaca and London

FOR PAUL LOVEJOY

Contents

Foreword / x

Acknowledgments / xiv

PART 1
The Cause of Contemporary Slavery

1 Contemporary Slavery as More Than Rhetorical Strategy?
   The Politics and Ideology of a New Political Cause / 5
   Annie Bunting and Joel Quirk

2 Contemporary Slavery and Its Definition in Law / 36
   Jean Allain

3 When Human Trafficking Means Everything and Nothing / 67
   Joel Quirk

4 Asylum Courts and the "Forced Marriage Paradox": Gender-Based Harm
   and Contemporary Slavery in Forced Conjugal Associations / 97
   Benjamin N. Lawrance

PART 2
Rhetoric

5 Narrating Wartime Enslavement, Forced Marriage,
   and Modern Slavery / 129
   Annie Bunting

6 Show and Tell: Contemporary Anti-Slavery Advocacy as Symbolic
   Work / 158
   Fuyuki Kurasawa

7 Methodological Debates in Human Rights Research: A Case Study
   of Human Trafficking in South Africa / 180
   Darshan Vigneswaran

8 Reparative Justice and the Post-Conflict Phase of Modern Slavery / 202
   Roy L. Brooks

PART 3
Practice

9 Modern Slavery from a Management Perspective: The Role of Industry
   Context and Organizational Capabilities / 229
   Andrew Crane

10 State Enslavement in North Korea / 255
   Rhoda E. Howard-Hassmann

11 Letting Go: How Elites Manage Challenges to Contemporary
   Slavery / 279
   Austin Choi-Fitzpatrick

12 Child Domestic Labour: Work Like Any Other, Work Like
   No Other / 301
   Jonathan Blagbrough

   Appendix: *Bellagio-Harvard Guidelines on the Legal Parameters
   of Slavery* / 329

   Selected Bibliography / 339

List of Contributors / 355

Index / 359

Foreword

By Gulnara Shahinian

Starting any new mandate is very challenging. This is especially true when the mandate comes with the very expansive title of United Nations Special Rapporteur on "contemporary forms of slavery, including its causes and consequences." As this book helps to demonstrate, the concept of contemporary slavery has frequently been used interchangeably with human trafficking. When we look closer, however, some important political and analytical differences begin to emerge. Ending human trafficking is a cause that has been embraced by states across the globe, with governments enthusiastically presenting all kinds of new laws, systems, and programs. This can be contrasted with slavery, which remains a taboo subject in many quarters. Governments may name-drop slavery to highlight how they feel about trafficking, but they are less comfortable with slavery as an independent category.

As Special Rapporteur, I routinely heard from government officials who maintained that the term "slavery" could not be legitimately applied to any number of contemporary issues. As far as slavery was concerned, they were only prepared to talk cautiously in terms of "vestiges" or "psychological remnants" associated with poverty and "negative traditions." Even the most limited affiliation with slavery evoked negative memories or images, which were frequently associated with colonialism. Ratification of the 1926 Slavery Convention was frequently equated with the end of slavery in its entirety. This widespread reluctance to talk about slavery as a specific category was reflected in the fact that it frequently proved very difficult to obtain an official invitation for a country visit, as governments considered an official invitation to be tantamount to a tacit acknowledgement of the existence of slavery. The same reluctance was on display during sessions of the United Nations Human Rights Council, where member states were comfortable asking questions related to trafficking in human beings, yet had remarkably little to say in relation to slavery.

Special Rapporteurs lack the power to directly compel action. They can only persuade via constructive dialogue and reasoned argument. Addressing the political sensitivities surrounding slavery therefore required careful diplomacy regarding the dimensions and applications of the term "slavery" on the basis of the 1926 Slavery Convention. It also meant documenting concrete cases that had been examined during country missions and demonstrating their correspondence to the legal criteria of the Convention. I often asked myself about the best ways of breaking through decades of silence that had relegated slavery to a relic from an earlier stage in history. Another related yet equally important exercise involved working through how political and economic structures could be changed in order to transform the power exercised by some over others, and to ensure that states who too often close their eyes in relation to structural problems such as child labour, child marriage, caste discrimination, and bonded labour can be convinced to take responsibility for the protection of their own citizens. The developmental mantra of "fighting poverty" as a catch-all cure has proved to be insufficient here, since it has become apparent that our actions need to be specifically targeted against larger patterns of exploitation and abuse.

It was therefore with the great excitement that I came across this collection. Many of the thoughts and challenges that I had while acting as Special Rapporteur have been carefully considered in the pages that follow. The chapters direct our attention to the problems associated with classification and representation, both legally and politically, and propose original and important alternatives from which to approach the underlying issues involved. They also provide new evidence from which to assess the inner workings of key institutions, such as immigration systems, courts, and prisons. In addition, they further help us to understand why specific practices take place; how they are experienced and justified; and what types of remedies, strategies, and interventions needs to be contemplated in order to chart alternative paths forward.

Of particular value here is the repeated emphasis on the relationship between slavery and personal and political authority. Slavery is perhaps the most political of all development issues, since it is frequently rooted in complex discriminatory practices that prevent millions of people from exercising their basic human rights, including even the right to identity, irrespective of universal birth registration. Many states fail to recognize or support millions of invisible people who work behind closed doors and in private properties. Some of these workers have never had identity documents, nor are they represented in the formal economy or included in any state programs.

Discriminatory practices and prejudice against certain groups of people on the basis of race, caste, gender, religion, specific traditional beliefs, and ethnicity exclude these vulnerable groups from development projects and from exercising to their rights, resulting in a condition of powerlessness and vulnerability. Our most important task is therefore to transform existing patterns of personal and political authority by helping vulnerable and marginalized peoples to effectively articulate and defend their own interests and agendas. There are still many things that we need to understand in more depth, but it is already evident at this point in time that our key goal must be to enable women, men, and children to exercise the freedom to choose their lives and future.

Our ideals and aspirations are currently being tested on many fronts. One of the most significant challenges stems from our accelerating global refugee and migration crisis. This crisis has multiplied already existing vulnerabilities, which have in turn been very publicly exposed via now all-too-common reports of death and deprivation involving migrants seeking sanctuary. It is here that this volume makes one of a number of important contributions by providing new strategies for rethinking questions of asylum, protection, vulnerability, and human security. Changing the terms upon which governments determine who

– and who is not – worthy of recognition and protection is central to any lasting remedy to vulnerability, abuse, and exploitation.

This volume is vital for a further reason. For many decades now, governments and international organizations have invested in a series of legal and institutional responses to slavery and related practices. It has become increasing evident that these ongoing investments have not been sufficient to overcome very significant obstacles to progress. It is here that this volume provides a number of additional resources and strategies from which to rethink the strengths and weaknesses of conventional models. Instead of upholding the status quo, we need to be thinking in terms of alternative approaches, which is once again where this volume makes a major contribution.

– Gulnara Shahinian
First United Nations Special Rapporteur on contemporary forms
of slavery, including its causes and consequences

Acknowledgments

This project is a product of academic matchmaking. The editors entered into a conversation – which later became a collaboration – thanks to an introduction from Paul Lovejoy, who saw the value in bringing together a lawyer who works on gender and rights and a political scientist who works on slavery and abolition. In the years that have followed, there have been many further conversations and a number of additional collaborations. Paul has remained a key inspiration and influence throughout, and it is for this reason – among many others – that we have dedicated this book to him.

This specific book started with a conversation about reinventing the wheel (there was also a metaphorical telescope involved, but this part of the conversation does not make as much sense with the benefit of hindsight). This conversation emerged from two observations. The first observation was that recent discussions regarding contemporary slavery and human trafficking – both academic and popular – often end up saying similar things in similar ways. The second observation was that many of the arguments and observations that are featured within these discussions have already been debated at length in other contexts. For decades now, scholars and activists have engaged in sustained and sometimes sophisticated deliberations regarding core themes such as migration and asylum; narrative and representation;

duties beyond borders; humanitarianism and human rights; poverty and protection; impunity; violence and complicity; reconciliation and rehabilitation; and sexism, racism, and discrimination. All of these now well-established bodies of research and experience have been notably absent from many recent discussions of slavery and trafficking, contributing to a situation where too many people have tried to reinvent the wheel unnecessarily.

This book tries to do things differently. From the outset, our primary goal has been to bring together experts from a variety of disciplines and perspectives and to have them apply insights and ideas from more established literatures towards a better understanding of the theory and practice of slavery and human trafficking. It was on this basis that we were able to secure funding from the Social Sciences and Humanities Research Council of Canada (SSHRC) to support an international workshop in Toronto. We are tremendously grateful for this financial contribution. This workshop was generously hosted by the Harriet Tubman Institute for Research on the Global Migrations of African Peoples (now called the Harriet Tubman Institute for Research on Africa and Its Diasporas) at York University. It was also supported by the Wilberforce Institute for the Study of Slavery and Emancipation (WISE) at the University of Hull; by further SSHRC funding via a major collaborative research initiative on slavery, memory, and citizenship; and by the Office of the Vice-President for Research and Innovation and the Dean's Office of the Faculty of Liberal Arts and Professional Studies at York University. Frank Luce, Dawn Ralph, and Sarah Whitaker at York were key to the success of the workshop.

We are especially grateful for the input and collaboration of very talented doctoral students at York University over the life of this project, including Karlee Sapoznik, who was our coorganizer and coapplicant on the SSHRC grant; Yael Machtinger for her skill and hard work in making the workshop a success; Nicholas Adeti Bastine and Katrina Keefer for acting as chair/discussants for panels; and Katrin Roots and Emily Lockhart for their careful editing of the book chapters. We are also very indebted to the participants and audience of the workshop that produced this collection, including Emily Rosser, Rebecca Scott, and Christien van den Anker.

It took longer than we expected to finalize the workshop papers for publication. During this phase of the process, we would like to especially acknowledge the patience and support of our contributors, the expertise and attention to detail provided by Randy Schmidt and the rest of the team at UBC Press, the miraculous editing skills of Cameron Thibos, and the excellent work of Emily Lockhart in preparing the manuscript for publication.

Finally, Annie would like to acknowledge and thank Michele Johnson, Director of the Tubman Institute, for her support and friendship; and Bruce Ryder for his patience, support, and good humour when listening to many hours of conversation about slavery and gender violence. Similarly, Joel would like to acknowledge and thank Stacey Sommerdyk, who has once again been indispensable in supporting this project to a successful conclusion.

Contemporary Slavery

PART 1
The Cause of Contemporary Slavery

Contemporary Slavery as More Than Rhetorical Strategy? The Politics and Ideology of a New Political Cause

Annie Bunting and Joel Quirk

Over the last two decades, contemporary slavery and human trafficking have emerged as major sources of popular fascination and political preoccupation.[1] This rapid and unexpected promotion to the front ranks of global conversations regarding exploitation and vulnerability has had far-reaching consequences. As many people working in this field will tell you, this new political cause of combatting "modern" or "contemporary" slavery – which has come to be chiefly understood in terms of fighting human trafficking – has experienced a remarkable degree of success in terms of popular awareness, institutional integration, and rhetorical support. What many people will not tell you, however, is that too many of the interventions that have followed in the wake of this remarkable success have not only struggled to make an impact, but they have also been complicit in a larger series of questionable political and ideological agendas.

All political causes invariably come with complications and limitations, so it should not be especially surprising that there have been problems aligning aspirations with outcomes. On this occasion, however, one of the main challenges has been reaching a minimum degree of clarity and consensus regarding exactly what "the cause" of combatting slavery – or human trafficking – actually entails. Two overlapping problems have been especially significant in this respect: (1) a widespread tendency to privilege activism over analysis and (2) a similar and related tendency to privilege rhetoric over substance. In the case of the former, the imperatives of activism frequently have found expression in a series of sensationalist, self-serving, and superficial interventions. Much of this activity has revolved around numerous efforts to harness the iconography of slavery in order to draw popular attention and institutional investment to a range of practices and problems. These diverse and sometimes competing agendas have in turn been loosely knit together in order to support the construction of a larger global cause: combatting "modern slavery," "contemporary forms of slavery," or "human trafficking." It is here, we would argue, that this global cause can be best understood as an unstable amalgamation of a wide range of diverse practices that go well beyond both legal definitions and historical experiences of slavery. Our chief goal in this collection is to interrogate the rhetorical dimensions and practical effects of this new political cause.

In keeping with long-standing trends within human rights activism more broadly, the construction of this global cause has been consolidated through the deployment of a series of frequently dubious "facts and figures" regarding the overall dimensions of contemporary slavery and human trafficking in the world today. Some prominent examples from this popular "facts and figures" genre include the following claims: (1) there are more "slaves now than at any point in human history";[2] (2) human trafficking is "the world's fastest growing criminal industry";[3] and (3) trafficking has become the third largest global criminal industry, following behind guns and drugs and generating "US $32 billion annually."[4] Despite usually having little or no credible methodological foundation, these "facts" have featured in countless speeches, books, and media reports over the last decade, thereby helping to both prioritize and publicize the cause. The main attraction of these types of sweeping assertions is their value as advocacy tools, so there has been a notable reluctance in many circles to interrogate how these "facts" have been calculated or to question whether or not they can be justified.[5] This theme is taken up in more depth by Darshan Vigneswaran in a later chapter focusing upon the politics of numbers in South African debates regarding human trafficking. For the moment, we would emphasize that this brand of activism has resulted in a situation where the cause of fighting contemporary slavery and trafficking now enjoys a high level of popularity and political support, yet the underlying issues continue to be very poorly understood.

Another related issue also needs to be factored into the equation here. While there is no doubt that the cause of fighting slavery and trafficking enjoys widespread global support, much of this support tends to be shallow to the point of sometimes being all but non-existent. In this particular context, "shallow" refers to both the limited range of issues that have been taken up (that is, most actors have narrowly focused upon a small number of locations and/or industries, rather than taking more holistic action on multiple fronts) and to a shallow level of commitment and investment (that is, most states have done little more than pass new legislation and have frequently been reluctant to make more substantial interventions that pose a more significant challenge to powerfully vested interests or the structural causes of exploitation). In theory, trafficking and contemporary slavery touch upon all kinds of problems and practices. In practice, only a small subset of specific cases within a much larger portfolio has been taken up in any sustained fashion.

This pattern of universal yet largely shallow support is by no means a new phenomenon. Governments and other actors have been rhetorically proclaiming their official commitment to the anti-slavery cause since the nineteenth century, yet their substantive policies and practices have routinely pulled in quite different directions.[6] This divide between rhetoric and substance is once again common to human rights activism more generally. Protecting human rights can frequently be costly and challenging, and relevant actors routinely lack the capacity or political will to follow through on their rhetorical and institutional commitments.[7] On this occasion, however, we also find a further political calculus at work. As we shall see later in this chapter, much of the appeal of the cause of "ending slavery" stems from the fact that it is perceived as being relatively "safe" from a political and ideological standpoint. This is because the cause has been selectively interpreted as being chiefly focused upon a small number of "aberrant" and "exceptional" cases, which are said to be concentrated within the "irregular" margins of the global economy and within so-called backward corners of the Global South.[8] This focus upon "exceptional" cases frequently ends up consolidating

– rather than challenging – dominant political and economic interests, especially in the Global North.

This political calculus is most apparent when it comes to campaigns that concentrate heavily upon various aspects of prostitution, since political and economic elites rarely have significant institutional investments in this specific area. However, there are also times when a narrow concentration upon the "worst of the worst" forms of labour exploitation can be politically attractive when it comes to tacitly minimizing, or otherwise legitimating, the much larger excesses of global capitalism. Over the last two decades, all kinds of leaders – ranging from George Bush to Robert Mugabe – have rhetorically declared their support for the cause of ending slavery and trafficking. While both the volume and ideological diversity of these voices is impressive at first glance, this type of "universal" global consensus is only possible because most of the actors and institutions involved have calculated that the political and economic stakes are relatively low and that there are likely to be reputational benefits and other advantages to offering rhetorical support to the cause.

Over the last two decades, a growing number of critics have taken issue with numerous aspects of the cause. The main focus of this now extensive critical literature has been discourses and policies associated with efforts to combat human trafficking, which have been heavily criticized from many different angles.[9] While competing approaches to human trafficking form a necessary part of our canvass in this book, they are not our main focus. In fact, we believe that there are at least some areas where it is increasingly difficult to break substantially new theoretical and conceptual ground, owing to the now extensive literature concerned with the strengths and weaknesses of competing positions. This increasing saturation is most notably – but by no means exclusively – evident when it comes to larger debates over human trafficking and its relationship to the legal status of prostitution, migration, and border protection, along with foundational questions of patriarchy, sexuality, and agency. We have no doubt that these are major global issues, but they are not issues that we seek to specifically prioritize in this volume.

Our goal instead is to pave the way for different perspectives and lines of inquiry. Much of the analysis that follows is designed to make the case for our preferred approach. To this end, we have divided this introduction into two sections, which also serve to both introduce and contextualize the subsequent chapters in the collection in light of our overarching arguments. In the first section, we provide a snapshot of the main actors, features, and fault lines that have emerged over the last two decades. Our primary argument is that the widespread presumption of a cohesive and singular global cause – fighting human trafficking and/or contemporary slavery – has ended up promoting a misleading and unhelpful picture of the divergent and frequently competing agendas, perspectives, and priorities in operation beneath the popular rhetoric of a shared global struggle. As we shall see, this state of affairs can often be further exacerbated by an emphasis upon sensational and exceptional cases. We argue that the widespread presumption of a cohesive and singular global cause frequently does more harm than good from an analytical standpoint, because it loosely aggregates very different problems under the rubric of a fictive global struggle. In many parts of the globe, the real action takes place primarily at a more localized and issue-specific level.

The second section builds upon this overall line of argument. We identify and analyze a number of ways in which the diverse themes now located under the rubric of "contemporary slavery" can be usefully disaggregated and connected to theories, experiences, and critiques found within established studies on various aspects of human rights and other allied fields. This analysis is not meant to be exhaustive, but instead draws upon a pluralistic framework in order to develop an introductory snapshot of where and how intersections and convergences might be developed further. Too many recent treatments of contemporary slavery and human trafficking have been predicated – either explicitly or implicitly – upon a politics of exceptionality, wherein "slavery" is promoted as a unique and exceptional evil that stands apart from other "lesser" challenges.

This hierarchical model promotes an unhelpful separation between "slavery" and many other experiences and literatures, contributing to insular conversations that too often involve attempts to reinvent the wheel, rather than drawing on more established precedents and ideas from other fields of academic inquiry and applied experience. At its worst, this hierarchical model can end up tacitly legitimating and/or de-prioritizing abusive practices and structures that are said to fall short of "true" slavery. Accordingly, we argue, contemporary slavery and trafficking should not be treated as singular, exceptional, and stratified categories, but instead need to be disaggregated into a series of smaller thematic and case-specific categories, which can in turn be best understood in combination with established literatures and applied experiences.

Contemporary Slavery and Human Trafficking: Rhetoric and Practice

Recent references to slavery and abolition(ists) invariably come with a great deal of historical and ideological baggage.[10] Many references to "slavery" have often been characterized by superficial efforts to appropriate both the infamy and iconography of slavery and its legal abolition, as Fuyuki Kurasawa later explores in his chapter in this volume. As we shall see, this dynamic has most commonly involved the history and language of slavery being strategically invoked as part of the effort to both prioritize and dramatize all kinds of current problems. This rhetorical strategy commonly involves a form of comparative analogy, wherein it is posited that there are sufficient similarities between historical slave systems (chiefly framed in terms of stylized images of transatlantic slavery) and more recent examples of exploitation, coercion, and violence. Numerous actors and institutions have used this rhetorical strategy in order to support larger arguments that specific sets of problems and practices should be regarded as a species of slavery and should therefore be prioritized ahead of "lesser" concerns.

The recent popularity of this rhetorical strategy has contributed to an environment where slavery means different things to different audiences. There are two further issues at stake here. On the one hand, there is widespread uncertainty regarding where slavery begins and ends as a category and on what grounds the determination of the status of a slave can and should be made.[11] On the other hand, there are competing visions of the nexus between slavery, human trafficking, forced labour, and other categories. This issue has been complicated by an unhelpful conflation of trafficking and slavery.[12] Both of these issues will be considered in more depth in subsequent chapters in this collection, where Jean Allain focuses on the question of defining slavery and Joel Quirk takes up the tensions between different conceptual schemes, such as slavery and trafficking. Since much of the heavy lifting takes place elsewhere, our main focus is on introducing and defending the main features of our approach to contemporary slavery as a political cause.

Numerous activists, academics, and policy-makers have sought to (re) define both the parameters of the anti-slavery cause and the link between slavery, trafficking, and "slave-like" practices. Some of the main actors here have been non-governmental organizations (NGOs) in the Global North, which are heavily concentrated in the United States in particular. Most NGOs in the Global North, such as the Polaris Project, chiefly define themselves as anti-trafficking organizations. While slavery still features prominently within this framework, it is mostly employed as a descriptor that underscores the problem of trafficking. The most common formula involves the depiction of "[h]uman trafficking [as] a form of modern-day slavery."[13] Within this formula, slavery frequently ends up as a rhetorical addendum that serves to underscore the severity of human trafficking, rather than as an independent or coherent category.

This framework can be contrasted with organizations that place slavery at the heart of a larger political agenda, of which human trafficking constitutes a subcategory. From their base in the United Kingdom, Anti-Slavery International (ASI) favours an expansive approach that places slavery at the heart of a broader portfolio of practices linked to slavery. According to ASI, slavery can be best understood as including bonded labour, forced labour, "early and forced marriage, trafficking, slavery by descent, and the worst forms of child labour."[14] From their base in the United States, Free the Slaves favours a similarly expansive approach, defining slavery as "the holding of people at a workplace through force, fraud or coercion for purposes of sexual exploitation or forced labor so that the slaveholder can extract profit."[15]

This expansive conception of slavery is broadly aligned with the recent work of the United Nations (UN) Special Rapporteur on contemporary forms of slavery, including its causes and consequences. The first rapporteur, Gulnara Shahinian, was appointed in 2008. Working with a limited budget and staff, she conducted a series of missions to Peru, Romania, Brazil, Ecuador, Mauritania, Haiti, Madagascar, and Kazakhstan. In keeping with the terms of their mandate, both Shahinian and her more recent successor, Urmila Bhoola (who was appointed in 2014), have broadly defined contemporary forms of slavery to include "debt bondage, serf-dom, forced labour, child slavery, sexual slavery, forced or early marriages and the sale of wives."[16] In addition to country reports, Shahinian has also produced thematic reports on the topics of domestic servitude (2010), child slavery in artisanal mining (2011), servile marriage (2012), and ways of combatting contemporary slavery (2013).

The position of this rapporteur supersedes the UN Working Group on Contemporary Slavery, which operated from 1975 to 2006, and complements the work of the UN Voluntary Trust Fund on Contemporary Forms of Slavery, which was founded in 1991. In 2004, the UN also established a new Rapporteur on Trafficking in Persons, focusing especially on women and children. The human trafficking rapporteur works in a similar fashion to the contemporary slavery rapporteur, with the main focus being country visits and thematic reports, which have recently included topics such as regional cooperation (2010), effective remedies for victims (2011), human rights and criminal justice (2012), trafficking and supply chains (2013), and organ trafficking (2013).[17]

Although the design of both rapporteur positions is similar, the human trafficking framework ultimately has a much higher profile than the contemporary slavery framework within the UN system. A good example of their relative prominence is the foundation of the UN Global Initiative to Fight Human Trafficking (UN.GIFT), which builds upon the notion that "human trafficking is a crime of such magnitude and atrocity that it cannot be dealt with successfully by any government alone."[18] Established in 2007, UN.GIFT is an ongoing high-profile partnership between the International Labour Organization, the International Organization for Migration, the Organization for Security and Co-operation in Europe, the UN Children's Fund, the UN Office on Drugs and Crime, and the Office of the High Commissioner for Human Rights. Building upon the terms of the 2000 Protocol to Prevent, Suppress and Punish Trafficking in Persons, especially Women and Children, UN.GIFT has divided human trafficking into four subcategories, which are recognized as regularly overlapping in practice.[19] These subcategories are sexual exploitation, forced labour, children, and the organ trade. While slavery is by no means absent from this equation, it most commonly serves once again as a rhetorical device for highlighting the "magnitude and atrocity" of human trafficking.

Another crucial player in this global story is the US government, which has been both celebrated and criticized in its self-appointed role as a global anti-trafficking "sheriff." The main focal point for debate has been the publication of annual trafficking in persons (TIPS) reports by the US State Department, which began in 2001. Both the origins and operations of these reports – along with the associated policy interventions and rankings of state performance – have already been closely documented and analyzed elsewhere.[20] For our purposes, it is sufficient to make several brief observations regarding the global contribution of US policies and priorities. First, it is important to keep in mind that the initial globalization of anti-trafficking under the auspices of the TIPS initiative chiefly took place under the administration of George W. Bush, which favoured a model that heavily prioritized human trafficking for the purposes of commercial sexual exploitation. While US policy shifted to a more expansive approach under Barack Obama, the cause of combatting commercial sexual exploitation – or even commercial sex of any form – has nonetheless been globalized as a dominant political priority thanks in part to the formative influence of early TIPS reports and activities.

Second, we need to keep in mind that there have been pronounced limits to US global power and influence under both administrations. While US hegemony has compelled numerous states to commit to the anti-trafficking cause both at a rhetorical and legislative level, these commitments have only been occasionally and episodically translated into substantive practices and pro-active policies and interventions. Numerous laws may well have been passed, but enforcement can often be another matter entirely.

This recurring divide between legal commitments and substantive practices is important on several levels. While all states and stakeholders are now ostensibly committed to a common cause, this rhetoric tends to be little more than a shallow veneer that masks both the differing political agendas and tremendous variations in the overall levels of interest and investment. During the late nineteenth century, the

Portuguese government passed numerous anti-slavery laws in their African colonies that were chiefly understood by insiders to be "*só para o inglês ver*" or "just for the English to see." Since these laws were geared towards alleviating outside British pressure for reform, they accomplished little in the way of substantive reform long after they were promulgated.[21] A comparable pattern can be found in many states that have recently passed – yet have rarely sought to pro-actively enforce – new laws against human trafficking in response to US pressure. There are many structural reasons for this widespread lack of enforcement, as we shall see in more detail later in this volume, but at least part of the issue is that external catalysts and categories can only go so far in the larger socio-economic and institutional reform. While the cause of combatting trafficking now commands broad support among governments globally, most of this support is shallow and selective.

There are some important exceptions to this overall pattern. As a growing number of scholars have documented, there have recently been a number of specific settings where more narrowly tailored projects and policy interventions have been taking place, such as the introduction of specialized teams in Brazil that focus upon the severe labour abuses[22] or rescue and rehabilitation schemes in India.[23] While political stakeholders across the globe are rhetorically committed to combatting many different variants of human trafficking or slavery, substantive action tends to be confined to specific priorities within specific locations. Once we look beyond the popular rhetoric of a cohesive and singular global cause – fighting trafficking and slavery – it quickly becomes apparent that there are only a relatively small number of locations and issue areas where sustained interventions are actually taking place. In many cases, these specific interventions also involve actors and organizations that do not self-identify as anti-slavery or anti-trafficking activists, but instead organize their activities around alternative referents, such as migrant rights, labour rights, or children's rights. Many of these activities become only part of the global anti-slavery cause via a process of creative aggregation.

Funding is also an important factor, since it is hard to get anything done without resources. On this front, the US government has once again played a major role in determining where and how specific interventions have occurred by making available hundreds of millions of dollars in funding to support anti-trafficking projects, both domestically and internationally.[24] As any number of human rights scholars have demonstrated, decisions about which types of projects get funded – and on what terms – can have a profound impact upon the types of languages that various organizations use and the types of issues and practices that they prioritize. The most infamous example of funding conditionality involves a requirement introduced by the Bush administration that organizations that receive US funding must first sign a pledge "explicitly opposing prostitution and sex trafficking."[25] This requirement is widely held to have complicated efforts to prevent HIV infection and to have greatly curtailed efforts to relax legal prohibitions against prostitution. It is worth noting, however, that funding conditionality extends well beyond the activities of the US government to encompass broader patterns associated with financial and institutional linkages between the Global North and the Global South. When funders in the Global North allocate resources to a specific project or issue, actors in the Global South are routinely obliged to align their activities with the interests and agendas of their external funders.[26]

This political economy of activism has not only contributed to the creation of new anti-trafficking organizations (mostly in relation to sex work but also sometimes on other fronts), but it has also encouraged established organizations to include anti-trafficking efforts (or rhetoric) within their existing portfolio of projects. Since anti-trafficking funding is often limited to a single funding cycle and anti-trafficking efforts often have shallow roots and few alternative means of support, the end of the funding can sometimes result in the end of the entire project or organization. There have also been additional cases, however, where established civil society groups and other actors have successfully extracted resources from the Global North in order to support preexisting projects. In various parts of West Africa, to take one notable example, NGOs such as Timidria (Niger), Temedt (Mali), and the *Initiative pour la Résurgence du Mouvement Abolitionniste* (Mauritania) have successfully leveraged renewed interest in human trafficking and contemporary slavery in the Global North in order to garner support and resources for their efforts to challenge the ongoing legacies of historical slave systems.[27]

It is often difficult to directly connect interventions in one part of the globe to parallel interventions taking place in other parts of the world. Brazilian activists seeking to end extreme exploitation in the agricultural sector have little to do with their counterparts seeking to combat the ongoing legacies of historical slave systems in Mali or Niger. Much the same can be said in relation to the activists concerned with state-sponsored forced labour in North Korea[28] compared with those concerned with bonded labour in India.[29] Activists in the United States who are concerned with "domestic minor trafficking" rarely look beyond their own borders (or even beyond sex work) when it comes to making substantive political and policy interventions. There can sometimes be broad similarities in the types of abuses that occur in these otherwise quite different contexts, but a fair amount of creative aggregation and extrapolation is required in order to translate broad similarities into the language of a common and cohesive global cause. Despite political rhetoric to the contrary, there is not one global anti-trafficking or anti-slavery movement. There are instead many different movements and organizations with numerous agendas and interests, most of which chiefly focus upon specific issues, priorities, and/or localized concerns.

This state of affairs has often been overshadowed by a widespread tendency to both reproduce and further entrench the fictive coherence of global struggle. Since the late 1990s, many researchers have framed their work in terms of – or at least rhetorically alluded to – the overarching notion of a global cause, which has in turn been promoted further via a number of influential and popular books.[30] Since states, NGOs, and international organizations have come to favour particular approaches and conceptual vocabularies, the scholars who study them have also tended to give pride of place to similar types of approaches and languages. There are some authors – the most influential being Kevin Bales[31] – who have devoted considerable energy seeking to define and demarcate global anti-slavery. However, there are also other authors who instead tend to make brief and fleeting references to some kind of global cause, often by way of ritual recitation of global "facts and figures," and then move to a more narrow focus on individual issues or locations.

It is at this juncture that a variety of more specific themes begin to take centre stage, since most scholars and activists are concerned primarily with specific (sub)themes, rather than seeking to give sustained attention to every aspect of the larger whole. These specific themes include commercial sex and prostitution;[32] hereditary bondage and descent-based discrimination;[33] forced and early marriage;[34] human trafficking, criminality, and crime control;[35] migration, asylum, and exploitation;[36] children in the global sex industry;[37] and domestic labour.[38] While different authors favour different approaches to these topics, the main point we want to emphasize here is that the addition of slavery and/or trafficking as overarching frames of reference does not always add very much in terms of analytical value. Instead of treating these numerous themes as subcategories of singular and cohesive global cause, we instead need to consider looking outward to more established literatures and applied experiences.

Broadening the Conversation(s)

Rhetorical appeals to the history of slavery and abolition can serve a number of different purposes and agendas. In the case of self-proclaimed "modern-day abolitionists," we can point to three main themes that have proven to be particularly significant.[39] First, rhetorical appeals to the history of anti-slavery have helped to position contemporary activists as the equivalents and/or descendants of earlier anti-slavery activists and campaigns. Second, rhetorical appeals to anti-slavery have helped to invest the anti-slavery or anti-trafficking cause with the same type of elevated moral status and urgency as previous historical campaigns to end legal slavery in the Americas. Finally, rhetorical appeals have been featured as part of the larger efforts to portray historical anti-slavery campaigns as key sources of inspiration and instruction, which can then be invoked in turn to demonstrate that seemingly impossible goals are obtainable with the right techniques and resolve.[40] Taken together, these themes have helped to establish – either implicitly or explicitly – a hierarchical conception of where the cause of ending slavery and trafficking should be situated in relation to other problems and practices. Within this hierarchy, slavery and trafficking are constructed as exceptional problems that should be accorded the highest possible priority. In turn, this perception has had the effect of establishing an informal separation between slavery and "lesser" problems.

This politics of exception can be unpacked in several different ways. One useful point of departure comes from Clifford Bob, who has sought to explain why and how some political causes have been able secure global recognition and support, while other causes continue to languish in relative obscurity. His analysis chiefly focuses upon the mechanics of competition associated with what he describes as a "global morality market," wherein activists in the Global South compete for resources and endorsements from their more privileged counterparts in the North.[41] This overall approach has important ramifications when it comes to the cause of contemporary slavery. According to Bob, there is no such thing as a "meritocracy of suffering, with the worse-off groups gaining the most help."[42] Instead, activists engage in fierce competition for resources, alliances, and popular and political attention. Within the context of this "global morality market," rhetorical appeals to (anti-)slavery appear to have played a key role in attracting interest and investment to the cause of ending slavery, since slavery is widely held to occupy a space alongside genocide in a "worst of the worst" category. In a world suffering from many serious problems, the cause of ending slavery enjoys several market advantages.

Others factors also need to be taken into account in order to fully develop this overall argument. As is well known, appeals to slavery and anti-slavery are not a new phenomenon. Activists of many different stripes have been seeking to harness slavery to support specific causes since the nineteenth century, including high profile yet highly problematic campaigns against "white" slavery.[43] Over the last two decades, references to "slavery" within the context of human trafficking and prostitution have frequently had much greater popular and political salience than references to "slavery" involving other types of practices, such as the abuse of domestic workers or forced labour for the state. Since some appeals to slavery have been more successful than others, we need to be cautious about assigning too much independent weight to "slavery" when it comes to the marketplace of activism and ideas.[44] While a full analysis of this theme is beyond the scope of this chapter, it should be evident from this overview that the recent success of the cause of ending slavery and trafficking cannot be explained as a "natural" or "organic" response to recent events but, instead, needs to be understood as emerging out of fierce competition between numerous causes, constituencies, and normative claims. To help explain this success, we need to reflect upon why this specific cause is now so popular.

This means interrogating how, why, and where anti-slavery rhetoric potentially aligns with other ideological, economic, and political agendas and what consequences follow from these alignments. Over the last two decades, the cause of ending trafficking and slavery has received significant rhetorical support from every corner of the political spectrum. This broad base of support has helped to foster a misleading, yet nonetheless widespread, impression that both anti-slavery and anti-trafficking are non-ideological and removed from "normal" politics, since strong rhetorical support comes from conservatives, liberals, traditionalists, and progressives. One good demonstration of this dynamic is the frequency with which recent anti-trafficking and anti-slavery legislation has enjoyed broad bipartisan support. Take, by way of example, the Victims of Trafficking and Violence Protection Act, which in 2000 sailed through both the US House of Representatives and Senate, which are otherwise notoriously polarized and deadlocked, and has since been renewed with similar bipartisan support in 2003, 2006, and 2008.[45] This was then admittedly followed by a period during which renewal was hijacked by larger political and ideological disputes between the Democrats and the Republicans, but these differences were later resolved without substantial change to the underlying legislation. Outside the United States, anti-trafficking legislation has been passed on a bipartisan basis in the vast majority of other countries and cases.

This self-presentation of the cause of ending slavery as one of those rare issues that should "transcend" everyday politics undoubtedly sounds good in theory, but to what extent is it actually borne out in practice? To help address this question, we need to ask why political and ideological adversaries have been able to reach – or appear to reach – common ground when it comes to ending slavery and trafficking. As is well known, political parties on both the left and the right generate at least part of their support via their potential capacity to both protect and promote the interests of various economic and social groups. In its most basic form, this often boils down to an expectation that politicians on the left will support the interests of workers and the public sector, while their counterparts on the right will support corporations and the private sector. While political realities are obviously far more complex in practice, there is nonetheless considerable merit to the basic notion that key groups within society have strategic interests and that these groups participate in politics in order to protect these interests.

So why have politicians and other actors been able to come together when it comes to this specific cause? One key consideration here is the degree to which contemporary slavery and human trafficking have been closely associated with commercial sex work. While commercial sex work is a topic that generates strong emotions, it is not an issue that frequently or directly threatens dominant economic and political interests (although larger gender relations within society are definitely a major part of the equation here). This political profile is important because it helps to explain why anti-trafficking has often been able to command an unusual level of bipartisan support. In stark contrast to historical campaigns to end legal slavery, which were firmly aimed at the profits and privileges of the rich and powerful, more recent global "anti-slavery" campaigns targeting human trafficking only rarely pose a direct threat to major political and economic interests. When "modern-day abolitionists" target abuses associated with commercial sex, their efforts do not directly challenge major economic and political interests or the foundations of our profoundly unjust global economy.

This calculation helps to explain why so much time and energy has been invested in various aspects of the relationship between slavery, trafficking, and prostitution. It is also important to keep in mind, however, that the status of prostitution also comes with its own internal dynamics and political fault lines, which can be best understood on their own terms rather than as a subcategory of a larger global struggle against slavery.[46] This starts with a now firmly polarized debate regarding the relationship between trafficking in persons and the status of prostitution, with one side of the argument invoking the cause of fighting trafficking in order to delegitimize prostitution and the other side maintaining that the cause of fighting trafficking has too often translated into policies that challenge the legitimacy and autonomy of all women engaged in sex work.[47]

In addition to this fundamental argument over prostitution, there have also been numerous other related critiques, starting with depictions of trafficking as a form of "moral panic," which is bound up in underlying social anxieties and legacies.[48] As part of this argument, critics have challenged popular narratives involving the construct of vulnerable "exotic" victims, whose "innocence" requires "rescue."[49] These narratives have in turn been linked to "celebritization" and popular tropes regarding "saviors" and "saved," wherein "human trafficking is not only susceptible to alluring, fetishistic and voyeuristic narratives, but plays into the celebrity-as-rescuer-of-the-victim ideal."[50] According to numerous critics, this "rescue" too often takes the form of paternalistic intervention, state "securitization," and/or border protection.[51] It should therefore come as no surprise that anti-trafficking remedies have ended up hurting, rather than helping, vulnerable groups.[52]

Two key observations can be extracted from the preceding analysis. First, we argue that it is essential to analyze individual components of the cause of ending slavery on their own terms, rather than taking the popular rhetoric of a larger common cause at face value. Second, we argue that political and economic interests play a central role in determining the degree to which "bipartisan" support is viable. There are numerous stakeholders who are deeply invested in the question of the legal status of prostitution who are not similarly invested in other topics. It costs relatively little for corporations and governments to take an official stand against abuses in the commercial sex industry, but once the topic shifts to global supply chains and exploitative labour practices, they quickly get apprehensive owing to their major economic interests relating to the legitimation and continuation of highly exploitative labour regimes. Much the same applies to labour abuses that are perpetrated by governments, such as the widespread abuse of migrant labourers in much of the Middle East. As Rhoda Howard-Hassmann demonstrates in her case study of forced labour in North Korea in this volume, governments have long been one of the most effective abusers of their citizens. A serious political challenge to global patterns of labour exploitation and vulnerability would rapidly and decisively fracture the current "bipartisan" appeal of the anti-slavery cause.

In light of these arguments, we further maintain that there is considerable analytical and political value in disaggregating the anti-slavery cause into key thematic areas, rather than treating so many different issues as aspects of a singular and cohesive global struggle. While different actors and institutions will invariably have different priorities and approaches, we think that the following list offers a provisional account of the substantive issues that currently uneasily coexist under the rhetoric of "ending slavery":

- prostitution and sexual exploitation
- migration and exploitation
- debt and exploitation
- child labour and exploitation
- domestic labour and exploitation
- global supply chains and exploitation
- hereditary bondage and descent-based discrimination
- wartime captivity and wartime abuses
- forced, servile and early marriage
- forced labour by the state.

This is obviously a huge and diverse list. It makes very little analytical sense to throw together such a diverse array of practices and issues under a singular banner, but this is nonetheless the current state of affairs that has emerged thanks to constant aggregation. Things get even messier when the list is further expanded to include themes such as prison labour and the carceral state or reparations for enslavement, which are both themes that are directly connected to the legacies of historical slave systems but that have to date been largely overlooked within discussions of contemporary slavery and trafficking.[53]

We believe that disaggregating the political rhetoric of anti-slavery and anti-trafficking will help to partially uncouple political agendas and political stakeholders from the empty rhetoric of "bipartisanship," where everyone is at least superficially assumed to be on the same side. Each of the themes listed above can and should be primarily understood as a distinct sphere of inquiry rather than as a subcategory whose primary function is to help illuminate different facets of a singular and cohesive field of global activism and inquiry. They should not be regarded primarily as "subcategories" within global anti-slavery or anti-trafficking movements. There may well be points of overlap and intersection between these different themes, but we would argue that these intersections should emerge at points where there are substantive areas of intersection rather than being artificially created through rhetorical aggregation and extrapolation.

It is here, we further argue, that existing scholarship and activism focusing upon "anti-slavery" and "anti-trafficking" also needs to engage more systematically with established literatures and practical experiences in related fields. As we have seen, the widespread popularity of the politics of exception has created an unhelpful and artificial separation between contemporary slavery and a range of "lesser" problems and practices. Disaggregating the rhetoric of anti-slavery into specific thematic areas should not only make it easier to prioritize practice over rhetoric. It should also make it easier to integrate arguments and insights from related areas of activism and inquiry. There is no need to reinvent the wheel to deal with a unique and exceptional case. The wheel has already been invented many times over in related fields. It just needs to be imported and adapted.

There are therefore two further steps to our overall argument in this volume. The first step involves a move from the singular and cohesive to the plural and distinct in order to disaggregate contemporary slavery into more specific themes. The second step involves placing these more specific themes alongside more established bodies of research. No list can ever be exhaustive, but for the purposes of illustration, we would point to the potential value of existing and ongoing research into the limits of law reform and rights advocacy,[54] human rights as discourse,[55] vernacularized mobilization of human rights norms,[56] the perils of human rights indicators,[57] feminist critiques of human rights protections,[58] and the larger relationship between human rights and social vulnerabilities.[59] We believe that reaching out to these and other literatures will help to highlight issues and dynamics that may have otherwise been overlooked or marginalized.

Many of the practices that violate contemporary human rights norms – think of age and consent to marriage, corporal and criminal punishments, and the lack of primary education – are featured prominently within earlier civilizing missions by European colonial powers, and the complications and limitations of current approaches and policies can be usefully approached within this larger context. Liberal conceptions of rights, which remain the dominant idiom of contemporary "anti-slavery" activism, have often ended up excluding rather than including.[60] Furthermore, human rights initiatives now regularly accompany neo-liberal global expansions of capital that have a very poor record of protecting against the excesses and logics of market competition.[61] It is within this larger context that Andrew Crane, a business ethicist who has written extensively on corporate citizenship, argues in this volume that slavery and exploitation should be approached as regularized management practices rather than as deviant exceptions.

These sorts of connections should not come as a surprise, but they have nonetheless too often been neglected or overlooked within recent scholarship and activism relating to contemporary slavery and trafficking. As Wendy Brown has incisively argued in the American context, the history of the civil rights movement shows that rights may reinforce the very structures of inequality that they aim to change.[62] This argument, in turn, helps to explain why and how the cause of ending slavery has ended up tacitly legitimating larger political arrangements involving exploitative labour systems and supply chains. To take a further example, it is also now well documented that law reform and liberal rights advocacy frequently fail to meet the needs of the most marginalized, yet, nonetheless, these solutions are what are frequently recommended when it comes to ending contemporary slavery and human trafficking. Similarly, in the area of housing rights and anti-poverty work, the rhetoric and politics of individual rights have proven to be a weak strategy for meaningful social change. If arguments based upon individual rights have not been particularly successful, then perhaps we should be thinking instead in terms of advancing collective organization and solidarity.

When viewed as discourse, human rights norms (like law more generally) need to be seen as contested and open to interpretation. A discursive approach "radically decenters international human rights law" and studies the way social practice produces human rights knowledge.[63]

Anti-slavery activists have recognized the power of rights as rhetoric, invoking the language of slavery to describe any number of different practices. However, it is also now well established within human rights scholarship that these types of rhetorical strategies are not limited to progressive social movements. The language of rights has frequently been mobilized by conservatives and reactionaries, such as vigilante justice groups and pro-gun lobbies. Daniel Goldstein's work in barrios in Bolivia has demonstrated how the language of the "right to security" can fuel vigilante justice when coupled with a suspicion of the state, police violence, and personal insecurity.[64]

In another fascinating example, the National Rifle Association from the United States assisted a local pro-gun lobby in Brazil in 2006 in order to turn the tide of popular opinion in a referendum on gun ownership. Exploiting fears of state intervention in the civil liberties of citizens, it used the approach that "if the government can restrict your right to self defense, what other rights will it restrict."[65] Much like the language of rights, the language of anti-slavery has proven to be highly malleable, and at least some of the political contexts where anti-slavery has been invoked have been similarly problematic.

These types of examples also underscore the importance of understanding the ways in which local contexts and political calculations interact with larger global discourses. As a now extensive literature has demonstrated, the "sites where human rights unfold in practice do matter, and that these sites are not simply nodes in a virtual network, but actual places in social space, places which can be law-like and coercive."[66] Not every location will be conducive to the politics of an international human rights campaign or anti-slavery strategy. There are often other competing and long-standing normative discourses for social justice and social change, including liberation theology, other religious discourse, party politics, unionization, and socialism. As Sally Engle Merry and colleagues have demonstrated in their study of gender violence and women's rights in five countries, social change is most challenging in cases where social norms are most intransigent.[67] These types of findings in turn invite further reflection and analysis regarding the extent to which lasting social change can be realized using the popular language of anti-slavery, or anti-trafficking, as a key platform for advocacy and change.

This literature also invites us to think further about how and why specific political interventions generate specific forms of political resistance and response. In his chapter for this volume, Austin Choi-Fitzpatrick focuses upon the degree to which human rights interventions, including those encouraging former slaves to challenge authority openly, have resulted in resistance from local elites as well as the development of new forms of social and economic oppression patterned on the basis of previous hierarchical relationships in operation under slavery.[68] In his 150 semi-structured interviews with former slaveholders, Choi-Fitzpatrick shows them as experiencing nostalgia, jealousy, confusion, and/or malice when confronted by a social movement of the former enslaved.

Existing literature on policy processes and alliances between private and public actors can also be tremendously valuable. As Darshan Vigneswaran argues in this volume, social scientists in general and human rights scholars in particular, regularly fail to recognize how epistemological differences with their "fellow travellers" in government, NGOs, and community organizations can undermine their collective ability to advance the cause of human emancipation.[69] Focusing upon the politics of numbers and human trafficking, Vigneswaran demonstrates that anti-trafficking policy processes and political conversations have remained largely impervious to criticism due to financial incentives, legitimation games, and sunken costs. His argument serves to highlight that not everyone will be – or can be – on the same political or ideological side and that appeals to "the evidence" are unlikely to be sufficient to adjudicate between competing positions.

This emphasis on policy processes also extends to legal processes. In his chapter for this volume, Benjamin Lawrance also explores how government officials and legal processes grapple with questions of classification. He specifically explores how the language of "forced marriage" ends up reproducing the troubling notion that conjugal relationships are akin to legal marriage for former "husbands" and "in-laws." Lawrance argues that this "forced marriage paradox" consists of two intertwined dynamics, namely the absence of a consistent set of definitions (based on evidence from UK and US courts), and the conundrum encountered by victims who cannot describe their experiences without employing language validating violent and illegitimate actions.

In a similar vein, Jonathan Blagbrough explores the language used by survivors and activists. In his work, Blagbrough argues that child domestic workers are narrowly construed as victims of exploitation in ways that neglect their full agency as decision makers, migrants, and children. Existing work on childhood is shown to have as much, if not more, to offer than the existing literature on slavery and human trafficking. This emphasis on the idiosyncrasies of lived experience is also taken up by Roy Brooks. Building upon his previous work on reparations for the history and legacies of slavery in the United States, Brooks seeks to extend his reparatory model to thinking about potential forms of redress for the harms associated with contemporary slavery. Here, as elsewhere, we encounter a now well-established critique of the limitations of criminal justice mechanisms, which remain the first port of call for many interventions.

As we have reiterated throughout this introduction, the term "contemporary slavery" is a provocative and powerful label applied by activists and others to signal the "worst forms of abuse." As Fuyuki Kurasawa deftly analyzes in his chapter for this volume, it draws on the histories and iconography of the transatlantic slave trade and American plantation slavery. As Joseph Slaughter argues in *Human Rights, Inc.: The World Novel, Narrative Form, and International Law*, the coming-of-age novel, *Bildungsroman*, "is the novelistic genre that most fully corresponds to – and, indeed, is implicitly invoked by – the norms and narrative assumptions that underwrite the vision of the free and full human personality development projected in international human rights law."[70] Slaughter is careful to qualify this claim by stating that he is talking about "dominant international legal construction of human rights" – in other words, not the discursive and dynamic understanding of human rights that we describe earlier in this introduction. Annie Bunting further develops these themes in her critical assessment of modern slavery narratives and legal testimonials in her chapter for this volume. She argues that should we limit our understanding of human rights violations and wartime violence to genres such as slave narratives or testimonies, we will miss the complexity and nuance of the experiences of survivors. This is particularly the case for survivors of gender violence in war, where the risks of voyeurism and narrative tropes are very prevalent.

Concluding Remarks

It has recently been argued that recent scholarship has been contributing to the emergence of a new field of "contemporary slavery studies."
According to Austin Choi-Fitzpatrick,

> scholars contributing to our understanding of trafficking and slav-
> ery are engaged in a nascent and emerging interdisciplinary field of
> contemporary slavery studies ... [that] ... bridges research and move-
> ment fields as it increasingly involves the voices and contributions
> of grassroots activists and survivors of slavery as well as scholars and
> policy makers.[71]

While this formula represents an advance upon orthodox approaches
that prioritize human trafficking, it nonetheless continues to treat the
cause of ending slavery and trafficking as a singular and cohesive object of analysis and activism. As we have sought to demonstrate in this
introduction, there are major limitations to this popular notion that
contemporary slavery constitutes a separate and distinct field of study.
It is instead preferable, we argue, to think in terms of multiple and overlapping spheres of activism and inquiry, which are nested within – and
do not stand apart from – a wide range of related scholarly literatures
and practical experiences. Slavery and trafficking should not only be
treated as separate and exceptional issues, but they also need to be disaggregated and merged into a model that focuses chiefly upon specific
themes and substantive practices.

As we have seen, too much of what takes place under the banner of
combatting human trafficking and contemporary slavery is sensationalist, self-serving, and superficial. Once we look beyond the popular rhetoric of a cohesive and singular global cause – fighting trafficking and
slavery – we quickly encounter a wide range of divergent and often
competing agendas, perspectives, and priorities. Despite political rhetoric to the contrary, many of these agendas and calculations are location
and issue specific, rather than subcategories within a much larger global cause. They are also not the sorts of issues or problems that tend to be
amenable to "bipartisan" or technocratic solutions. The idea that anti-
slavery is one of those rare issues that "transcends" politics or ideology

is only sustainable because the underlying issues at stake have been constructed and demarcated in a way that minimizes direct challenges to dominant political and economic interests. In order to move forward, both politically and analytically, we have to be prepared to discard both the politics of exception and the fiction of a shared and universal global struggle.

Notes

1 For the earlier history, see Suzanne Miers, *Slavery in the Twentieth Century: The Evolution of a Global Problem* (Walnut Creek, CA: AltaMira Press, 2003); Joel Quirk, *The Anti-Slavery Project: From the Slave Trade to Human Trafficking* (Philadelphia: University of Pennsylvania Press, 2011).

2 See, for example, Melissa Hogenboom, "A Tipping Point in the Fight against Slavery?" 18 October 2012, *British Broadcasting Corporation*, http://www.bbc.co.uk/news/magazine-19831913 (accessed 31 July 2012).

3 "The Problem", *A21*, http://www.a21.org/content/human-trafficking/gl0ryw?permcode=gl0ryw&site=true, (accessed 2 November 2016).

4 "Slavery"; "Human Trafficking"; "Factsheet on Human Trafficking," *UN Office on Drugs and Crime*, http://www.unodc.org/documents/human-trafficking/UNVTF_fs_HT_EN.pdf (accessed 31 July 2012).

5 See Sally Engle Merry, *The Seductions of Quantification: Measuring Human Rights, Gender Violence, and Sex Trafficking* (Chicago: University of Chicago Press, 2016). See also other work on indicators, which are available at http://www.iilj.org/research/indicatorsproject.asp.

6 See, for example, Benjamin Lawrance and Richard Roberts, eds., *Trafficking in Slavery's Wake: Law and the Experience of Women and Children* (Athens, OH: Ohio University Press, 2012); Quirk, *The Anti-Slavery Project*.

7 See, for example, Thomas Risse, Stephen C. Ropp, and Kathryn Sikkink, eds., *The Power of Human Rights: International Norms and Domestic* (Cambridge: Cambridge University Press, 1999); Alexander Betts and Phil Orchard, "Introduction: The Normative Institutionalization-Implementation Gap," in Alexander Betts and Phil Orchard, eds., *Implementation and World Politics: How International Norms Change Practice* (Oxford: Oxford University Press, 2014), 1–28.

8 This despite Free the Slaves and Human Rights Watch's work on extreme exploitation in the United States.

9 See, for example, Julia O'Connell Davidson, "New Slavery, Old Binaries: Human Trafficking and the Borders of 'Freedom,'" *Global Networks* 10, 2 (2010): 244–61; James Hathaway, "The Human Rights Quagmire of 'Human Trafficking,'" *Virginia Journal of International Law* 49, 1 (2008): 25–42: Janie Chuang, "Rescuing Trafficking from Ideological Capture: Prostitution Reform and Anti-Trafficking

Law and Policy," *University of Pennsylvania Law Review* 158, 6 (2010): 1655–1728: Nandita Sharma, "Anti-Trafficking Rhetoric and the Making of a Global Apartheid," *National Women's Studies Association (NWSA) Journal* 17, 3 (2005): 88–111.

10 Karen Bravo, "Exploring the Analogy between Modern Trafficking in Humans and the Trans-Atlantic Slave Trade," *Boston International Law Journal* 25, 2 (2007): 207–95: Ariel Gross, "When Is the Time of Slavery? The History of Slavery in Contemporary Legal and Political Argument," *California Law Review* 96, 1 (2008): 283–321; Joel Quirk, "Uncomfortable Silences: Contemporary Slavery and the 'Lessons' of History," in Alison Brysk and Austin Choi-Fitzpatrick, eds., *From Human Trafficking to Human Rights: Reframing Contemporary Slavery* (Philadelphia: University of Pennsylvania Press, 2012), 25–43: Gretchen Soderlund, "Running from the Rescuers: New US Crusades against Sex Trafficking and the Rhetoric of Abolition," *NWSA Journal* 17, 3 (2005): 64–87; Gretchen Soderlund, *Sex Trafficking, Scandal, and the Transformation of Journalism, 1885–1917* (Chicago: University of Chicago Press, 2013).

11 Jean Allain and Robin Hickey, "Property Law and the Definition of Slavery," *International and Comparative Law Quarterly* 61, 4 (2012): 915–38; Jean Allain, ed., *The Legal Understanding of Slavery: From the Historical to the Contemporary* (Oxford: Oxford University Press, 2012).

12 See, for example, Shiro Okubo and Louise Shelley, *Human Security, Transnational Crime and Human Trafficking: Asian and Western Perspectives* (New York: Routledge, 2011); Cornelius Friesendorf, ed., *Strategies against Human Trafficking: The Role of the Security Sector* (Geneva: Centre for the Democratic Control of Armed Forces, 2009).

13 "Human Trafficking."

14 "What Is 'Modern Slavery'?," *Anti-Slavery International*, http://www.antislavery.org/english/slavery_today/what_is_modern_slavery.aspx (accessed 2 November 2016).

15 "Slavery Questions and Answers," *Free the Slaves*, https://www.freetheslaves.net/wp-content/uploads/2015/03/Slavery-Questions-and-Answers.pdf (accessed 2 November 2016).

16 Special Rapporteur on Contemporary Forms of Slavery, United Nations, Office of the High Commission for Human Rights, http://www.ohchr.org/EN/Issues/Slavery/SRSlavery/Pages/SRSlaveryIndex.aspx (accessed 2 November 2016).

17 The United Nations (UN) had previously appointed Gay McDougall in 1997 as a special rapporteur with a narrower mandate on "systematic rape, sexual slavery and slavery-like practices in armed conflict." McDougall reported in 1998 and 2000.

18 "Forms of Human Trafficking and Other Issues," *UN Global Initiative to Fight Human Trafficking (UN.GIFT)*, http://www.ungift.org/knowledgehub/en/about/index.html (accessed 2 November 2016).

19 Discussed further by Joel Quirk, "When Human Trafficking Means Everything and Nothing," in this volume. Protocol to Prevent, Suppress and Punish Trafficking in Persons, especially Women and Children, 15 November 2000, 40 ILM 335 (2001).

20 See, for example, Anthony DeStefano, *The War on Human Trafficking: US Policy Assessed* (New Brunswick, NJ: Rutgers University Press, 2008); Bromfield Footen,

The Hijacking of Human Trafficking Legislation during Its Creation: A US Public Policy Study (Saarbruken, Germany: VDM Verlag, 2010); Anne Gallagher, "Human Rights and Human Trafficking: A Reflection on the Influence and Evolution of the US Trafficking in Persons Reports," in Austin Choi-Fitzpatrick, ed., *From Human Trafficking to Human Rights: Reframing Contemporary Slavery* (Philadelphia: University of Pennsylvania Press, 2012), 172–94.

21 See, for example, James Duffy, *Question of Slavery* (Oxford: Clarendon Press, 1967); Eric Allina, *Slavery by Any Other Name: African Life under Company Rule in Colonial Mozambique* (Charlottesville, VA: University of Virginia Press, 2012).

22 Siobhán McGrath, "Many Chains to Break: The Multi-Dimensional Concept of Slave Labour in Brazil," *Antipode* 45, 4 (2013): 1005–28.

23 Austin Choi-Fitzpatrick, "Letting Go," in this volume.

24 See, for example, "U.S. Government Funded Anti-Trafficking Programs," *US Department of State*, http://www.state.gov/j/tip/response/grants/ (accessed 5 May 2013).

25 Edi Kinney, "Appropriations for the Abolitionists: Undermining Effects of the US Mandatory Anti-Prostitution Pledge in the Fight against Human Trafficking and HIV/AIDS," *Berkeley Journal of Gender Law and Justice* 21 (2006): 161.

26 See, for example, Darshan Vigneswaran, "Methodological Debates in Human Rights Research," in this volume; Mike Dottridge, ed., "Following the Money: Spending on Anti-Trafficking," *Anti-Trafficking Review* 3 (2014): 3–175.

27 Lotte Pelckmans and Eric Hahonou, "Citizenship Struggles: Social Movements and Slavery in West Africa," *Vienna Journal of African Studies* 20 (2011): 141–62.

28 Rhoda Howard-Hassmann, "State Enslavement in North Korea," in this volume.

29 Choi-Fitzpatrick, "Letting Go."

30 See, for example, David Batstone, *Not for Sale: The Return of the Global Slave Trade and How We Can Fight It* (New York: HarperCollins, 2007); Benjamin Skinner, *A Crime So Monstrous* (Edinburgh: Mainstream Publishing, 2008); Victor Malarek, *The Natashas: The Horrific Inside Story of Slavery, Rape, and Murder in the Global Sex Trade* (Boston: Arcade Publishing, 2004).

31 See, for example, Kevin Bales, *Disposable Peoples: New Slavery in the Global Economy* (Berkeley, CA: University of California Press, 1999); Kevin Bales, *Ending Slavery: How We Free Today's Slaves* (Berkeley, CA: University of California Press, 2007).

32 See, for example, Karen Beeks and Delila Amir, *Trafficking and the Global Sex Industry* (Lanham, MD: Lexington Books, 2006); Siddharth Kara, *Sex Trafficking: Inside the Business of Modern Day Slavery* (New York: Columbia University Press, 2009).

33 See, for example, Benedetta Rossi, ed., *Reconfiguring Slavery: West African Trajectories* (Liverpool, UK: University of Liverpool Press, 2009); Ann McDougall, "The Politics of Slavery in Mauritania: Rhetoric, Reality and Democratic Discourse," *Maghreb Review* 35, 3 (2010): 259–86: Zekeria Salem, "8 Bare-foot Activists: Transformations in the Haratine Movement in Mauritania," in Stephen Ellis and Ineke van Kessel, eds., *Movers and Shakers: Social Movements in Africa* (Leiden: Brill, 2009), 157–77;

Alice Bellagamba, Sandra Green, and Martin Klein, eds., *The Bitter Legacy: African Slavery Past and Present* (Princeton, NJ: Marcus Wiener Publishers, 2013).

34 See, for example, Annie Bunting, "Stages of Development: Marriage of Girls and Teens as an International Human Rights Issue," *Social and Legal Studies* 14, 1 (2005): 17–38; Annie Bunting, "Forced Marriage in Conflict Situations: Researching and Prosecuting Old Harms and New Crimes," *Canadian Journal of Human Rights* 1, 1 (2012): 165–85.

35 See, for example, Maggie Lee, *Trafficking and Global Crime Control*, (London: Sage Publications, 2011); Louise Shelley, *Human Trafficking: A Global Perspective* (New York: Cambridge University Press, 2010).

36 See, for example, Rutvica Andrijasevic, *Migration, Agency and Citizenship in Sex Trafficking* (Basingstoke, UK: Palgrave Macmillan, 2010); Hannah Lewis et al., *Precarious Lives: Forced Labour, Exploitation and Asylum* (London: Polity Press, 2014); Pardis Mahdavi, *Gridlock: Labor, Migration, and Human Trafficking in Dubai* (Stanford, CT: Stanford University Press, 2011); Bridget Anderson, "Where's the Harm in That? Immigration Enforcement, Trafficking, and the Protection of Migrants' Rights," *American Behavioral Scientist* 56, 9 (2012): 1241–57.

37 See, for example, Julia O'Connell Davidson, *Children and the Global Sex Trade* (Cambridge: Polity Press, 2005); Virginia Kendall and Markus Funk, *Child Exploitation and Trafficking: Examining the Global Challenges and US Responses* (Lanham, MD: Rowman and Littlefield, 2012).

38 See, for example, Bridget Anderson, *Doing the Dirty Work: The Global Politics of Domestic Labour* (New York: Zen Books, 2000); Jonathan Blagbrough, "Child Domestic Labour: A Modern Form of Slavery," *Children and Society* 22, 3 (2008): 179–90.

39 See, for example, "I Am a Modern-Day Abolitionist," *Not for Sale*, http://www.notforsalefilm.com/about.html (accessed 2 November 2016).

40 Quirk, "Uncomfortable Silences."

41 Clifford Bob, *The Marketing of Rebellion: Insurgents, Media, and International Activism* (Cambridge: Cambridge University Press, 2005); 4.

42 Ibid., 6.

43 See, for example, Jo Doezema, *Sex Slaves and Discourse Masters: The Construction of Trafficking* (London: Zed Books, 2010); Jessica Pilley, *Policing Sexuality: The Mann Act and the Making of the FBI* (Cambridge, MA: Harvard University Press, 2014).

44 See, for example, Margaret Keck and Katherine Sikkink, *Activists beyond Borders: Transnational Advocacy Networks and International Policy* (Ithaca, NY: Cornell University Press, 1998); Thomas Risse, Stephen Ropp, and Katherine Sikkink, eds., *The Persistent Power of Human Rights: From Commitment to Compliance* (Cambridge: Cambridge University Press, 2013); Thomas Risse, Stephen Ropp, and Katherine Sikkink, eds., *The Power of Human Rights: International Norms and Domestic* (Cambridge: Cambridge University Press, 1999); Charli Carpenter, "Studying Issue (Non)-Adoption in Transnational Advocacy Networks," *International Organization*

61 (2007): 643–67; Clifford Bob, ed., *The International Struggle for New Human Rights* (Philadelphia: University of Pennsylvania Press, 2009); Assem Prakesh and Mary Gugerty, eds., *Advocacy Organizations and Collective Action* (Cambridge: Cambridge University Press, 2010); Sidney Tarrow, *Power in Movement: Social Movements and Contentious Politics* (Cambridge: Cambridge University Press, 2011).

45 Victims of Trafficking and Violence Protection Act, 2000, PL 106-386.

46 Quirk, "When Human Trafficking Means Everything."

47 See, for example, Kamala Kempadoo, Jyoti Sanghera, and Bandana Pattanaik, eds., *Trafficking and Prostitution Reconsidered: New Perspectives on Migration, Sex Work, and Human Rights* (Boulder, CO: Paradigm Publishers, 2005); Bridget Anderson and Rutvica Andrijasevic, "Sex, Slaves and Citizens: The Politics of Anti-Trafficking," *Soundings* 40 (2008): 135–45.

48 See, for example, Joe Doezema, *Sex Slaves and Discourse Masters: The Construction of Trafficking,* (London: Zed Books, 2010); Chandre Gould, "Moral Panic, Human Trafficking and the 2010 Soccer World Cup," *Agenda: Empowering Women for Gender Equity* 24, 85 (2010): 31–44.

49 See, for example, Laura Maria Agustín, *Sex at the Margins: Migration, Labour Markets and the Rescue Industry* (London: Zed Books, 2007); Makau Mutua, "Savages, Victims, and Saviors: The Metaphors of Human Rights," *Harvard International Law Journal* 42, 1 (2001):201–46; Jonas Todres, "Law, Otherness, and Human Trafficking," *Santa Clara Law Review* 49, 3 (2009): 605–72.

50 Dina Franscesca Haynes, "The Celebritization of Human Trafficking," *Annals of the American Academy of Political and Social Sciences* 653 (2014): 25.

51 See, for example, Jacquline Berman, "(Un)Popular Strangers and Crises (Un) Bounded: Discourses of Sex Trafficking, the European Political Community and the Panicked State of the Modern State," *European Journal of International Relations* 9, 1 (2003): 37–86; Cornelius Friesendorf, "Pathologies of Security Governance: Efforts against Human Trafficking in Europe," *Security Dialogue* 38, 3 (2007): 379–402; Claudia Aradau, "The Perverse Politics of Four-Letter Words: Risk and Pity in the Securitisation of Human Trafficking," *Millennium: Journal of International Studies* 33, 2 (2004): 251–77.

52 See, for example, Elizabeth Bernstein, "Militarized Humanitarianism Meets Carceral Feminism: The Politics of Sex, Rights, and Freedom in Contemporary Antitrafficking Campaigns," *Signs: Journal of Women in Culture and Society* 36, 1 (2010): 45–71; Global Alliance against Traffic in Women, *Collateral Damage: The Impact of Anti-Trafficking Measures on Human Rights around the World* (Bangkok: Amarin Publishing, 2007); Anne Gallagher, ed., "Special Issue: Where's the Accountability?" *Anti-Trafficking Review* 1 (2012): 1–168.

53 Joel Quirk, "Reparations Are Too Confronting: Let's Talk About Modern-Day Slavery Instead," Beyond Trafficking and Slavery, openDemocracy, 7 May 2015, https://www.opendemocracy.net/beyondslavery/joel-quirk/reparations-are-too-confronting-let's-talk-about-'modernday-slavery'-instead (accessed 23 June 2015).

54 Wendy Brown, "Revisiting the Jewish Question," in Austin Sarat and Thomas R. Kearns, eds., *Identities, Politics, and Rights* (Ann Arbor, MI: University of Michigan Press, 1997), 85–130.

55 Mark Goodale, *Human Rights at a CrossRoads* (New York: Oxford University Press, 2013); Mark Goodale and Sally Engle Merry, eds., *The Practice of Human Rights: Tracking Human Rights between the Local and the Global* (New York: Cambridge University Press, 2007).

56 Sally Engle Merry, *Human Rights and Gender Violence: Translating International Law into Local Justice* (Chicago: University of Chicago Press, 2006).

57 Sally Engle Merry, "Measuring the World: Indicators, Human Rights, and Global Governance," *Current Anthropology* 52, 3 (2011): 83–95; Kevin E. Davis, Benedict Kingsbury, and Sally Engle Merry, "Indicators as a Technology of Global Governance," *Law and Society Review* 46, 1 (2012): 71–104; André Broome and Joel Quirk, "Governing the World at a Distance: The Practice of Global Benchmarking," *Review of International Studies* 41, 5 (2015): 819–41.

58 See, for example, Doris Buss, "Rethinking 'Rape as a Weapon of War,'" *Feminist Legal Studies* 17 (2009): 145–63: Kamari Maxine Clarke, *Fictions of Justice: The International Criminal Court and the Challenge of Legal Pluralism in Sub-Saharan Africa* (Cambridge: Cambridge University Press, 2009).

59 See, for example, Anne Gallagher, *The International Law of Human Trafficking* (Cambridge: Cambridge University Press, 2010); Goodale and Merry, *Practice of Human Rights*; Mahmood Mamdani, ed., *Beyond Rights Talk and Culture Talk: Comparative Essay on the Politics of Rights* (New York: Palgrave Macmillan, 2000); Merry, *Human Rights and Gender Violence*; Austin Sarat and Thomas R. Kearns, eds., *Human Rights: Concepts, Contests, Contingencies* (Ann Arbor, MI: University of Michigan Press, 2001).

60 Hannah Arendt, *The Origins of Totalitarianism* (Orlando, FL: Harcourt Brace and Company, 1973), 267–302.

61 Sarat and Kearns, *Human Rights*.

62 Brown, "Revisiting the Jewish Question."

63 Mark Goodale, "Locating Rights, Envisioning Law Between the Global and the Local" in Goodale and Merry, *Practice of Human Rights*, 8.

64 Daniel M. Goldstein, "Human Rights as Culprit, Human Rights as Victim: Rights and Security in the State of Exception" in Goodale and Merry, *Practice of Human Rights*, 49–77.

65 Joshua Kurlantzick, "Global Gun Rights?" *New York Times Magazine*, 17 September 2006.

66 Goodale and Merry, *Practice of Human Rights*, 13.

67 Sally Engle Merry et al., "Law from Below: Women's Human Rights and Social Movements in New York City," *Law and Society Review* 44, 1 (2010): 101–28.

68 Choi-Fitzpatrick, "Letting Go."

69 Vigneswaran, "Methodological Debates."

70 Joseph Slaughter, *Human Rights, Inc: The World Novel, Narrative Form, and International Law* (New York: Fordham University Press, 2007), 40.

71 Austin Choi-Fitzpatrick, "Rethinking Trafficking: Contemporary Slavery," in Alison Brysk and Austin Choi-Fitzpatrick, eds., *From Human Trafficking to Human Rights: Rethinking Contemporary Slavery* (Philadelphia: University of Pennsylvania Press, 2012), 14.

Contemporary Slavery and Its Definition in Law

2

Jean Allain

Had Olaudah Equiano, Abraham Lincoln, or William Wilberforce been able to look into the future to the twenty-first century, what they may have been most struck by was not how far we had come in ending slavery and suppressing human exploitation but, rather, that we had yet to agree on what in fact the term "slavery" means. This is a rather intriguing puzzle, as a consensus has existed for more than ninety years among states as to the legal definition of slavery. Yet, this definition has failed to take hold among the general public or to "speak" to those institutions interested in the ending of slavery.

At first blush, this is not so hard to understand since the definition, drafted in the mid-1920s by legal experts, is rather opaque and seems to hark back to a bygone era. The definition found in the 1926 Slavery Convention reads: "Slavery is the status or condition of a person over whom any or all of the powers attaching to the right of ownership is exercised."[1] At first sight, the definition really does not convey much to the reader, but for the fact that it appears to require that a person own another. As the ownership of one person by another has been legislated out of existence – again – it appears that this definition should have no traction in the contemporary world. Yet, this is not so since the legal definition of slavery established in 1926 has been confirmed twice: first, by being included in substance in the 1956 Supplementary Convention on the Abolition of Slavery, the Slave Trade, and Institutions and Practices Similar to Slavery (Supplementary Convention) and, more recently, in the 1998 Rome Statute of the International Criminal Court (Rome Statute).[2] Further, the definition's contemporary relevance has been validated by international courts and been given its most in-depth consideration by the High Court of Australia in the 2008 case *The Queen v Tang*.[3] Thus, we know that the definition holds, but what we do not truly know is what it means.

This chapter unpacks the 1926 definition of slavery to demonstrate the manner in which it can and should be read so as to give it substance both as a legal tool – to assist in the prosecution of individuals involved in enslaving others, be it through the trafficking process or otherwise – and as an advocacy tool meant to aid in bringing contemporary slavery to the forefront of public consciousness, in suppressing slavery, and in assisting the victims. This chapter starts unpacking the definition by providing guidance as to how the property paradigm of the definition can be translated so as to reflect both the lived experiences of slaves and to provide its legal parameters, so as to give the term slavery legal certainty. That is to say, it provides a manner to read the definition and apply it. The chapter then works backwards in time, putting in place the background and evolution that allow for this contemporary understanding to emerge by further unpacking the 1926 definition and considering its various elements with reference to the *Tang* judgment. The chapter then concludes by going back still further in time, to consider the evolution of the 1926 definition and to show the dynamics that have been at play, which first marginalized its use but later breathed new life into the definition. In setting out this chapter in this manner, it will read like a "how to" manual, giving the reader both the ability to understand what slavery means in legal terms and, if need be, to follow its genealogy backwards to provide further understanding if need be.

Understanding the Definition of Slavery

Over a two-year period, from 2010 through to 2012, more than a dozen experts in the area of slavery and the law came together to develop the *Bellagio-Harvard Guidelines on the Legal Parameters of Slavery*.[4] This Research Network on the Legal Parameters of Slavery, established through funding of the United Kingdom's Arts and Humanities Research Council, was built on three pillars, personified by Anthony Honoré, whose classic article on ownership was published more than fifty years ago; by Seymour Drescher, Stanley Engerman, and Orlando Patterson, who represent the historical study of slavery; and by Kevin Bales, who is the leading scholar and activist dealing with contemporary issues of slavery. The research network sought to provide guidance to defence counsel, judges, juries, and prosecutors as to the legal parameters of slavery so as provide legal certainty, thus ensuring the integrity of the legal process through fair trials and respect for the rights of the accused to know the charges against him or her.

The research network provided more than an interpretation of the 1926 definition of slavery; it provided an understanding of this definition that is applicable in a contemporary setting where slavery is no longer legally allowed. In so doing, it shows that the property paradigm of the 1926 definition does in fact capture the essence of slavery, be it contemporary or otherwise. In considering the work of the research network, it is worth repeating the 1926 definition of slavery to give it emphasis: "Slavery is the status or condition of a person over whom any or all of the powers attaching to the right of ownership is exercised."

The focus was to try to understand what constitutes those "powers attaching to the right of ownership." By unpacking this phrase, it would be expected that the parameters of what was and was not to be considered slavery would become evident. The research question was, if you wish: what powers does one exercise when one owns a person? The answer, it seems to me, comes on two counts from Anthony Honoré, emeritus regius professor of civil law at Oxford University. First, in his seminal piece entitled "Ownership," which appeared in the 1961 *Oxford Essays in Jurisprudence*, he develops, at the level of first principles, what constitutes ownership, by setting out its various instances. These instances provided a framework for the approach of the network in seeking to apply a property paradigm to slavery. Second, in an essay meant as his contribution to the research network, Honoré considers the very notion of slavery from both a legal and philosophical perspective, pointing out that ultimately what we object to in slavery is the inability of a person to exercise their natural capacities when they find themselves in a "state of unlimited subordination to another individual."[5]

The link between this property paradigm and slavery is, in a word: control. In any situation of ownership, the owner controls the thing owned. This is normally understood as a possession. Typically, possession means physical possession, but it can also mean the ability to control access to a thing, such as when a person possesses the content of their house by simply controlling access to that house by means of the front door key. With this in mind, slavery should be understood as the ability of one person to control another as they would possess a thing. Ownership implies such a background relationship of control. Where a slave is concerned, this control is tantamount to possession. It is control exercised in such a manner as to significantly deprive that person of their individual liberty. Normally, this control is exercised through violence and later through threats of violence or coercion, but it may also emerge through deception and/or coercion. One need not physically control a person, in the same way that one need not physically possess the contents of one's house; control tantamount to possession of a person goes beyond their physical control.

In the language of the 1926 definition of slavery, possession is one of the powers attaching to the right of ownership. To exercise possession over a person is foundational to the concept of slavery. It is the hallmark of slavery. Slavery can only be present if possession is present; if control tantamount to possession is being exercised. It is foundational, as the *Bellagio-Harvard Guidelines on the Legal Parameters of Slavery* make plain – possession is a hallmark of slavery – and only if possession is exercised can any or all of the other powers attaching to ownership be exercised. Thus, one cannot sell something if one does not first possess it. In the same manner, one cannot sell a person if one does not control him or her in a manner that is tantamount to possession. In a related manner, the ability to sell a person will be indicative of the presence of control tantamount to possession. The reverse also holds: possession allows for the ability to sell; selling indicates possession.

What then are the other powers attaching to the right of ownership? Well, the power to buy or sell a person – to involve a person as the object of a transaction – may provide evidence of slavery. It is worth emphasizing that it *may* provide evidence of slavery. It is sometimes said that athletes are slaves because they are bought and sold. While it may be true that their services are being bought and sold, such transactions fail to meet the threshold of slavery if there is a lack of control over the athlete that would amount to possession. While the football player having been sold to another club and forced to move cities may deem it unfair; he or she will not be compelled to go be it under threats of violence or otherwise. The athlete may not like it, but he or she can always walk away. In cases of slavery, somebody is exercising control in such a manner as to significantly deprive the enslaved of her or his individual liberty. The person enslaving is dictating what the enslaved is to do and backing up these dicta with violence either actual or latent. So, it is not enough in meeting the threshold of slavery to say that a person has been bought or sold, though it may indicate that slavery is present. What is required is to establish whether control tantamount to possession is present. The same would be true where other such transactions involving human beings are concerned, such as bartering, exchanging, or gifting a person to another.

A second power attaching to the right of ownership is the ability to use a person. Again, one person can use another, but this need not amount to slavery. Nevertheless, such use may amount to slavery if the background relationship of control is present to such an extent that it is tantamount to possession. By using a person, what is meant is the deriving of benefit from his or her service or labour. In the case of slavery, such benefit might be the savings incurred as a result of paying little or no salary for labour or the gratification from sexual services. Closely associated with the use of a person is the power attaching to the right of ownership manifest in the ability to manage the use of a person. In general terms, it goes without saying that to manage a person is not to enslave them. Division of labour is such that employers make legitimate decisions on a daily basis about the management of workers. Where it will amount to slavery is when there exists control tantamount to possession, and then management of the use of a slave takes place. Such management will include direct management, where, for instance, a brothel owner delegates powers to a day manager in a case of slavery within the context of sex work. It may also include more abstract management, where a person manages the use of a slave by isolating them from their previous social relationships and forging a new identity of that person through the compelling of a new religion, language, place of residence, and/or even marriage.

Beyond the case of both the management and the use of a person may be added the power attaching to the right of ownership of profiting from the use of a person. In the case of slavery, this will be where, once control tantamount to possession has been established over a person, money can be made from his or her use. Thus, the use of the slave is translated into the making of money for the enslaver, but such profit might also entail the mortgaging of a person, being let for profit, or being used as collateral. In concrete terms, this would mean that a slave is used and the money received from the toil of that slave – either his or her salary or the product of his or her labour – goes to the person who has enslaved. Thus, to exercise the power of profiting from the use of a person, in the case of the enslavement of an agricultural worker would entail the establishment of control (ordinarily through violence, coercion, and/or deception) that would amount to possession. Having established this control, the agricultural worker is made to harvest crops, and the profit from that labour, along with the salary that was meant to go to the worker, is appropriated by the enslaved.

A further power attaching to the right of ownership that is often thought to be less common, yet fits into the property paradigm, is the ability to transfer a person to an heir or successor. In this situation, it would be difficult to see how such a transfer would be able to truly take place without the background element of control tantamount to possession being in place. Regardless, such control would need to be present for such an inheritance to constitute slavery. Lest it be thought that such cases of inheritance are a thing of the past, they are not. There are a number of systematic cases of widow inheritance in various countries. The case of Igbo and Hausa-Fulani of Nigeria is instructive. Among these communities, "widows are considered part of the estate of their deceased husband and, therefore, have no inheritance rights themselves," and, as such, certain customary laws prescribe that a widow be "inherited" by "a male relative of the former husband."[6]

In the language of property law, it is said that ownership can entail the ability to use up property; to exhaust a thing owned; to consume it. You can use a car until you run it into the ground; you can exhaust a pack mule; you can consume food. In the case of slavery, this power attaching to the right of ownership may be understood in relation to the disposal, mistreatment, or neglect of a person. Having established control tantamount to possession, slavery will be manifest where the disregard for the well-being of the person is evidenced by severe physical or psychological exhaustion, which, if allowed to carry on to its logical conclusion, would entail the death of the enslaved. In this case, the destruction of the person is a process of physical or psychological exhaustion; the person is broken and, over time, he or she grows frail, either in body or in mind.

A final power attaching to the right of ownership is worth mentioning, but more for its inapplicability to human beings then for its value in seeking to establish evidence of slavery taking place. With regard to what in property law is called "security of holding," the owner of property can exercise a power attaching to the right of ownership against an attempt by the state to expropriate. Such security of holding will not mean that expropriation is not allowed but, rather, that there is due process, a public interest, and that fair, market value, compensation will be provided. However, in a contemporary setting where individuals can no longer own slaves *de jure*, such ownership of slaves is no longer protected from expropriation by the state. Of course, the corollary is that expropriation cannot take place because the state cannot then take over the deed of ownership of a person. Instead, where slavery is concerned, one might think of an "insecurity of holding," a duty on the state to "expropriate"; to confiscate human beings held in situations tantamount to possession, so as to liberate them. What I am thinking of here is the positive obligation on the state to suppress slavery. In human rights law, there is established, at minimum, a positive obligation to bring about the end of slavery and to effectively criminalize such enslavement.[7]

Having set out the various powers attaching to the right of ownership, one gets a sense of what will constitute slavery in law. Having established a background relationship of control that would amount to possession, the exercise of powers attaching to the right of ownership will include the buying, selling, using, managing, profiting, and even the destruction of another person. In seeking to make a determination as to whether slavery exists in such a situation, it would be important to evaluate the specific circumstances and not make a judgment based on what the specific practice might be called. This is important as there is confusion within the realm of human exploitation, as certain terms, such as "slavery" and "practices similar to slavery" are terms of law, whereas other terms such as "contemporary forms of slavery" and "slavery like practices" are terms of art, which have no legal currency. As result, it is best to look at the substance of the relationship and simply ask: is there an exercise of any or all of the powers attaching to the right of ownership?

Where one is asked to consider the distinction in law between, say, slavery and forced labour or slavery and one of the "practices similar to slavery" (that is, one of the servitudes set out in the 1956 Supplementary Convention: debt bondage, serfdom, servile marriage, or child exploitation), it may be best to start by looking at the more serious of the offences and ask whether any or all of the powers attaching to the right of ownership are exercised in a given situation; if so, then slavery is present. In a case where one is making a decision between slavery and forced labour and slavery is not present, then one would look to the International Labour Organization's 1930 Forced Labour Convention, which establishes that "the term 'forced or compulsory labour' shall mean all work or service that is exacted from any person under the menace of any penalty and for which the said person has not offered himself voluntarily."[8] If it can be demonstrated that in the case at hand a person has been compelled to work under a menace of a penalty and that they did not offer themselves voluntarily, then this will, in law, constitute forced labour.

Likewise, in cases where the conventional servitudes found in the 1956 Supplementary Convention are at play – as between slavery and debt bondage, serfdom, servile marriage, or child exploitation – reference would first be made to the more serious of the offences, and, if the circumstances do not meet the threshold of the exercise of any or all of the powers attaching to the right of ownership, reference would then be made to the definition of those conventional servitudes as set out at Article 1(a)–(d) of the 1956 Supplementary Convention so as to determine if the situation has met a specific definitional threshold. Thus, by reference to the established legal definitions found in international instruments, conceptual clarity emerges and, with it, the ability to disaggregate concepts such as "trafficking," "modern slavery," "contemporary forms of slavery," or other umbrella terms meant to capture various forms of exploitation.[9]

The Contemporary Relevance of the 1926 Definition of Slavery

Having provided, up front, an explanation of the manner in which the definition of slavery can be understood and applied in a contemporary setting, this chapter now works backward to further unpack the definition so as to demonstrate how, in fact, the 1926 definition has contemporary relevance. In other words, before we could consider what constituted the various powers attaching to the right of ownership, a more fundamental question has to be asked of the definition: does the 1926 definition only apply to situations of chattel slavery or historical types of slavery where one owns – de jure – a slave? De jure enslavement is, in other words, ownership in the legal sense, where a right of ownership could be vindicated in a court of law in regard to a dispute between two individuals claiming ownership over an enslaved person. If the 1926 definition of slavery was only applicable de jure and not to de facto situations of ownership, then it would have little contemporary relevance, and, thus, the elaboration of the content of the powers attaching to the right of ownership would be a moot exercise. However, as we shall see, just as with illegal drugs or illegal weapons, one can exercise the power that attaches to ownership without actually owning such drugs or weapons in the legal sense. The question then turns on whether the wording of the definition of slavery found in the 1926 Slavery Convention allows for an interpretation that gives it contemporary relevance.

It bears repeating that the definition of slavery found in Article 1(1) of the 1926 Slavery Convention states: "Slavery is the status or condition of a person over whom any or all of the powers attaching to the right of ownership is exercised." One would be led to believe that, internationally, the definition has contemporary relevance since states negotiating the 1956 Supplementary Convention reproduced the substance of the 1926 definition in their text. Likewise, in 1998, states negotiating the establishment of an International Criminal Court once more reproduced in substance the 1926 definition of slavery in the Rome Statute. In its 1998 version, the text sets out a definition of "enslavement" under the heading of a crime against humanity. This definition reads: "'Enslavement' means the exercise of any or all of the powers attaching to the right of ownership over a person and includes the exercise of such power in the course of trafficking in persons, in particular women and children."[10]

I say that the definition is "reproduced in substance" since the latter half of the sentence does not add anything new to the substance of the definition. Instead, this is a common legislative tool used to bring to the attention of judges, prosecutors, and so on, that they should pay particular attention in cases of trafficking to those instances where women or children may be involved. Thus, in international law, the definition of slavery, as first set out in 1926, is very much the definition accepted by states. But the question remains: does the 1926 definition of slavery have contemporary relevance?

As late as 2005, the question was answered in the negative by the European Court of Human Rights (ECtHR) in the *Siliadin v France*.[11] In this case, the ECtHR, in considering the fate of a Togolese girl who had been exploited as a domestic worker by her French hosts, determined that both forced labour and servitude had transpired in breach of Article 4 of the Convention for the Protection of Human Rights and Fundamental Freedoms (ECHR), but it failed to find a case of slavery.[12] By reference to the 1926 definition, the court stated that

> this definition corresponds to the "classic" meaning of slavery as it was practiced for centuries. Although the applicant was, in the instant case, clearly deprived of her personal autonomy, the evidence does not suggest that she was held in slavery in the proper sense, in other words that Mr and Mrs B. exercised a genuine right of legal ownership over her, thus reducing her to the status of an "object."[13]

It might be added here that the ECtHR has, by reference to its 2010 judgment in *Rantsev v Cyprus and Russia*, moved away from its 2005 position, recognizing, in the case of trafficking into Cyprus for the purposes of prostitution – which had left a young Russian woman dead

– that it "considers that trafficking in human beings, by its very nature and aim of exploitation, is based on the exercise of powers attaching to the right of ownership" although there was no question of de jure ownership transpiring in this case.[14]

A more thorough consideration of the definition of slavery has come about not via human rights courts but, rather, through criminal courts, where, I would argue, the process is much more rigorous as there are competing human rights at play: the prohibition against slavery versus the rights of the accused to know the charges laid. In this regard, the 2002 judgment of the International Criminal Tribunal for the former Yugoslavia (ICTY), in the *Prosecutor v Kunarac et al.* case, is instructive.[15] The case dealt with the Serbian commanders of the ethnically cleansed town of Foca, Bosnia-Herzegovina, who, in maintaining a detention centre, used it as a means for regularly raping scores of Muslim women. With regard to this case, the Appeals Chamber accepted

> the chief thesis of the Trial Chamber that the traditional concept of slavery, as defined in the 1926 Slavery Convention and often referred to as "chattel slavery," has evolved to encompass various contemporary forms of slavery which are also based on the exercise of any or all of the powers attaching to the right of ownership.[16]

The Appeals Chamber did not recognize that the definition applied only to cases of ownership – that is de jure ownership – of a person since it stated that

> The Appeals Chamber will however observe that the law does not know of a "right of ownership over a person." Article 1(1) of the 1926 Slavery Convention speaks more guardedly "of a person over whom any or all of the powers attaching to the right of ownership are exercised." That language is to be preferred.[17]

A further case that shines much light on the definition of slavery is the 2008 *Tang* case, which was decided by the High Court of Australia. This case, which involved five Thai women who were sold and bonded into prostitution in Melbourne, allowed the highest court in the land to consider whether the definition of slavery had contemporary relevance. In other words, the Court decided whether the definition was applicable to cases of de jure slavery as the ECtHR intimated in its 2005 *Siliadin* judgment or whether it applied in de facto situations where a person did not legally own another person but, instead, exercised powers of ownership in a factual manner.

Before setting out the reasoning of the High Court of Australia in the *Tang* case, it might be worthwhile to take the reader through "Treaty Interpretation 101." The reference point for interpreting a provision like the definition of slavery is the 1969 Vienna Convention on the Law of Treaties (VCLT), which provides guidance on all things related to international agreements, including how treaties should be interpreted. The general rule is that a provision of a treaty should be interpreted in good faith, that one should look to the ordinary meaning of the words, considering them in their context (both in relation to other provisions of the treaty and to the treaty as a whole), and, finally, that the interpretation should be made in light of the object and the purpose of the treaty. If the outcome of an interpretation, in the language of the VCLT, "leads to a result which is manifestly absurd or unreasonable" or, more germane to our considerations, "leaves the meaning ambiguous or obscure," then "recourse may be had to the supplementary means of interpretation, including the preparatory work of the treaty and the circumstances of its conclusion." These supplementary means are thus the legislative history of the negotiations or, in the parlance of international diplomacy, the *travaux préparatoires*. The final element of treaty interpretation found within the VCLT relates to treaties negotiated in two or more languages. Where each of these texts is deemed authoritative, it may transpire that there exists a divergence between them. In such cases, and where the general rules and the supplementary rules of treaty interpretation do not eliminate the need, reference can be had to "the meaning which best reconciles the texts, having regard to the object and purpose of the treaty." These, then, are the interpretive tools set out in the VCLT that allows us now to consider the definition of slavery as first set out in the 1926 Slavery Convention. [18]

It will be recalled that the definition speaks of "slavery as the status or condition of a person over whom any or all of the powers attaching to the right of ownership is exercised." Turning first to consider the ordinary meaning of the terms "status or condition." The *Oxford English Dictionary* defines status, in the legal sense, as: "The legal standing or position of a person as determined by his membership of some class of persons legally enjoying certain rights or subject to certain limitations; condition in respect, e.g., of liberty or servitude, marriage or celibacy, infancy or majority."[19] Inference as to the term "status" being used in the legal sense can be drawn from the *travaux préparatoires* where, for instance, it was noted that the "most important measure for the gradual abolition of slavery is that the status of slavery should no longer be recognised in the eye of the law."[20]

In the definition of slavery, legal status is juxtaposed by the conjunction "or" with the term "condition," which may be deemed a "mode of being, state, position, nature." It is further described by the *Oxford English Dictionary* as a "characteristic, property, attribute, quality (of men or things)."[21] While "condition" has a legal meaning, this meaning is not relevant here since it speaks of a condition as a prerequisite for receiving, for instance, an inheritance on condition of the heir having reached the age of majority.[22] Thus, while "condition" in the legal sense is not applicable in the context of the definition, the juxtaposition of it with regard to legal "status" (that is, reading it "in context"), accompanied by its ordinary meaning as being an attribute of a person and a mode of being, speaks to slavery in factual terms. Such a reading of the phrase "status or condition," it might be noted, was confirmed by the High Court of Australia in *Tang.* The Court noted that "status is a legal concept. Since the legal status of slavery did not exist in many parts of the world, and since it was intended that it would cease to exist everywhere, the evident purpose of the reference to 'condition' was to cover slavery de facto as well as de jure."[23]

While it might be said that it is enough to base an understanding of the definition of slavery as being applicable in both de jure and de facto situations by reference to a reading of the phrase "status or condition," I would argue that there are two more elements that speak to this understanding of the definition, thus confirming it. Both deal with the phrase "powers attaching to the right of ownership" that is found in the definition of slavery. With regard to the first element, it will be recalled that the Appeals Chamber of the ICTY noted that "the law does not know of a 'right of ownership over a person,'" but, in fact, the definition speaks of the exercise of the "powers attaching to the right of ownership." The phrase is a step removed from ownership. One does not need to own the thing but, instead, to exercise a power attaching to the right of ownership. In the context of the definition of slavery, it does not speak of having a right of ownership over a person – a legal right of ownership – but, rather, of exercising powers of ownership even when, for instance, such ownership might be legally impossible. Here, one might draw an analogy to a case of a kilogram of heroin. While a court will not determine a "right of ownership" of the prescribed drug, for this is impossible, it will ask instead: who exercised "a power attaching to the right of ownership," such as possession, and sentence accordingly. In this manner, we see that the definition goes beyond the strict confines of the exercise of a right of ownership over person and, instead, speaks of the exercise of a power attaching to a right of ownership. Thus, the definition goes beyond a legal right of ownership (de jure ownership) and encompasses the exercise of such powers in de facto situations.

The second element touching on the phrase "powers attaching to the right of ownership" turns on the difference in meaning found in the authentic French and English versions of the 1926 Slavery Convention; more specifically with regard to the phrase "powers attaching to," which in the French text appears as "*les attributs.*" *Les attributs* can be translated to English literally so that the phrase would now read "the attributes of the right of ownership."[24] Since the object and purpose of the 1926 Slavery Convention, as noted in its preamble, is "securing the complete suppression of slavery in all its forms," the meaning of the term between "powers attaching to" and "*les attributs*" that best reconciles the texts would appear to be the one that allows for an expansive, rather than a restrictive, interpretation of the phrase. As a result, in speaking of the attributes of a right of ownership, the French text appears to go beyond the legal interpretation that gives credence to the general and supplementary rules of treaty interpretation, thus speaking to the definition of slavery going beyond the legal and being applicable also in situations of de facto ownership.

This interpretation of the definition of slavery, taking into consideration the rules of interpretation of the VCLT, produces the same outcome that the High Court of Australia arrived at in the *Tang* case – namely that the definition of slavery has contemporary relevance as it is applicable not only in situations of de jure ownership but also in situations where one does not own another person in a legal sense – since this is almost impossible today – but, in fact, exercises a power attaching to the right of ownership. Let us now turn to the *Tang* case in more detail.

In 2005, a Melbourne brothel owner was found guilty of five counts of both "intentionally possessing a slave, and ... of intentionally exercising over a slave a power attaching to the right of ownership." Thus, in the Australian context, the definition of slavery was incorporated in its domestic legislation. The case revolved around five sex workers who had been escorted to Australia and each sold for AUS $20,000 – that is to say, in the language of the buyers quoted by the High Court of Australia, "'the amount for this girl,' 'the amount of money we purchased this woman' and 'the money for purchasing women from Thailand to come here.'"[25] These women where then bonded through a debt of between AUS $42,000 and AUS $45,000 related to their purchase, travel, and accommodation expenses, which was to be repaid through sex work. In summary, the Court noted that

> while under contract, each complainant was to work in the respondent's brothel in Melbourne six days per week, serving up to 900 customers over a period of four to six months. The complainants earned nothing in cash while under contract except that, by working on the seventh, "free," day each week, they could keep the $50 per customer that would, during the rest of the week, go to offset their contract debts.[26]

The reasoning in the *Tang* judgment is instructive in two ways. First, the majority judgment of the court, penned by its chief justice, Murray Gleeson, sets out the legal reasoning, which demonstrates the contemporary relevance of the definition of slavery. Second, the concurring opinion of Justice Kenneth Madison Hayne takes a different approach, asking fundamental, normative questions in seeking to understand the applicability of the definition in a contemporary situation. Gleeson CJ sets out the reasoning of the court on the contemporary relevance of the definition of slavery and its reading of the exercise of "powers attaching to the right of ownership" as being applicable in de facto as well as de jure situations in the following manner.

He notes that in 1926 many of the states party to the Slavery Convention had already abolished the legal status of slavery and that the declared object of the parties was to bring about "the complete abolition of slavery in all its forms." The court goes on to state that:

> [i] It would have been a pitiful effort towards the achievement of those ends to construct a Convention that dealt only with questions of legal status. The slave trade was not, and is not, something that could be suppressed merely by withdrawal of legal recognition of the incidents of slavery. It is one thing to withdraw legal recognition of slavery; it is another thing to suppress it. The Convention aimed to do both.
>
> In its application to the de facto condition, as distinct from the de jure status, of slavery, the definition was addressing the exercise over a person of powers of the kind that attached to the right of ownership when the legal status was possible; not necessarily all of those powers, but any or all of them ... On the evidence it was open to the jury to conclude that each of the complainants was made an object of purchase (although in the case of one of them the purchaser was not the respondent); that, for the duration of the contracts, the owners had a capacity to use the complainants and the complainants' labour in a substantially unrestricted manner; and that the owners were entitled to the fruits of the complainants' labour without commensurate compensation.[27]

The court goes on to state that

> it is important not to debase the currency of language, or to banalise crimes against humanity, by giving slavery a meaning that extends beyond the limits set by the text, context, and purpose of the 1926 Slavery Convention. In particular it is important to recognise that harsh and exploitative conditions of labour do not of themselves amount to slavery. The term "slave" is sometimes used in a

metaphorical sense to describe victims of such conditions, but that sense is not of present relevance ... An employer normally has some degree of control over the movements, or work environment, of an employee. Furthermore, geographical and other circumstances may limit an employee's freedom of movement.[28]

While the Court would go on to consider the textual make-up of the wording of the Australian Criminal Code and the determination of its lower Court of Appeal, it followed on its previous pronouncement by concluding that

powers of control, in the context of an issue of slavery, are powers of the kind and degree that would attach to a right of ownership if such a right were legally possible, not powers of a kind that are no more than an incident of harsh employment, either generally or at a particular time or place.[29]

While Hayne J concurs with the reasoning of Gleeson CJ, he considers the notion of "ownership," stating that it "must be read as conveying the ordinary English meaning that is captured by the expression "dominion over" the subject matter.[30] Where ownership is a legal relationship, Hayne J relates, "an 'owner' has an aggregation of powers that are recognised in law as the powers permissibly exercised over the subject matter. It is a term that connotes at least an extensive aggregation of powers, perhaps the fullest and most complete aggregation that is possible."[31] Since ownership of a person is impossible in the Australian context, Hayne J states that "what the alleged offender has done must then be measured against a factual construct: the powers that an owner would have over a person if, contrary to the fact, the law recognised the right to own another person."[32] In considering the powers attaching to a right of ownership, Hayne J sees in possession the power of dominion over a person; he thus uses ownership and possession as being synonymous, stating that "possession, like ownership, refers to a state of affairs in which there is the complete subjection of that other by the first person." He then continues, stating that one, and perhaps the most obvious, way in which to attempt to give practical content to the otherwise abstract ideas of ownership or possession (whether expressed by reference to subjection, dominion or otherwise) is *to explore the antithesis of slavery.* That is, because both the notion of ownership and of possession, when applied to a person, can be understood as an exercise of power over that person that does not depend upon the assent of the person concerned, it will be relevant to ask *why* that person's assent was irrelevant. Or, restating the proposition in other words, in asking whether there was the requisite dominion over a person, the subjection of that person, it will be relevant to ask whether the person concerned was deprived of freedom of choice in some relevant respect and, if so, what it was that deprived the person of choice.[33]

Having turned to, and considered, the jurisprudence related to issues of slavery and "involuntary servitude" in the United States, Hayne J draws a number of insights, the first being that the American cases "show that some assistance can be obtained in the practical application of the abstract concepts of ownership and possession by considering the antithesis of slavery and asking whether, and in what respects, the person alleged to be a slave was free." Hayne J then continues: "Asking what freedom a person had may shed light on whether that person was a slave. In particular, to ask whether a complainant was deprived of choice may assist in revealing whether what the accused did was exercise over that person a power attaching to the right of ownership."[34] As a result of this analysis, which moves us closer to understanding not the criminality of the accused but, rather, the deprivations of the victim, Hayne J gets to the heart of the normative understanding of slavery and provides further guidance, beyond the majority judgment in *Tang*, as to the application of the definition of slavery in a contemporary setting.

The 1926 Definition of Slavery
Having worked backwards in the previous section to demonstrate the contemporary relevance of the definition of slavery manifest both in the wording of the definition and in the *Tang* case and, thus, grounding

the opening section of this chapter that considered the parameters of those powers attaching to the right of ownership, this section will take one further step back to consider the very foundation of the definition. This section considers the genesis of the definition of slavery as well as the reasons why it failed to take hold and have relevance throughout much of the twentieth century. The final point is worth emphasizing as throughout the twentieth century, the definition of slavery slipped further and further into obscurity so that, as the new millennium approached, its applicability was near naught; only to be given new life at the dawn of the twenty-first century by the work of the research network that developed the *Bellagio-Harvard Guidelines*.

The definition of slavery, and the Slavery Convention itself, was developed within the context of a League of Nations that was a European colonialist club, seeking to end slavery beyond its membership while curbing the excesses of servile labour while leaving it intact within the colonies. The genesis of the 1926 Slavery Convention emerged out of the provisions of Articles 22 and 23 of the 1919 Covenant of the League of Nations, which dealt with the Mandate Territories that were transferred from the vanquished to the victors of the First World War and, more specifically, those colonial possessions of Central Africa.[35] Article 22 states that among the responsibilities of the new mandate holders was "the prohibition of abuses such as the slave trade," while under Article 23, the Covenant required the members of the League of Nations to "endeavour to secure and maintain fair and humane conditions of labour for men, women, and children" as well as granting "general supervision over the execution of agreements with regard to the traffic in women and children."

Action with regard to these provisions was first precipitated by a memorandum circulated by Sir Frederick Lugard, a British member of the Permanent Mandates Commission, which proposed that Ethiopia, an independent, non-member state of the League, be placed under a mandate for its inability to suppress the slave trade.[36] This led to a chain of events that not only saw Ethiopia join the League of Nations but also the establishment of an instrument suppressing the slave trade, slavery, and forced labour.[37] The League of Nations established a body of experts, the Temporary Slavery Commission, whose work in 1924 and 1925 would be the DNA of the legal provisions related to forced labour, slave trade, slavery, and the convention servitudes that emerged thirty years later in the 1956 Supplementary Convention.

Where the 1926 Slavery Convention is concerned, while most of its provisions have been superseded by other obligations found in more recent treaties, what remains applicable are its definitions of both slavery and the slave trade. Where the slave trade is concerned, the convention sets out the following definition:

> The slave trade includes all acts involved in the capture, acquisition or disposal of a person with intent to reduce him to slavery; all acts involved in the acquisition of a slave with a view to selling or exchanging him; all acts of disposal by sale or exchange of a slave acquired with a view to being sold or exchanged, and, in general, every act of trade or transport in slaves.

With regard to the definition of slavery, it will be recalled that Article 1(1) of the Slavery Convention reads: "Slavery is the status or condition of a person over whom any or all of the powers attaching to the right of ownership is exercised." This definition, while it was considered by a drafting committee, found its final form through the pen of Robert Cecil, that is: Viscount Cecil of Chelwood.[38] Viscount Cecil, having considered feedback from states as to his proposed definition, reiterated his understanding of the definition of slavery as "the maintenance by a private individual of rights over another person of the same nature as the rights which an individual can have over things."[39] At the prompting of the Union of South Africa, Viscount Cecil made plain that unless a practice reached the threshold of the exercise of powers attaching to the right of ownership, it did not constitute slavery as defined by the 1926 Slavery Convention.[40]

This point was brought home in 1936, when the League of Nations' Committee of Experts on Slavery considered the issue of serfdom, emphasizing that one must make a distinction between slavery as defined in the convention and other forms of exploitation:

It is important, however, to keep the fundamental distinction clearly in mind, and to realize that the status of "serfdom" is a condition "analogous to slavery" rather than a condition of actual slavery, and that the question whether it amounts to "slavery" within the definition of the Slavery Convention must depend upon the facts connected with each of the various systems of "serfdom."[41]

The Committee of Experts on Slavery was more explicit in regard to its considerations of debt slavery, noting that at least theoretically:

Debt slavery is only a temporary form, for the assumption is that the slavery ends as soon as the debt is repaid. In practice, however, the conditions in which the debt-slave lives are often of the nature that repayment is an impossibility and the debtor is therefore a slave for life. Even worse than this may sometimes happen, for in some systems there are cases in which the debt is "hereditary" and, after the death of the debtor, it is transmitted to the children and children's children. It is right, perhaps, that one should realise quite clearly that the system – *whatever form it may take in different countries – is not "slavery" within the definition set forth in Article 1 of the 1926 Convention, unless any or all the powers attaching to the right of ownership are exercised by the master.*[42]

Despite such an understanding of the definition of slavery, shortly after the establishment of Slavery Convention, another stream emerged that sought to read into the definition of slavery an interpretation that went beyond its ordinary meaning so as to encompass lesser servitudes or types of human exploitation.[43] While this had its genesis in abolitionist groups that had to reinvent themselves in the wake of the 1926 Slavery Convention, it reached its fullest expression during the United Nations (UN) era. In 1956, the UN adopted an instrument meant to supplement the 1926 Slavery Convention. Though originally meant to suppress various servitudes, for reasons related to the obligations to be undertaken and not to the normative standards set, the term servitude was dropped, and the instrument was entitled the 1956 Supplementary Convention on the Abolition of Slavery, the Slave Trade, and *Institutions and Practices Similar to Slavery*. While the reasons for this change need not concern us here, what is important is the recognition that servitudes were now to be understood as "institutions or practices similar to slavery" or, in its shorter form, as "practices similar to slavery."[44]

This distinction is important since 1956 was a watershed for international relations. The previous year's Bandung Conference had created what would come to be known as the Non-Aligned Movement, while, in 1957, Ghana became the first African state to gain its independence from European colonial powers. The decolonization process would realign the UN as the original fifty-one member states would lose their democratic majority as newly independent states joined the organization, ultimately raising the Organization's membership by a factor of four. This loss of dominance within the democratic bodies of the UN (that is, excluding the UN Security Council) meant that newly independent states could set the agenda. Where slavery was concerned, this agenda related to the legacy of colonialism, including the African slave trade, but moreso to the apartheid regimes of southern Africa, which were considered to be aligned with contemporary manifestations of slavery. If it was not slavery, then at least servitude – that is, at least, in the language of the 1956 Supplementary Convention: "a practice similar to slavery."

Consider the main proponent of this approach, Waldo Waldron-Ramsey, the representative of Tanzania, who, in 1966, stated:

> The policy of apartheid followed by South Africa in its own territory and in South West Africa, by the racist, traitorous and illegal regime in the Colony of Rhodesia and the colonialist methods applied by the Portuguese Government in the so-called Portuguese territories of Mozambique, Angola, and Portuguese Guinea, were flagrant examples of slavery. It was manifest that the methods traditionally used by the colonialist must be regarded as practices similar to slavery.[45]

However, the advocacy of apartheid (and, to a lesser extent, colonialism) as slavery or as a practice similar to slavery was not accepted by the old guard. Despite having lost their majority, the original members of the UN held enough seats to be the gatekeepers of international law since the route to establishing a new legal norm through treaty law was via an international conference, which, procedurally, required a two-thirds majority throughout. For newly independent states, the numbers did not add up. Thus, the link between slavery and practices similar to slavery, on the one hand, and apartheid and colonialism, on the other hand, could not be sustained in legal terms.

Realizing this, Waldron-Ramsey changed tactics – though he was not happy – and, ultimately, what would emerge from the UN Economic and Social Council was a compromise found in a 1966 resolution that would see the creation of a term not of law but, rather, of art – a political term – that would gain much currency in the UN system.[46] This resolution decided "to refer the question of slavery and the slave trade in all their practices and manifestations including the *slavery-like practices* of apartheid and colonialism, to the Commission on Human Rights."[47] This term would add a layer of confusion to the regime of human exploitation – beyond what was created when "servitude" was replaced with a "practice similar to slavery" in the 1956 Supplementary Convention – since there was now the term of art "slavery-like practice," which was a near replica of the legal term "practice similar to slavery."

Having sowed confusion by this nomenclature, any momentum that might have been generated in addressing issues of slavery was lost from 1966 onwards. It might be noted, as Suzanne Miers has shown, that the emphasis on apartheid and colonialism by newly independent states deflected attention away from its "entrenched customs," such as child marriage and widow inheritance, which were legislated against in the 1956 Supplementary Convention.[48] That said, the confusion would lead to a loss of direction most evident in the work of the UN Working Group on Contemporary Forms of Slavery (1975–2006), which by the end of its tenure had overseen the collapse of the applicability of slavery at the international level. The working group failed to grasp the distinction between the political and the legal, utilizing the term "slavery-like practice" to mean provisions under the 1956 Supplementary Convention, coining the phrase "contemporary forms of slavery," which went beyond the definition of slavery to include situations that moved quite far away from the legal. Under the heading of "contemporary forms of slavery," the working group considered a number of social ills, including trafficking in persons, exploitation of prostitutes (in 1989); child pornography, children in armed conflict (1990); child soldiers (1991); removal of organs (1992); incest (1993); migrant workers, sex tourism (1994); illegal adoption (1996); early marriages, and detained juveniles (1997). Many of its considerations strayed very far from the status or condition of a person over whom any or all of the powers attaching to the right of ownership are exercised.

Where the legal came into play, and the definition of slavery gained some traction, which would lead to its contemporary application, was the move internationally within the realm of international criminal law. Towards the end of the twentieth century, what emerged was a "neo-abolition era," which was based, like its predecessor, on religious convictions that were backed by coercive legislation imposed by the most dominant state of the era. Thus, history repeated itself. Just as Quaker activism and Anglican evangelicalism laid the foundation for the British abolitionist campaign, which would first end the transatlantic slave trade and, in its wake, lead to the end of the slave trade on land and the abolition of slavery, so too did the "religious right" in the United States influence the American Congress in passing the 2000 Victims of Trafficking and Violence Protection Act (Victims of Trafficking Act).[49] Just as British dominance of the seas during the nineteenth century allowed it to force a network of bilateral "right to search" treaties that effectively authorized it to police the seas, controlling commerce in such a manner as to force the end of the slave trade at sea, so too did the Victims of Trafficking Act and its progeny force states – by threatening non-complying states with the prospect of losing foreign aid and multilateral assistance, and even have the United States vote against them at the World Bank and International Monetary Fund – to implement domestic legislation criminalizing the trafficking of people.[50]

While the United States may consider itself the enforcer; it is enforcing international criminal law in the guise of an international instrument, as its anti-trafficking legislation is based on the UN's 2000 Protocol to Prevent, Suppress and Punish Trafficking in Persons, especially Women and Children (Trafficking Protocol).[51] The Trafficking Protocol sets out a definition of trafficking in persons that, in essence, renews obligations previously undertaken to suppress slavery and also, most importantly for our purposes, other types of exploitation domestically. Article 3(a) of the protocol reads:

> "Trafficking in persons" shall mean the recruitment, transportation, transfer, harbouring or receipt of persons, by means of the threat or use of force or other forms of coercion, of abduction, of fraud, of deception, of the abuse of power or of a position of vulnerability or of the giving or receiving of payments or benefits to achieve the consent of a person having control over another person, for the purpose of exploitation. Exploitation shall include, at a minimum, the exploitation of the prostitution of others or other forms of sexual exploitation, forced labour or services, slavery or practices similar to slavery, servitude or the removal of organs.

The dominant position that the United States holds has allowed it, through informal empire, to require states to pass legislation that criminalizes the trafficking of persons for various purposes including slavery, servitude, and forced labour. Just as in the United States' later legislation, the 2008 William Wilberforce Trafficking Victims Protection Reauthorization Act, the original 2000 legislation makes it "the policy of the United States not to provide non-humanitarian, nontrade-related foreign assistance to any government that (1) does not comply with minimum standards for the elimination of trafficking; and (2) is not making significant efforts to bring itself into compliance with such standards."[52] As a result, states have turned their thoughts to slavery as a criminal offence in ways they had not during the twentieth century.

Further, the emergence of slavery in legal terms has also benefited from the criminal law paradigm as a result of the development of international criminal law manifest primarily in the jurisprudence of the ICTY in the *Kunarac* case and the establishment of the crime against humanity of enslavement in the Rome Statute. In *Kunarac* case, the Appeals Chamber's determination of enslavement was "based on the exercise of any or all of the powers attaching to the right of ownership."[53] This reference to the definition of slavery and the willingness to utilize it in international criminal law was confirmed by the definition's inclusion in the 1998 Rome Statute. The statute establishes the crime against humanity of enslavement as "the exercise of any or all of the powers attaching to the right of ownership over a person and includes the exercise of such power in the course of trafficking in persons, in particular women and children."[54] This definition is supplemented by the secondary legislation of the International Criminal Court (ICC) and its 2002 Elements of the Crimes, which seek to give more flesh to the bare bones of the crimes as set out in the Rome Statute. Where enslavement is concerned, the Elements of the Crimes set out the following, *inter alia*: "The perpetrator exercised any or all of the powers attaching to the right of ownership over one or more persons, such as by purchasing, selling, lending or bartering such a person or persons, or by imposing on them a similar deprivation of liberty."[55] This provision brings us full circle as it provides a short list of the "powers attaching to the right of ownership," which are considered in the opening section of this chapter, while pointing to the fundamental element of slavery – "the loss of personal liberty of the victim" – though it might be added: where it reaches the threshold of control tantamount to possession.

Conclusion

The Trafficking Protocol and the Rome Statute are fundamental to understanding the reemergence of the legal definition of slavery in the twenty-first century. As a result of these instruments, a majority of states – that is, well over a hundred states – have had to bring their domestic legislation into conformity with their international obligations by ensuring that slavery is criminalized, albeit transnationally and internationally. In so doing, and with the possibility of the ICC looking into issues of systematic enslavement within a country and the United States tying World Bank assistance to the suppression of trafficking of persons for the purposes of, among other things, slavery, it goes a long way to explaining the emergence of our contemporary neo-abolitionism era. Having considered the genesis of the definition of slavery from the League of Nations through to the United Nations era, a sense emerges as to why it was not utilized throughout most of the twentieth century. The *Tang* judgment flows from the criminal law side of the equation and truly engages with the definition of slavery by reading contemporary relevance into the 1926 definition. Having determined that the definition of slavery held not only in de jure situations but also in de facto situations, the Research Network on the Legal Parameters of Slavery took it upon itself to elaborate the *Bellagio-Harvard Guidelines on the Legal Parameters of Slavery*, which flesh out the exercise of powers attaching to the right of ownership in situations of slavery. The fundamental understanding of the definition of slavery then, if Olaudah Equiano, Abraham Lincoln, or William Wilberforce were interested, is the controlling of another person as one would possess a thing. Having established such control, the powers attaching to the right of ownership will include the buying, selling, use, management, profit, transfer, or even the destruction of a person held in slavery.

Notes

1 Slavery Convention, 25 September 1926, 60 LNTS 253.
2 Supplementary Convention on the Abolition of Slavery, the Slave Trade, and Institutions and Practices Similar to Slavery, 7 September 1956, 226 UNTS 3 (Supplementary Convention); Rome Statute of the International Criminal Court, 17 July 1998, 2187 UNTS 90 (Rome Statute).
3 *The Queen v Tang*, [2008] HCA 39.
4 The listing of the members of the Research Network on the Legal Parameters of Slavery is found within the *Bellagio-Harvard Guidelines on the Legal Parameters of Slavery*, which are reprinted in the appendix in this volume. Research Network on the Legal Paramaters of Slavery, *Bellagio-Harvard Guidelines on the Legal Parameters of Slavery*, 2010–11.
5 Anthony Honoré, "Slavery: From Ancient to Modern," in Jean Allain, ed., *The Legal Understanding of Slavery: From the Historical to the Contemporary* (Oxford: Oxford University Press, 2012), 9–39.
6 Immigration and Refugee Board of Canada, *Nigeria: Levirate Marriage Practices among the Yoruba, Igbo and Hausa-Fulani; Consequences for a Man or Woman Who Refuses to Participate in the Marriage; Availability of State Protection, February 2006*, Doc. NGA101045.E, 16 March 2006, http://www.unhcr.org/refworld/docid/45f1478811.html (accessed 18 October 2016).
7 In the European context, the positive obligations with regard to slavery are wider, as a result of the 2010 Rantsev case before the European Court of Human Rights. See ECtHR, *Rantsev v Cyprus and Russia*, Application no. 25965/04, 7 January 2010. Consider also Jean Allain, "*Rantsev v. Cyprus and Russia*: The European Court of Human Rights and Trafficking as Slavery," *Human Rights Law Review* 10 (2010): 546–57; Jean Allain, *The Law and Slavery* (Leiden: Martinus Nijhoff, 2015), 217–29.
8 Forced Labour Convention, 28 June 1930, 39 UNTS 55.

9   See generally Jean Allain, *Slavery in International Law* (Leiden: Martinus Nijhoff, 2013). Beyond the considerations of the High Court of Australia, the recent developments before the Inter-American Court of Human Rights should be noted, where the Court utilized the conceptual framework set out in the 2012 *Bellagio-Harvard Guidelines on the Legal Parameters of Slavery* to determine what constitutes those "powers attaching to the rights of ownership":

In this sense, the so-called powers attaching to the right of ownership must be understood in the present day as the control exercised over a person that significantly restricts or deprives him of his individual freedom with intent to exploit through the use, management, benefit, transfer, or divestment of a person. In general, this exercise will be supported and will be obtained through such means as violence, deception, and/or coercion.

See IACtHR, *Workers of Fazenda Brasil Verde vs Brazil*, judgment, 20 October 2016, para. 271 (translated from the Spanish.)

10   Rome Statute, Article 7(2)(c).

11   ECtHR, *Siliadin v France*, Application no. 73316/01, 26 July 2005.

12   Convention for the Protection of Human Rights and Fundamental Freedoms, 4 November 1950, 213 UNTS 221.

13   *Siliadin*, para. 122.

14   *Rantsev*, 280.

15   ICTY, *Prosecutor v Kunarac et al.*, Case nos. IT-96–23 and IT-96–23/1-A, 12 June 2002.

16   Ibid., para. 117.

17   Ibid., paras. 118–19.

18   See Articles 31 and 32, Vienna Convention on the Law of Treaties, 23 May 1969, 1155 UNTS 331.

19   *Oxford English Dictionary* (Oxford: Oxford University Press, 1989), 2nd ed., Volume 16, 573.

20   Temporary Slavery Commission, League of Nations, *Report of the Temporary Slavery Commission adopted in the Course of its Second Session, 13th July –25th July 1925*, Doc. A.19.1925.VI, 25 July 1925, 3.

21   *Oxford English Dictionary*, (Oxford: Oxford University Press, 1989), 2nd ed., Volume 3, 684.

22   The *Oxford English Dictionary* reads: "In a legal instrument, e.g. a will, or contract, a provision on which its legal force or effect is made to depend" – that is, "something demanded or required as a prerequisite to the granting or performance of something else; a provision, a stipulation." See *Oxford English Dictionary*, (Oxford: Oxford University Press, 1989), 2nd ed., Volume 3, 683.

23   *Tang*, 13 (emphasis added).

24   See *Oxford English Dictionary*, 2nd ed., Volume 1, (Oxford: Oxford University Press, 1989), 775, where it states that "attribute" "as a mental act", is "to ascribe *to* as belonging or proper; to consider or view as belonging or appropriate *to*. Italics in the original.

25 Ibid., 8.

26 Ibid., 9.

27 Ibid., 13 (emphasis added). Note also the confirmation of this reading in the following 2016 determination by the Inter-American Court of Human Right (translated from the Spanish): "The first element (status or condition) refers to both the *de jure* and *de facto* situation, ie., the existence of a formal document or a legal standard for the characterization of this phenomenon is not essential, as in the case of Chattel or traditional slavery." IACtHR, *Workers of Fazenda Brasil Verde vs Brazil*, judgment, 20 October 2016, para. 270.

28 *Tang*, 16.

29 Ibid., 16. Criminal Code Act 1995 (Cth).

30 Ibid., 60; Hayne J follows by explaining in more detail his understanding of dominion:

> As explained earlier, to constitute "ownership," one person would have dominion over that other person. That is, the powers that an owner of another person would have would be the powers which, taken together, would constitute the complete subjection of that other person to the will of the first. Or to put the same point another way, the powers that an owner would have over another person, if the law recognised the right to own that other, would be powers whose exercise would not depend upon the assent of the person over whom the powers are exercised.

31 Ibid., 60.

32 Ibid., 60.

33 Ibid., 62.

34 *Tang*, 65.

35 Covenant of the League of Nations, 28 June 1919, 225 Parry 195.

36 Suzanne Miers, *Slavery in the Twentieth Century: The Evolution of a Global Problem* (Walnut Creek, CA: AltaMira Press, 2003), 103.

37 See Jean Allain, "Slavery and the League of Nations: Ethiopia as a Civilised Nation," *Journal of the History of International Law* 8 (2006): 213–44; see also Allain, *The Law and Slavery*, 121–58.

38 See Jean Allain, *The Slavery Conventions: The Travaux Préparatoires of the 1926 League of Nations Convention and the 1956 United Nations Convention* (Leiden: Martinus Nijhoff, 2008), 51–60.

39 League of Nations, *Slavery Convention: Report Presented to the Assembly by the Sixth Committee*, Doc. A.104.1926.VI, 24 September 1926, 1–2.

40 See Allain, *The Slavery Conventions*, 76–79.

41 League of Nations, *Slavery: Report of the Advisory Committee of Experts, Third (Extraordinary) Meeting of the Advisory Committee*, Doc. C.189(I).M.145.1936.VI, 13–14 April 1936, 27.

42 Ibid., 24–25 (emphasis added).

43 See, for instance, Report of the International Commission of Inquiry into the Existence of Slavery and Forced Labour in the Republic of Liberia, (United States Department of State: Government Printing Office, Washington, DC) 8 September 1930.

44 For those interested in a fuller elaboration of the move from servitude to "practice similar to slavery," see Jean Allain "On the Curious Disappearance of Human Servitude from General International Law," *Journal of the History of International Law* 11 (2009): 303–32; see also Allain, *The Law and Slavery*, 297–324.

45 United Nations Economic and Social Council, Social Committee, *Summary Record of the Five Hundred and Thirty-Sixth Meeting*, 7 July 1966, UN Doc. E/AC.7/SR.536, 14 December 1966, 5.

46 Consider Waldo Waldron-Ramsey's words, as the Greek representative proposed that a conference be convened to settle the issue:

> The Committee was not asked to go back to the 1926 or 1956 Conventions, to which the Greek representative had referred, but to deal with slavery in 1966. Some delegations interpreted the notion of slavery in a limited technical sense and were endeavouring to restrict its definition to suit their own ends; he was not fooled by their humbug.
>
> They drew attention to the slavery alleged to exist in India and Pakistan where it was supposed to result from traditional debtor-creditor relationships, or in the High Andes of Peru and Bolivia, where it was said to stem from landlord-tenant relationships. In point of fact there was no slavery either in those Asian countries or in Latin America, but slavery undoubtedly existed in the African counties he had mentioned [re: South Africa, Rhodesia, etc.].
>
> Similarly, it had been claimed that forms of slavery were to be found in certain Islamic customs, particularly polygamy. He protested against such allegations which were designed purely to camouflage other motives. Forms of bondage similar to slavery might be said to exist in certain European and American countries particularly in the Anglo-Saxon countries where prostitution and drug addiction were rife, as he remembered from the time when he had practised as a barrister in London.
>
> Nor could the question of racialism be excluded, for it was the direct corollary of slavery. In his opinion, the classic definition of slavery he had given should either be accepted or extended to include all related manifestations of it without exception.

United Nations Economic and Social Council, *Summary Record of the Five Hundred and Thirty-Sixth Meeting*, 5.

47 United Nations, Economic and Social Council, Social Committee, *Slavery, Algeria, Gabon, Cameroon, Iran, Iraq, Morocco and the United Republic of Tanzania: Draft Resolution*, UN Doc. E/AC.7/L.492, 14 July 1966 (emphasis added).

48 Miers, *Slavery in the Twentieth Century*, 362.

49 See Christopher Leslie Brown, *Moral Capital* (Chapel Hill: North Carolina Press, 2006); Ronald Weitzer, "The Social Construction of Sex Trafficking: Ideology and Institutionalization of a Moral Crusade," *Politics & Society* 35 (2007): 447–75. Victims of Trafficking and Violence Protection Act, 2000, PL 106-386 (Victims of Trafficking Act).

50 See Jean Allain, "Nineteenth Century Law of the Sea and the British Abolition of the Slave Trade," *British Yearbook of International Law* 78 (2008): 342–88 (as reproduced in Allain, *The Law and Slavery*, 46–100); Victims of Trafficking Act, s. 110.

51 Protocol to Prevent, Suppress and Punish Trafficking in Persons, especially Women and Children, 15 November 2000, 40 ILM 335 (2001).

52 Victims of Trafficking Act, s. 110. William Wilberforce Trafficking Victims Protection Reauthorization Act of 2008, PL 106-386. These minimum standards related to legislating criminal liability for those involved in trafficking in persons require that the state "should make serious and sustained efforts to eliminate severe forms of trafficking in persons." According to the *Trafficking in Persons Interim Assessment Report*, the US Department of State has placed fifty-eight states on its special watch list, as it was deemed that these States, *inter alia*: "(a) had a very significant or significantly increasing number of trafficking victims, [and] (b) had failed to provide evidence of increasing efforts to combat TIP from the previous year." See US Department of State, *Trafficking in Persons Interim Assessment Report*, 5 April 2011, http://www.state.gov/g/tip/rls/reports/2011/160017.htm (accessed on 18 October 2016).

53 *Kunarac et al.*, para. 117.

54 Rome Statute, Article 7(2)(c).

55 International Criminal Court, Assembly of States Parties, *Elements of the Crimes*, Doc. ICC-ASP/1/3, 9 September 2002, 117. Note that attached to these *Elements of the Crimes* is a footnote that reads:

> It is understood that such deprivation of liberty may, in some circumstances, include exacting forced labour or otherwise reducing a person to a servile status as defined in the Supplementary Convention on the Abolition of Slavery, the Slave Trade, and Institutions and Practices Similar to Slavery of 1956. It is also understood that the conduct described in this element includes trafficking in persons, in particular women and children.

When Human Trafficking Means Everything and Nothing

3

Joel Quirk

In August 2010, the United Nations (UN) launched yet another new initiative to combat human trafficking. Describing trafficking as "slavery in the modern age," UN Secretary General Ban Ki-moon offered the following snapshot: "Every year thousands of people, mainly women and children, are exploited by criminals who use them for forced labour or the sex trade. No country is immune. Almost all play a part, either as a source of trafficked people, transit point or destination."[1] Since the mid-1990s, there have been many similar speeches launching many similar initiatives. At an international level, these initiatives now include the UN Global Initiative to Fight Human Trafficking (2007), the creation of the UN Special Rapporteur on Trafficking in Persons, Especially in Women and Children (2004), EU Directive 2011/36 on Preventing and Combating Trafficking in Human Beings and Protecting Its Victims (2011),[2] the African and European Union's joint Ouagadougou Action Plan to Combat Trafficking in Human Beings (2006),[3] and the Asian Regional Initiative against Trafficking in Women and Children (2000).[4] Governments, corporations, and large parts of global civil society have all rallied around the anti-trafficking cause, displaying a level of commitment – at least at a rhetorical level – that distinguishes anti-trafficking from many other human rights campaigns that either languish in obscurity or arouse fierce official opposition.

These recent initiatives build upon a series of common propositions, which continue to dominate official documents and public statements regarding human trafficking. The most important of these propositions include the following: (1) the scale of human trafficking continues to rapidly increase globally; (2) the main driving forces behind trafficking are globalization, organized crime, migration, and poverty; and (3) trafficking is one of the most pressing human rights issues of our time, which means that it should be prioritized over other "everyday" problems and practices. It is via this last proposition that the aforementioned connection with slavery becomes especially prominent, since slavery is both popularly regarded and legally defined as an exceptional category, which is frequently placed alongside genocide in terms of unusual severity. As we shall see, all of these propositions are highly suspect, but they have nonetheless helped to justify and orientate the now substantial amounts of time, energy, and money that continue to be expended on anti-trafficking initiatives.

This chapter takes its initial point of departure from a now extensive critical literature that maintains that recent efforts to both conceptualize and combat human trafficking have been profoundly flawed and have consequentially ended up doing more harm than good on multiple occasions.[5] This critical literature now dates back around three decades, and it has had a substantial impact upon academic debates. Outside the academy, however, the picture is very different. With the notable exception of debates over the legal status of prostitution, there has been remarkably little engagement with critical voices regarding trafficking at either a political or popular level. Critical voices have been largely ignored, rather than engaged, and established orthodoxies continue to be uncritically reproduced, rather than publically justified or explicitly defended.

This does not mean, however, that there have been no significant changes in recent times. As we shall see, human trafficking has proven to be a remarkably elastic concept, so its overall dimensions and political effects have been subject to a continual process of reformulation and contestation. There have been many additions and revisions over the last two decades, such as the notable inclusion of "child domestic trafficking" within the anti-trafficking agenda in the United States.[6] In this chapter, I am chiefly concerned with one notable recent revision: the widespread embrace of a "maximalist" version of trafficking, which has seen human trafficking become synonymous with all forms of "modern" or "contemporary" slavery. When human trafficking first broke through as an issue in the mid-1990s, there was a pronounced emphasis on commercial sexual exploitation. During this formative period, the essence of trafficking was widely understood in terms of three core characteristics: (1) the exploitation of migrants by (2) organized criminals for the purposes of (3) commercial sex. While this narrow version continues to have considerable resonance, the last decade has been marked by a move to (re)classify many other practices and problems as forms of trafficking.

The increasing influence of this "maximalist" version of trafficking is important on a number of levels. First, it can be potentially interpreted as an example of adaptive or strategic learning. As we shall see, one of the main criticisms that has been – and continues to be – levelled at the narrow version of human trafficking is that narrowly focusing upon commercial sexual exploitation has ended up excluding – or, at the very least, de-prioritizing – other equivalent problems elsewhere. Recent efforts to expand the anti-trafficking agenda to incorporate other problems can therefore be at least potentially regarded as an example of the "mainstream" responding to critical voices. If learning can take place on this front, then perhaps learning can take place elsewhere?

Second, the reclassification of many different practices as forms of human trafficking raises a series of questions about the political and analytical effects of this increasingly dominant vocabulary. Does reclassifying a variety of practices as forms of human trafficking help us to understand them better? Perhaps reclassifying can also help to generate additional levels of public interest and political investment? Finally, we have the nexus between trafficking and other alternative forms of classification. As we shall see, trafficking and slavery have increasingly become synonymous and interchangeable, while a third relevant category – forced labour – remains present but less resonant.

The main argument of this chapter is that the conflation of trafficking and slavery has resulted in a situation where trafficking increasingly means everything and nothing. The maximalist version of trafficking is not only analytically incoherent, it is also unlikely to generate high levels of further investment since this maximalist political rhetoric is only weakly connected to practical action. The original core version of trafficking – migrants, criminals, and commercial sex – continues to cast a very long shadow, and most recent efforts to expand anti-trafficking frequently have shallow roots within both political practice and popular consciousness. Furthermore, the numerous problems that critics have identified with the theory and practice of anti-trafficking are exacerbated, rather than corrected, by maximalist inflation. To help develop this overall line of argument, I have divided the chapter into two sections. In the first section, I provide a brief snapshot of the historical genesis and defining features of human trafficking in both theory and practice, paying particular attention to the key arguments found in a now substantial critical literature. Building upon this initial point of departure, the second section goes on to consider the strengths and weaknesses of recent efforts to expand human trafficking so that it is synonymous with slavery and forced labour.

Human Trafficking and Its Critics

Human trafficking can be best understood as a new way of (re)classifying a variety of long-standing problems and practices. Until relatively recently, the concept of human trafficking – or trafficking in persons – rarely featured in either policy circles or popular discussions. While the wide range of problems now described as forms of human trafficking have deep historical roots, they were previously classified and analyzed using different vocabularies, including slavery, sexual slavery, prostitution, or child labour.[7] The most prominent historical precursor to what is now understood as human trafficking concerned earlier campaigns focusing upon prostitution under the banner of "white slavery" or, less commonly, traffic in persons. While some recent scholars have begun to project the concept of human trafficking backwards through time, this retroactive reclassification tends to overstate the similarities between different conceptual vocabularies and practices by positing a false equivalence with human trafficking.

Within the context of this overall argument, the mid-1990s can be regarded as a decisive sea change since it was during this period that we see the emergence of a distinctive vocabulary, infrastructure, and cause in relation to human trafficking. While the backstory behind the emergence of this new cause still requires further research, it is widely agreed that at least some of the immediate impetus came from the internationalization of campaigns around sexual violence and abuse working in combination with increasing post-Cold War anxieties regarding international migration. In the decade that followed, the cause of ending human trafficking was rapidly embraced by governments, human rights activists, and international organizations, culminating in a situation today where trafficking is now firmly established as the preeminent way of conceptualizing and combatting numerous forms of human bondage.

The remarkable rise of anti-human trafficking as a political cause has not gone unchallenged. For over two decades now, a growing number of critics – both academics and activists – have questioned both the conceptual foundations and practical ramifications of both public and private efforts to combat trafficking. Many topics could be potentially discussed here, since different critics have developed different lines of argument. In this context, I will briefly focus my analysis on eight main themes. At the risk of overgeneralizing, I would suggest that human trafficking has been most commonly critiqued as (1) a form of "moral panic," which is predicated upon (2) unhelpful, paternalistic, and neo-colonial models of "innocence," "rescue," and "savoirs" and the "saved," which, in turn, (3) paves the way for collateral damages and carceral responses that too often end up hurting vulnerable populations. In addition, we have further lines of critique that contend that (4) prominent estimates of scale, distribution, and growth lack a credible methodological foundation, that (5) anti-trafficking has frequently been used as a strategic tool for political efforts to resist the decriminalization of sex work and (6) the extension and legitimation of punitive government policies to police migration. Finally, we have the critiques that (7) anti-trafficking policies remain heavily indebted to the troubling preoccupations and policies of the US government and that they have also (8) tended to overlook – and sometimes even legitimate or normalize – forms of exploitation that take place outside commercial sex. It is this last point that will be the major focus of the second section of this chapter.

The politics of – and the conceptual slippage that often accompanies – the relationship between human trafficking and sex work has long been a major focal point for both critical scholarship and political mobilization. It is chiefly in this context that human trafficking has been repeatedly denounced as a form of moral panic or political myth. One of the leading exponents of this critique is Joe Doezema, who has drawn upon parallels between historical "white slavery" campaigns and more recent anti-trafficking campaigns in order to advance her central argument that "narratives of trafficking in women, like those of 'white slavery', appear to be descriptions of reality, but are actually mythical narratives closely bound up with ideologies concerning sexuality, race and the state."[8] By drawing upon the language of mythology and ideology, Doezema focuses attention upon the causes, constituencies, and consequences associated with the reproduction of themes of "innocent" victimhood, paternalism, salvation, organized criminality, sexual danger, and national honour.

The main point of departure for this overall argument is the history and legacies of campaigns against "white slavery" in Britain and the United States during the late nineteenth and early twentieth centuries. Doezema observes that "white slavery" generated a tremendous amount of popular interest and political activity, yet there is now a widespread consensus among historical specialists that "white slavery" campaigns offered a grossly distorted and exaggerated picture of the issues involved, with few – if any – actual practices closely corresponding with dominant depictions of "innocent victims." According to Doezema, recent trafficking discourses do not closely align with the underlying empirical realities but, instead, should be approached as an "arena in which shifting ideas around sexuality, the role of women and ideas of labour and citizenship [are] contested."[9] While this line of argument is especially concerned with popular iconographies, it also has applications to recent debates over policy responses at a national and international level.[10] It is also within this context that further critiques regarding the politics of rescue, or the "rescue industry," come into focus.

The politics of rescue can be best understood in terms of a series of binaries between saviour and supplicant, protector and victim, or "civilized" and "backward." Some individuals and institutions are treated as actors, while others are tacitly assumed to be *acted upon*. This formula finds practical expression in, among other things, the "raid and rescue" model, which has emerged as the favoured strategy of many anti-trafficking organizations and operations. This model is predicated upon the idea that victims need rescuing, yet critics have suggested that in many cases rescue can actually be unwelcome, transient, and/or un-helpful. On the one hand, there are practical concerns regarding the poor implementation of rescue projects, with those who are "rescued" frequently being abused, deported, or neglected. On the other hand, there are philosophical concerns regarding the politics and the ideolo-gy of rescue, where self-congratulatory narratives of benevolence and paternalism have the tacit effect of legitimating and validating posi-tions of privilege while denying agency to those who are "rescued." This dynamic is further complicated by the popularity of highly stylized models of "innocent victimhood," which contribute to thresholds be-tween deserving and undeserving.[11] In a world where exploitation and abuse are ubiquitous, the "rescue industry" focuses upon a small subset of prospective victims, leaving numerous others outside its orbit of concern.

It should be evident from the above analysis that efforts to combat human trafficking are frequently said to end up doing more harm than good. Researchers studying the impact of anti-trafficking policies have come to describe this disconnect between aspirations and outcomes in terms of "collateral damage." Especially troubling is an increasing body of research that argues that anti-trafficking policies tend to inflict the most damage upon marginalized and vulnerable populations. Common examples include police abusing those they are supposed to assist, im-migration systems mistreating migrants with impunity, and people "rescued" from trafficking being subject to forms of incarceration, ex-ploitation, and abuse.[12] Rather than providing a solution, the state and its agents (and private actors in a number of cases) can instead end up making things worse. On the one hand, we have a widespread and in-creasing reliance on surveillance, incarceration, and even militarization, which results in heavy-handed and coercive interventions. On the other hand, we have bureaucratic systems that prove unfit for their purpose, often resulting in unjust detention, deportation, or prosecution.

Governments and campaigners generally agree that only a relatively small group of trafficking victims (however the term is defined) eventually come to public notice, while a much larger population remain uncounted and undocumented. The exact size of this larger population has also been a persistent source of controversy. Many different estimates of scale, distribution, and growth have been widely – and often uncritically – championed over the years. As is now well known, the key sticking point is the methodological grounds upon which estimates are created. A useful example of this overall line of argument comes from Laura María Agustín, who dismisses the vast majority of recent estimates of trafficking as "mostly fantasies," since

> many of the sources referred to, when investigated, are simply small local NGOs, local police and embassy officials, extrapolating from their own experience and from reports in the media. Most of the writing and activism on this issue does not seem to be based on empirical research, even when produced by academics. Many authors lean heavily on media reports and statistics published with little explanation of methodology or clarity about definitions.[13]

Many anti-trafficking initiatives have been at least partially justified on the grounds that trafficking has been increasing rapidly, but the evidence for this claim now appears to be speculative at best. This applies to both global and country-specific estimates.[14] Moreover, it is also clear that efforts to calculate the scale of trafficking tend to be implicated in underlying political and financial agendas. As part of a larger survey of the recent history of trafficking estimates, David Feingold concludes that "global estimates of trafficking do not serve any serious policy purposes. However, they do serve a socio-political purpose: to advocate for and justify the expenditure of resources."[15] If the scale of human trafficking is not actually increasing, or is perhaps on a much smaller scale than has been widely reported, then it becomes harder to make a case for supporting established policies and constituencies.

Financial considerations not only help to explain a widespread reluctance to question dubious statistics. They also help to at least partially explain the recent global proliferation of anti-trafficking organizations and interventions. Numerous organizations, both old and new, have calculated that (re)-badging their work in terms of "anti-trafficking" will help increase their chances of generating new funding streams and recruiting allies and audiences. Highly polarized arguments over the legal status of prostitution become especially important at this juncture.[16] Much of the energy that has been mobilized under the banner of "fighting trafficking" is ultimately directed towards preventing the decriminalization of sex work.[17] Opposition to the decriminalization of sex work has a long pedigree, but during the 1990s various conservative and reactionary voices (together with a smaller number of feminist abolitionists) were able to successfully (re)frame their position in terms of anti-trafficking. This new vocabulary proved to be very valuable as a funding strategy and political tool.[18]

The vast majority of funding that has been directed towards anti-trafficking causes has focused upon commercial sex, and this convergence between anti-trafficking and anti-decriminalization has proved to be a potent weapon in political and ideological arguments with sex worker organizations and their allies campaigning for decriminalization and greater protections for sex workers.[19] One of the most well-known examples of this political argument took place during the negotiations over the drafting of the 2000 Protocol to Prevent, Suppress and Punish Trafficking in Persons, Especially Women and Children (Trafficking Protocol).[20] Political conservatives and feminist abolitionists made a concerted effort to formally link trafficking with all forms of prostitution, while sex workers sought instead to ensure that trafficking would not be invoked to obstruct or otherwise penalize consensual sex work.[21]

Political, ideological, and financial calculations go a long way towards explaining the degree to which trafficking has shaped debates over sex work. It has also become clear, however, that other campaigners have sought to (re)-badge their work along broadly similar lines. On this front, a useful snapshot comes from Julia O'Connell Davidson and Bridget Anderson, who argue that

> the woolly and imprecise nature of the term "trafficking" ... makes it possible for so many people to clamber aboard the trafficking gravy train. And – to extend the metaphor – few of them agree on where

the train is or should be heading ... In one carriage we find feminist abolitionists who recognize no distinction between forced and free choice prostitution, and who have leapt in the hope of advancing a struggle against the commercial sex trade in general ... In another carriage we may find human rights NGOs that have joined the train out of desire to combat a human rights violation that they deem to constitute a form of "modern slavery." For these NGOs, it is not important whether the victims end up in the sex industry or another sector.[22]

The second part of this passage touches upon the recent move towards a maximalist model of human trafficking, which will be considered in more depth in the following section. For the moment, it is sufficient to observe that the cause of ending human trafficking has emerged as a major platform for both political contestation and political cooptation by many different causes and constituencies.

This in turn brings us to another line of critique, which revolves around the political relationship between trafficking, border protection, and criminality. This is primarily an issue in relation to international migration, where trafficking forms one element of a larger series of institutional responses to – and popular anxieties over – the global movement of peoples, particularly from developing to developed countries.[23] In an era of tightening immigration controls, a number of critics have identified human trafficking as providing further rhetorical ammunition for efforts to curb "undesirable" migration.[24] This line of argument is not only limited to institutional responses, but it is also said to reflect stylized images of the dangers of movement per se. One prominent exponent of this view is Ratna Kupur, who argues that

anti-trafficking initiatives are based upon assumptions about trafficked persons, especially women, as "victims" incapable of choosing to cross borders ... responses focus on border controls and the prosecution of "traffickers," who range from transport agents to the victims' families who consent to the movement. Discouraging women's mobility and stigmatizing her (third world) family therefore conveys a simple message: to keep the "native" at home.[25]

This critique shares affinities with the "open borders" approach, where migration is not something to be restricted and deterred but, instead, is to be facilitated and supported.

On this front, there have also been additional suggestions that recent anti-trafficking and anti-immigration efforts may ultimately be counterproductive because they increase expenses and hazards associated with migration without coming to terms with the complex reasons people seek to move in the first place.[26] This stance does not automatically align with popular images associated with the nefarious activities of organized criminal networks – which can at least sometimes be exaggerated – but it does direct our attention to the vulnerabilities that accompany migrants with the "wrong" type of passport or immigration status.[27] As many scholars have observed, undocumented migrants "are more vulnerable to threats because they know that efforts to seek legal recourse can result in protracted immigration detention, criminal prosecution, and, of course, removal."[28] Here, as elsewhere, governments tend to play a key role in enabling and encouraging the exploitation of migrants, yet their role tends to overshadowed by a focus upon criminals and illicit movements.[29]

There is one key exception to this lack of attention to governments: the recent anti-trafficking policies of the US government. This issue has both domestic and international dimensions, and it proved to be especially contentious under the presidency of George W. Bush, who was widely reported as having being "captured" – at both an ideological and institutional level – by "an unlikely alliance of feminists, conservatives, and evangelical Christians who have used the anti-trafficking movement to pursue abolition of prostitution around the globe."[30] The most commonly cited example of the influence of this alliance has been a legislative "gag rule" that officially prevented any organization that advocated the decriminalization of sex work from receiving funding. Since funding tends to be the lifeblood of all forms of political activism, this political economy of anti-trafficking ended up at least partially privileging certain approaches. Several commentators have examined which groups got funding and for what types of projects, and they have concluded that not only did anti-prostitution voices receive most of the resources on offer, but other voices may also have ended up at least partially reconfiguring their political platforms in an effort to secure financial resources.[31]

The influence of this anti-prostitution alliance has also been widely reported in relation to another central instrument of US anti-trafficking policy: the trafficking in persons (TIPS) reports by the US State Department. The first of these reports was published in June 2001 in order to help satisfy a series of requirements under the terms of the Victims of Trafficking and Violence Protection Act (Victims of Trafficking Act).[32] This Victims of Trafficking Act enshrined, among other things, a series of compliance standards for assessing anti-trafficking efforts. The inaugural 2001 report evaluated eighty-three countries, and this total has steadily increased with the passage of time. Using the criteria established by the Act, the annual reports rank the anti-trafficking efforts of each of these countries, dividing them into Tier 1, Tier 2, Tier 2 "Watch List," and Tier 3. The lowest ranking – Tier 3 – can be invoked by the US president to deny non-humanitarian and non-trade-related assistance to the countries involved.[33] From the outset, this ranking process has attracted considerable scrutiny. The key enduring issues have been a tendency to conflate trafficking and prostitution, a suspicion that foreign policy considerations have sometimes influenced the ranking process (with allies receiving more favourable treatment than enemies), the use of opaque and/or unreliable sources of information, and further complications associated with the United States appointing itself as a "global sheriff" on human trafficking.[34]

The Bush presidency played a key role in a formative stage of international anti-trafficking policy. Some of the worst features of this early period were reduced, but not entirely eliminated, once Barack Obama took office. Annual reports started to include human trafficking within the United States as an object of analysis, thereby partially addressing charges that there was a double-standard in only evaluating other countries (although the US prison industrial complex remains a notable omission). In addition, there was also a stronger effort to give more attention to practices and problems outside sex work and prostitution. Under Bush, the TIPS office published its own estimates of human trafficking. In 2004, for example, the estimate given was a figure of "600,000 to 800,000 men, women, and children trafficked across international borders each year," with approximately 80 percent being women and girls and up to 50 percent being minors.[35] In 2006, 2007, and 2008, the figure given was 800,000 annually, with millions more said to be trafficked within countries.

Under Obama, the TIPS office has given greater emphasis to estimates from outside sources. What is particularly important, at least for my purposes here, is the degree to which trafficking has come to be regarded as being synonymous with both contemporary slavery and forced labour. In 2009, greater prominence was given to research by the International Labour Organization (ILO), with particular emphasis placed on its finding that "there are 12.3 million people in forced labor, bonded labor, forced child labor, and sexual servitude at any given time."[36] While the earlier figure of 800,000 was also included in 2009, it would be notably absent from later reports and has not yet been updated. Significantly, both estimates in 2009 were found under a subheading entitled "The Scope and Nature of Modern-Day Slavery." In 2010, the same figure of 12.3 million appeared instead under a subheading on "Human Trafficking by the Numbers."[37] More recent reports have continued to collapse the distinction between trafficking, slavery, and forced labour. In 2013, the report declared that "as many as 27 million men, women, and children are trafficking victims at any given time."[38] As is well known, the figure of 27 million began as an estimate of contemporary slavery in the late 1990s, yet it has here been repurposed as an estimate of global trafficking. In 2014, we heard from John Kerry, the US secretary of state, about "20 million victims of trafficking."[39] Once again, this figure did not begin as an estimate of human trafficking but instead emerged via research on forced labour. During the Obama years, human trafficking has increasingly become interchangeable with slavery and forced labour, resulting in a situation where it too often means everything and nothing.

The Maximalist Approach to Human Trafficking

This expansive approach to trafficking can be at least partially traced to a larger debate over the relative significance of commercial sexual abuse in comparison to other problems and practices. Since at least the early 2000s, a growing number of critics have argued that the priority accorded to abuses associated with commercial sex have ended up at least indirectly marginalizing, or otherwise excluding, a variety of related problems and practices. There are at least two distinct strands to this overall line of argument. In the first variant, the main axis of comparison takes place within a trafficking framework. A good example of this approach comes from Janie Chuang, who has argued that "neo-abolitionist legal reforms ... have promoted criminal justice responses that target prostitution and leave unquestioned the exploitative labour practices and migrant abuse that characterize the majority of trafficking cases."[40]

In the second variant, the axis of comparison takes place between trafficking and forced labour or contemporary slavery. A good example of this approach comes from James Hathaway, who has argued that the Trafficking Protocol has "enabled governments to hive off a tiny part of the global problem of slavery as the focus of international attention and resources, leaving the overwhelming majority of slaves to depend on largely irrelevant and ineffective supervisory structures.[41] Both variants draw upon estimates and extrapolations that are subject to the same underlying methodological problems identified above, so the types of evidence cited to support both lines of argument must once again be approached with caution.

One of the most important early sources of information that was invoked to support arguments that labour abuses outside the commercial sex industry were being neglected was a 2005 ILO report entitled *A Global Alliance against Forced Labour*.[42] It was this report that was responsible for the aforementioned finding that a minimum of 12.3 million people were being subject to forced labour. In keeping with the terms of the 1930 ILO's Forced Labour Convention, the report defined forced labour as "all work or service which is exacted from any person under the menace of any penalty and for which the said person has not offered himself voluntarily."[43] The 2005 report also generated a series of regional (rather than country-specific) estimates, with the three regions with the largest concentrations of forced labour being reported as Asia and the Pacific (9,490,000), Latin America and the Caribbean (1,320,000), and sub-Saharan Africa (660,000). While these figures were methodologically flawed, they nonetheless proved to be politically significant because they included a key finding that the vast majority of cases of forced labour involved private agents and economic exploitation, with forced prostitution accounting for between 8 and 10 percent of regional cases. A different pattern was reported in wealthy industrialized countries, where forced prostitution was calculated to account for around 55 percent of an overall total of 360,000.[44] These figures provided ammunition for critics who argued that sex had been "oversold."

Even more significant was an additional finding that the minimum number of persons in forced labour at a given moment as a result of trafficking was 2,450,000 or 20 percent of the overall total of 12.3 million. The ILO therefore concluded in 2005 that a "large majority of forced labour globally is not linked to trafficking."[45] Yet when the ILO later published a follow-up report in 2012, their earlier position on trafficking underwent a major redefinition. Accordingly, their new survey concluded that there were now 20.9 million people who were

> victims of forced labour globally, trapped in jobs into which they were coerced or deceived and which they cannot leave. Human trafficking can also be regarded as forced labour, and so this estimate captures the full realm of human trafficking for labour and sexual exploitation, or what some call "modern-day slavery."[46]

Here, as elsewhere, we find categories merging into one another. It becomes much harder to argue that anti-trafficking polices have neglected labour when trafficking covers everything.

While critics such as James Hathaway have employed a comparatively narrow approach to trafficking, a number of recent defenders of a human trafficking framework instead maintain that trafficking actually covers far more practices and problem areas than has sometimes been appreciated. One influential example of this approach comes from Anne Gallagher, who has argued that "it is difficult to identify a 'contemporary form of slavery' that would not fall within [the] generous parameters" of the Trafficking Protocol.[47] Gallagher's position here is primarily based upon a legal analysis of the requirements of the Trafficking Protocol, which defines trafficking in the following terms:

The recruitment, transportation, transfer, harbouring or receipt of persons, by means of the threat or use of force or other forms of coercion, of abduction, of fraud, of deception, of the abuse of power or of a position of vulnerability or of the giving or receiving of payments or benefits to achieve the consent of a person having control over another person, for the purpose of exploitation. Exploitation shall include, at a minimum, the exploitation of the prostitution of others or other forms of sexual exploitation, forced labour or services, slavery or practices similar to slavery, servitude or the removal of organs.[48]

This complex formula clearly goes beyond the confines of commercial sex to incorporate many practices, which can therefore be regarded – at least formally – as forms of trafficking.

This does not, however, mark the end of the conversation. The Trafficking Protocol was established as one of three supplements to the 2000 Convention against Transnational Organized Crime, so it is necessary for states to sign up to the "parent" convention before they can sign up to any of the protocols.[49] As its name suggests, this lengthy convention is designed to strengthen cooperation against organized crime, and it contains a series of provisions criminalizing "safe havens," money laundering, corruption, and other related matters. Significantly, these provisions only apply to "serious crimes" with a transnational dimension and an organized criminal element (a structured group of three or more persons). These conditions extend to the supplementary protocols, which means that if both traffickers and trafficked operate within the boundaries of a single state, they may not be formally covered by the protocol. In response to this lacuna, Gallagher points to a further obligation in the parent convention that "requires that the offense of trafficking be established in the domestic law of every State Party, independently of its transnational nature."[50]

There is no question that this further obligation has been reflected in practice, since anti-trafficking legislation typically covers both international and domestic practices. In Gallagher's view, there are therefore solid legal grounds for applying a human trafficking framework to virtually all forms of enslavement. Accordingly, the idea of slavery and trafficking being in competition is actually a non-issue

> While much remains to be done ... international human rights mechanisms have, particularly over the past decade, demonstrated a growing willingness to consider issues of private exploitation such as trafficking, debt bondage, forced labor, forced marriage, child sexual exploitation, and child labor, occurring *within*, as well as between, countries. It is this fact, more than any other, that lays to rest any concerns that the global campaign against trafficking has wasted effort and resources that could better have been spent on the "broader" problem of enslavement.[51]

This formula is not only confined to legal analysis but also extends to an explicitly political argument. Not only are the relevant legal structures in place, there is also said to be a growing willingness to combat many forms of abuse under the rubric of trafficking.

As I have already indicated, this more expansive reading of trafficking has also featured prominently in the recent incarnations of the US annual TIPS reports. In 2015, for example, we learned that trafficking in persons and modern slavery are "used as umbrella terms." Furthermore, human trafficking is now said to cover practices as diverse as "the sale of women and children by terrorists in the Middle East, the sex trafficking of girls lured from their homes in Central Europe, the exploitation of farm workers in North America, or the enslavement of fishermen in Southeast Asia."[52] Understood in these terms, human trafficking can be further divided into many different forms, including sex trafficking, child sex trafficking, forced labour, bonded labour or debt bondage, domestic servitude, forced child labour, unlawful recruitment, and the use of child soldiers.

Perhaps most problematically, the 2015 report follows several years of precedent by removing any requirement for victims to have been involved in migration, declaring that

> human trafficking can include, but does not require, movement. People may be considered trafficking victims regardless of whether they were born into a state of servitude, were exploited in their hometown, were transported to the exploitative situation, previously consented to work for a trafficker, or participated in a crime as a

direct result of being subjected to trafficking. At the heart of this phenomenon is the traffickers' goal of exploiting and enslaving their victims and the myriad coercive and deceptive practices they use to do so.[53]

This clearly marks a decisive departure from the migrants, criminals, and commercial sex formula that was the central model for discussion of human trafficking in the late 1990s.

As I have already indicated, I think it is likely that this maximalist approach to trafficking has been at least partially developed in response to earlier critics regarding the relative neglect of issues that fell outside the original parameters of migrants, criminals, and commercial sex. By incorporating different practices and problems, the maximalist approach at least potentially undercuts charges of "ideological capture" in relation to commercial sex. By incorporating practices that take place within – as well as between – sovereign borders, it potentially undercuts charges that ending human trafficking is ultimately little more than a further pretext for border protection. If a human trafficking framework can be successfully adapted to incorporate at least some of the issues that critics have argued have been neglected or distorted, then perhaps the energy and resources that have recently been invested in anti-trafficking can now be channelled towards a more inclusive and effective political agenda. Maybe this new approach is not ideal, but is there not at least a utilitarian case to be made that it nonetheless marks a major advance upon earlier models of political activism and analysis?

While I can understand the logic behind such arguments, I would nonetheless argue that recent efforts to promote a maximalist understanding of trafficking should be resisted rather than welcomed. This conclusion rests upon three main considerations: (1) the analytical incoherence that quickly arises when human trafficking is interpreted in maximalist terms; (2) the serious challenges involved in convincing key stakeholders to invest in this new understanding of trafficking beyond the level of political rhetoric; and (3) the degree to which the expanding parameters of human trafficking are likely to end up exacerbating, rather than correcting, the existing problems that numerous critics have already identified regarding anti-trafficking in theory and practice.

The maximalist approach to trafficking is subject to all kinds of analytical challenges. As any number of commentators have observed, trafficking has never been easy to define or apply. Not everyone uses the concept in the same way, and even in cases where a definition has been agreed upon there remains scope to disagree over whether or not individual cases meet relevant thresholds. One of the main points at issue here is the complex relationship between trafficking and migration. Despite frequent – and often highly ritualized – comparisons between slave trading and human trafficking, the vast majority of individuals who come to be defined as trafficking victims actually migrate voluntarily, yet do so on the basis of imperfect or fraudulent information. While kidnapping and abductions are not entirely unheard of, trafficking tends to be chiefly defined by what happens after migrants reach their eventual destination. The archetypal case revolves around international migration. Until trafficking victims arrive at their destination, there can be very little to distinguish them from other categories of migrant. As the now extensive literature on international migration can attest, the pursuit of sanctuary and/or a better life regularly propels tens of millions of people to migrate, either legally or illegally. If these migrants manage to circumvent restrictions on movement, they routinely end up being framed as a menace to the socio-economic order by "host" populations opposed to the "wrong" types of immigration. If these migrants find a way of circumventing migrations controls, yet then end up trapped in bondage, they can end up as victims of trafficking and, hence, (qualified) objects of sympathy. There is not one path for migrants and one path for trafficking victims but, rather, many overlapping paths with many overlapping destinations. This can make it difficult to determine – both in theory and in practice – where trafficking ends and where people smuggling, asylum seeking, or economic migration begins. Importantly, this is not simply a technical or analytical exercise. It is also a political question, with governments routinely manipulating the language of trafficking to serve their interests.

The conceptual challenges associated with trafficking are evident in the definition of trafficking found in the Trafficking Protocol, which comprises over a hundred words and a series of qualifying clauses revolving around transit (for example, recruitment, transportation, transfer), technique (for example, force, coercion, abduction), and terms of exploitation (for instance, sexual exploitation, forced labour, slavery). When trafficking first emerged as a major issue in the mid-1990s, one of the major initial policy responses was – and remains – to offer training for public servants (police, customs officials, prosecutors, and so on) regarding what the definition of trafficking meant and how it should be applied. Despite the production of numerous training manuals and training courses, there continues to be consistent reports of relevant officials misunderstanding and misapplying trafficking legislation.[54] While these definitional challenges are by no means unique to trafficking, there is nonetheless a level of complexity at work here that means that trafficking presents a series of challenges at the best of times.

These challenges are greatly exacerbated when trafficking is defined in maximalist terms. This is most obviously an issue when human trafficking is applied to cases where no movement takes place. Various forms of heredity bondage remain a significant problem in a number of parts of the globe, most notably in parts of West Africa and the Indian subcontinent, and it is very difficult to apply either the "transit" or "technique" component of the Trafficking Protocol to such cases. This is not to say that movement is entirely absent in such cases, but it can be difficult to regard it as a defining or central feature in a significant number of cases. Similar problems arise when it comes to the topical nexus between trafficking and supply chains. The most recent TIPS report gave prominent billing to supply chains, observing that

> human trafficking has no boundaries and respects no laws. It exists in formal and informal labor markets of both lawful and illicit industries, affecting skilled and unskilled workers from a spectrum of educational backgrounds. Victims include adults and children, foreign nationals and citizens, those who travel far – whether through legal or illegal channels – only to be subjected to exploitation, and those who have been exploited without ever leaving their hometowns.[55]

Setting aside movement as a defining criteria leaves us with a version of trafficking that is a long way removed from what most people commonly understand trafficking to look like.

Trafficking is hard to describe at the best of times, but without movement it becomes an incoherent mess. Once these and other related practices – such as forced marriage, the abuse of child soldiers, or forced labour for the state – are treated as forms of trafficking, we rapidly reach a point where trafficking frequently becomes a hollowed out placeholder, while other concepts do all the analytical work. As the preceding statement makes clear, the maximalist approach to trafficking does not do away with the other ways of classifying exploitation and abuse, such as slavery or forced labour, but instead regards them as synonymous with trafficking. It is by no means clear, however, what additional analytical value or conceptual insight is derived by the addition of a human trafficking framework. At the heart of the trafficking framework is a concern with forms of private exploitation and criminal activities that arise as a consequence of vulnerabilities and abuses associated with migration. This point of departure becomes incoherent in cases where migration is peripheral or inconsequential.

This brings us back to the idea that the motivations at work for expanding trafficking are political rather than analytical. As we have seen, the politics of human trafficking have always been rather murky, since trafficking is not so much a singular issue as a powerful lodestone for a variety of often competing interests, orientations, and agendas. In this context, our task becomes to identify the underlying issues or agendas that help explain recent moves towards a maximalist approach. From a political activism standpoint, the primarily strategic logic behind a maximalist approach to human trafficking is based upon the idea that this rebadging will draw additional attention to problems that might otherwise have slipped below the radar. If invoking a human trafficking framework can help to generate political pressure and additional resources to combat serious human rights abuses, then perhaps the charge of analytical incoherence is not very relevant. Should we prioritize politics over analysis?

While this logic cannot be entirely dismissed out of hand, it also requires further contextualization. At this juncture, it is important to keep in mind that there are already many non-governmental organizations (NGOs) working on many different practices and problems. In the Indian sub-continent, to take but one example, efforts to combat bonded labour date back to the 1970s, with contributions coming from the Bonded Labour Liberation Front, Volunteers for Social Justice, the South Asian Coalition on Child Servitude, the Gandhi Peace Foundation, the Human Rights Commission of Pakistan, the Pakistan Institute of Labour, Education and Research, the Bonded Labour Liberation Front of Pakistan, Backward Society Education, and the Informal Sector Service Centre. These NGOs also have links with NGOs in the North such as Human Rights Watch and Anti-Slavery International, along with international organizations such as the ILO and the International Organization for Migration, creating a relatively dense institutional network that predates the emergence of this new approach to human trafficking. In this context, any assessment of the maximalist approach needs to consider (1) whether the addition of trafficking gives additional value to established activities and (2) whether the addition of trafficking complicates or compromises established efforts. Any assessment of these issues requires case-specific analysis, which goes well beyond the scope of this chapter, but the basic point here is that it does not automatically follow that adding a trafficking framework adds political value or useful visibility. Given all of the problems that critics have identified, adding trafficking may very well make things worse.

However, this does not mark the end of the political calculus that is at work. On this front, we also need to take into account the persistence of political interests and economic agendas that are likely to resist a maximalist approach. The main danger here is that the maximalist approach becomes little more than a rhetorical gesture, or superficial commitment, while the real energy and expertise remain concentrated on the "core business" of migration, criminals, and commercial sex. The Trafficking Protocol and other similar instruments may well formally apply to a variety of practices, but it does not necessarily follow that this legal theory is reflected in substantive practices. If governments chiefly understand trafficking as a migration, prostitution, and border protection issue, then they are likely to resist efforts to expand trafficking to include other related practices, especially if this means confronting major economic interests (such as cheap labour and supply chains) or institutional complicity (such as forced labour for the state or abuses tied to official migrant labour schemes).

While this subject once again requires further case-by-case investigation, it is also worth keeping in mind that it is not simply a question of political interests but also a question of popular consciousness. As many critics have noted, popular impressions of trafficking tend to be heavily informed by stylized narratives of "innocent" victimhood, whereby naive girls (autonomous women being largely absent) are tricked or abducted into sexual slavery, where they endure a range of horrific abuses. These "innocent" victim narratives frequently have an underlying subtext of sexual voyeurism, but even in their less problematic incarnations they can nonetheless establish a series of expectations against which actual practices can end up being at least partially evaluated. This iconography can mean that vulnerable and abused individuals find it difficult to gain a sympathetic hearing because their personal histories do not correspond to the "innocent" victim model.[56] Since popular impressions of trafficking tend to be tied to a specific set of expectations, it remains an open question whether the general public is likely to be truly receptive to this maximalist approach. And if this approach is not taken up, then the politics of trafficking are likely to remain focused upon topics that attract the most public interest and political activity: commercial sex.

As we have already seen, the cause of ending trafficking is subject to numerous problems. These problems will not be resolved by moving towards a maximalist approach. Estimates of scale are not going to get better once there are more things to count. The strategic manipulation of anti-trafficking for the purposes of border protection is likely to continue. We are still left with the problems associated with moral panic, collateral damage, and the politics of rescue. If the collateral damage critique is substantially correct, it really does not seem like a very good idea to extend anti-trafficking to other practices and issues. Given all of these considerations, it would be better perhaps to make trafficking conceptually and politically smaller rather than expand its parameters to such a significant and indeterminate degree.

Concluding Remarks

The last two decades have been characterized by a marked improvement in the global profile of human trafficking. While most commentators have welcomed this trend, there have also been a growing number of critical voices that have challenged the conception and execution of anti-trafficking efforts. The main focus of these critiques, which first emerged around the turn of the century, has been the contentious relationship between prostitution, trafficking, and border protection. Official efforts to combat trafficking have generally proved remarkably resilient in face of these critiques, with the dominant response being to maintain course (with perhaps slightly more defensiveness than in the past). There has been, however, one area where a recent shift can be identified: the move to place a variety of practices alongside commercial sex under the anti-trafficking rubric. Faced with criticism that anti-trafficking efforts have narrowly focused upon a subset of the overall problem, influential voices and institutions – most notably the US government – have gradually embraced a new conception of human trafficking that now formally extends to many different practices and problems.

This chapter has sought to demonstrate that this maximalist approach to human trafficking is both analytically incoherent and politically problematic. The analytical rationale for expanding trafficking is weak and unnecessarily complicated, especially in relation to cases where movement is not a defining feature of the cases at hand, and the underlying political agendas driving anti-trafficking efforts are likely to reduce this maximalist approach to little more than a rhetorical flourish while the core action takes place elsewhere. Moreover, there remain so many problems with how anti-trafficking policies have been both conceptualized and implemented that it is hard to see why their remit should be expanded. As we have seen, the impulse to aggregate and lump together as many issues as possible under a common rubric has clearly had a major influence upon the politics of trafficking and contemporary slavery. This impulse is increasingly proving to be problematic. Not everything belongs together.

Notes

1   "UN Launches Global Action Plan to Combat Scourge of Human Trafficking," 31 August 2010, http://www.un.org/apps/news/story.asp?NewsID=35777 (accessed 5 November 2016).

2 EU Directive 2011/36 on Preventing and Combating Trafficking in Human Beings and Protecting Its Victims [2011] OJ L 101/1.

3 Ouagadougou Action Plan to Combat Trafficking in Human Beings, 22-23 November 2006, https://ec.europa.eu/anti-trafficking/sites/antitrafficking/files/ouagadougou_action_plan_to_combat_trafficking_en_1.pdf, (accessed 5 November 2016).

4 Asian Regional Initiative against Trafficking in Women and Children (2000), www.humantrafficking.org/events/88, (accessed July 2013).

5 For an introduction to this literature, see "Beyond Trafficking and Slavery," https://www.opendemocracy.net/beyondslavery (accessed 30 June 2015).

6 See, for example, Jennifer Musto, *Control and Protect: Collaboration, Carceral Protection, and Domestic Sex Trafficking in the United States* (Berkeley, CA: University of California Press, 2016); Alexandra Lutnick, *Domestic Minor Sex Trafficking: Beyond Victims and Villains* (New York: Columbia University Press, 2016).

7 See, for example, Roger Sawyer, *Slavery in the Twentieth Century* (London: Routledge and Kegan Paul, 1986); Roger Sawyer, *Children Enslaved* (London: Routledge and Kegan Paul, 1988); C.W.W. Greenidge, *Slavery* (London: Allen and Unwin, 1958). The term "trafficking" does not appear in the index of any of these global surveys, despite the fact that they cover what is now familiar ground.

8 Joe Doezema, *Sex Slaves and Discourse Masters: The Construction of Trafficking* (London: Zed Books, 2010), 46. See also Ronald Weitzer, "The Growing Moral Panic over Prostitution and Sex Trafficking," *Criminologist* 30, 5 (2005): 3–5; Ronald Weitzer, "The Mythology of Prostitution: Advocacy Research and Public Policy," *Sexuality Research and Social Policy* 7 (2010): 15–29.

9 Doezema, *Sex Slaves and Discourse Masters*, 172.

10 For further examples of this type of argument, see John Frederick, "The Myth of Nepal-to-India Sex Trafficking: Its Creation, Its Maintenance, and Its Influence on Anti-Trafficking Interventions," in Kamala Kempadoo, Jyoti Sanghera, and Bandana Pattanaik, eds., *Trafficking and Prostitution Reconsidered: New Perspectives on Migration, Sex Work, and Human Rights* (Boulder, CO: Paradigm, 2005), 127–47; Julia O'Connell Davidson, *Children in the Global Sex Trade* (Cambridge: Polity, 2005); Jyoti Sanghera, "Unpacking the Trafficking Discourse," in Kempadoo, Sanghera, and Pattanaik, eds., *Trafficking and Prostitution Reconsidered*, 4–6; Alison Murray, "Debt-Bondage and Trafficking: Don't Believe the Hype," in Kemala Kempadoo and Joe Doezema, eds., *Global Sex Workers: Rights Resistance and Redefinition* (New York: Routledge, 1998), 51–64; Ana Paula da Silva, Thaddeus Gregory Blanchette, and Andressa Raylane Bento, "Cinderella Deceived: Analyzing a Brazilian Myth Regarding Trafficking in Persons," *Vibrant: Virtual Brazilian Anthropology* 10, 2 (2013): 377–419; Edward Snajdr, "Beneath the Master Narrative: Human Trafficking, Myths of Sexual Slavery and Ethnographic Realities," *Dialectical Anthropology* 37 (2013): 229–56; Erin O'Brien, "Human Trafficking

Heroes and Villains: Representing the Problem in Anti-Trafficking Campaigns," *Social and Legal Studies* 25:2 (2016): 205–24; Jonathan Todres "Law, Otherness, and Human Trafficking," *Santa Clara Law Review* 49 (2009): 605–72; Jeff Gulati, "News Frames and Story Triggers in the Media's Coverage of Human Trafficking," *Human Rights Review* 12 (2010): 1–17.

11 See, for example, Christine M. Jacobsen and May-Len Skilbrei, "'Reproachable Victims'? Representations and Self-representations of Russian Women Involved in Transnational Prostitution," *Ethnos: Journal of Anthropology* 75, 2 (2010): 190–212; Carole Vance, "Innocence and Experience: Melodramatic Narratives of Sex Trafficking and Their Consequences for Law and Policy," *History of the Present* 2, 2 (2012): 200–18; Julia O'Connell Davidson, "Will the Real Sex Slave Please Stand up?" *Feminist Review* 83 (2006): 4–22; Jayashri Srikantiah, "Perfect Victims and Real Survivors: The Iconic Victim in Domestic Human Trafficking Law," *Boston University Law Review* 87, 1 (2007): 157–211.

12 See, for example, Global Alliance against Traffic in Women (GAATW), *Collateral Damage: The Impact of Anti-Trafficking Measures on Human Rights around the World*, (Bangkok: GAATW, 2007); Elizabeth Bernstein, "Militarized Humanitarianism Meets Carceral Feminism: The Politics of Sex, Rights, and Freedom in Contemporary Antitrafficking," *Signs* 36, 1 (2010): 45–71; Jennifer Lynne Musto, "Carceral Protectionism and Multi-Professional Anti-Trafficking Human Rights Work in the Netherlands," *International Feminist Journal of Politics* 12, 3–4 (2010): 381–400; Niki Adams, "Anti-Trafficking Legislation: Protection or Deportation?" *Feminist Review* 73 (2003): 135–39.

13 Laura María Agustín, *Sex at the Margins: Migration, Labour Markets and the Rescue Industry* (London: Zed Books, 2007), 38, 39.

14 See, for example, Thomas M. Steinfatt, "Sex Trafficking in Cambodia: Fabricated Numbers versus Empirical Evidence," *Crime Law and Social Change* 56 (2011): 443–62; Chandre Gould, *Selling Sex in Cape Town: Sex Work and Human Trafficking in a South African City* (Pretoria, South Africa: Institute for Security Studies, 2008); Jerry Markon, "Human Trafficking Evokes Outrage, Little Evidence: US Estimates Thousands of Victims, But Efforts to Find Them Fall Short," *Washington Post*, 23 September 2007; Nick Davies, "Inquiry Fails to Find Single Trafficker Who Forced Anybody into Prostitution," *The Guardian*, 20 October 2009.

15 David A. Feingold, "Trafficking in Numbers: The Social Construction of Human Trafficking Data," in Peter Andreas and Kelly M. Greenhill, eds., *Sex, Drugs and Body Counts: The Politics of Numbers in Global Crime and Conflict* (Ithaca, NY: Cornell University Press, 2010), 55. For additional perspectives, see Patrick Belser and Michaelle de Cock, "Improving Forced Labour Perspectives," in Beate Andreas and Patrick Belser, eds., *Forced Labour: Coercion and Exploitation in the Private Economy* (Boulder, CO: Lynne Reinner, 2009), 173–94; Gillian Wylie, "Doing the Impossible: Collecting Data on the Extent of Trafficking" in Christien van den Anker and Jeroen Doomernik, eds., *Trafficking and Women's Rights* (Houndmills,

UK: Palgrave, 2006), 70–88; Frank Laczko, "Introduction," in Frank Laczko and Elzbieta Gozdziak, eds., *Data and Research on Human Trafficking: A Global Survey* (Geneva: International Organization for Migration, 2005), 5–16; Ronald Weitzer, "Flawed Theory and Method in Studies of Prostitution," *Violence Against Women* 11, 7 (2005): 934–49.

16 See, for example, Wendy Chapkis, *Live Sex Acts: Women Performing Erotic Labour* (London: Cassell, 1997); Kemala Kempadoo and Joe Doezema, eds., *Global Sex Workers: Rights Resistance and Redefinition* (New York: Routledge, 1998); Jill Nagle, ed., *Whores and Other Feminists* (New York: Routledge, 1997); Jay Levy and Pye Jakobsson, "Abolitionist Feminism as Patriarchal Control: Swedish Understandings of Prostitution and Trafficking," *Dialectical Anthropology* 37 (2013): 333–40.

17 For overviews, see Kate Sutherland, "Work, Sex, and Sex-Work: Competing Feminist Discourses on the International Sex Trade," *Osgoode Hall Law Journal* 42, 1 (2004): 139; Joyce Outshoorn, "The Political Debates on Prostitution and Trafficking of Women," *Social Politics: International Studies in Gender, State and Society* 12, 1 (2005): 141.

18 See, for example, Michelle Madden Dempsey, "Sex Trafficking and Criminalization: In Defence of Feminist Abolitionism," *University of Pennsylvania Law Review* 158, 6 (2010): 1729; Sheila Jeffreys, *The Industrial Vagina: The Political Economy of the Global Sex Trade* (London: Routledge: 2009); Catherine MacKinnon, *Are Women Human? And Other International Dialogues* (Cambridge, MA: Harvard University Press, 2006); Kathleen Barry, *Female Sexual Slavery* (Englewood Cliffs, NJ: Prentice-Hall, 1979).

19 See, for example, Agustín, *Sex at the Margins*, 36–41; Doezema, *Sex Slaves and Discourse Masters*, 6–7; Feingold, "Trafficking in Numbers," 51–53; Kristina Hahn, "NGOs' Power of Advocacy: The Construction of Identities in UN Counter-Human Trafficking Policies," in Jens Steffek and Kristina Hahn, eds., *Evaluating Transnational NGOs: Legitimacy, Accountability, Representation* (Houndmills, UK: Palgrave, 2010), 226–36.

20 Protocol to Prevent, Suppress and Punish Trafficking in Persons, especially Women and Children, 15 November 2000, 40 ILM 335 (2001).

21 See, for example, Janie A. Chuang, "Rescuing Trafficking from Ideological Capture: Prostitution Reform and Anti-Trafficking Law and Policy," *University of Pennsylvania Law Review* 158, 6 (2010): 1672–77; Doezema, *Sex Slaves and Discourse Masters*, 106–44; Anne Gallagher, "Human Rights and the New UN Protocols on Trafficking and Migrant Smuggling: A Preliminary Analysis," *Human Rights Quarterly* 23, 4 (2001): 1002–3; Outshoorn, "Political Debates on Prostitution and Trafficking of Women," 148–52; Elizabeth Bernstein, "The Sexual Politics of the 'New Abolitionism,'" *Differences* 18, 3 (2007): 128–51.

22 Julia O'Connell Davidson and Bridget Anderson, "The Trouble with 'Trafficking,'" in Christien van den Anker and Jeroen Doomernik, eds., *Trafficking and Women's Rights* (Houndmills, UK: Palgrave, 2006), 24.

23 See, for example, Joel Quirk and Darshan Vigneswaran, "Mobility Makes States," in Joel Quirk and Darshan Vigneswaran, eds., *Mobility Makes States: Migration and Power in Africa* (Philadelphia: University of Pennsylvania Press, 2015), 1–34.

24 See, for example, Jacqueline Berman, "(Un)Popular Strangers and Crises (Un) Bounded: Discourses of Sex-Trafficking, the European Political Community and the Panicked State of the Modern State," *European Journal of International Relations* 9, 1 (2003): 49–53; Davidson and Anderson, "The Trouble with 'Trafficking,'" 15–21; James Hathaway, "The Human Rights Quagmire of 'Human Trafficking,'" *Virginia Journal of International Law* 49, 1 (2008): 25–42; Nandita Sharma, "Anti-Trafficking Rhetoric and the Making of a Global Apartheid," *National Women's Studies Association Journal* 17, 3 (2005): 94. For a critique of some elements of this argument, see Anne Gallagher "Human Rights and Human Trafficking: Quagmire or Firm Ground? A Response to James Hathaway," *Virginia Journal of International Law* 49, 4 (2009): 833–46.

25 Ratna Kupur, "Migrant Women and the Legal Politics of Anti-Trafficking Interventions," in Sally Cameron and Edward Newman, eds., *Trafficking in Human Beings: Social, Cultural and Political Dimensions* (Tokyo: United Nations University Press, 2008), 113.

26 See, for example, Berman, "(Un)Popular Strangers and Crises (Un)Bounded," 41–46; Peter Andreas, "The Transformation of Migrant Smuggling across the U.S.-Mexican Border," in David Kyle and Rey Koslowski, eds., *Global Human Smuggling Global Human Smuggling: Comparative Perspectives* (Baltimore: Johns Hopkins University Press, 2001), 107–22; Jennifer M. Chacón, "Tensions and Trade-Offs: Protecting Trafficking Victims in the Era of Immigration Enforcement," *University of Pennsylvania Law Review* 158, 6 (2010): 1609–53; Kamala Kempadoo, "From Moral Panic to Global Justice: Changing Perspectives on Trafficking," in Kempadoo, Sanghera, and Pattanaik, *Trafficking and Prostitution Reconsidered*, xvi–xix; Khalid Koser, "The Smuggling of Asylum Seekers into Western Europe; Contradictions, Conundrums, and Dilemmas," in Kyle and Koslowski, eds., *Global Human Smuggling*, 58–72.

27 See, for example, Catherine Dauvergne, *Making People Illegal: What Globalization Means for Migration and Law* (Cambridge: Cambridge University Press, 2008); Toby Shelley, *Exploited: Migrant Labour in the New Global Economy* (London: Zed Books, 2007); Craig McGill, *Human Traffic: Sex, Slaves, and Immigration* (London: Vision, 2003).

28 Chacón, "Tensions and Trade-Offs," 1612.

29 Joel Quirk, *The Anti-Slavery Project: From the Slave Trade to Human Trafficking* (Philadelphia: University of Pennsylvania Press, 2011), 251–52.

30 Chuang, "Rescuing Trafficking from Ideological Capture," 1658. See also Anthony M. DeStefano, *The War on Human Trafficking: US Policy Assessed* (New Brunswick: Rutgers University Press, 2008), 109–17; E. Benjamin Skinner, *A Crime So Monstrous* (Edinburgh: Mainstream Publishing, 2008), 74–77, 82–85, 133–43; Moshoula

Capous-Desyllas, "A Critique of the Global Trafficking Discourse and US Policy," *Journal of Sociology and Social Welfare* 34, 4 (2007): 57–79; Svati P. Shah, "South Asian Border Crossings and Sex Work: Revisiting the Question of Migration in Anti-Trafficking Interventions," *Sexuality Research and Social Policy* 5, 4 (2008): 19–30.

31 See, for example, Chuang, "Rescuing Trafficking from Ideological Capture," 1683–93; Mike Dottridge, ed., "Special Issue: Following the Money: Spending on Anti-Trafficking," *Anti-Trafficking Review* 3 (2014).

32 Victims of Trafficking and Violence Protection Act, 2000, PL 106-386.

33 For an overview of the recent history of the reports, see Anne Gallagher, "Human Rights and Human Trafficking: A Reflection on the Influence and Evolution of the US Trafficking in Persons Reports," in Alison Brysk and Austin Choi-Fitzpatrick, eds., *From Human Trafficking to Human Rights: Reframing Contemporary Slavery* (Philadelphia: University of Pennsylvania Press, 2012).

34 See, for example, Janie A. Chuang, "The United States as Global Sheriff: Using Unilateral Sanctions to Combat Human Trafficking," *Michigan Journal of International Law* 27, 2 (2006): 437–94; Chuang, "Rescuing Trafficking from Ideological Capture," 1677–94; DeStefano, *The War on Human Trafficking*, 118–27; Kay B. Warren, "The Illusiveness of Counting 'Victims' and the Concreteness of Ranking Countries," in Andreas and Greenhill, eds., *Sex, Drugs and Body Counts*, 110–26.

35 US Department of State, *Trafficking in Persons Report*, June 2004, 6.

36 US Department of State, *Trafficking in Persons Report*, June 2010, 7.

37 Ibid., 7.

38 US Department of State, *Trafficking in Persons Report*, June 2013, 7.

39 US Department of State, *Trafficking in Persons Report*, June 2014, 2.

40 Chuang, "Rescuing Trafficking from Ideological Capture," 1659.

41 Hathaway, "The Human Rights Quagmire," 57.

42 International Labour Organization (ILO), *A Global Alliance against Forced Labour: Global Report under the Follow-up to the ILO Declaration on Fundamental Principles and Rights at Work* (Geneva: ILO, 2005).

43 Forced Labour Convention, 28 June 1930, 39 UNTS 55.

44 ILO, *Global Alliance against Forced Labour*, 12–14.

45 Ibid., 14.

46 ILO, *Global Estimate of Forced Labour: Results and Methodology* (Geneva: International Labour Organization, 2012), 13.

47 Gallagher "Human Rights and Human Trafficking," 814.

48 Trafficking Protocol, article 3.

49 Convention against Transnational Organized Crime, 15 November 2000, 40 ILM 335 (2001).

50 Gallagher, "Human Rights and Human Trafficking," 812.

51 Ibid., 824.

52 US Department of State, *Trafficking in Persons Report*, June 2015, 2.

53　Ibid., 7.

54　See, for example, Anne Gallagher and Paul Holmes, "Developing an Effective Criminal Justice Response to Human Trafficking," *International Criminal Justice Review* 18, 3 (2008): 318–43.

55　US Department of State, *Trafficking in Persons Report*, June 2015, 13.

56　Elizabeth Bruch, "Models Wanted: The Search for an Effective Response to Human Trafficking," *Stanford Journal of International Law* 40 (2004): 1–45; Wendy Chapkis, "Trafficking, Migration and the Law: Protection Innocents, Punishing Immigrants," *Gender and Society* 17, 6 (2003): 930; Joe Doezema, "Forced to Choose: Beyond the Voluntary v. Forced Prostitution Dichotomy," in Kempadoo and Doezema, *Global Sex Workers, Rights Resistance and Redefinition*, 43–47.

Asylum Courts and the "Forced Marriage Paradox": Gender-Based Harm and Contemporary Slavery in Forced Conjugal Associations

4

Benjamin N. Lawrance

The applicant's account of events ... appeared to be a fabrication ... why [have we] accepted her account that she had been threatened with the cultural institution of "forced marriage" and there are many types of marriage which in Western liberal society are described as "forced" but are not ... The consequence is to suggest that every un-married young woman in Guinea is at risk of forced marriage and that every single mother is at risk of persecution.
– Deputy Judge Shaerf, Upper Tribunal, 9 March 2015

The world has woken up to the fact that women as a sex may be persecuted in ways which are different from the ways in which men are persecuted and that they may be persecuted because of the inferior status accorded to their gender in their home society.
– Baroness Hale of Richmond, *SSHD v K and Fornah v SSHD*,
18 October 2006

In recent years, what is colloquially referred to as "forced marriage" has emerged as an increasingly important basis for asylum petitions and refugee status determinations. "Forced marriages" emerge from a variety of social and cultural contexts, including, but not limited to, conflict-driven impressment and sexual exploitation, "arranged" marriages and betrothal contracts, and Islamic marriages *in absentia*. Perhaps because most asylum petitions emerge from the "Global South," developing countries appear overrepresented in scholarly and lay attempts to establish the parameters of "forced marriage." And whereas Western jurisdictions have a disproportionate role in adjudicating asylum, the definition of forced marriage is applied with frustrating inconsistency as Judge Shaerf's comments in the above epigraph demonstrate.

While some "forced marriage" practices may be familiar to Western legal practitioners and expert witnesses, asylum seekers struggle to find terms to describe the circumstances and the individual(s) from which they seek protection. Legal scholars Jenni Millbank and Catherine Dauvergne state that "the understanding of forced marriage, has been limited, and arguably misunderstood, in American asylum law."[1] Indeed, the authors contend that US asylum policy pertaining to "forced marriage" is almost exclusively concerned with child marriages (that is, minors) and that incipient federal legislative action emerging from a focus on human trafficking is currently redefining "forced marriage" to exclude adults. Yet this is only part of the problem. Confusion and ambiguity surrounding "forced marriage" is not confined to the United States; globally, it spans all jurisdictions.[2] The urgency for nuanced and careful definitions of exploitative contexts is paramount in asylum adjudication. Paralleling the introduction by the editors of this volume and their critique of the conflation of slavery terminology, "forced marriage" is here offered as an example of the dangers of homogenizing language and simplistic categories such as the collapsing of "forced marriage" and "servile marriage" into the Walk Free Foundation's Global Slavery Index.[3]

The origins of this chapter reside with my personal encounters with asylum applicants struggling to explain their stories of "forced marriage." The primary role of the expert witness in asylum hearings is to contextualize the claims of the applicant and render comprehensible to the court, cultural, social, and linguistic concepts as well as other terminology.[4] One of my goals as an expert witness is to avoid using phrases that may subject the asylum seeker to further violence, but this not always easy to accomplish.[5] One awkward phrase – often repeated in oral and written testimony by applicants – illustrates the difficulty of achieving the goal of representing the enactor of the violence without simultaneously granting him a legal status to which he is not entitled, namely "the man who purports to be my husband." This phrase, designed to avoid granting an enactor of violence the honorific "husband," usually emerges from the interaction between asylum seekers and their respective legal counsel, and many discussions about how to render (and often translate) terms from different cultural milieus. It is but one example of the difficulties encumbered by the phrase "forced marriage."

Several recent asylum petitions by African women alleging "forced marriage," wherein both the asylum seeker and the survivor's counsel struggled to describe the basis for asylum, form the basis for this chapter. All of the claimants speak a mother tongue other than English. All of the references to individual asylum applicants are pseudonyms, and no dates, names, or locations (beyond countries) correspond to the real individuals. All individuals made initial contact with me via their counsel and consented in person, in writing, and/or via their legal counsel to provide pseudonymous information. All court documents are published public records. All individuals discussed in this chapter are heterosexual women.[6] Some of the individuals were granted protection.

In this chapter, I contend that the phrase "forced conjugal association" (FCA) better captures the complexity of what is generally called "forced marriage" in asylum claims, and I advocate for renewed attention to conceptualizing and defining FCA, drawing on asylum jurisprudence about gender-based harms and the slavery conventions. The phrase "forced conjugal association" emerged first in the Special Court for Sierra Leone to distinguish the expansive experiences of "forced marriage" from the relatively narrow crime of "sexual slavery."[7] If sexual slavery consists of the deprivation of liberty, withholding the right of property, and coerced sexual acts, "forcible conjugal association" represents "forcing a person" into "the veneer of a conduct" by a variety of means, including threats, violence, and coercion. As such, it affirms the illegitimacy and illegality residing at the heart of the practices from which the asylum applicant has sought refuge.[8]

FCA provides an alternative avenue to the awkwardness described above. And its relative novelty may encourage people to reconsider or to realize that claims are often more complicated than they first appear. The term also resonates with Baroness Hale's view in the epigraph above that courts have the potential to be a site of institutional remedy for gender violence.[9] But, as I demonstrate below, the true value of FCA has yet to be realized. FCA is exceptionally useful because by drawing on the expansive conceptualization resonating with emerging definitions of contemporary slavery, it incorporates actions and actors beyond those of the classic male perpetrator, such as the behaviours and practices of kinsmen and women, religious officials, government agents, and many others.

This chapter contributes to conceptualizing the relatively new phrase FCA by shifting the focus to the institutional constraints on asylum claims invoking "forced marriage," namely the courts and the bureaucracy that they inhabit. I argue that it is a court's responsibility to employ consistent definitions and terminology to assure the dignity and respect necessary for justice and protection. I first describe the "forced marriage paradox" as consisting of two intertwined dynamics, namely a reluctance to apply definitions consistently (based on evidence from UK and US courts), and the conundrum encountered by asylum-seekers who cannot describe their experiences without employing language validating violent and illegitimate actions. Subsequently, a deeper analysis of the textuality of the asylum process reveals the dynamic producing the paradox and the nature of the violence perpetrated by courts against asylum-seekers. Examples of this paradox include: the action(s), attempted action(s), or purported action(s) before and after the event or act occurs; the textuality of the initial statement; the process of translation; and the reception and subsequent use of the applicant's statement by the court. The "forced marriage paradox" thus describes an asylum process that furnishes asylum-seekers a diminished capacity to describe their experience without employing legitimating terminology. FCA eclipses the "forced marriage paradox," but its full capacity as a definition of gender-based harm has yet to be realized. The chapter concludes with suggestions for an enhanced definition of FCA informed by recent jurisprudence emerging from contemporary prosecutions of gender-based harm and slavery.

Asylum Courts and the "Forced Marriage Paradox"

Consistent terminology and language are central to a transparent and equitable asylum determination process.[10] As Judge Shaerf's comments demonstrate, however, courts and bureaucracies are conservative and highly ethnocentric, engaging newer terms cautiously and reluctantly.[11] The ongoing reluctance to apply coherent language to "forced marriage" asylum claims is deeply troubling and contrasts with a variety of other gender-based harms, such as forced genital cutting.[12] The "forced marriage paradox" thus consists of two oppositional, but intertwined, dynamics – the inconsistent application of "forced marriage" definitions in asylum claims, coupled with the institutional pressures borne by asylum seekers to describe their experiences in terms applicable only to legal consensual marriage. Courts and tribunals operate globally under a variety of national rules, guidance, and regulations concerning what is generally referred to as "forced marriage." The asylum seeker navigating complex court procedures is often compelled to employ the very terminology of legitimate marriage (such as husband, in-laws, and so on) to describe the experiences and parties from which they are seeking protection.

Whereas other gender-based harms lend themselves to graphic and affirmative terminology, those individuals fleeing coercion into conjugal unions often appear to carry a negative burden, insofar as they must stipulate how their specific experience constitutes an aberration from a legitimate marriage or marital context. Immigration officers and courts already struggle to describe and translate the activities and circumstances into clear, sensitive, and unambiguous English. In addition, asylum seekers face a heavy burden in the adversarial context of tribunals and courts to avoid cementing inaccuracies. The claims process and immigration courts play a primary and preeminent role in manufacturing this paradox. And, in so doing, these institutions further perpetuate violence against the asylum seeker.

In the United States, asylum is strictly a discretionary relief.[13] To qualify, an alien must demonstrate a "well-grounded fear of persecution" upon return to the country of such person's nationality on account of race, religion, nationality, membership in a particular social group, or political opinion.[14] Female genital cutting (that is, female genital mutilation) became a basis for asylum within the framework of a "particular social group."[15] The Executive Office for Immigration Review provides extensive documentation for consultation by its officers and judges. The "Gender Guidelines for Overseas Refugee Processing" notes that "forced marriages" are among the "forms of harm that are unique to, or more common to, women."[16] The United States also attends to the UN High Commissioner for Refugees guidelines.[17] Gender-based claims are interpreted within steadily expanding parameters.

Refugees from "forced conjugal associations" must explain precisely what it is they are seeking protection, and they must identify the perpetrators. In many instances, they must describe situations and relationships and employ terms about which consensus has yet to be reached. They often infer or allege actions that are crimes in one country, such as "spousal rape" or sexual assault within marriage, but that are indistinguishable from legal, consensual marriage in another. Consider, for example, Ghana's 2007 Domestic Violence Act 732, which omits criminalizing rape within marriage, rending it impossible for a Ghanaian subjected to a contractual betrothal or wedding ceremony to seek the prosecution of her would-be spouse for rape in her country.[18] The incapacity of government prosecutors to indict men for rape and the persistent unavailability of state protection may thus meet US requirements for asylum.

In contrast with the United States, British legislation governing asylum is relatively new.[19] A person may apply to remain in the United Kingdom if removing them would be in breach of their rights laid down in the 1950 Convention for the Protection of Human Rights and Fundamental Freedoms (ECHR), often called a human rights claim.[20] The ECHR contains a number of "articles" of protected rights. Most human rights claims are anchored on Article 3 (prohibition on torture and inhuman or degrading treatment) or Article 8 (right to respect for family life and private life). A human rights claim can be part of an asylum claim under the 1951 Convention Relating to the Status of Refugees (Refugee Convention) or it can stand apart.[21] Under the Refugee Convention, asylum seekers need to show that they have a "well-founded fear of persecution" due to their race, religion, nationality, political opinion, or membership in a particular social group and are unable or unwilling to seek protection from the authorities in their own country. As the definition is often interpreted as being forward looking, an asylum seeker alleging trafficking for sexual exploitation in the United Kingdom, for example, and who has suffered significant harm in Britain may not prevail if there is no future risk of "re-trafficking" in the country of origin. A "forced marriage" claim may be sustained on asylum grounds as a future persecutory harm if the actors are demonstrably still pursuing the claimant. As in the United States, it is not necessary to demonstrate past persecution in order to have a future risk – sometimes events that occur after a person's arrival in the United Kingdom can give rise to a future risk of persecution in their own country (*"sur place"* claims).

European law also impacts how "forced marriage" claims are adjudicated in the United Kingdom. The United Kingdom is party to EC Directive 2004/83 on Minimum Standards for the Qualification and Status of Third Country Nationals or Stateless Persons as Refugees or as Persons Who Otherwise Need International Protection and the Content of the Protection Granted, which creates a common European asylum system.[22] All asylum or human rights claims are considered in light of its provisions to ensure the application of common criteria for identifying people in need of international protection and the granting of a minimum level of benefits. The waters around "forced marriage" were further muddied with the passage in the United Kingdom of the Forced Marriage (Protection) Act of 2007–08 and the Modern Slavery Act of 2015.[23] These laws – at the centre of which is the "forced marriage protection order," designed to protect a person at risk or who has already been coerced into marriage – emerged partly because of domestic concerns about UK citizens being "duped" into going abroad and succumbing to unions against their will.[24] As a precursor to the 2008 law, the United Kingdom first raised the age for "sponsored" visas, supposedly because maturity increases an individual's capacity to resist a "forced marriage."[25] At the heart of the 2008 definition of "forced marriage" is a distinction between "forced" and "arranged," and at the heart of this distinction resides the concept of "consent."[26]

In the United Kingdom and the United States, as well as in Australia, Canada, New Zealand, and elsewhere, individuals have prevailed with asylum claims that employ the phrase "forced marriage." A claim may surface as part of a wider domestic violence allegation. A claim may be situated within the broader context of "honour crimes" which, in turn, may or may not be part of an allegation of homophobia or discrimination based on sexuality.[27] A claim may emerge from the context of warfare, such as in Sierra Leone, and independently from an allegation of slavery or sexual violence. In many cases, the distinction between "forced marriage" and "arranged marriage" is blurred, and the question of "consent" and what constitutes "consent" becomes the subject of intense scrutiny.[28] In the United States, a claim of "forced marriage" must navigate the wider concerns about "continuing harm," which have emerged from gender-related claims about forced sterilization and, more recently, female genital cutting. Survivors of "forced marriage" must also combat broader structural and ideological biases that "portray an ideological distinction between 'marriage for us' and 'marriage for them.'"[29]

This conflicting spectrum of guidelines, regulations, and statutes sits in tension with emerging international law. Forced conjugal association in the context of abduction by soldiers during war was recently recognized in international humanitarian law as an "inhuman act" independent of sexual assault and sexual slavery.[30] Notwithstanding this recognition, Dauvergne and Millbank contend that "a threatened or actual forced marriage is rarely held to trigger protection obligations per international treaties." Instead, their analysis of refugee decisions "revealed a profound and on-going reluctance to accept that forced marriage was, in and of itself, a persecutory harm."[31] Indeed, since 1990, James Hathaway has argued cogently that "forced marriage" should be clearly understood as a persecutory harm.[32] So how do we account for the apparent imbalance in terms of how courts and immigration officials view "forced marriage" and the difficulties encountered by applicants?

For Millbank and Dauvergne, the reason why asylum seekers have a difficulty winning their cases is structural and ideological and part of the wider failures of refugee law. They write:

> Forced marriage provides a key site for understanding and explaining the persistent failure of refugee law to fully embrace human rights norms, especially as they relate to gender and sexuality. This failure is caused by the structure of refugee law, which is erected on a foundation of "othering" and is sustained by a recurrent division between "us" and "them."[33]

Millbank's and Dauvergne's powerful critique of structure targets the core biases of the international refugee community vis-à-vis the universality of rights. They are careful to point out that many asylum cases have included a "forced marriage" claim as part of a set of rights violations, yet they are rarely featured as "central criterion for any refugee claim."[34] As I hope to demonstrate, the development of structural binaries is very important. But I see this a little differently, however, insofar as I identify the court and the process together as important originators of some of this bias. To be sure, there exists demonstrable bias with regard to the applicability of human rights in gender-basis claims more broadly. Yet where "forced marriage" is concerned, bias has its greatest impact at the moment of entrance into the asylum process.

Applicants' capacities to express the persecutory harm they endure or face are severely limited in terms of the language they can draw upon to describe their experience. Individuals must routinely use terms and phrases that pertain to legitimate and legal marriages. In so doing, they are counterintuitively undercutting their allegations, insofar as the terminology of legitimate marriage resonates with the bureaucratic and judicial audience as legal and non-persecutory. Furthermore, by using terms such as "husband" or even phrases such as "the man who purports to be my husband," the asylum seeker effectively raises the persecution threshold. Instead of clarifying the narrative and strengthening the basis for asylum, such language weakens the individual claim, injects implausibility into the determination context, and possibly renders success more elusive.

How can we imagine justice for asylum seekers if their very testimony renders their claims less plausible? Evidence from several national jurisdictions demonstrates that no single strand of jurisprudence prevails in "forced marriage" asylum. Framed in US legal parlance, the "nexus" of "forced marriage" is still very much a matter of contestation.[35] Millbank and Dauvergne may well argue that "forced marriage" should constitute "a paradigm of 'persecution.'"[36] But the great spectrum of cultural and legal contexts within which "forced marriage" cases arise demonstrates that nothing is further from the truth. While there are many avenues to a "forced marriage" asylum petition in different jurisdictions, they are all paved with isomorphic difficulties. Whereas Millbank and Dauvergne see the issue as a structural problem and a "key site for understanding and explaining the persistent failure of refugee law to fully embrace human rights norms, especially as they relate to gender and sexuality," my focus on the language deployed in the courts recasts the obstacle to "forced marriage" claims as chiefly institutional and the remedy as conceptual.[37]

Notwithstanding the inconsistent application of definitions, allegations of "forced marriage" operate within a primarily Western legal context that craves certainty and clarity. Defining and characterizing the relationships and actions of parties, which may include soldiers and officers, fathers and mothers, and extended family, matchmakers, or clerics and clergymen – is central to asylum, regardless of the basis of persecution. And the application process (of which translation is a crucial aspect) and the terminology employed in courts form a large part of this impediment.

Asylum Seekers and the "Forced Marriage Paradox"

There is no obvious place to begin to disassemble the "forced marriage paradox" from the perspective of the asylum seeker. The asylum seeker's narrative and the court's interpretation of language and its own terminology are of equal importance. There is no simple division between applicant and adjudicator: the process is dialectical.[38] The textuality of the application must also be treated as the product of a dialogic process. However, because the linear process of an asylum petition begins at the moment of filing, I also begin with the petition of the applicant and then consider the role of the courts.

Texts and Textuality of the Asylum Process

The texts I examine came to me via the applicant's legal counsel, and they differ in form and structure. I did not collect them, and I did not independently interview individual applicants. I offer no pretense of scientific method or sample, and there is no control case. The data contained in asylum application documents is qualitative and anecdotal; I leave it to others to assess the applicability of my generalized conclusions. In some cases, the "rawest" data comes in the form of the initial intake interview conducted by a government agent and rarely in the presence of an attorney. But when I see the case, the narrative of the applicant is usually in the form of a sworn statement or affidavit. The narrative has been massaged and polished so significantly that it is unrecognizable as a dialogue, the form from which it ultimately originated.

In some instances, when I encounter the case, it has already moved into the adversarial judicial process, and I am presented simultaneously with the transcript of the interview, the intake notes, the statement, and a determination wherein the narrative is interpolated and interpreted. In one instance, a case came to me via a second legal representative, after the first application failed and a new claim was filed. The original interviews and statements were not available, and I had to reconstruct the narrative of the individual based on the fragments of original statements quoted or interpolated in negative administrative and judicial determinations and of the paraphrased account of the applicant in those same determinations.

Among the more important factors in the textuality of the asylum process is the process of translation, whereby terms, phrases, and idioms are rendered into English for the benefit of the court. Translating rights and the language of humanitarianism has been acknowledged as a site of significant contestation.[39] The role of court translators is an important site of research: they may have extraordinary influence on the outcome of a case.[40] Translation in the context of asylum tribunals and immigration courts is a site of particularly significant problems. Ilene Durst has argued that "[m]any negative determinations of credibility can be explained by the inability of the asylum applicant, or his attorney, to translate the persecution suffered into a narrative graspable by the adjudicator, and/or the adjudicator's inability to transcend the barriers created by the inherent otherness of trauma, culture, and language."[41] However, it is not always judges who construct barriers. As Muneer Ahmad argues, lawyers may also object to the interference of a translator in the "dyadic norm" of lawyer-client and "view interpreters with suspicion."[42] My experience strongly suggests that translating plays a central role in grounding those same references in the language of legitimate and legal unions, thereby further weakening the capacity of the asylum seeker to demonstrate reasonable grounds or a well-founded fear of persecution.

Other textual matters merit consideration, but my focus here is the dialogic character and translated product as well as the violence perpetuated against asylum seekers during the process. When I encounter the claim, it has usually passed through several stages, including possibly a judicial hearing and appeal. Below I describe three key stages of the "forced marriage paradox," namely the role of the petition and statement, the process of translation, and the reception of the statement by courts and tribunals, including the paraphrasing, citing, and interpolating of language from asylum seekers.

How the Narrator Tells the Story:
Petitions and the Forced Marriage Paradox

The asylum seeker encounters the forced marriage paradox at the moment they claim asylum. In some instances, this begins the minute they have cleared customs and immigration in the country in which they wish to claim asylum (for example, the United Kingdom). In other cases, petitioners may await up to one year to file a claim according to domestic law (such as in the United States). But regardless of the date of the application, the paradox unfolds from the outset. In the first interview, the asylum applicant is asked to explain the grounds for asylum. The first interview becomes the basis for subsequent testimony. It often becomes the text against which future statements are compared and from which any departures must be adequately explained.[43] The statement that originates with the interview remains the primary document for the entire asylum application process and any subsequent appeals. And it is possible to track changes in language and terminology through this process.

The narrative that emerges from the outset and forms the basis for the case is anchored by references to legitimate and legal unions. From the first moment that the actors of the narrative are outlined, they are afforded the status of legitimate familial terminology. Take, for example, the case of Massa (not her real name) from Togo, who fled to the United States, only to have her case bungled by an infamous attorney now in federal prison. Massa stated in writing: "When I was twenty years old, my uncle chose my husband for me. The man he chose was thirty-five at the time. When my mother and father informed me that a husband had been chosen for me, I told them I was not ready." In this example, the protagonist and (primary?) perpetrator is identified as a "husband." Massa describes how she fled Togo in order to escape the coercion, but the impression that the individuals causing her flight had acted legitimately is pervasive.

In a similar way, the relationship envisioned for the individual fleeing is framed as a legal union, and the language adopted by the survivor is that of a legitimate union. Another example given by Kane (not her real name), from Côte d'Ivoire, illustrates how difficult it is to avoid such language. Kane fled an Islamic ceremony in absentia, and the hostage taking of one of her children. She stated:

> I told my father that since he is no longer supporting me, he can no longer tell me what to do with my life. During this exchange, my father was mean and insulting. He said that as a woman, I only need a high school diploma and that I should just get a menial job until I am married. He said that a woman only needs to know how to read and write and nothing more.

Kane has difficulty in describing what she was subjected to without invoking marital terminology. Kane stated: "My father said that the marriage was decided and was final, that I had been promised to the Imam and would marry him shortly. I thought that my father arranged the marriage as a punishment for continuing my studies and because he wanted to thwart my education plans." Thus, even instances and moments cited as examples of contestation between herself and the other parties inscribe legitimacy.

A legitimating language of legal unions is not omnipresent, to be sure. Individual applicants for asylum may deploy alternative terms when referring to protagonists. But while not every attempt to narrate context requires reference to protagonists employing the terminology of legal unions, the example of Akua (not her real name) from Ghana, as told through her counsel, highlights the reliance on terms of legitimate marriage to describe at least the practices, if not the actors. Akua stated that the man she was told to marry was very old, slim, and frail. She recalls being taken to his house. There were older people there, who she assumed to be his adult children. They took the lead. She did not want him to look at her. She looked down most of the time. She did not speak directly to him. She explains that when someone is old, they do not refer to him or her by name, but he was referred to as "*afeto*" or old man. Akua's case was complicated by the fact that the arrangement constituted part of a punishment for alleged criminal activities. While Akua consistently refused to identify the individual as her "husband," or even (through her counsel) as "the man who purported to be her husband," choosing instead "old man," the process into which the perpetrators, including her parents, attempted to subject her is described as a marriage by use of the verb "marry."

The difficulties encumbered by victims are often amplified by the marital status of the participants. Perpetrators gain legitimacy in the eyes of the law insofar as they may already be legally married to one or more spouses. Konda (not her real name) fled Togo and sought sanctuary in the United Kingdom. In her initial application for asylum, she was granted removal from withholding because she was a minor. After reaching maturity, she again petitioned for asylum and appealed a negative determination. Whereas the political grounds for the first ruling were still valid, Konda's second and ultimately successful attempt to remain in the United Kingdom was coupled with a description of a "forced marriage" that had not been part of the original statement. Konda explained: "I fled Togo owing to a number of political problems and also because I was pressured to marry a man who was already married with four wives." In so doing, her claim was undermined by the existence of other legal unions. In this instance, Konda's explanation was used to discredit her claim, insofar as the alleged perpetrator was viewed as law-abiding and upstanding.

How the Audience Hears the Narrative:
Translation and the Forced Marriage Paradox
Translating cultural idiom into English, whether from another European language such as French or from an African language such as Yorùbá, encumbers similar levels of difficulty and hazard. The translation experience encountered between asylum applicants and their legal counsel is a site of comprehension, attempted understanding, and miscomprehension. In some instances, the asylum applicant renders

phrases and terms from a Ghanaian language, such as Twi or Ewe, directly into English. In other cases, an attorney may infer the English meaning of a French term, which was translated into French by a bilingual applicant. A legal counselor may also make the decision to use the original word in the original language. This provides for an intentional moment of miscomprehension in a court context, which perhaps counterintuitively may provide for an opening for an expert witness to speak in more detail and with greater influence and more independent knowledge. But such decisions and moments are rare.

The court's determination text and the judge also engage in a form of translation, usually in the absence of an expert. What may appear to be a reasonable effort to understand or render comprehensible a specific ethnicized or cultured term, oftentimes constitutes a unilateral undertaking. A term from the Moba language of Togo and Burkina Faso, for example, rendered into French and then into English by the applicant and her counsel, may be remolded or retranslated by a judge by the process of analogy. In this way, asylum seekers lose control of their narrative and later struggle to address the inconsistency, mischaracterization, and mistranslation inserted into the official record.

Delicate cultural details, including appellations, are often the first element to be erased in the process of translation. Complex appellations – affixes and suffixes – in many West African languages enable the conversers to distinguish between different levels of proximity in familial relationships. It is difficult to discern the effect of the erasing of relationships on asylum petitions, but when I read a translated statement, such as Massa's, I am acutely aware of the cultural flattening that has been imposed on the narrative. Massa stated:

> According to ... custom, a sibling chooses the spouses of a younger sibling's children and the youngest sibling selects the spouses of the oldest sibling's children ... My father is the oldest of three children. He has a sister who is the middle child and a brother who is the youngest. Because my father's brother (my uncle) is the youngest child, my uncle is expected to choose the spouses of my father's children.

The flattening caused by the imposition of culturally inappropriate terminology on naming practices, which attend to bloodline proximity and speak intuitively to power dynamics, is profound. If this is lost on a Western audience, it may be problematic because the type of power or capacity to perpetuate violence against an individual is central to asylum adjudication. For example, if in one culture a senior uncle of a matriline is responsible for arranging marriages in a community, then identifying him by his appellation highlights his capacity and agency. But such cultural subtly is evacuated by the flattening of translation.

Idiomatic concepts and practices are rendered innocuous or mute by translation, with unknown consequences. What may appear to be a relatively straightforward anecdote may be imbued with rich cultural meaning that specifically addresses the nature of power or violence at the hands of the perpetrator. Asylum seekers often invoke contractual obligations or negotiations, but the court rarely addresses or acknowledges the context. Massa's story provides one example. She noted: "Once my uncle distributed the kola nuts to family members, the marriage was ceremonially complete according to [our] cultural practices." It is difficult for members of a court or immigration officials to comprehend the sanctity of the exchange of kola nuts. Whereas lying under oath or contempt of court, for example, are violations of cultural codes with attendant criminal consequences, the implications of disavowing a ceremony concluded with the breaking of a kola nut is lost in translation.

Metonyms and metonymic phrases also illustrate the perils of translations. Witchcraft and witchcraft accusations are arriving in asylum and immigration tribunals with increasing frequency.[44] Sorcery or "juju" may feature as the primary basis for an application, such as women forced to live in "witch camps" in northern Ghana or western Senegal. But in asylum applications, forms of witchcraft or animist practices are frequently invoked as examples of the type of physical and psychological retribution visited upon those who resist. Akua described the context of her punishment ritual before a shrine: "The fetish priest takes you through cleansing rituals. These are a form of torture until you confess. Either you are tortured until you die or you confess to something you did not do." But the UK courts doubted Akua's claims for two reasons: first, her claims of "torture" were not believed because no "objective evidence" supported the claim of this type of punishment by shrine priests and, second, because of her age and background, she was not the "usual" individual subjected to "witchcraft accusations." Explaining Akua's claims to the court was very difficult.

While a specific term, such as "witch" may trip up a judge, other terms have powerful non-equivalents in European languages, with a Western intellectual life of their own. This intellectual life may be conveyed as part of the process of translation. Bride price is frequently the source of misunderstanding. When the concept of "bride price" or "bride wealth" payments surface in the petitions of asylum seekers, they have usually already undergone translation, and the specific cultural details and practices attendant to each cultural act are rarely the subject of discussion. Massa's experience in Togo highlights the double jeopardy encumbered when a "bride price" becomes part of the testimony. Massa stated: "They told me that it was too late for anything to be done, and that the bride-price had been paid even before my uncle had called them. The bride-price is part of [our] culture. A bride-price can include money or other property." Thus, the invocation of "bride-price," "bride wealth," or even "dowry" is especially complicated because the undescribed and often unwitnessed ceremonies are a standard element of legitimate marriages.

In an effort to mitigate some of the damage wrought by translation of cultural practices, asylum seekers may use passionate or intense language that sits uncomfortably with courts or immigration officials. Seemingly aware of the court's disinterest in the role of her "uncle" in the contractual negotiations, Massa tried to speculate or hypothesize about what might happen if hierarchies and attendant obligations and influence were ignored. She stated that the "custom of siblings selecting spouses for another sibling's children is very strong in [our] culture and cannot be resisted or challenged. Had I refused the *husband* selected by my uncle, my uncle would have killed me and the entire village would have supported his actions." Whereas this hypothetical scenario was imagined to convey the power of hierarchy and dangers of disobedience, speculative assertions frequently do further damage to an individual's credibility. Judges or immigration officials may accuse them of hyperbole or embellishment.

Translation may also be a silencing process insofar as an image or document displayed in the context of asylum adjudication may convey legitimacy to a process inadvertently or unintentionally. Konda fled from Togo because of her political activities, but her claim expanded because her parents attempted to force her into a union in order to ameliorate the damage her political actions had allegedly caused her family. To accomplish this, they arranged for a story to be published in a Togolese newspaper that gave the impression that she was lost and needed help, and they included a photograph of her in full *hijab*. In my expert statement that featured prominently in her successful appeal, I stated:

> The narrative portrays her as a misguided girl, who has fallen into bad company[,] who needs rescuing. It is designed effectively as a mechanism of entrapment whereby an unwitting bystander or resident seeing [Konda] might take pity on her plight and bring her whereabouts to the attention of the authorities and her estranged family ... The article features a photograph of [Konda], and the photograph is in the manner of a betrothal photograph, the type of image produced by parents to facilitate the arrangement of a marriage.

I examined the article and photograph carefully and concluded that it conveyed an unmistakable message to an urban Muslim readership, namely that she was a runaway bride. Whereas Konda's political grounds for asylum had been questioned by the UK Border Agency, the violence awaiting her upon her return was embedded in the betrothal photograph and accompanying text.

How the Court Reframes the Narrative:
Determinations and the Forced Marriage Paradox

When misunderstanding or "errors of law" form the basis for an appeal or "leave to appeal," the damage affected by the language deployed in asylum narratives is already well underway. Courts and immigration officials are actively engaging in reframing the survivors' narratives and, in so doing, perpetuate violence in two distinct ways. They deepen the deleterious impact of the previous narrative structuring, restructuring, and translation. They also contribute to emerging narratives of the survivor in unique and frustrating ways by making determinations about the meaning, import, and validity of the terms and phrases.

Courts and immigration officials deepen the impact of earlier language restrictions. Fear of witchcraft and reprisals for witchcraft, as part of an asylum claim, is intensely scrutinized in the United Kingdom, and an individual's claims are compared with existing case law and government reports on the prevalence of the specific practices. One judge observed:

> It is not clear from your further submissions from the passage on "Ritual Servitude and Sexual Abuse" and "Women Accused of Witchcraft" how both the [Minister] and the Immigration Judge misunderstood the objective material. The passage[s] referred to do not establish that it is likely that a 19 year old girl would be sent to a fetish shrine on account of an accusation of witchcraft. The former refers to the practice of offering a pre-pubescent girl to a fetish shrine in order to atone for past deeds while the latter ... to the fate of women who are accused of witchcraft who are forced to live in "witch camps." It is considered that these are quite distinct issues. You point to no further objective material which establishes that it is reasonably likely that a 19-year-old girl would be sent to a fetish shrine after being accused of witchcraft.

At first glance, it may seem thorough to compare a claimant's narrative with "objective evidence," data anchored by scholarly knowledge and expert evidence. But, in reality, it creates a set of parameters within which all future claims must fit. Akua's extraordinary story fails to fit neatly within the "objective evidence" about "witch camps" in the north of Ghana and "fetish shrines" in the south because at the heart of her claim is an unusual form of punishment including gender-based harms. Explaining why her claim was plausible requires knowledge of the local language and highlights a sequence of poor translations of cultural and gendered terms that entered the official record several years earlier.

Courts and tribunals also perpetuate violence when they attempt to disentangle elements of a complex claim. As a matter of order and process, it may seem sensible to consider different elements of a claim as distinct and separate bases for protection. However, as Akua's story indicates, attempts to disentangle her "forced marriage" claim from witchcraft enabled a judge to conclude that because the "old man" was now deceased, there was no continuing fear of "forced marriage." The judge stated:

> Your client claims to have been accused of being a witch by the family following the death of her father and aunt. When [Akua] was around 16 or 17 years of age she claims that she was taken to a village ... in the Volta region, where she was to marry a village elder. Your client ran away only to return to her family when she was 19 years of age. On her return the man that it was intended that she marry died.

In this way, the "forced marriage" component was dismissed as not being credible because the prospective individual was deceased. In reality, however, the ongoing punishment for "witchcraft," which itself included forced bondage to a man in a shrine and repeated sexual assault, was only exacerbated by the death of the "old man." The initial "witchcraft" accusation arose from Akua's alleged role in the deaths of her father and aunt, to which the death of the "old man" was then coupled. By separating these elements, the court restructured Akua's narrative and diminished the nexus of vulnerability.

A similar bias was perpetuated against Kane, when the abduction of her children by an imam, which was conveyed by her parents, was set aside as a separate claim. Hostage taking has been used in West Africa as a mechanism for controlling labour and families for centuries.[45] But, for Kane, the abduction of her children was not treated as an element of FCA. Kane observed:

> In the summer of 2009, I found out that my son ... had been forced to live in the Imam's household. My mother was trying to hide this news from me but had to tell me eventually when I became suspicious that he was never around to speak over the phone. When the Imam found out that I would not be returning to the Ivory Coast soon as my father had promised, he became very angry and insisted that [my son] come and live with him and his other wives and children. My sister later told me that it was my father who agreed to

give [my son] away to the Imam earlier in the year. Since the Imam wields a lot of power in my community, my mother could not go against his will either.

Kane was made party to an illegal union in absentia, which is discussed below. But the violence expressed against Kane by her family members and the other perpetrators was the primary motivating factor for the illegal child conveyance and abduction. The goal of the imam was to force Kane to return from the United States and submit herself; the children held hostage operated as an illegal means to an illegitimate end. But for reasons that remain unclear, the court was disinterested in the nexus of power and violence at the heart of the claim.

In the course of separating distinct elements of a narrative, a court determination or an asylum tribunal hearing further perpetuates violence by historicizing specific components. Historicizing, or rendering into the historical past, is one of the many powers a court can wield when adjudicating a case. Kane explained in her narrative that she was punished for making herself "unmarriable" by becoming pregnant and then refusing to abort the pregnancy. She stated:

When my siblings and I were living on our own ... I dated a man who lived in our neighborhood, whom I no longer keep in contact with. I got pregnant and gave birth to my son ... when I was 18. My father had initially tried to pressure me to have an abortion. I refused to have the abortion and my father forced me to stop attending school for about a year.

Whereas her narrative strongly indicates that her father's violence towards her, including the later "forced marriage," began much earlier, the court relegated this component of her story as prehistory. By historicizing earlier examples of violence or attempted violence against Kane, the court and the asylum process generally detracts from her capacity to argue that there existed a pattern of gender violence, of which the "forced marriage" was only the most egregious example.

More perplexing is the role documentation plays in substantiating claims. Kane fled from Côte d'Ivoire and learned when she was in the

United States that an Islamic ceremony had been performed in absentia. Whereas the United States does not recognize as legally binding any contractual union not entered into willingly by both parties, and to the best of my knowledge no Ivoirian civil court has upheld such ceremonies, Kane was under considerable pressure to document the existence of such a ceremony. Kane explained:

> My father found out that I left the country in February 2009. He said he was going to continue planning the marriage without me since he had given the Imam his word. My father thought that I would only stay ... [abroad] for a short while and would be forced to return to the Ivory Coast when my visa expired, which is what the Imam also believed. My mother and M. told me that a religious ceremony took place in March 2009, where I was married to the Imam. They said the marriage was performed at the Imam's mosque ... with my mother, my father and M. present. I was not even there for the marriage and I do not believe it to be valid in any way.

I examined the document, which was introduced to the court as evidence. Since neither the United States nor Côte d'Ivoire would recognize the validity of such a ceremony, the document was not a marriage certificate but, rather, a fraudulent and invalid simulacrum. While the documentation was a powerful component of Kane's successive asylum claim, the court, and indeed all of the parties to the dispute, consistently referred to it as a marriage certificate.

Narration, Translation, and Determination

In summary, the asylum petition process and the immigrations courts are deeply complicit in manufacturing the "forced marriage paradox." The paradox is pervasive and powerful and unfolds from the outset. From the moment the petitioner attempts to narrate her experience, she is constrained by terminology and language. She is unable to describe the situation from which she has fled without deploying terms from legitimate and legal unions. The paradoxical nature of "forced marriage" claims is exacerbated by translation. Not only are specific terms and concepts rendered inert and innocuous, but the cultural flattening of translation is also accompanied by metonymic phrases and silencing that frustrate the asylum applicant. Even attempts to undo the damage wrought by translation that is caused by lawyers or judges or others may give rise to accusations of exaggeration and diminish the credibility of a claimant. And courts intensify this misrepresentation in receiving and determining claims. Judges may separate and segment different components of claims. They test claimants' language against "objective evidence," and they reify imagery, ideas, and documents from illegal and invalid attempts to compel an individual by repeatedly identifying them with terminology appropriate only to legitimate unions.

Forced Conjugal Association: Slavery by Another Name?

"Forced marriage" claims continue to be misunderstood because a paradox resides at the heart of the asylum process. Western legal forums and national refugee and asylum policies operate under multiple and conflicting definitions and guidelines, and individuals seeking refugee status must routinely deploy terminology and language appropriate to legal and legitimate marriages in order to describe that which is anything but a valid union. This context is basically a linguistic conundrum; it has a direct bearing on the capacity of individuals to make legitimate and credible claims. "Forced marriages" involve perpetrators whose power, background, motivations, and mechanisms require elaboration and theorization for more effective asylum petitions and refugee status determinations, but a focus on the human perpetrators is only one part of a many faceted issue. Instead of adopting a unitary definition within which claims are argued, courts and tribunals place the burden on asylum seekers and refugees to describe the context and parameters. The institutions in which asylum claims and refugee status determinations are made constitute the crucible of the forced marriage paradox. How can we imagine justice in asylum claims if the language routinely used, at best, infringes on the plausibility of the claimant but, at worst, perpetuates violence against the most vulnerable in our society?

One solution involves mandating that all parties to international asylum and refugee statutes update their gender violence protocols to lay open the multiple practices, language, and terminology. This would entail considerable discussion and negotiation, with no guarantee that domestic tribunals would adhere to international protocols. Another approach might be to advance the issue within domestic immigration courts, aggressively promoting the adoption of the term "forced conjugal association" in "forced marriage" cases, with the hope that a precedent-setting ruling would restore balance. Such an approach is fraught with danger, not the very least of which is the possibility of a powerfully negative determination or precedent.

A third possibility is for scholars to further invigorate the definition of FCA by highlighting the textuality of the narratives. As an emergent category of gender-based harm, FCA provides a skeleton framework for understanding how "forced marriage" differs from sexual slavery, but the full import of this distinction has yet to be realized. We can go further and identify the indicia of FCA, namely the spectrum of actors and actions involved. Reading survivor narratives for language that resonates with established asylum jurisprudence and international slavery conventions focuses attention on the multivalent actions comprising FCA. The stories of Konda, Massa, Akua, Kane, and others demonstrate how the actions and activities of those perpetrating FCAs bears striking similarity to well-documented and well-established practices of slavery and enslavement. From contractual exchanges of goods in place of people, via hostage taking and sexual assault, to attempts to control labour, remuneration, fertility, and reproduction, the tales of women from Africa who flee FCAs are richly illustrated with the actions characteristic of contemporary enslavement practices. Rather than pursuing legislative or litigation to carve out an appropriate space for those fleeing FCAs, perhaps a just asylum process is within reach.

The potential value of an expanded definition of FCA as remedy to the "forced marriage paradox" is paralleled by the important 2008 Australian High Court decision, *The Queen v. Tang*.[46] In the prosecution of Wei Tang for the forced prostitution of several Thai women, the court wrestled with how to address slavery in a system that does not recognize its existence. Tang's barristers argued that the definition of slavery was limited to "chattel slavery" or, specifically, the treatment of a person as property – a narrow definition that is not recognized in Australia. The court, however, ruled that the "scope of slavery," pursuant to the 1926 Slavery Convention, consisted of *de facto* and *de jure* slavery: de jure being a status and de facto being a condition.[47] The Slavery Convention was signed and ratified by a number of states that did not recognize slavery as a status and that actively sought to extend this situation universally. Subsequent to this distinction, the court ruled that the indicia of slavery resided in the terms of its statutory definition of the "exercise of powers attaching to the right of ownership," which, in this particular case, involved the enslaver's conduct and her capacity to exercise dominion over the other women.[48] Slavery was thus distinguished from mere exploitation. The final component of the description of slavery from the *Tang* case concerned the role of consent. The court ruled that whereas an absence of consent is not necessarily an attribute of slavery, the nature of what constituted consent shifts once an individual has entered into a slave relationship.

The experiences of the victims of Wei Tang provide an interesting parallel with which to illustrate the value of describing and cementing a comprehensive and coherent definition of FCAs. In this case, prosecutors were attempting to describe an experience and status that was not legally possible. In order to effect the conviction, crown prosecutors had to return to established definitions and implied understandings of slavery in a largely dormant convention to which Australia had been party for many decades. The ruling has provoked much interest because it demonstrates how a sensitivity to language and meaning not only provided a resolution to a central problem confronting anti-slavery practitioners and scholars but also afforded justice to victims with respect and dignity. The initial definition of forced conjugal association laid out by the Sierra Leone court is part of the process. It now falls on scholars and experts to fully realize the value and power of this framework and to ensure that survivors who bring their stories before asylum courts are treated with the same respect and dignity accorded the victims of slavery.

Notes

1 Jenni Millbank and Catherine Dauvergne, "Forced Marriage and the Exoticization of Gendered Harms in United States Asylum Law," *Columbia Journal of Gender and Law* 19, 3 (2011): 6.

2 Jenni Millbank and Catherine Dauvergne, "Forced Marriage as Harm in Domestic and International Law," *Modern Law Review* 73, 1 (2010): 57–88.

3 http://www.globalslaveryindex.org (accessed 31 October, 2016).

4 For further discussion, see Benjamin N. Lawrance et al., "Law, Expertise, and Protean Ideas about African Migrants," in I. Berger, B.N. Lawrance, T. Hepner Redeker, J. Tague, and M. Terretta, *African Asylum at a Crossroads: Activism, Expert Testimony, and Refugee Rights* (Athens, OH: Ohio University Press), 1–37.

5 At the Sierra Leone International Court, Justice Doherty identified the term wife as "indicative of forced marital status which had lasting and serious impacts on the victims." SCSL, *Prosecutor v Brima, Kamara, and Kanu*, Case no. SCSL-2004–16-PT, 20 June 2007, at 590, paras 1009–12 (citing the prosecution's final brief). The term wife caused mental trauma and stigmatization and negatively impacted the victims' ability to reintegrate into their communities. See Ann Palmer, "An Evolutionary Analysis of Gender-Based War Crimes and the Continued Tolerance of 'Forced Marriage,'" *Northwestern University Journal of International Human Rights* 7 (2009): 133. See also Jennifer Gong-Gershowitz, "Forced Marriage: A 'New' Crime against Humanity?" *Northwestern University Journal of International Human Rights* 8 (2008): 53.

6 I concur with Millbank and Dauvergne that forced conjugal association affects women and men and particularly gay men and lesbians. Millbank and Dauvergne, "Forced Marriage and the Exoticization"; Millbank and Dauvergne, "Forced Marriage as Harm," 69.

7 *Brima, Kamara, and Kanu.*

8 Sonja C. Grover, *Prosecuting International Crimes and Human Rights Abuses Committed Against Children: Leading International Court Cases* (New York: Springer, 2010), 451–56.

9 *SSHD v K and Fornah v SSHD* (2006) UKHL 46 at para. 86 (Baroness Hale of Richmond).

10 For the best discussion of this see, Anthony Good, *Anthropology and Expertise in the Asylum Courts* (New York: Routledge-Cavendish, 2007).

11 For another example, consider a preference for viewing "honour crimes" as "cultural" rather than "gender based," which has significant implications for asylum claims. See Rupa Reddy, "Gender, Culture and the Law: Approaches to 'Honour Crimes' in the UK," *Feminist Legal Studies* 16 (2008): 305–21.

12 For a great discussion, see Karen Musalo, "The Evolving Refugee Definition: How Shifting Elements of Eligibility Affect the nature and Focus of Expert Testimony in Asylum Proceedings," in *African Asylum at a Crossroads*, I. Berger et al, eds., (Athens: Ohio University Press, 2015), 75-101.

13 Asylum, 8 USC §§ 1158(a), 1101(a)(42).

14 "INS [Immigration and Naturalization Service] Gender Persecution Guidelines," *Interpreter Releases* 72, 22 (1995): 771.

15 *In re Kasinga*, 21 I & N Dec 357, 365 (BIA 1996) (holding that persecution was on account of applicant's membership of a social group comprising of the young women of the Tchamba-Kunsuntu Tribe); see also *Niang v Gonzales*, 422 F.3d 1187, 1200 (10th Cir. 2005) (holding that for purposes of female genital mutilation, a social group can be defined by both gender and tribal membership).

16 Executive Office for Immigration Review, Department of Justice, "Gender Guidelines for Overseas Refugee Processing" (2000) (Update 2012) https://www.uscis.gov/sites/default/files/USCIS/About%20Us/Directorates%20and%20Program%20Offices/RAIO/Gender%20Related%20Claims%20LP%20(RAIO).pdf (accessed 31 October 2016).

17 "Gender Guidelines for Overseas Refugee Processing." UN High Commission for Refugees (UNHCR), "Guidelines on International Protection: Gender-Related Persecution within the Context of Article 1A(2) of the 1951 Convention and/or Its 1967 Protocol Relating to the Status of Refugees," Doc. HCR/GIP/02/01, 2002; UNHCR, "Guidance Note on Refugee Claims Relating to Sexual Orientation and Gender Identity," 2008; UNHCR, "Guidelines on International Protection: Child Asylum Claims under Articles 1(A)2 and 1(F) of the 1951 Convention and/or 1967 Protocol Relating to the Status of Refugees," 2009.

18 Domestic Violence Act, 2007 Act 732 (3 May 2007); see Saida Hodžić, "Unsettling Power: Domestic Violence, Gender Politics, and Struggles over Sovereignty in Ghana," *Ethnos* 74, 3 (2009): 331–60.

19 The Asylum and Immigration Appeals Act of 1993; the Asylum and Immigration Act of 1996; and the Immigration and Asylum Act of 1999 govern asylum and refugee determinations in the United Kingdom.

20 Convention for the Protection of Human Rights and Fundamental Freedoms, 4 November 1950, 213 UNTS 221.

21 Convention Relating to the Status of Refugees, 28 July 1951, 189 UNTS 150.

22 EC Directive 2004/83 on Minimum Standards for the Qualification and Status of Third Country Nationals or Stateless Persons as Refugees or as Persons Who Otherwise Need International Protection and the Content of the Protection Granted [2004] OJ L 304/12.

23 Forced Marriage (Civil Protection) Act 2007 (UK), s. 63A; Modern Slavery Act 2015 (UK).

24 For a 2003 incident, see Jan McGirk, "Court frees Briton Imprisoned and Tricked into Marriage," *The Independent*, 7 May 2003; for another example, see "Teenager battered for refusing arranged marriage after father sold her as £10,000 bride," *The Daily Mail*, 23 February 2011.

25 Geetanjali Gangoli and Khatidja Chantler, "Protecting Victims of Forced Marriage: Is Age a Protective Factor?" *Feminist Legal Studies* 17 (2009): 267–88.

26 Sundari Anitha and Aisha Gill, "Coercion, Consent and the Forced Marriage Debate in the UK," *Feminist Legal Studies* 17 (2009): 165–84.

27 See Benjamin N. Lawrance and Charlotte Walker-Said, "Resisting Patriarchy, Contesting Homophobia: Expert Testimony and the Construction of African Forced Marriage Asylum Claims," in Anne Bunting, Benjamin N. Lawrance, and Richard L. Roberts, eds., *Marriage by Force? Contestation over Consent and Coercion in Africa* (Athens: Ohio University Press, 2016), 199–24.

28 See Annie Bunting, Benjamin N. Lawrance, and Richard L. Roberts, "'Something Old, Something New': Conceptualizing Forced Marriage in Africa," in Bunting, Benjamin N. Lawrance, and Richard L. Roberts, *Marriage by Force?* 1-40.

29 Millbank and Dauvergne, "Forced Marriage as Harm," 63.

30 See *Brima, Kamara, and Kanu*; SCSL, *Prosecutor v Sesay, Kallon and Gbao*, Case no. SCSL-04-15-T RUF, 25 February 2009.

31 Millbank and Dauvergne, "Forced Marriage as Harm," 57.

32 James Hathaway, *The Law of Refugee Status* (Toronto: Butterworths, 1991), 112.

33 Millbank and Dauvergne, "Forced Marriage as Harm," 57.

34 Ibid.

35 *INS v Elias-Zacarias* 502 US 478, 483 (1992). For a critique of "nexus," see Shayna S. Cook, "Repairing the Legacy of INS v. Elias-Zacarias," *Michigan Journal of International Law* 23 (2002): 223. See also Stephen Castles and Nicolas Van Hear, "The Migration-Asylum Nexus: Definition and Significance," Oxford University, COMPASS, 27 January 2005, http://www.compas.ox.ac.uk/ (accessed 31 October 2016); Good, *Anthropology and Expertise*.

36 Millbank and Dauvergne, "Forced Marriage as Harm," 57.

37 Ibid., 58.

38 See Benjamin N. Lawrance and Galya Ruffer, "Witness to the Persecution? Expertise, Testimony, and Consistency in Asylum Adjudication," in Benjamin N. Lawrance and Galya Ruffer, eds., *Adjudicating Refugee and Asylum Status: The Role of Witness, Expertise, and Testimony* (Cambridge: Cambridge University Press, 2015), 1–24.

39 Shira Shapiro, "She Can Do No Wrong: Recent Failures in America's Immigration Courts to Provide Women Asylum from 'Honor Crimes' Abroad," *American University Journal of Gender, Social Policy and the Law* 18 (2009): 293; See also Ann Elizabeth Mayer, *Islam and Human Rights: Tradition and Politics*, 3rd edition (Boulder, CO: Westview Press, 1999), 21. Generally, see Sally Engle Merry, *Human Rights and Gender Violence: Translating International Law into Local Justice* (Chicago: University of Chicago Press, 2006).

40 Benjamin N. Lawrance, "*La Amistad*'s 'Interpreter' Reinterpreted: James 'Kaweli' Covey's Distressed Atlantic Childhood and the Production of Knowledge about Nineteenth-Century Sierra Leone," in Suzanne Schwarz and Paul Lovejoy, eds., *Slavery, Abolition and the Transition to Colonialism in Sierra Leone* (Trenton, NJ: Africa World Press, 2014), 217–56.

41 Ilene Durst, "Lost in Translation: Why Due Process Demands Deference to the Refugee's Narrative," *Rutgers Law Review* 53 (2000): 127.

42 Muneer Ahmad, "Interpreting Communities: Lawyering across Language Difference," *University of California Los Angeles Law Review* 54 (2007): 999.

43 See Durst, "Lost in Translation," 139, considering *Balasubramanrim v INS*, 143 F.3d 157, 158 (3d Cir. 1998).

44 Kate Luongo, "Allegations, Evidence, and Evaluation: Asylum-Seeking in a World with Witchcraft," in Berger et al., *African Asylum*, 183–85.

45 For example, Paul E. Lovejoy and David Richardson, "The Business of Slaving: Pawnship in Western Africa, c. 1600-1810," *Journal of African History* 42 (2001): 12.

46 *The Queen v Tang*, [2008] HCA 39. For further discussion, see Irina Kolodizner, "*R v Tang*: Developing an Australian Anti-Slavery Jurisprudence," *Sydney Law Review* 31 (2009): 487; University of Queensland Human Trafficking Working Group, "Case Report (Criminal) – R v. Wei Tang." See https://www.unodc.org/cld/case-law-doc/traffickingpersonscrimetype/aus/2009/r_v_wei_tang_2009_23_vr_332.html?tmpl=old (accessed 31 October 2016); Rachel Harris, "Modern-Day Slavery in Australia: The Queen v Wei Tang," Paper presented at the thirteenth Annual Public Law Weekend, National Museum of Australia, Canberra, 1 November 2008, 6.

47 Slavery Convention, 25 September 1926, 60 LNTS 253.

48 *The Queen v Tang*, (2008) 237 CLR 1, 19 (Gleeson CJ).

PART 2
Rhetoric

Narrating Wartime Enslavement, Forced Marriage, and Modern Slavery

5

Annie Bunting

"Tell Your Story"

"Feel free, go on, tell your story," the social worker prompted, and they each recited what happened to them during the conflict in Sierra Leone. Each of the dozen women present seemed shy yet accustomed to narrating their experiences to a foreigner, a complete stranger.[1] I also perceived that since the social worker was the person with whom they worked and through whom they would be participating in UN Women (UNIFEM) skills training, they were reluctant *not* to speak. Only one woman chose to be silent. Another woman had given evidence to investigators from the Special Court for Sierra Leone (SCSL) but did not testify at trial. She had also made a claim for reparations through the National Commission for Social Action (NaCSA). It was very difficult to hear their experiences and to receive their stories.

While women have told me on this and other occasions that they are grateful I am interested in their experience and willing to listen, this experience was, or could be characterized as, an uncomfortable moment in "trauma tourism,"[2] or what John Lennon and Margaret Mitchell call "dark tourism."[3] Journalists, researchers, human rights investigators, prosecutors, students, and non-governmental organizations (NGOs) ask survivors to tell their story. Our work depends on it. Writing complete history depends on it. And prosecuting crimes against humanity depends on it. But, all the while, it is not clear what women and men who have endured sometimes years of violence and captivity gain from the "performative enactment of testimony."[4]

Some participants in interviews with researchers and local NGO groups express that, with the telling of their story, some form of healing takes place. As one woman told me, "once I get it out of my chest ... it is healing."[5] Others say that hearing from those with similar experiences helps them deal with the stigma of sexual violence. Still others articulate that they seek justice and want history to include the extreme violations that took place against them. As Binaifer Nowrojee wrote in *Your Justice Is Too Slow*,

> when asked what they want from the international tribunal [ICTR], Rwandan women above all mention the law: they say they are looking for public acknowledgement of the crimes committed against them. They want the record to show that they were subjected to horrific sexual violence at the hands of those who instigated and carried out genocide.[6]

And some survivors may participate in trials that seek to bring accused war criminals to justice, but these are very few of the many survivors who offer up their stories for public consumption.

In this chapter, I explore the question of how testimonials of wartime enslavement are produced and circulated in different forums and with varied consequences. I am interested in the question of how victims' narratives of abduction and captivity are treated in legal investigations and in claims for reparations in comparison to self-authored memoirs by "survivors," "child soldiers," or "modern slaves." In particular, I will examine the emphasis placed on women's accounts of rape, sexual slavery, forced labour, impregnation, and forced marriage in international criminal trials, Truth and Reconciliation Commissions (TRCs), and other proceedings in post-conflict situations. My focus is on locations where there have been international criminal indictments and/or TRC processes such as in Liberia, Sierra Leone, Rwanda, and

Uganda.[7] I explore the tension between "stealing the pain of others"[8] and representing or animating the "silenced voices" of women.[9] Here I build on the insights from human rights and feminist scholarship concerned with the treatment of testimonials, narratives, and witnessing.[10] Put another way, I am interested in the way the documentation of gender violence in various forms and in different fora is part of a broader political economy of trauma in which modern slavery activism participates.[11]

Second, I compare testimonies given in court, TRCs, and reparation processes with so-called modern slavery memoirs or slave narratives. I will provide a close reading of the autobiography of Sierra Leonean Mariatu Kamara, *The Bite of the Mango*, as one example of a memoir of contemporary war. Emblematic of the child soldier memoirs are those of Ishmael Beah, also from Sierra Leone (*A Long Way Gone*), Emmanuel Jal from the Sudan (*War Child*), Grace Akallo from Uganda (*Girl Soldier*), and the collection *Stolen Angels: The Kidnapped Girls of Uganda*. Some of the well-known narratives of modern slavery include *Restavec* by Jean-Robert Cadet (Haiti), *Slave* by Mende Nazer (Sudan), and the collection by Kevin Bales and Zoe Trodd, *To Plead Our Own Cause*.[12] While self-authored (or coauthored) memoirs offer some response to the limits of legal testimonies, I have found that some popular biographies and nascent scholarly work in the area of contemporary slavery are characterized by emotive, often decontextualized, accounts. The narratives found on modern slavery websites and in trials are more prone to these tropes of de-contextualized accounts than full-length biographies. Memoirs, by contrast, can be what Richard Delgado calls "counterstories" to challenge oppression.[13]

The "new slave narrative," as Kelli Lyon Johnson states, is a "body of stories [that] constitutes both a continuation and transformation of the slave narrative tradition of the eighteenth and nineteenth centuries."[14] She goes on to argue that "contemporary slave narratives offer an interpretive framework of what I am calling *narrative advocacy*."[15] The majority of "slave narratives" Lyon Johnson examines (95 of 149) are from the collection *To Plead Our Own Cause*. Like Lyon Johnson, Laura T. Murphy, in her book *Survivors of Slavery: Modern-Day Slave Narratives*, relies on

Bales's sociological definition of slavery and acknowledges the limitations of only working with narratives of people who have had access to NGOs, in particular, in the United States.[16] These challenges include representativeness, mediation, and translation.[17] If what we come to know of the experiences of human bondage and exploitation are those made popular through these often brief "slave narratives," we may neglect many other experiences of child soldiers, forced marriage, and wartime casualties, which may be less hopeful about the human spirit and resilience. Further, if the majority of our understanding is produced through narration for advocacy, other consequent silencing may result. All genres have conventions, yet we should work against a narrative advocacy genre that flattens the culturally diverse ways of "telling stories and producing social meaning" and be receptive to the risks of stories produced for commodification and circulation in English.[18]

This chapter draws from the fields of anthropology of human rights,[19] contemporary slavery studies,[20] and recent scholarship that critically assesses international criminal trials.[21] My approach, however, is focused primarily on testimonies of women rather than on the legal dimensions of the trial decisions,[22] the "monumental history" produced by courts,[23] or the political economy/geopolitics of international tribunals.[24] Thus, I will not explore the role of experts, lawyers, and judges in international transitional justice but, rather, the voices of survivor victims.[25]

I will argue that while we have to be attentive – constantly critically reflexive – to the dangers of appropriating and consuming the suffering of women, I am not convinced that those dangers outweigh the scholarly and political imperatives to work with women to bring those voices to the fore and the need to fill the gaps in indictments, tribunal evidence, official histories, and popular understandings of conflict. In this endeavour, there is richer potential in narrative and life story writing than in relying on limited legal testimonies. In particular, in the cases of "modern slavery" and sexual violence (where voyeurism is a real problem), it is important to engage with narratives not produced through legal or activist lenses. At the same time, the engagement with survivors and their stories cannot be what Lawrence Langer describes in the context of one Holocaust memoir, *Fragmented*, as a "sentimental response to details of childhood pain [which] smothered the critical intelligence."[26]

Naming Gender Violence as Crimes against Humanity or Modern Slavery

There is nothing new about gender violence in war. Indeed, scholars have documented the role of sexual violence and other gender crimes in conflict situations in historical contexts related to war and enslavement.[27] The role of gender violence in contemporary conflicts is also well known and documented by scholars and NGOs such as Human Rights Watch (HRW), Amnesty International, and Médicins Sans Frontières.[28] Holding perpetrators responsible for those crimes against women, however, is a relatively new phenomenon in international criminal law.[29] Even after the Second World War, the Japanese commanders and soldiers who sexually enslaved women were not subject to criminal prosecution for the mass rapes of the so-called comfort women.[30] And on the other side of the world, "Robert Jackson, the Chief Prosecutor of the Nuremberg Tribunal, decided not to present sexual crimes in the cases against the Nazi leaders."[31]

Over the past three decades, there has been an increasing recognition of the crimes suffered by women in times of war. Since the Second World War when gender crimes were not included in war crimes tribunals, this recognition of gender crimes could be described as a sea change in international criminal law. Included in this law reform is the recognition of rape as an indictable offence rather than a part of the spoils of war; rape as a tool of genocide; sexual slavery; forced impregnation; and so on. These are now listed in the Rome Statute for the International Criminal Court as well as in statutes for the ad hoc tribunals.[32] Forced marriage is not listed as its own indictable offence in these statutes.[33] Abduction of a woman and designating her as a "wife" in times of war and relative peace, however, has been described in recent legal decisions and popular discourse as sexual slavery, enslavement, servile marriage, or modern slavery.

Interpreting and naming experiences of gender violence in war as modern slavery, sexual slavery, or crimes against humanity has risks and contradictory outcomes for activists and "victims" affected by violence in war.[34] There is a complicated economy of storytelling, recognition, and reparations. Testimonies in international courts facilitate a judicial purpose, which is not of the survivors' making. Testimonies to human rights organizations and journalists serve to bring attention to the plight of survivors and may or may not have been solicited by victims. In contrast, claims made to reparations bodies or human rights agencies are more often initiated by survivors for the purpose of reparations. And personally authored memoirs or biographies of wartime violence are written both for educational and commercial purposes. As I discuss in the section below on modern slavery biographies, readers of modern slavery narratives are not necessarily entering into what Anne Cubilié calls a "reciprocal relationship" that transcends the spectacle and voyeurism of wartime violence.[35] Indeed, I will argue that while some of the recent child soldier memoirs are less sensational and voyeuristic than other modern slavery memoirs (notably the human trafficking narratives found on many NGO websites), they circulate in a context of spectacle and politics of shock.

Kay Schaffer and Sidonie Smith's work on "'Grandmothers' telling stories of forced sexual slavery during WWII" exemplify these critiques well.[36] They argue that there were a number of "framing constraints" on the stories told by women years after their wartime enslavement, and they contend that

> the women have been held hostage to the ur-narrative of crimes against humanity. Rights activists require for their activism and expect from their informants a particular story of victimization: the ur-story of childhood poverty, abduction, forced sexual slavery and lonely survival. Changing the story, going beyond the expected narrative can be seen as a deviation from the work of collective remembering. Moreover, the narrator is expected to position herself as a ... victim of the "past" not an active agent in the present.[37]

The legal system and the general public will interpret testimonies of wartime sexual slavery against "schemata and scripts," as Richard Sherwin illustrates.[38] The "script" of an innocent victim from humble beginnings who suffers in silence for many years is one way of understanding the story. As Sherwin notes, "other mental representations ... also help us organize information in such a way as to give it meaning. They include metaphors, stereotypes, narrative genres, and recurrent plot lines."[39] Much like my experiences of hearing testimonies from the women in Sierra Leone, Schaffer and Smith found repetition in the story of Korean survivors, identifying "common plotting" in the stories of the "innocent victims" and the fact that the victims had to tell and retell their story.[40] And as in other discussions of rape and gender violence, there are "stories told and untold." In particular discussions of poverty, "rape in wartime occludes the discussion of systematic discrimination against women."[41]

More generally, over the past decade, there has been a growing critique of these developments in international criminal law. These critiques are similar to the concerns voiced about domestic prosecutions for sexual violence as well as the particular critiques aimed at the International Criminal Tribunals for Rwanda (ICTR) and for the former Yugoslavia (ICTY), the SLSC, and the International Criminal Court (ICC). I would summarize these critiques under four types. First, commentators argue that there is a particular gendered subject who is seen as the appropriate "helpless victim" of sexual and other violence and in need of protection from international law and humanitarian institutions.[42] As in national trials of violence against women, therefore, they point to the risks of revictimization in international trials for women and men who may or may not fit the stereotype. Indeed, there have been documented instances of humiliation and disrespect of witnesses at the ICTR.[43] The gendered stereotype lacks the complexities of victimhood and identity[44] and obfuscates the discussion of other forms of violence that women may have endured or inflicted. Women's role as fighters, as well as victims, for example, is often unexplored.[45]

Second, critics argue that the gendered victim in international tribunals is dependent on the construction of an African "warlord" or perpetrator.[46] This critique is part of a broader post-colonial criticism of international criminal law that sees it as a new form of imperialism. Third, it is argued, certain things may be silenced through the international criminal law and TRC proceedings. Emphasis is placed on the sexual violence but not on economic and other structural violence.[47] And, finally, critics have pointed out that a partial view of history is told through these narrations of victimization placed before the courts, commissions, and the public.[48] I agree with Richard Wilson's assessment that the records [archives] produced by the trials may indeed be "indispensable" for historians of the conflicts in the former Yugoslavia and Rwanda.[49] The historical narrative produced in these trial judgments, however, may not in fact provide rich and nuanced history. When one considers the exclusion of women's experience from official histories, the likelihood of partial history being told through international trials is much more certain.

Thus, we have calls to end impunity for gender-based violence in conflict situations and critiques of the justice systems that are set up to end impunity. In the following section, I am going to map out what I see as the challenges and complexities of trying to bring diverse women's voices into the international criminal proceedings and public discourse in order to document the harms experienced in times of war. In particular, I will focus on enslavement for the purposes of forced marriage, seen as a new crime in international law ("conjugal slavery" in the SCSL's decision in *Prosecutor v Charles Ghankay Taylor*).[50] I will proceed to argue that, despite the dangers, we should continue to work with women who narrate their experiences of suffering and make demands for "justice." The real potential of narratives of forced marriage and enslavement lies not in legal testimonies but, rather, in the collaborative storytelling told in respectful environments for social justice, despite, or outside, the court processes.

Legal Representations of Gender Violence and Forced Marriage

People prefer stories to be neat. Recognizable characters, familiar motives, and recurring scenarios of conflict and resolution are typical elements of our workday narrative world. Legal narratives are no different. And trial lawyers, especially prosecutors and defence attorneys, are only too glad to indulge a preferred image or storyline if it will help win a case. The trouble with having one's stories neat, however, is that they tend to leave things out – the things that make a story messy and hard to keep in mind. Of course, such infelicitous details can be dealt with. That is what recurring storylines, familiar genres and plots, and typical characters, conflicts, and resolutions are for. They keep the messiness out.[51]

In this section, I will focus on the ways in which legal proceedings produce knowledge about gender violence. As early as September 1994, Africa Rights published its comprehensive report on the Rwandan genocide, *Rwanda: Death, Despair and Defiance*, which included reports of rape and the abduction of women and children.[52] In 1996, HRW published its report on rape during the genocide in Rwanda, *Shattered Lives: Sexual Violence during the Rwanda Genocide and Its Aftermath*. Ironically, legal prosecutions of the crimes committed during the genocide in Rwanda started with a silence about rape and other gender violence. This was, as Nowrojee has stated, despite the fact that it was general knowledge that sexual violence was widespread in the 1994 genocide[53] and that the tribunal investigators were aware of the sexual violence. In the first few years, however, there was a lack of political will and devoted resources on the part of the Office of the Prosecutor at the ICTR.[54]

Like Nowrojee, Doris Buss notes the paradox of the ICTR's record on sexual violence prosecutions. While there was widespread acknowledgment of rape during the genocide, the conviction rate was dismally low. The vast majority of cases proceeded without rape indictments. Of the cases that included gender violence charges, only five men were found guilty, or approximately 10 percent of the cases.[55] In Buss's careful analysis of the ICTR decisions on rape as a tool of genocide/weapon of war, she argues that the narrative produced by the legal judgments is one that "limits what women can speak of."[56] She goes on: "The Rwanda Tribunal decisions, while laudable in many respects, can be read as narrating a limited conception of harm and the complex dimensions of violence in 1994 Rwanda."[57]

The ICTR's decision in *Prosecutor v Jean-Paul Akayesu* (1998) was the tribunal's first judgment and included the precedent-setting finding of rape as a tool of genocide for which Akayesu was found guilty.[58] In the context of the ICTR, the world came to know about rape and sexual violence through the testimony of the UN forces, including General Roméo Dallaire as well as witnesses and victims. Women gave evidence about sexual violence, mutilations, and extreme brutality to ICTR investigators, and some women testified in court. Major Brent Beardsley, Dallaire's assistant, gave evidence in *Prosecutor v Theoneste Bagosora, Gratien Kabiligi, Aloys Ntabakuze, and Anatole Nsengiyumva* in 2004 (ten years after the genocide).[59] He stated: "It seemed that everywhere we went, from the period of 19th April until the time we left, there was rape everywhere near these killings sites."[60]

When women did testify in court about gender violence and rape, "rape of individual women has largely been absent from the record."[61] Others spoke on their behalf and represented their pain; rape was a phenomenon not an individual's suffering. Buss refers to this phenomenon as the "hyper-visibility and un-visibility of sexual violence."[62] Rape of women was everywhere but individual victims of rape were nowhere to be seen. The hyper-visibility also comes dangerously close to a "pornographic" consumption of the suffering of women during the genocide in Rwanda – not an indignation that would move people to "outrage," solidarity, and action.[63] When women did appear before the court, it was not an "enabling environment."[64] Shame also plays an important cultural role in women's testifying to rape and can "lead women to silence themselves."[65] Cubilié writes: "Shame and its connection to gender and other differences help to make testimonial witnessing of atrocity a zone that is unstable and unsafe but from which these witnesses seek to build forms of ethics that can negotiate such issues while also acknowledging difference."[66] Certainly, survivors of the Rwandan genocide continue to speak out, despite the serious risks to their security and health.

With respect to the case of enslavement for forced marriage, the silence was even deeper. The complicated cases where women were kept alive, subjected to repeated rapes, sometimes referred to as wife or temporary wife, and provided with a measure of protection disrupts the available script of rape during the genocide. Africa Rights reported in 1994: "Many young women were taken as 'wives' – often second 'wives' by their abductors. From the behaviour of these men, they clearly intended to keep the women indefinitely."[67] The report documents cases where women were abducted by militiamen, "distributed" among the *interahamwe,*[68] or "bought" during an ad hoc tribunal.[69] These cases of forced marriages during the genocide clearly meet the definition of slavery.[70] Despite the fact that HRW's report *Shattered Lives* and Africa Rights' report *Death, Despair and Defiance* include reference to forced marriages, no indictments for enslavement for forced marriage were included, and the issue was never taken up by the ICTR or human rights investigators.[71]

Monika Kalra, an associate legal officer for the ICTY, writes in 2001:

> The prosecutor's office is aware of the existence of forced marriage
> during the 1994 genocide, yet it has not prosecuted the crime. In
> *Akayesu*, Witness NN clearly testified that Rafiki took her out of the
> group to be his wife. She also described the nature of her "marriage"
> and the sexual violence she endured therein. The reasons for not
> prosecuting forced marriage are unknown but may be due to the
> OTP's lack of resources.[72]

The testimony from NN in *Akayesu* follows:

> 434. Two days after arriving at the bureau communal, Witness NN
> recounted seeing an Interahamwe called Rafiki, whom she had
> known previously and who had previously told her that he wanted
> to live with her. When he saw her at the bureau communal, she said
> he told her that he was going to rape her and not marry her ...
> 435. ... Subsequently, Witness NN said on two consecutive days
> she was taken with a group of several hundred people, mostly wom-
> en and children, to a hole near the bureau communal where the In-
> terahamwe were intending to kill them with a grenade. The first day
> they were apparently unable to find a grenade. On the second day,
> they were beaten and brought back to the hole. At that time Witness
> NN said Rafiki, the Interahamwe who had locked her in his house,
> took her out of the group and said that she was his wife.[73]

Testimonies of forced marriage during the genocide, such as those of
NN, Josianne, Juliana, and Vestine collected by Africa Rights, include
accounts of women spared execution while not knowing their fate.[74]
Josiane was twenty years old when she was interviewed by Africa Rights
in Gitarama in 1994:

> They decided that I should be kept as a hostage. Some soldiers arrived
> and asked why I had not yet been killed. They told them "She is our
> hostage." The soldiers left and proceeded to finish off the survivors. The

interahamwe grouped me and three women together. One was a married woman. They distributed the other three women amongst themselves. One of the woman, a student aged nineteen, was later killed. Her crime is that she is not only a Tutsi, but an educated Tutsi woman.

They collected some other women as we walked along. They handed me over to a married man. He took me to his home. His wife was heavily pregnant. The next day he told me that my ten-year-old sister had been found in a house. He brought her to me. Even though I had been "given" to him, he was not confident that the other interahamwe would let him keep me.[75]

The SCSL also heard testimony from women about their experiences of gender-based violence, including abduction, rape, and forced marriage. The trial judgment in *Prosecutor v Issa Hassan Sesay, Morris Kallon, Augustine Gbao* found that "forced marriage was important to the RUF [Revolutionary United Front] both as a *tactic of war and means of obtaining unpaid logistical support for troops.*"[76] The SCSL's Trial Chamber II heard expert testimony in 2005 in *Prosecutor v Alex Tamba Brima, Brima Bazzy Kamara, and Satigie Borbor Kanu* from Zainab Bangura (now United Nations Special Representative on Sexual Violence in Conflict) on the issue of forced marriage.[77] The prosecution commissioned her report about both the Armed Forces Revolutionary Council (AFRC) and the RUF, and, in it, "forced marriage was captioned as the 'Bush Wife Phenomenon'":[78]

According to Zainab Bangura, forced marriage arose when a young girl/ woman was abducted during the war, came under the total control and command of a rebel/soldier (captor) claiming her to be his wife. This happened when the captor proclaimed *yu na mi wef*, in the Krio lingua franca meaning "you're my wife." At this point the victim was left with no option to accept the "marriage" ... In return, the "bush husband" ensured that he provided protection and support in terms of food and clothing.[79]

The following exchange comes from the defence cross-examination of Ms. Bangura:[80]

Mrs. Bangura, I put it to you that the marriages you referred to as forced marriages which took place in the bush or at the jungle, were mere relationships, social relationships. They were never marriages.

A. Well, that's not how the girls see them, because the issue of wife was used. The word "wife" was used. They will tell you, "I was married." Even the communities, the stigmatisation – when people come they tell you "this my rebel wife." And even in Freetown, you know that in Freetown, that people are pointed and they said, "This now junta wife." In Freetown here, people who had relationship, they point fingers to them and say, "This now junta wife." That is referring to the AFRC.

This narrative plot of abduction and complete control by a "bush husband" or rebel husband became the storyline of enslavement for the purposes of forced marriage in the Sierra Leone conflict. While the SCSL investigators took witness statements and the court heard testimony about forced marriage from individual women, the narrative in circulation was that articulated by the expert witness. This is a similar finding to the research that Buss completed in the context of the ICTR.

Further, such oversimplified accounts were repeated in the statements given to the reparations commission. The NCSA took 32,000 claims for reparations, of which 3,579 concerned sexual violence.[81] Of those women who made claims pertaining to sexual violence, 650 received some form of skills training as reparations and 235 received benefits. The following is one example of a statement made by a claimant for reparations:

When the RUF entered the town. They captured at me. The[y] went with me to the bush. Five RUF raped me. They virginated me immediately. I married to the bush boss of the RUF. I was with them for four years. I escaped to them, g came back to my people at Kabala. [as written].[82]

We can see in the claims being made to the Reparations Program in Sierra Leone that the applicants were being "held hostage" to a particular narration; indeed it appears that they were not in control of the narration in this context. Survivors of the conflict gave evidence to a bureaucrat in towns across the country or in Freetown. The conditions of these interviews were not always private and secure. Further, the bureaucrat would take notes on a reparations claim form titled "Circumstances leading to the human rights violation" with tick boxes for different violations. Of a random sample of 321 women's claims for reparations for human rights abuse, approximately one-quarter of the women talked about the designation of "wife," while others spoke of rape and other losses. Years of captivity in the bush are reduced to five lines of "testimony" for reparations:

> According to the victim, she was captured at Moyamba at night, and was brought to Mill 91, where she was used by one of the commander as his wife. How often forced her to have sex with him [as written].
>
> When the rebels entered Allen Town east end of Freetown, I together with five other women were captured and taken away. I was with the rebels for 6 months and three of the rebels used me as their wife, whenever they want. (sex slave) [as written].[83]

Circumstances where women were forced to kill – sometimes to kill other women with their own hands – were extremely traumatic, but they did not find their way into the reparations claims. For women in northern Uganda, the designation of wife was also experienced as a harm in itself, but such a harm did not fit the common understanding of sexual violence crimes. I would argue that the narrative arc of gender violence cases in the Democratic Republic of Congo (DRC) and at the SCSL repeats this paradox of visibility and witnessing. This is one way in which memoirs can add nuance and depth to our understanding of wartime violence.

In the case of the Korean women who gave testimony about their experience of enslavement for forced sexual labour in the Second World War, Schaffer and Smith argue that there was a "backdrop of prostitution as an alternative way of understanding" their experience. Therefore, they argue, women had "the need to tell stories of resistance" to their captivity and rape.[84] Similarly, for women held for years by rebels in Sierra Leone, Liberia, or northern Uganda, there is the fear that their families and communities will see them as colluding with rebels (rebel wife, junta wife, or bush wife) and, in fact, that they are staying with them by "choice." In the testimonial statements given by women about so-called forced marriage in conflict situations, women talk of trying to escape and being controlled by commanders and rebel husbands. The alternative understanding of complicity with the rebels needs to be denied. But the following statement makes clear that forced marriage during and after the war in Sierra Leone could also offer some measure of protection, especially when family and community structures were destroyed during the war:

> I was captured by the rebels since 1994 ... my parents were killed while I was raped and abducted by the rebels. I was abducted to two years period and after gaining freedom by Gov't troops, I have no where to stay in Kenema so I decided by forced to marriage to one [Soso?] man who brought me to [this] district up to date [as written].[85]

I have argued that in the ICTR and the SCSL, as well as in the reparations process in Sierra Leone, testimonies of wartime enslavement are all too often brief, repetitive, and lacking context. Testimonies of sexual violence and enslavement are either excluded or limited. Experts' version of their experience stand in for the more varied experiences of forced marriage in war – such experiences become the "bush wife phenomenon" in Sierra Leone and "rape as genocide" in Rwanda.

War Memoirs and Modern Slavery Narratives

The limiting constraints of legal representations of gender violence and forced marriage are not confined to formal settings such as criminal investigations and reparations processes. Indeed, researchers and activists also participate in the extraction of testimonies from survivors and cannot completely escape the problematics described in the previous section. Feminists (and here I include myself and the work of the coalition of which I am a member) and anti-slavery activists, while aware of the structural constraints of narratives of gender violence, have participated in pushing the agenda of international criminal law to include rape, forced marriage, and other gender violence indictments. This process of law reform and advocacy is dependent on the collaboration and testimonies of survivors. Further, the emphasis placed on rape as torture, rape as an act of genocide, and forced marriage as a crime against humanity means that other dimensions of harm and violence experienced in war may not be documented and discussed. Forced marriage has also been categorized as a form of modern slavery with similar consequences. When framed as modern slavery and seen as "one of the worst crimes," the complexity of the causes of enslavement for the purposes of forced marriage and the nuance of the relationships may be lost.

In this section, I turn to some modern slavery narratives and memoirs of war. Free the Slaves (FTS) in the United States, a sister organization to Anti-Slavery International, has a rich collection of "slave narratives" and published research on the topic. Cofounder Kevin Bales, along with his colleagues and coauthors, has documented cases ranging from indentured labour in India, debt bondage, trafficking for sexual exploitation, child domestic servitude, slavery in mines, and forced marriage in DRC. In the collection, *To Plead Our Own Cause: Personal Stories of Today's Slaves*, Bales and Trodd include ninety-five narratives and an introduction that places the collection in the "literary tradition of slave narratives." Bales also explains, on the FTS website, the motivation behind the book:

> The truth of slavery is in the lived experience of people who have been enslaved, we will never understand that truth unless they can speak freely and in their own voices. In this book we did not edit, correct grammar, or change in any way the words of these remarkable survivors. The result is a richness and a power beyond anything we've seen.[86]

These "modern-day slave" narratives do offer a richness that is not found in legal testimonies that are mediated through rules of procedure and evidence and shaped to the needs of the prosecution. And the narratives collected in *To Plead Our Own Cause* are not repetitive stories of exploitation followed by freedom, survival, and personal triumph.

Nonetheless, no collection is an unmediated random sample of memories and stories. They are stories of "survivors," placed in a context of the politics of shock and action.[87] Readers are to be moved into activism on behalf of those who are living in slavery or who have experienced slavery. I question whether, on reading the short narratives of modern-day slaves, the audience is in a "reciprocal" relationship:

> Our ethical engagement as witnesses to this survivor witnessing is a crucial element of the forms that state violence takes in relation to human rights discourse, and these survivors all testify to the importance of an engaged, ethical witnessing of atrocity that opposes the disengaged, guilt-ridden viewing of atrocity-as-spectacle that many forms of spectatorship take.[88]

A close reading of the survivors' stories in *To Plead Our Own Cause* demands such "ethical engagement" and attention to the complexity and loss included in their testimonies.

In the book-length memoirs from "child soldiers" and "modern-day slaves" that are most popular in the English language, the authors are those survivors who have migrated to North America. These memoirs are less calls to collective action, however, than to collective witnessing – to read or to hear about the experiences of abduction, hunger, loss, and violence. In the case of Emmanuel Jal, Mariatu Kamara, and Ishmeal Beah, the authors are also spokespersons and advocates for the UN Children's Fund, the Coalition to Stop the Use of Child Soldiers, War Child, or Make Poverty History. The author of *Restavec*, Jean-Robert Cadet, also migrated to the United States from Haiti, and the subtitle of his memoir is *From Haitian Slave-Child to Middle-Class American*.[89]

The literature of trauma and personal memoir writing began with the Holocaust survivors. These are very powerful personal accounts, coming years after the Second World War. Many Holocaust survivors only spoke of their experience when they were in their eighties, much like the Korean "grandmothers" speaking about wartime atrocities. Some Holocaust survivors as well as Rwandan genocide survivors have talked about feeling compelled to speak as they neared the end of their lives since they were the only remaining members of their family and their family history would otherwise die with them. However, here too, certain parts of women's stories are silenced or remain untold for much longer.[90]

While none of these memoirs could reach the iconic status of Anne Frank's *Diary of a Young Girl*, it is nonetheless helpful to remember what Lawrence Langer cautions in his reading of the *Diary*. Sometimes the popularity of a memoir may tell us more about our cultural response to atrocity and genocide than it does about the history of the events narrated in the text.[91] In his essay "Anne Frank Revisited," Langer writes:

> [The passages] seem to offer concrete support for the welcome notion that in the midst of chaos, even the chaos of mass murder, the human imagination, to say nothing of other features of the self, can remain untainted by the enormity of the crime ... Her irrepressible enthusiasm for life triumphs over threats to her security, furnishing a template for managing those threats that can be transferred to her readers.[92]

Mariatu Kamara's memoir, titled *The Bite of the Mango* is written with Canadian journalist Susan McClelland and tells of her experience during the war in Sierra Leone and her journey to Canada.[93] Kamara was approximately twelve years old at the time the war came to her area. She was brutally attacked by rebels in Manarma, near her village of Magborou, when she was going to collect water. The rebels amputated both of her hands. She walked alone for days to Freetown. Her memoir disrupts simple understandings of young people's experience of war. Rather than a short account of the wartime abuses, *The Bite of the Mango* offers readers a sense of her life before the conflict, her time in the refugee camp, which included begging in the streets, and the challenges of learning to adapt to daily living without hands. She lingers on moments that are uncomfortable and atypical. She shares, for example, her anger at well-intentioned benefactors who wished to provide prosthetic hands. She recounts moments of real loneliness and sadness. And she shares her challenge in adapting to Canadian culture and education.

While the reader often wants to think of an author's account of being a child in war as typical or representative, most of these biographies are in fact atypical. They are the young people who survived, who developed skills in displaced persons' camps or in the bush, sought education and emigration, and, subsequently, wrote about their experiences. About Anne Frank, Langer writes:

> She would have rejected with scorn Levin's charge that she spoke for six million perished souls. She was not a representative victim, and certainly not a representative teenager. Her feminist instincts long before the birth of the movement set her apart from the average young girl of her time. Her insistence on being treated as "Anne-in-her-own-right" rather than the typical adolescent her father thought she was confirms how much the attempt to universalize her experience violates her independent spirit.[94]

In her book, Kamara also recounts the story of being interviewed by journalists after arriving in the refugee camp in Freetown. After being skeptical and reluctant at first to speak with journalists because she was "thinking about all the money I would be missing by not begging," Kamara agreed to meet the international journalists, and she writes of the encounter as follows:

> "Can you tell them what happened to you?" the camp representative jumped right in.
> I didn't know where to begin, so I sat quietly thinking. The lady with the red hair turned to the representative, who turned to me. "She wants to know if you are with your family."
> "Yes," I replied. That was an easy question.
> The representative translated another question from the woman. "Do you need anything?"
> "Vegetables, clean water, soap, new clothes, dishes." I am not sure where the answer came from, but I found myself reciting a long list of everything we didn't have at the camp that we'd had back at Magborou.
> *I then broke into my story, or at least a small portion of it: "My name is Mariatu. I am a victim of the rebel attack on Manarma. Child soldiers held me hostage for ten hours and then cut off my hands. I now live in*

Aberdeen with my cousins Adamsay, Ibrahim, and Mohamed, who were also in the Manarma attack. They don't have hands either."

"How old is your baby?" the red-haired woman asked.

"His name is Abdul" I replied. "He is five months old"

My first interview with the media lasted about 15 minutes ...

It would be many years before I read the articles written about me ... Every one of them would come back to haunt me. The journalists all said the rebels had raped me and that I had conceived Abdul in the attack on Manarma ...

Many years later ... "I was traumatized that day because I had learned for the first time [in school in Canada] that much of the information written in those articles was wrong. The most glaring mistake the journalists had made was stating that the rebels had raped me."[95]

In this excerpt, we see the dynamic of storytelling in a context of commodification and public consumption where the teller is not in control of her story. While the journalist was, in Kamara's experience, respectful and put her at ease, the articles written about her were factually incorrect. She had been raped by a family friend, an older man she called an uncle, just before the rebels attacked her village. She became pregnant from that rape. And while she did not speak of the sexual assault to the journalists, the narrative of rape by rebels overtook her story.

Second, you can read in this excerpt the "story" she breaks into, which is the script of wartime violence, a repeated tale of being held by rebels. It reads as almost a separate voice from that of her own story being told in the memoir. In the script of "representative victim" for journalists, there is a detachment and lack of detail and emotion from the author. It is similar in its tone and brevity to the statements given for claims for reparations about human rights violations or the statements made to researchers and investigators. One of the things that is so rich for the purposes of my inquiry about *The Bite of the Mango* is Kamara's reflection on the interviews and the articles produced about her.

In Emmanuel Jal's memoir *War Child*, we also read of his numerous interviews with journalists and aid workers, *khawajas*, as he came to speak as one of the Lost Boys of Sudan. Like Kamara, he is an extraordinary person who at a very young age was subjected to horrific treatment in war. In his case, he was recruited into the fighting forces of the Sudan People's Liberation Army (SPLA) and travelled to Ethiopia and then back to southern Sudan. He was finally taken to Nairobi and removed from the fighting forces. He survived, in part, due to his charm and skills with language. He was often asked by SPLA superiors to speak to journalists and to ask for more food from humanitarian aid agencies. However, he was not a "typical war child"; the pages of his memoir remind us of the many children who died walking for days without food, simply dropping off the line of refugees, or the children who died in combat or from disease in the refugee camps. Jal does not avoid or exclude these stories from his account. (In some ways, it feels relentless.) Rather when read from this perspective, his book is about children who died in war all around him, while he somehow avoided death from beatings, starvation, disease, and war. He writes:

> The line of soldiers stretched into the dusk as troops walked through the forest. Lam was behind me but we didn't speak. I knew that he, like me, didn't want to open his mouth and let death slip slowly inside as we talked. All around us lay corpses, which the sun had warmed throughout the day. They were everywhere – bones, skeletons, and fresh bodies – and their rotten smell hung in the air. This was the front of the front line, and even the vultures did not fly away in surprise when they saw us. Death was everything here while the living went unnoticed.[96]

Langer argues that Holocaust testimonial evidence is as much about death and near death as it is about survival. Indeed, his work directs attention towards the ways in which modern slavery narratives and child soldier memoirs are accounts of "endurance" rather than survival,[97] or "deathlife" rather than living.[98] In this way, Langer argues, Holocaust survivors experienced living as "their missed destiny of death," which stays with them as they recollect.[99] In Jal's autobiography, there are many places in the book where he too "brushes" with death and many others around him die.

One has to be cautious not to oversimplify slave narratives as stories of survival and hope but, rather, to read them as complex remembering(s) of loss. Jal, for example, tells the reader of his struggles to feel any emotion when he is reunited with his siblings after he started a successful music career. His book ends with those relationships unresolved. Cadet, the author of *Restavec*, closes his memoir with a short afterword, almost a corrective to the more optimistic final paragraph of his book:

> Although the birth of [my son] Adam filled the void in my chest, I still became clinically depressed at times, especially during the holidays when everyone I knew seemed to be on the way to reconnect with family members ... As I watched Adam in the arms of his grandma, reaching for her smiling face, I felt like the silent victim of rape. Then I realized that Adam too was a victim, a casualty of restavec servitude. Had my former country abolished all forms of slavery, Florence's treatment of me would have never been socially condoned ... Restavec slavery is wrong. It is the worst crime imaginable, because the victims are incapable of resisting their adult predators.[100]

In the memoir by Kamara, we find others who brand her story as a story of triumph. Her publisher packages her book as a story of "courage, resilience and hope." In her own words, hers is a journey from "poor village girl to war amputee to activist living in Canada," touring with her book to raise awareness.[101] What is clear from reading her book and hearing her speak is that she tells her story as a form of advocacy, politics, and fundraising for her foundation in Sierra Leone. Of course, it is also a story of "courage, resilience and hope," but it is not only that story. In Ishmael Beah's "Foreword" to *Bite of the Mango*, he writes: "In my culture, every story is told with the purpose of either imparting knowledge, repairing a broken bond, or transforming the listener and the teller. Mariatu's story embodies all of these elements. I have been waiting for such a story, one that reminds us all of the strength and resilience of the human spirit."[102]

Conclusions

Just as Wilson argued in relation to larger historical narratives produced by international criminal trials, I would argue that the documentary evidence from legal proceedings concerning gender violence and enslavement for forced marriage is very valuable. In other words, the archive of witness statements and trial transcripts are valuable to students of the atrocities in Sierra Leone, Liberia, Rwanda, and elsewhere. While the narratives produced by courts about gender violence and forced marriage are problematic and limited, the evidentiary background to the cases is very valuable and often untapped. Even these sources are mediated through the legal frame. By contrast, first-person narratives and memoirs provide readers with much more nuanced and complicated views of abduction, captivity, and gender violence in war.

Chris Coulter writes in her book *Bush Wives and Girl Soldiers: Women's Lives through War and Peace in Sierra Leone* that human rights reports and data of gender violence in war – and I would add modern slavery accounts – "records and illustrates but does little in the way of providing a deeper understanding of the war and the people in it, but, to be fair, this is not the objective of such data."[103] Coulter demonstrates in her rich ethnography the value of anthropological studies of atrocity and mass human rights violations. She states: "Explaining social relations, issues of agency, notions of self, culture and cosmology is a project better suited to anthropology [than] UN and NGO studies [which] work from a human rights framework."[104] Even excellent ethnographic work, such as that done by Coulter in Sierra Leone, is still part of a broader "commodification of suffering."[105]

Erica Caple James, in her compelling ethnography of trauma counselling and humanitarian aid work in Haiti, explores the paradox that the "effort to rehabilitate the citizens ... ends up reinforcing the very practices of predation, corruption and repression that they were intended to repair.[106] James argues that with the "commodification of suffering" in both terror economies and compassion economies, "individual and collective pain and suffering was extracted and remade into something productive but with opposite goals."[107] Activists and scholars working with survivor groups have the potential through life story narratives to demand a better politics of representation. I would argue that the composite of testimonies gathered by human rights reporters, personal self-authored memoirs, and ethnographies provide a more complex picture of gender violence and enslavement than any one form of knowledge can provide. I have argued here that legal testimonies and legal knowledge offer limited accounts of experience in conflict situations. Produced for a different purpose than scholarly research or political advocacy, legal testimonies are an important, but partial or incomplete, source of information. At the same time, memoirs and even interviews with anthropologists cannot completely avoid the "framing constraints" of narratives of violence, abduction, captivity, and enslavement.

Notes

1 Interview with author, Freetown, August 2010.
2 Laurie Beth Clark, "Coming to Terms with Trauma Tourism," *Performance Paradigm* 5.2, October 2009, http://www.performanceparadigm.net/index.php/journal/article/view/76 (accessed Nov. 1, 2016).
3 J. John Lennon and Margaret Mitchell, "Dark Tourism: The Role of Sites of Death in Tourism," in Margaret Mitchell, ed., *Remember Me: Constructing Immortality – Beliefs on Immortality, Life, and Death* (New York: Routledge, 2007), 167–78.
4 Anne Cubilié, *Women Witnessing Terror: Testimony and the Cultural Politics of Human Rights* (New York: Fordham University Press, 2005), 10.
5 Interview with author, Freetown, August 2010.
6 Binaifer Nowrojee, "Your Justice Is Too Slow: Will the ICTR Fail Rwanda's Rape Victims?" United Nations Research Institute for Social Development Occasional Paper 10, 2005, 4. See also Binaifer Nowrojee, "Making the Invisible War Crime Visible: Post-Conflict Justice for Sierra Leone's Rape Victims," *Harvard Human Rights Journal* 18 (2005): 85-105.
7 To a lesser extent, I will rely on surveys done by Maria Eriksson Baaz and Maria Stern, "A Critical Analysis of Sexual Violence in the Democratic Republic of Congo (DRC)," Swedish International Development Cooperation Agency Working Paper on Gender based Violence, 2010.
8 Sherene Razack, "Stealing the Pain of Others: Reflections on Canadian Humanitarian Responses" *Review of Education, Pedagogy and Cultural Studies* 294 (2007): 375–94.
9 Nowrojee, "Your Justice Is Too Slow"; And see Rhonda Copelon, "Gender Crimes as War Crimes: Integrating Crimes against Women into International Criminal Law," conference paper available at www.iccwomen.org/publications/articles/docs/Gender_Crimes_as_War_Crimes.doc (accessed Nov. 1, 2016) 1-19.
10 Doris Buss, "Rethinking 'Rape as a Weapon of War,'" *Feminist Legal Studies* 17, 2 (2009): 145–63; Jean-Robert Cadet, *Restavec: From Haitian Slave Child to Middle-Class American* (Austin, TX: University of Texas Press, 1998); Cubilié, *Women Witnessing Terror*; Kay Schaffer and Sidonie Smith, *Human Rights and Narrated Lives: The Ethics of Recognition* (New York: Palgrave Macmillan, 2004).

11 Erica James, *Democratic Insecurities: Violence, Trauma, and Intervention in Haiti* (Berkeley, CA: University of California Press, 2011).

12 Mariatu Kamara with Susan McClelland, *The Bite of the Mango* (Richmond Hill, ON: Annick Press, 2008); Ishmael Beah, *A Long Way Gone: Memoirs of a Boy Soldier* (Vancouver, BC: Douglas and McIntyre, 2007); Emmanuel Jal, *War Child: A Child Soldier's Story* (New York: St. Martin's Griffin, 2009); Faith J.H. McDonnell and Grace Akallo, *girl soldier: A Story of Hope for Northern Uganda's Children* (Grand Rapids, MI: Chosen Books, 2007); Kathy Cook, *Stolen Angels: The Kidnapped Girls of Uganda* (Toronto: Penguin Group, 2007); Jean-Robert Cadet, *Restavec*; Mende Nazer and Damien Lewis, *Slave: My True Story* (New York: Public Affairs, 2003); and Kevin Bales and Zoe Trodd, *To Plead Our Own Cause: Personal Stories by Today's Slaves* (Ithaca: Cornell University Press, 2008).

13 Richard Delgado, "Storytelling for Oppositionists and Others: A Plea for Narrative," *Michigan Law Review* 87, 2411 (1989) 2436–37.

14 Kelli Lyon Johnson, "The New Slave Narrative: Advocacy and Human Rights in Stories of Contemporary Slavery," *Journal of Human Rights* 12, 2 (2013): 243. See Henry Louis Gates Jr., ed., *The Classic Slave Narratives* (New York: Signet Classics, 2012), containing "The Life of Olaudah Equiano," "The History of Mary Prince," "Narrative of the Life of Frederick Douglass," and "Incidents in the Life of a Slave Girl."

15 Johnson, "The New Slave Narrative" (emphasis in original).

16 Laura T. Murphy, *Survivors of Slavery: Modern-day Slave Narratives* (New York: Columbia University Press, 2014), 7.

17 Johnson, "The New Slave Narrative," 246.

18 Schaffer and Smith, *Human Rights and Narrated Lives*, 139–40.

19 Chris Coulter, *Bush Wives and Girl Soldiers: Women's Lives through War and Peace in Sierra Leone* (Ithaca, NY: Cornell University Press, 2009); Mark Goodale and Sally Engle Merry, *The Practice of Human Rights: Tracking Law between the Global and the Local* (Cambridge: Cambridge University Press, 2007).

20 Alyson Brysk and Austin Choi-Fitzpatrick, eds., *From Human Trafficking to Human Rights* (Philadelphia: University of Pennsylvania Press, 2012).

21 Buss, "Rethinking 'Rape as a Weapon of War'"; Kamari Maxine Clarke, *Fictions of Justice: The International Criminal Court and the Challenge of Legal Pluralism in Sub-Saharan Africa* (Cambridge: Cambridge University Press, 2009); Richard A. Wilson, *Writing History in International Criminal Trials* (New York: Cambridge University Press, 2011).

22 Valerie Oosterveld, "Sexual Slavery and the International Criminal Court: Advancing International Law," *Michigan Journal of International Law* 25 (2004): 605–51.

23 Wilson, *Writing History in International Criminal Trials*, 86.

24 Clarke, *Fictions of Justice*.

25 In this way, I am disagreeing with Kamari Clarke's assertion that victims are ghosts. I do not think they are mere specters; they are present, but the dimensions of their stories are certainly limited and flattened through legal proceedings. Clarke, *Fictions of Justice*.

26 Lawrence Langer, *Using and Abusing the Holocaust* (Bloomington, IN: Indiana University Press, 2006), 55.

27 Paul Lovejoy, "Internal Markets or an Atlantic-Sahara Divide? How Women Fit into the Slave Trade of West Africa," in Gwyn Campbell, Suzanne Miers, and Joseph C. Miller, eds., *Women and Slavery* (Athens, OH: Ohio University Press, 2007), 259–80.

28 Doris Buss, Joanne Lebert, Blair Rutherford, Donna Sharkey, and Obijiofor Aginam, eds., *Sexual Violence in Conflict and Post-Conflict Societies: International Agendas and African Contexts* (New York: Routledge, 2014); Neha Jain, "Forced Marriage as A Crime Against Humanity: Problems of Definition and Prosecution." *Journal of International Criminal Justice* 6 (2008), 1013–32; Susan McKay and Dyan Mazurana, *Where are the Girls? Girls in the Fighting Forces in Northern Uganda, Sierra Leone and Mozambique: Their Lives During and After War* (Montreal: Rights and Democracy, 2003).

29 Nowrojee, "Making the Invisible War Crime Visible"; Copelon, "Gender Crimes as War Crimes."

30 Gay J. McDougall, Special Rapporteur on Contemporary Forms of Slavery, "Systematic Rape, Sexual Slavery and Slavery-Like Practices during Armed Conflict," Doc. E/CN.4/Sub.2/1998/13, 1998.

31 Luis Moreno Ocampo, "Keynote Address – Interdisciplinary Colloquium on Sexual Violence as International Crime: Interdisciplinary Approaches to Evidence" (2010) 35, 4 *Law & Social Inquiry* 839, 842.

32 Rome Statute of the International Criminal Court, 17 July 1998, 2187 UNTS 90.

33 Annie Bunting, "Forced Marriage in Conflict Situations: Researching and Prosecuting Old Harms and New Crimes," *Canadian Journal of Human Rights* 1, 1 (2012): 165–85.

34 William Hague, British Secretary of State for Foreign and Commonwealth Affairs, "Sexual Violence in War Is Our Generation's Slave Trade," *Huffington Post*, 28 January 2013, http://www.huffingtonpost.com/william-hague/sexual-violence-in-war-is_b_2551284.html (accessed 1 November 2016).

35 Cubilié, *Women Witnessing Terror.*

36 Schaffer and Smith, *Human Rights and Narrated Lives*, 123.

37 Ibid., 136–37.

38 Richard K. Sherwin, "Law Frames: Historical Truth and Narrative Necessity in a Criminal Case," *Stanford Law Review* 47, 1 (1994): 49–51.

39 Ibid., 51.

40 Schaffer and Smith, *Human Rights and Narrated Lives*, 137.

41 Ibid., 138.

42 Katherine Franke, "Gendered Subjects of Transitional Justice," *Columbia Journal of Gender and Law* 153 (2006): 813–28.

43 Nowrojee, "Your Justice is Too Slow," 23–24.

44 Clarke, *Fictions of Justice*; Buss, "Rethinking 'Rape as a Weapon of War.'"

45 Coulter, *Bush Wives and Girl Soldiers*, 126. See also Erin Baines, *Buried in the Heart: Women, Complex Victimhood and the War in Northern Uganda* (Cambridge: Cambridge University Press, 2016).

46 Clarke, *Fictions of Justice*.

47 Baaz and Stern, "A Critical Analysis of Sexual Violence."

48 Buss, "Rethinking 'Rape as a Weapon of War.'"

49 Wilson, *Writing History in International Criminal Trials*, 69.

50 SCSL, *Prosecutor v Charles Ghankay Taylor*, Case no. SCSL-03-01-A, 26 September 2013.

51 Sherwin, "Law Frames," 40.

52 African Rights, *Rwanda: Death, Despair and Defiance* (London: African Rights, 1994), 410–49.

53 Nowrojee, "Your Justice is Too Slow," 3.

54 Ibid., 9.

55 Buss, "Rethinking 'Rape as a Weapon of War,'" 151; Nowrojee, "Your Justice is Too Slow," 3.

56 Buss, "Rethinking 'Rape as a Weapon of War,'" 146.

57 Ibid., 151. Nowrojee puts it more strongly: "Let us not continue to treat rape victims with the callous disregard that has often characterized the ICTR experience. Let us not deny rape victims international justice ... Let us not build international justice at the expense of the victims, who can least afford to make more sacrifices." Nowrojee, "Your Justice is Too Slow," 27.

58 ICTR, *Prosecutor v Jean-Paul Akayesu*, Case no. ICTR-96-4-T, 2 September 1998.

59 ICTR, *Prosecutor v Theoneste Bagosora, Gratien Kabiligi, Aloys Ntabakuze, and Anatole Nsengiyumva*, Case no. ICTR-98-41-T, 28 September 2004.

60 Nowrojee, "Your Justice is Too Slow," 1. Razack notes how in a process of national witnessing, we identify with Dallaire and the UN forces and do not see and feel the pain of Rwandans or take responsibility for our own implication in this history. Rather, Rwandans disappear as the suffering and injustice is about UN forces: "In this way, trauma narratives furnish middle power nations such as Canada with a homemade, that is to say a specifically national, version of the politics of rescue." Razack, "Stealing the Pain of Others," 381.

61 Buss, "Rethinking 'Rape as a Weapon of War,'" 153.

62 Ibid., 153.

63 Razack writes: "What happens to us after we read of such pornographic details? What has happened to you as I say them or you read my repetition of them?" Razack, "Stealing the Pain of Others," 384.

64 Nowrojee, "Making the Invisible War Crimes Visible," 23.

65 Cubilié, *Women Witnessing Terror*, 15; Sara Sharratt, *Gender, Shame and Sexual Violence: The Voices of Witnesses and Court Members at War Crimes Tribunals* (Farnham: Ashgate, 2011).

66 Cubilié, *Women Witnessing Terror*, 14.

67 African Rights, *Rwanda: Death, Despair and Defiance*, 437.

68 Ibid., 438.

69 Ibid., 440–42.

70 Jean Allain, "The Definition of Slavery in International Law," *Howard Law Journal* 52, 2 (2009): 239–76.

71 African Rights, *Rwanda: Killing the Evidence: Murder, Attacks, Arrests and Intimidation of Survivors and Witnesses* (London: Africa Rights, 1996), 33–34.

72 Monika Satya Kalra, "Forced Marriage: Rwanda's Secret Revealed," *University of California Davis Journal of International Law and Policy* 7 (2001): 197.

73 *Akayesu*, 1998: 178 (paras 434–35).

74 All of these names are pseudonyms in African Rights, *Rwanda: Death, Despair and Defiance*.

75 African Rights, *Rwanda: Killing the Evidence*, 438–39.

76 SCSL, *Prosecutor v Issa Hassan Sesay, Morris Kallon, Augustine Gbao*, Case no. SCSL-04-15-T, 2 March 2009, para. 2107 (*RUF* case) (emphasis added).

77 SCSL, *Prosecutor v Alex Tamba Brima, Brima Bazzy Kamara, and Satigie Borbor Kanu*, Case no. SCSL-04-16-T, 16 June 2005 (*AFRC* case).

78 Ibrahim Jalloh, "Analyzing Bush Wife Phenomenon at the Special Court Trials," International Commission on Transitional Justice (ICTJ), May 2006 (on file with author).

79 Ibid.

80 *RUF* case, 38, lines 21–29.

81 The Truth and Reconciliation Commission for Sierra Leone took 8,000 statements.

82 On file with author.

83 On file with author, with permission from the Truth and Reconciliation Commission for Sierra Leone.

84 Schaffer and Smith, *Human Rights and Narrated Lives*, 139.

85 On file with the Truth and Reconciliation Commission for Sierra Leone.

86 *Free the Slaves*, http://www.freetheslaves.net/building-awareness/books/ (accessed 1 November 1, 2016).

87 "Stories of Survivors," *Free the Slaves*, http://www.freetheslaves.net/about-slavery/survivor-stories/ (accessed 1 November 2016).

88 Cubilié, *Women Witnessing Terror*, 10–11. I would argue that the reciprocal relationship of "ethical witnessing" discussed by Cubilié could be present between the researchers and participants in the process of the work by Free the Slaves; anonymous witnessing risks the narratives being spectacular.

89 Cadet, *Restavec*.

90 Sara R. Horowitz, *Voicing the Void: Muteness and Memory in Holocaust Fiction* (New York: State University of New York Press, 1997).

91 Langer, *Using and Abusing the Holocaust*, 21.

92 Ibid., 19.

93 Mariatu Kamara, with Susan McClelland, *Bite of the Mango* (Richmond Hill, ON: Annick Press, 2008).

94 Langer, *Using and Abusing the Holocaust*, 23.

95 Kamara, with McClelland, *Bite of the Mango*, 104–05, 192.

96 Emmanuel Jal, *War Child: A Child Soldier's Story* (New York: St. Martin's Griffin, 2009), 150.

97 Langer, *Using and Abusing the Holocaust*, 96.

98 Ibid., 14.

99 Ibid.

100 Cadet, *Restavec*, 183.

101 Kamara, with McClelland, *Bite of the Mango*.

102 Ishmael Beah, "Foreword," in Kamara, with McClelland, *Bite of the Mango*, 7.

103 Chris Coulter, *Bush Wives and Girl Soldiers*, 11.

104 Ibid., 8.

105 James, *Democratic Insecurities*, 26.

106 Ibid., 7.

107 Recall the quotation from the woman quoted earlier from Sierra Leone: "Once I get it out of my chest … it is healing." Interview with author, Freetown, August 2010.

Show and Tell: Contemporary Anti-Slavery Advocacy as Symbolic Work

6

Fuyuki Kurasawa

In this chapter, I want to shift the focus of research on contemporary slavery from descriptions of specific instances of slavery or the analysis of its systemic causes and effects to the constitution of slavery as a problem to be addressed within Euro-American public spheres.[1] Thus, rather than taking slavery for granted as a social object – whose self-evident status as a morally abhorrent fact serves as an unquestioned point of analytical departure – the chapter examines some of the major processes and mechanisms through which anti-slavery advocacy groups produce such an object as a moral evil, against which public opinion can be mobilized by supporting steps to prevent or stop its various manifestations around the world. Understanding how slavery becomes established as a publicly significant problem represents a greater puzzle when considering the fact that campaigns about various forms of enslavement operate on a socio-political terrain composed of competing claims in national and global civil societies about human rights violations and injustices around the world. Non-governmental organizations (NGOs) and social movements are constantly publicizing seemingly more urgent and spectacular situations, notably those involving intensive and large-scale situational violence that garner greater media coverage and geopolitical importance than slavery (for example, civil war, genocide).[2] In such an over-saturated setting, how can anti-slavery be transformed into a distinctive and prominent cause within Western arenas of public debate today, one that morally and politically would interpellate segments of civil society to convert it into involved publics?

The answer to such a question does not lie strictly in an institutional analysis of anti-slavery campaigns' informational strategies, which consist of them comprehensively documenting and enumerating various forms of slavery in order to lobby states and alert Euro-American publics about the existence of such forms. Likewise, the answer is not to be found solely in a legally formalistic study of these same campaigns, which would concentrate on the enshrining of multilateral conventions and international treaties (against human trafficking, indentured and forced labour, and so on) as well as on the prosecution of those responsible for, or directly exploiting, enslaved persons. Hence, rather than employing either an institutionalist or a formalist approach, adopting a culturally attuned critical sociology enables us to gain a fuller understanding of the oft-neglected symbolic work that underpins anti-slavery advocacy.

More precisely, this chapter considers one of the principal, yet hitherto under-analyzed, means by which such advocacy groups have attempted to position slavery at the centre of public discourse, namely their extensive reliance on images coded to represent facets and instances of enslavement. Indeed, throughout their history, anti-slavery NGOs and social movements have sought to harness the iconographic power of visual material to gain socio-political traction in Western public spheres. To a considerable extent, the capacity of these actors' campaigns to affect public opinion substantially has depended upon their engaging in the politico-symbolic labour of generating or circulating paintings and photographs presented as illustrations of the suffering of slaves and the indignities inflicted upon them. Together with their associated textual commentary, whether of a more didactic, poetic, or politicized nature, such illustrations have played an essential role in practices of slavery being acknowledged as immoral in Euro-American social imaginaries and in convincing the public that something must and can be done to put an end to them.

If the use of images' iconographic power to sway public opinion is a hallmark of all organizations (states, private corporations, civil society actors, and so on), what distinguishes the visually grounded symbolic work of anti-slavery groups is their engagement in a process of historically derived analogical juxtaposition built around the transatlantic slave trade. The socio-cultural consensus about the latter's status as a universal signifier of evil can be mobilized, through the use of visual tropes and conventions, to establish a moral equivalence between it and contemporary modes of enslavement.[3] Therefore, the first section of the chapter explains how analogical juxtaposition operates through what can be designated as mediating and metonymic icons, which function together to designate certain present-day practices as types of slavery as well as to produce a moral proximity between these practices and the transatlantic slave trade.

In the chapter's second part, I analyze more precisely how the symbolic work of analogical coding is far from indeterminate since it is structured by the reoccurrence of specific visual conventions to represent enslavement. Drawing on an analysis of images of the transatlantic slave trade used by the abolitionist movement and of pictures appearing on the websites of anti-slavery NGOs, the second part of the chapter denotes three types of these visual motifs: personification, which underscores the experiential dimensions of a particular slave's circumstances; massification, which illustrates the scale of slavery by portraying an undifferentiated group of enslaved subjects; and rescue, which depicts in racialized terms the freeing of slaves of colour by their white "saviours."

Finally, the third section discusses the ambiguous political legacy of the iconographic history of the representations of slavery, whose indexical referentiality adds moral weight to contemporary anti-slavery campaigns while also introducing potential pitfalls for such campaigns by compromising their capacity to generate a discrete, non-analogically dependent iconography capable of strongly mobilizing public opinion. We can thus speak of the paradox of analogical juxtaposition, which is simultaneously the greatest symbolic asset of contemporary anti-slavery advocacy and its most problematic mechanism. It should be noted that the following pages do not offer a comprehensive history of the visual representation of slavery, which would go well beyond the scope of this chapter. Instead, I have chosen to compare contemporary anti-slavery iconography to that popularized by the abolitionist movement from the late eighteenth to the mid-nineteenth century, since the latter established the dominant visual motifs that are reproduced today.[4]

Explaining Analogical Juxtaposition

Historically derived analogical juxtaposition operates through visual symbols that perform two functions, namely mediation and metonymy. At the first level, such symbols can be seen as mediating icons, which attempt to demonstrate a historical and moral continuity between past and current practices and situations of enslavement. Instead of creating a moral economy of strict equivalence, contemporary representations of slavery operate via a logic of symbolic analogy designed to construct normative parallels with the transatlantic slave trade in order to draw on the latter's cultural status as a universal moral evil to gain public and political support for anti-slavery causes. At the same time, anti-slavery advocates tend to eschew analogically coding images in a manner that would aim to collapse the substantial differences in intensity and scale between present-day types of enslavement and the transatlantic slave trade, since suggesting the exact factual or moral correspondence of the two would risk trivializing the systemic global effects of the latter (the dislocation of African societies, the birth of capitalism and modernity, the socio-cultural entrenchment of racism in the North and South Atlantic worlds, and so on) while missing the distinctiveness of ongoing forms of slavery (for example, the reproduction of gender and racial inequalities, Western states' creation of illegality to designate vast portions migrant populations, and the lax enforcement of existing labour legislation). Put simply, anti-slavery advocacy seeks to draw on the past to acquire moral weight in public spheres in the present, while avoiding the suggestion of an easy moral and structural equation of the present with this past. Therefore, analogical juxtaposition in current campaigns operates on a dual interpretive register, which can be explained in Saussurian terms as the employment of contemporary visual signifiers whose meanings are derived less from their relations to referents of existing types of slavery than to another set of signifiers designating an iconography of historically established forms of enslavement (chains, whips, slave ships, and so on). This process is explained in Figure 6.1:

Figure 6.1 Visual analogical juxtaposition in anti-slavery campaigns

CVS: contemporary visual signifier
CR: contemporary referent
HVS: historical visual signifier
CS^1: 1st chain of signification
CS^2: 2nd chain of signification
CS^3: 3rd chain of signification

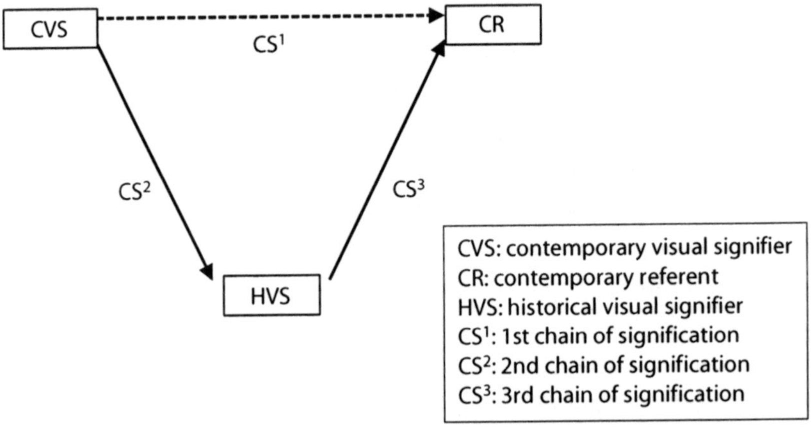

Whereas a standard chain of signification (CS^1 in Figure 6.1) operates through a non-analogical process, according to which a contemporary visual signifier (CVS) would acquire meaning by symbolically designating a contemporary referent (CR), the perceived lack of moral heft and social prominence of such contemporary referents of present-day instances of slavery has compelled anti-slavery campaigns to devise and rely upon an indirect, analogical process of signification (CS^2 + CS^3). Thus, a contemporary visual signifier (CVS) of slavery must be linked through a signifying chain (CS^2) to a one of its historically established visual signifiers (HVS), which morally and culturally amplifies a corresponding contemporary referent (CR) in the second part of the analogical process (CS^3). In short, the mechanism of analogical juxtaposition of current and past visual symbols of slavery is vital in order for anti-slavery advocacy to gain public traction since a more semiotically and chronologically direct process is inadequate to achieve this objective in and of itself.

In addition to performing a mediating function, visual symbols are metonymic icons whose role is not to portray slavery per se but, rather, to embody and refer to the racialized structures of domination upon which slavery depends as well as the suffering inflicted onto a slave's body. The iconography of chains, whips, and the slave ship stand in for the system of enslavement and the dehumanizing treatment of those subjugated to it, while also suggesting modes of physical, symbolic, and structural violence that cannot be fully captured by the image's frame and the camera's gaze and, thus, whose intensity and scale can only be alluded to metonymically.

Taken together, then, these mediating and metonymic roles point to a defining lacuna in the visual representation of contemporary slavery – that is to say, the ongoing difficulty in establishing an iconography that is distinctive vis-à-vis its historical iterations because it is not excessively derived from the latter. The aforementioned dual interpretive register of anti-slavery advocacy constitutes a political and representational inadequacy since such advocacy must rely on culturally shared symbols of the transatlantic slave trade imbedded in the collective memory of Euro-American societies in order for its campaigns to mobilize public opinion. To date, anti-slavery groups have been mostly unable to portray the current situations of enslavement as rhetorically discrete, with historical mediation and symbolic analogy being the principal mechanisms through which the meanings of these situations as morally abhorrent and socially intolerable practices and structures become apparent. In other words, an image of enslavement today is not inherently distinguishable or recognizable as such by viewers, and processes of textual designation ("this is a type of slavery" or "this is an enslaved person") implicitly or explicitly must draw on past signifiers of slavery for audiences to acknowledge the image's purpose and importance.

Therefore, to parry this iconographic lacuna, anti-slavery advocates have had to foreground representational conventions of enslavement inaugurated during the transatlantic slave trade within their campaigns' visual material, drawing from a historically constituted symbolic index and set of motifs to produce publicly recognizable depictions of slavery. However, how can such an iconographic typology be discovered? In the first instance, we have to proceed by surveying the imagery that abolitionist groups produced from the late eighteenth to the mid-nineteenth centuries in order to observe the historical formation of specific visual patterns,[5] which can then serve as a taxonomic foundation to classify visual material generated by contemporary anti-slavery advocates.[6] Through such classification and corresponding coding of pictures, I

Table 6.1 Distribution of website images across the three visual conventions

NGO (number of images)	Personification % (number of images)	Massification % (number of images)	Rescue % (number of images)
Anti-Slavery International (144)	56.3 (81)	11.8 (17)	31.9 (46)
Free the Slaves (125)	50.4 (63)	16.8 (21)	32.8 (41)
International Justice Mission (98)	27.6 (27)	23.5 (23)	48.9 (48)
Not for Sale (67)	34.3 (23)	17.9 (12)	47.8 (32)
Polaris Project (32)	84.4 (27)	12.5 (4)	3.1 (1)
Total (N = 466)	47.4 (221)	16.5 (77)	36.1 (168)

Notes: A total of 1758 JPEG and GIF image files were collected from the five websites. 768 of these files (those of less than ten kilobytes) were not viewed because they were assumed to be thumbnails, buttons, icons, banners, and other design elements. Of the 990 remaining images that were viewed, 524 were excluded because they focused on organizational publicity rather than on anti-slavery per se, depicting staff members receiving awards, biographical information about staff and officers, and meetings. Such pictures of organizational publicity represented the largest category of all images for four of the five NGOs studied here, the exception being Anti-Slavery International. The remaining 466 images included in the analysis were classified into the three visual conventions of personification, massification, and rescue, according to the distribution outlined in Figure 6.1.

discerned a typology of three visual conventions consistently reproduced throughout the history of visual representation of Euro-American anti-slavery struggles: personification (a lone slave, drawing out the experiential aspects of his or her condition), massification (an undistinguishable mass of slaves, illustrating the scale of slavery), and rescue (racialized slaves from the Global South being freed by white Westerners). As detailed in Table 6.1, contemporary anti-slavery iconography is distributed across these three conventions.

In aggregate terms as well as for three of the five websites in question, personification constitutes the most common convention, although rescue is also a significant type in most websites, notably for those NGOs underscoring direct action (the International Justice Mission) and grassroots involvement (Not for Sale).

The Historical Reproduction of Iconographic Conventions

Aside from the specific results outlined in Figure 6.1, what is significant is the fact that the visual field of anti-slavery advocacy is anchored in the three conventions noted here in a manner that remains remarkably consistent across historical periods in the Western world. Each of these conventions should be explained in turn.

Personification

Personification is an iconographic convention defined by the representation of a single enslaved subject, notably of his or her personal experience of suffering and loss of human dignity. A personified image is primarily designed to underscore the intensity of such suffering for a particular slave, frequently employing an expressivist aesthetic and rhetorical style in order to graphically capture and convey to viewers the physical, mental, and emotional condition of slavery. The slave's face and racialized body is inscribed with symbolic traces of this condition, in the process becoming a signifier of the extremes of human pain and indignity. In order to humanize the slave in the eyes of white, Euro-American audiences and foster the latter's experiential and sentimental identification with the former, personification aims to express his inner feelings and state of mind while often communicating details about her everyday life. Thus, personification can be understood as a device of phenomenological transposition, whereby viewers are prompted through visual and textual symbols to exercise their moral imaginations in a manner that would allow them to transpose themselves momentarily in the place of the enslaved subject. Conversely, personified images frequently contain visual or textual markers of the institutional causes or perpetrators of slavery, so as to identify for viewers – and morally condemn – the structures and actors responsible for the slave's abject state.

Two motifs of personification appear repeatedly throughout the history of the visual representation of slavery. The first of these – the enslaved body – was captured in William Blake's famous engraving "A Negro Hung Alive by the Ribs to a Gallows" (1796), the symbolic elements of which set a number of conventions employed for the particularization of enslavement and the aesthetic reconstruction of how it is experienced by a specific person.[7] Most strikingly, Blake's image portrays the slave's tortured and contorted body, his flesh torn by a hooked chain that suspends him by the ribs as his gaze meets that of the viewers. The visual scaling and structuring of the engraving suggest a deliberate thematic emphasis on communicating the enslaved subject's experience of suffering since his body is positioned in the foreground of the image and is proportionally much larger than the other visual components in the frame.[8] Blake also incorporates signs clearly linking the slave's torture to the institution of slavery itself, notably through the illustration of devices to inflict pain upon him (the gallows and hooked chain) as well as the presence of a slave ship on the horizon.

The survey and analysis of abolitionist material published in Britain and the United States between the late eighteenth and early nineteenth centuries conducted for this chapter (*The American Anti-Slavery Almanacs* from 1838, 1839, and 1843) indicate that the motif of the enslaved subject became a staple of the struggle to end the transatlantic slave trade. Widely circulated publications from the American Anti-Slavery Society were replete with images of slaves being flogged, tortured, or humiliated by slave owners in a manner that not only captured their suffering but also morally implicated and condemned those perpetrating, supporting, or benefiting from the system of slavery as a whole. For example, an illustration published in *The Anti-Slavery Record* portrays a male slave owner whipping a female slave's back, with the caption "The Flogging of Females: 'What! – the whip on Woman's shrinking flesh!'" while a white woman looks upon the scene with detachment and a group of black slaves (two adults and a child) witness the scene with horror.[9] An illustration from the September 1838 issue of *The American Anti-Slavery Almanac* is equally exemplary of this trope of the body in pain since it represents a male slave, hung by the wrists and ankles, being whipped by a slave owner, while two other slaves writhe on top of each other and another is being held to the ground by his head and wrists. The graphic caption reads: "Sometimes a slave is tied up by the wrists, while the ankles are fastened to a staple in the floor. In this position, they are punished with the whip or with the paddle. This is an instrument of torture bored full of holes, each hole raising a blister."[10] Clearly, recreations of scenes such as these, expressivist in their attempts to explicitly display the suffering of the enslaved subject and the cruelty of the slave owners, were designed to cultivate moral revulsion and outrage among Anglo-American viewers and, thus, sympathy for slaves themselves and abolitionism as a political movement. And one of the most famous images of the abolitionist campaign, reproduced in books and other print material as either a photogravure (taken anonymously in 1836), or its illustrated or woodblocked facsimile bearing the title *Gordon*, was that of a male slave with his denuded back turned to the camera in order to expose numerous scars and wounds caused by flogging, which had turned this part of his body into a deformed mound of flesh, graphically exposing viewers to the corporeal torture that was integral to slavery.[11]

The enslaved body remains a common trope of personification in imagery from contemporary anti-slavery campaigns, as found in our analysis of websites of anti-slavery NGOs and printed US governmental reports, although the shift from illustrated to photographic material corresponded to a parallel transition from the depiction of corporeal pain in itself to that of the labouring body. Hence, images portray enslaved persons practising various forms of indentured or forced labour, ranging from plantation and farm work to domestic servitude and sex work. Despite this shift, the representational objective remains identical, namely to capture and reconstruct the slave's experience of suffering for viewers. For instance, an iconic photograph in these campaigns depicts a Brazilian worker at an Amazonian charcoal-producing farm. His denuded torso is coated in sweat and soot, while he strains under the weight of a large basket filled with charcoal pieces.[12]

The second motif of personification consists of testimony, the attempt to humanize the enslaved subject by creating and distributing images and text aiming to generate sentimental and ethical ties between this subject and Western audiences. Thus, in describing the everyday reality of the slave's experience, testimonial pictures and accompanying poetic or descriptive captions are designed symbolically to counteract racist or civilizationally chauvinistic discourses by elevating her moral stature and demonstrating her ordinary personhood whose existential make-up is similar to that of Euro-American viewers and, conversely, expressing how slavery violates a fundamental norm of human dignity through the slave's merciless exploitation, humiliation, or treatment that reduces her to the status of an animal or thing. William Cowper's

"The Negro's Complaint" (1788), a narrative poem illustrated with co-loured woodcut prints, stood as one of the defining testimonial documents of the abolitionist struggle. Written in the first-person voice of a black African slave in England, it served visually and discursively to bear witness to the experiential dimensions of the transatlantic slave trade.[13] Similarly, several images from the *Anti-Slavery Record* and other abolitionist publications attempted to personify the condition of being enslaved while depicting the numerous moral injuries that such a condition inflicted upon a subject. Today, photographs and videos containing enslaved persons' testimonial accounts are a mainstay of various anti-slavery campaigns since their websites and printed materials prominently feature the voices of current or former slaves describing the hardships and distress that they have been made to endure.[14]

Massification

The second visual convention used in anti-slavery advocacy can be termed massification for it includes images that represent slaves less as specific individuals than as an undifferentiated mass that is subjected, collectively, to the institutionalized mechanisms of enslavement. Massification is employed to produce visual material that emblematizes the scale or extent of slavery around the world, gesturing towards the sizable numbers of enslaved persons and their shared state of being owned by others. The group of slaves in a specific picture stand as symbolic microcosms of their peers suffering under similar circumstances in numerous territories. Furthermore, while images of massification are less prone towards phenomenological reconstruction than their personified counterparts described above, their depictions of a group of persons degraded to the status of objects or tools indistinguishable from each other are designed to suggest to Western viewers that slavery constitutes a collective experience of dehumanization of racialized groups. In iconographic terms, massification functions within a realist aesthetic genre, which tends towards an unadorned, visually and rhetorically restrained reflection of an observable reality.

Considered to be abolitionism's most iconic and widely circulated image, the diagram of the "Brookes" slave ship exemplifies the characteristics of massification mentioned here. The print depicts the hold of a transatlantic slave ship carrying African subjects, whose bodies are crammed and arranged into every conceivable bit of space. In the late eighteenth and early nineteenth centuries, the rhetorical power of this picture in the British public sphere was considerable for it "seemed to make an instantaneous impression of horror upon all who saw it, and was therefore instrumental, in consequence of the wide circulation given it, in serving the cause of the injured Africans."[15] By illustrating the conditions of transportation of the enslaved in an architectural and quasi-forensic rendering of the ship's haul, the image could portray the latter as a technology of mass subjection of peoples of colour transformed into human cargo, deprived of individuality and dignity because they were packed like cattle or goods being carried along colonial trade routes.[16] The iconicity of the "Brookes" slave ship image remains unsurpassed, becoming a symbolic convention of massification that can be repurposed infinitely. It was partially resignified by anti-slavery advocates during Anti-Slavery International's 2007 "Trafficking Is Modern Slavery" campaign. In it, above the text stating "The Methods Have Changed But People Are Still Suffering," can be found an illustration of a jumbo jetliner, into the cabin of which is transposed a reproduction of the Brookes's haul and its enslaved subjects.[17]

The repetition of symbolic patterns of massification can be found in other genres in the iconography of anti-slavery. Nineteenth-century paintings of groups of black slaves at work on sugarcane or cotton plantations in the Caribbean and the US South, such as William Clark's "Cutting the Sugar Cane, Antigua" (1823),[18] present slavery as a highly structured system of mass manual labour in which the enslaved persons themselves appear as collective extensions of their tools – that is to say, a cluster of machine-like, racialized bodies without hearts or souls. In our age, photographs of forced or indentured agricultural work tend to reproduce similar iconographic elements, representing migrants or other subordinate segments of populations operating on farms as undifferentiated bundles of manual labour power. The massifying effects of such pictures can assist Euro-American audiences in quantitatively scaling up their perceptions of slavery since they capture a single instance of a structural relation of domination that affects millions of persons in the North Atlantic region and elsewhere in the world.

Rescue

Rescue forms the third visual convention of interest because of the constant repetition of images portraying the freeing or saving of slaves by their "rescuers" throughout the representational history of anti-slavery advocacy. This convention fits within the broader narrative and iconography of salvation, fuelled by the racial and civilizational economy of global geopolitics, through which the passivity, vulnerability, and lack of agency of enslaved persons of colour are contrasted to the heroic qualities, agentic capacities, and compassionate nobility of their white "liberators." According to such a logic, slaves cannot free themselves but must be freed by others. A symbolic and compositional tension appears in more recent pictures produced by anti-slavery groups, for such groups seemingly aim to dampen or mask the explicit racial and civilizational hierarchies by depicting their workers as eyewitnesses standing in solidarity with and beside slaves rather than as deus ex machina rescuers imbued with a superior moral stature. Nonetheless, this apparent attempt to create more egalitarian visual scenarios is undermined by the ongoing dependence of portions of the anti-slavery movement – notably its Christian evangelical wing – on discursive and iconographic means, which sustains the belief that the rescuing of enslaved populations in the Global South remains a post-colonial "white man's burden," akin to missionary work and the self-aggrandizing heroism of colonialism's civilizational mission.

François-Auguste Biard's "L'abolition de l'esclavage dans les colonies françaises (27 avril 1848)"[19] is one of the classic works in the rescue genre. Set in a generic French Caribbean colony at the moment that slavery was abolished by France in 1848, the painting features a white colonial official engaging in the performative act of making the announcement of the abolition to a group of formerly enslaved black subjects, who are celebrating their newly declared freedom through a variety of dramatized poses. Two of them at the centre of the frame embrace each other, looking skyward with their arms upright while holding their chains and open shackles, while others lie prostate on the ground in front of the colonial official and other white French colonial settlers. Striking in Biard's portrait is the gratitude of the former slaves towards their colonial masters and, by symbolic extension, the French Republic that granted them their freedom because of its supposed compassion towards their plight and its universalist humanism.[20]

As Table 6.1 indicates, photographs of rescue are used widely by anti-slavery NGOs on their websites. Although contemporary pictures are structured in a manner devised to attenuate the racial and civilizational subjugation displayed in Biard's image and others produced in the late eighteenth and nineteenth centuries, the fundamental symbolic structure of the rescue motif established in these paintings is faithfully reproduced in recent pictures. Indeed, the latter typically include a white, Western NGO staff member posing for the camera with formerly enslaved subjects, who are most commonly children of colour somewhere in the Global South. Featured on several pages of International Justice Mission's website, for instance, is a photograph of one of the agency's staff members sitting beside a young girl and other adults in a Kenyan village,[21] while the Not for Sale Campaign's website similarly contains multiple pictures of smiling, newly freed children surrounding one of its staff members in Asia or Africa. These and numerous other images falling under the iconographic rubric of rescue serve multiple functions for a NGO vis-à-vis its Euro-American audiences. Initially, they seek to cultivate empathy or pity towards the ex-slaves being portrayed; they encourage identification of such audiences with the staff members, transposing themselves into the heroic role of freeing slaves; and they illustrate the logistical effectiveness of this NGO on the ground and in the field, thereby demonstrating that donations will serve to achieve results and that something can be done to stop slavery. Overall, then, the convention of rescue inserts itself into a familiar mode of thinking, namely that only Western benevolence and intervention can prevent permanently vulnerable populations – particularly "innocent" children and women – from becoming enslaved and thus subjected to lives of extreme exploitation and misery. Consistent with this worldview, only Western subjects have the capacity to avert such a fate for others and, accordingly, bear a self-appointed responsibility to liberate slaves and permanently abolish slavery in every part of the globe.

Living in the Shadows of the Past

Derived from the reproduction of the three visual conventions explained above, the powerful iconographic legacy of abolitionism generates a paradox at the heart of contemporary anti-slavery advocacy. On the one hand, this legacy inscribes symbols and motifs of the transatlantic slave trade into the collective memory and social imaginaries animating public discourse in Euro-American societies, forming a visual template that is indexical in character – that is to say, composed of a well-established set of symbolic conventions to which socio-political actors can refer and upon which they can draw. This public indexicality and referentiality considerably reduce the discursive and iconographic labour that anti-slavery NGOs must expend in public spheres, since they can exploit the potency of abolitionism's visual template to enhance their campaigns' impact and reach. In turn, Western audiences already familiarized with these early modern visual conventions can easily link them to their intended meaning as signifiers of slavery in present-day images, thus facilitating the process of public sense making and symbolic recognition. If a picture contains visual or textual symbols of enslavement (chains, human cargo, and so on) and fits within the modes of personification, massification, or rescue, it can readily be recognized as such by ordinary citizens.

On the other hand, this same legacy can create difficulties for advocacy groups aiming to make a case for public acknowledgment of, and concern about, particular instances of slavery. In the first instance, audiences may reject or contest the legitimacy of the processes of analogical juxtaposition that such NGOs and social movements pursue when drawing on historical symbols of enslavement to publicize the latter's present-day manifestations. Such problems became apparent in 2007 during commemorations of the bicentenary of the abolition of slavery in Britain. At the time, groups at the London Print Studio, outside of the York Castle Museum, and on the Palace Green in Durham recreated the image of the Brookes slave ship by having people lie down beside each other in patterns replicating those depicted in the original print. A controversy arose regarding the pertinence of restaging the image by using largely white participants to do so, notably whether this constituted an appropriation of an icon of collective suffering rooted in communities of African descent as well as whether such a restaging and its transposition of participants into the role of slaves was a suitable means of gaining a better understanding of slavery in the past and present.[22]

In addition, contemporary recreations of iconic pictures of enslavement may be perceived as desacralizing the status of the transatlantic slave trade as a universal evil because they create an inappropriate, trivializing relation of moral equivalence between this publicly recognized evil and what are believed to be less brutal and extensive manifestations of slavery today. Issues such as these may in fact have the unintended consequence of creating a "backlash" in public opinion, whereby the perceived illegitimacy of employing symbolic equivalence – dismissed by critics as morally dubious "publicity stunts" – may taint contemporary anti-slavery campaigns and thereby prompt ordinary persons to ignore or politically devalue the causes that such campaigns are advocating and to underestimate both the severity of slavery today and the imperative to take action to prevent or stop it.

Second, the mnemonic and symbolic weight of the transatlantic slave trade compromises attempts by advocacy groups to establish the gravity of forms of contemporary slavery in public spheres. Indeed, since most recent anti-slavery campaigns have relied on the indexicality of past visual symbols to gain socio-political traction, they have not been able to generate a distinctive and discrete iconography – that is to say, one that is semiotically and morally self-referential by being built around visual icons easily recognized by audiences as signifiers of existing situations of enslavement and as morally abhorrent on their own terms in social imaginaries and public discourses.

The failure of NGOs and social movements to produce such an iconography and have it publicly validated can inadvertently condemn current instances of slavery to appear as symbolically and morally impoverished reiterations of their historical antecedents, pale imitations or lesser versions of "original" or earlier manifestations of enslavement that are themselves socially established as forms of universal evil. The aforementioned 2007 campaign by Anti-Slavery International that transposed the Brookes slave ship into the cabin of a jetliner is a case in point since the text below the image of the plane reads: "Trafficking Is Modern Slavery" "The Methods Have Changed But People Are Still

Suffering." By selecting slogans that analogically refer to such earlier types of slavery, Anti-Slavery International and other organizations employing similar visual and discursive strategies are implicitly admitting that no symbol of human trafficking and other modes of contemporary enslavement has a public impact comparable to that of early modern iconography and, thus, that it cannot act as a discrete signifying system capable of appreciably affecting public opinion unless it uses the moral revulsion towards the transatlantic slave trade – "people are *still* suffering." Audiences can only become concerned about, and grasp the suffering inflicted on, persons being trafficked today by drawing upon the collective memory, moral discourses, and social imaginaries that emerged out of the slave trade, yet this suffering is presented reiteratively as an experience whose significance is acquired derivatively by symbolic association with the past.

Conclusion

In a culture saturated by images, contemporary anti-slavery activism must adopt representational strategies that break with audiences' indifference or fatigue towards forms of suffering and exploitation around the world. In this chapter, I have argued that anti-slavery groups have attempted to work around this problem by pursuing types of iconographic coding that draw upon techniques of historically derived analogical juxtaposition built around the transatlantic slave trade. These techniques mobilize the latter's socially recognized status as a universal signifier of evil to morally amplify and culturally pollute present-day modes of enslavement via pictorial tropes and the visual conventions of personification, massification, and rescue.

Although effective and thus widely used by anti-slavery groups today, analogical juxtaposition introduces its own set of dilemmas. At one level, the visibility of symbols of physical coercion and violence in depictions of the transatlantic slave trade (chains, whips, and the like) may inadvertently diminish the perceived significance of images of contemporary instances of enslavement in which such symbols frequently are absent or hidden (for example, bonded labour, human trafficking). At another level, the public recognition of certain situations as forms of slavery may well depend upon reproducing a problematically racialized and

gendered representational economy in which women of colour are positioned as passive victims awaiting rescue, whereas white, Western, male
subjects are portrayed as their saviours. Put differently, the task for anti-
slavery groups is to draw attention to their cause without reproducing,
and thereby giving validity to, a salvation narrative rooted in the colonial
logic of the "white man's burden." Over the next few years, the willingness and capacity to negotiate this tension likely will determine the success and legitimacy of the anti-slavery movement's pictorial campaigns.

Notes

1 Throughout this chapter, I use the legal definition of slavery employed by the
Research Network on the Legal Parameters of Slavery, led by Jean Allain (Queen's
University, Belfast), which relies on Article 1(1) of the 1926 Slavery Convention,
25 September 1926, 60 LNTS 253: "Slavery is the status or condition of a person
over whom any or all of the powers attaching to the right of ownership are exercised." Slavery Convention, 25 September 1926, 60 LNTS 253.

2 By contrast, contemporary slavery, caused by complex systemic factors (economically induced migration, forced labour arrangements, and so on) and defined by
their "low-intensity" suffering, is a manifestation of structural violence that is thus
much less likely to garner attention than forms of situational violence.

3 In this way, the transatlantic slave trade functions much like the Holocaust, in that
the public case for moral condemnation of a contemporary event is frequently
made by seeking to establish a moral rapprochement between it and these universal evils. Jeffrey Alexander, *The Meanings of Social Life: A Cultural Sociology* (Oxford:
Oxford University Press, 2003).

4 This is not to claim that anti-slavery iconography remained unchanged during the
period from the mid-nineteenth to the late twentieth century, which is not analyzed here. Rather, it is to contend that such iconographic transformations – if
they did take place – did not have a significant impact on contemporary campaigns, which consistently return to abolitionist visual tropes rather than those
that may have been created subsequently.

5 The following sources were surveyed: three major abolitionist publications from
the American Anti-Slavery Society (the *Anti-Slavery Record*, *The Slave's Friend*, and
the *Anti-Slavery Almanac*), which were included on the website of Uncle Tom's
Cabin and American Culture project (directed by Stephen Railton at the University
of Virginia) (see http://utc.iath.virginia.edu/abolitn/abgall.html (accessed 9 August
2011); the archive of images (using "esclavage" and "abolition de l'esclavage" search
terms) on the *L'Histoire par l'image* website from Réunion des musées nationaux de
France (see https://www.histoire-image.org/index.php (accessed 20 June 2011);

anti-slavery images contained on the British Library's *Campaign for Abolition* website (see http://www.bl.uk/learning/histcitizen/campaignforabolition/sources/antislavery/antislaverysources.html (accessed 19 June 2011); and studies of the visual and material representation of slavery (Marcus Wood, *Blind Memory: Visual Representations of Slavery in England and America* [New York: Routledge, 2000]; Jane Webster, "Looking for the Material Culture of the Middle Passage," *Journal for Maritime Research* 7, 1 (2005): 245–58).

6 Photographs from the websites of five major non-governmental organizations (NGOs) were collected and analyzed: Anti-Slavery International, Free the Slaves, the International Justice Mission, the Not for Sale Campaign, and the Polaris Project. Among all of the websites of anti-slavery organizations, the selection of these five NGO sites was done on the basis of their popularity and level of influence, as determined by two criteria measured by Alexa (a leading Internet information company): traffic, as measured by the number of "hits" and "visits" per month and number of external links from other websites back to these NGO websites. See, respectively, http://www.antislavery.org/english/ (worldwide rank of 1,372,014 and 707 external website linkages); http://www.freetheslaves.net/ (worldwide rank of 1,002,594 and 437 external website linkages); http://www.ijm.org/ (worldwide rank of 542,454 and 549 external website linkages); https://www.notforsalecampaign.org/ (worldwide rank of 361,465 and 322 external website linkages); and https://polarisproject.org/ (worldwide rank of 901,784 and 319 external website linkages) (accessed and compiled 2–3 August 2011 by Steve Tasson). The web-specific methodology for this analysis follows that specified by Marcus Wood. Marcus Wood, "Significant Silence: Where Was Slave Agency in the Popular Imagery of 2007?" in Cora Kaplan and John Oldfield, eds., *Imagining Transatlantic Slavery* (Basingstoke, UK: Palgrave Macmillan, 2010). Using Microsoft Explorer's *Offline Web Pages*, websites were consulted and saved on 2–3 August 2011, going to a minimum number of three links deep from their homepages.

7 Blake's engraving was first published in John Stedman's *Narrative of a Five Years' Expedition against the Revolted Negroes of Surinam* (London: J. Johnson and T. Payne, 1806 [1796]).

8 Wood, *Blind Memory*, 38–40.

9 *The Anti-Slavery Record*, Vol. 1, No. 10 (October 1835), from Schomburg Center for Research in Black Culture, Manuscripts, Archives and Rare Books Division, New York Public Library Digital Collections, http://digitalcollections.nypl.org/items/510d47da-7549-a3d9-e040-e00a18064a99 (accessed 5 November 2016).

Another illustration from the same publication captioned "Cruelties of Slavery" depicts a scene consisting of a black male slave bent on one knee with outstretched arms being whipped by a white male slave owner, the latter dangling by one arm a black infant who appears to have been yanked away from the slave. See *The Anti-Slavery Record*, Vol. 1, No. 5 (May 1835), from Uncle Tom's Cabin and American Culture Multimedia Archive, University of Virginia, http://utc.iath. virginia.edu/abolitn/gallasrf.html (accessed 5 November 2016).

10 *The American Anti-Slavery Almanac*, Vol. 1, No. 3 (September 1838), from Uncle Tom's Cabin and American Culture Multimedia Archive, University of Virginia, http://utc.iath.virginia.edu/abolitn/gallaaaf.html (accessed 5 November 2016).

11 See *Harper's Weekly*, 4 July 1863, 429, among other publication venues. One version of it can be viewed via the Library of Congress, *Prints and Photographs Online Catalogue*, http://www.loc.gov/pictures/item/89716298/ (accessed 19 April 2013). For an analysis of the image, see Wood, *Blind Memory*, 266–71.

12 For the original photograph, see http://www.eduardomartino.com/?portfolio= modern-day-slavery-in-brazil, image 8 (accessed 5 November 2016).

13 An extract from "The Negro's Complaint" captures its testimonial and humanizing qualities:

> Still in thought as free as ever,
> What are England's rights, I ask,
> Me from my delights to sever,
> Me to torture, me to task ?
> Fleecy locks and black complexion
> Cannot forfeit nature's claim;
> Skins may differ, but affection
> Dwells in white and black the same.

For illustrations and extracts from Cowper's poem, including the passage cited here, see http://www.bl.uk/learning/images/makeanimpact/large9017.html (accessed 19 June 2011).

14 To take one example among many, Anti-Slavery International provides a PowerPoint slideshow for educators containing a photograph of a child domestic worker in the Philippines named Mila, accompanied by the following testimonial:

> Each day I had to get up at 5.00am, to carry out household chores such as taking care of my employers' children, cooking, cleaning, doing the laundry and ironing. On top of this, I was given additional work including helping out in a pre-school, making deliveries, and in one case, looking after pigs.
>
> In one place I lived in a shed, with no light, no mattress, and only one bucket of water a week for washing.
>
> I worked for 11 employers in total but only one of them gave me any salary, and that was just 500 pesos (£5.30) a month.

15 The illustration dates from 1787, but most famously was published in Thomas Clarkson, *History of the Rise, Progress, and Accomplishment of the Abolition of the African Slave Trade by the British Parliament* (London: Longman, Hurst, Rees, and Orme, 1808), from which the cited passage also originates, as cited on the following British Library webpage: https://www.bl.uk/collection-items/diagram-of-the-brookes-slave-ship (accessed 5 November 2016).

16 One of the later versions of the illustration of the "Brookes" slave ship contained the following note, which explained the crowding and inhumane conditions in the haul in sober yet detailed terms:

> The "Brookes" after the Regulation Act of 1788, was allowed to carry 454 Slaves, She could stow this number by following the rule adopted in this plate. Namely of allowing a space of 6 ft. by 1 ft. 4 in. to each man; 5 ft. 10 in. by 1 ft. 4 in. to each woman, and 5 ft. by 1 ft. 2 in. to each boy, but so much space as this was seldom allowed even after the Regulation Act. It was proved by the confession of the Slave Merchant that before the above Act the Brookes had at one time carried as many as 609 Slaves. This was done by taking some out of Irons and locking them spoonwise (to use the technical term) that is by stowing one within the distended legs of the other.

See *Herb: Social History for Every Classroom*, http://herb.ashp.cuny.edu/items/show/1226 (accessed 12 March 2012).

17 See *British Library*, http://www.bl.uk/learning/citizenship/campaign/myh/photographs/gallery2/image3/trafficking.html (accessed 19 June 2011).

18 See *British Library*, http://www.bl.uk/onlinegallery/onlineex/carviews/c/022zzz000 1786c9u00004000.html (accessed 20 April 2013).

19 François-Auguste Biard, "L'abolition de l'esclavage dans les colonies françaises (27 avril 1848)," Musée du château de Versailles, France, http://ressources. chateauversailles.fr/spip.php?article90 (accessed 5 November 2016).

20 See Mathilde Larrère, "Analyse et interprétation," *L'histoire par l'image* https://www. histoire-image.org/pleincadre/index.php?m=esclavage&d=1&i=3 (accessed 18 March 2012).

21 It should be noted that this photograph's connection to a scenario of slavery may be tenuous since the caption accompanying it on the International Justice Mission's (IJM) website is as follows: "Miriam (lower right) watches her great-granddaughter sing a song for IJM staff celebrating IJM's help in restoring her family's property after wealthy neighbors attempted to seize it. The legal battle for Miriam's property rights lasted over five years, and her victory made national headlines in Kenya." See http://www.ijm.org/who-we-are (accessed 19 March 2012). While the IJM presents itself as a direct-action anti-slavery organization, it also appears that it is active in the protection of private property rights, with the connection between these two causes being left ambiguous.

22 See *1807 Commemorated*, http://www.history.ac.uk/1807commemorated/exhibitions/museums/brookes.html (accessed 21 March 2012); *Durham University*, https://www.dur.ac.uk/durham.first/winter07/slaveship (accessed 21 March 2012).

Methodological Debates in Human Rights Research: A Case Study of Human Trafficking in South Africa   **7**

Darshan Vigneswaran

This chapter thinks through the difficulties involved in maintaining the credibility of an "abolitionist" humanitarian campaign. Anti-slavery campaigners aspire to the complete eradication of slavery in all of its forms. This "zero tolerance" approach has proven to be effective in many respects, particularly in providing governments and international organizations with a clear sense of how to decide when work, recruitment, migration, inter-personal relationships, discrimination, and punishment become unacceptable forms of bondage. However, the closer abolitionists move to their ultimate goal, the harder they find it to maintain a consistent position on the question of what levels of resources their campaign requires. When there are many victims of slavery, anti-slavery activists commonly rest their arguments for state intervention on the grounds of proportionality: more resources are needed to deal with a large problem. However, as the number of victims declines, abolitionists rarely argue in favour of reduced levels of enforcement. This is due to the fact that a true abolitionist does not believe that the success of their campaign can be measured numerically in terms of lives affected and abuses prevented. Rather, success is measured by the absence of numbers. Until there is evidence to suggest that practices akin to slavery no longer exist, any amount of effort to abolish slavery can be deemed to have been insufficient.

This chapter suggests that if the campaign against modern forms of slavery is to be successful it has to be wary of this potential for inconsistency. In part, this is due to the fact that the material resources and humanitarian goodwill available to tackle modern forms of slavery are finite and must be used in an efficient manner. In part, this is due to the fact that inconsistency undermines the ability of anti-slavery campaigners to maintain coalitions. When campaigners appear to neglect the implicit practical lessons in the numbers, they not only risk losing the attention of neo-liberal politicians and "bean-counting" bureaucrats. They also risk losing the support of some of their closest potential allies, particularly their empirically oriented colleagues in the academy, who may not share a purist ideal of what "abolition" means. Finally, abolitionists and their scholarly colleagues need to address this issue of proportionality because a poorly calibrated abolitionist campaign can have deeply negative effects on the lives of many. Law enforcement campaigns invariably produce a significant amount of collateral damage, particularly due to the fact that the countries where slavery is a prominent problem are usually also countries where law enforcement officials commonly abuse human rights.

This chapter develops this argument through a contextual reading of a debate about issues of prevalence in the South African anti-trafficking campaign. I specifically examine the debate – or, rather, frustrating encounter – between the scholars and practitioners engaged in this campaign. The chapter begins by critically examining scholars' implicit assumptions regarding the potential for reasoned debate to produce progressive change. I briefly survey some prominent ideas in the history of intellectual thought to explain why scholars should attempt to understand the social and ideational forces that explain what their interlocutors are trying to say.

The next part of the chapter uses this contextual approach to explore the failure of scholarly and practitioners to reach common ground. I identify how funding priorities have made practitioners' interested in the issue of numbers. I then go on to identify the ideational factors that have prevented practitioners from engaging meaningfully with scholarly efforts to answer these questions. Here, I point to abolitionists' unwillingness to accept that any calculation of the number of victims in

South and Southern Africa could potentially warrant a decision to divert campaign and state resources in alternative directions. However, rather than attributing this avoidance to practitioners' pure instrumentalism, or messianic zeal, I suggest that scholars and practitioners have collectively failed to think through how we address the thorny issue of proportionality in an abolitionist enforcement campaign.

The chapter then explains why it is important for campaigners to move beyond this stalling point in their relationship. I explore some of the negative humanitarian consequences of the poorly calibrated anti-trafficking campaign in South Africa. I pay attention to the failures of campaigners to effectively use their available resources and goodwill and the potential indirect outcomes of this misdirected criminalization campaign for migrants and workers. The chapter then concludes with an attempt to understand how scholars can more fruitfully engage with policy-making and implementation on issues of migration, labour, and exploitation in Southern Africa.

Scholarship and Dialogue with Practitioners

The argument in this chapter rests on a particular philosophy of knowledge, its social construction, and its meaning. These "first order" questions are given short shrift in most analyses of contemporary humanitarian and human rights issues. Most scholarship on human rights begins with an implicit commitment to human emancipation, and scholars then tend to gravitate towards, and endorse, those social groups and organizations that share these commitments, while engaging critically and constructively with those who do not. However, they rarely consider how their scholarly commitments often create conflicts with those who share the same normative positions in human rights debates.

Scholars' core epistemological assumptions often differ significantly from those of their principal interlocutors in public debates. Scholars themselves adopt a wide range of different positions on the subject of epistemology. Here, I am going to radically simplify by pointing out the temptations and possible limitations of one particularly prominent position. The earliest origins of this position stem as far back as the Socratic method, which holds that dialogue and debate between opposing positions will conclusively lead to the collective production of greater insight and collective acceptance of a common reason. This basic principle underpins a wide range of forms of social scientific analytical techniques and methodological frameworks; has fundamentally shaped contemporary academic ritual and procedure; and has informed the manner in which scholars create and organize academic disciplines and institutions. Most importantly, it informs the way we conceptualize the nature, purpose, and functioning of the public realm. The most prominent exponent of this argument is Jürgen Habermas who defines modernity in terms of the progressive transformation in Western European public culture from a representational age to one of reasoned debate and decision-making in the public sphere.[1]

This idea of a progressive, truth-discovering dialogue has not crowded out other positions on the social construction of knowledge. Thomas Kuhn is perhaps the most famous proponent of the notion that scientific knowledge and "progress" is the product of indeterminate contests between incommensurate and historically constituted traditions of knowledge production.[2] While this basic truth has led many scholars into repeated inter-paradigmatic warfare and personal bouts of self-analysis and critique, it is surprising how commonly we forget this dictum when we try to understand the positions adopted by our interlocutors in the public sphere.

In order to combat this tendency, many have argued in favour of a methodological principle: that the interpretation of ideas should always involve a consideration of motivations and context. Ludwig Wittgenstein argues that theories of human behaviour, society, and politics consist of a series of speech acts whose true meaning cannot be interpreted and genuinely understood outside of their unique historical contexts – as efforts to simultaneously speak truth, shape discourse, and change the world around us.[3] This latter position has been developed into a form of applied philosophy by the Cambridge School's histories of ideas. This literature argues that we cannot understand the reasons why ideas sometimes shape reality in progressive ways and why sometimes they do not if we fail to pay attention to the material forces and ideological positions that shape the core assumptions of the various interlocutors engaged in a particular debate. The crucial upshot of this position for the current study is that these secondary factors will ultimately shape how practitioners interpret and receive the "truths" or "insights" generated by academic labour.

The ensuing discussion helps to contextualize scholarly engagements with practitioners in the debate on human trafficking in two important ways. First, it serves to highlight the notion that despite making important concessions to social constructivists and tipping our hat at postmodernity, academics who work on human trafficking commonly work within a knowledge framework that at least gives credence to the notion that the force of the best argument will generally win a debate. We commonly believe that our cold-hearted commitment to respect the basic facts and healthy commitment to the principles of logic uniquely equips us to shape public debates. The more scholars generate truths and compel practitioners to engage in discussions about these truths, the more likely it is that we will have good policy and practice.

Second, it suggests that if scholars are to more effectively contribute to processes of progressive change, we need to think through the epistemological commitments of our interlocutors. The lack of impact of social scientific research does not always stem from our failure to meet academic standards of credibility but often has to do with the instrumental and ideological commitments of practitioners, which commonly lead them to avoid debates or develop reasons why research is wrong. This is not because practitioners are dim-witted but, rather, because they are committed. Scientists who study the effects of cigarettes, air pollution, and climate change are familiar with the way in which organized interests can effectively and consistently discredit high quality research. However, social scientists, in general, and human rights scholars, in particular, regularly fail to recognize how epistemological differences with their "fellow travellers" in government, non-government organizations (NGOs), and community organizations can undermine their collective ability to achieve emancipatory ends.

Studying the Trafficking Campaign

If you want to understand how these dissonances develop, you need to get your hands a little dirty – to participate in the production of knowledge in a humanitarian campaign. In this respect, I draw on approximately four years of participant observation, as an advocacy-oriented researcher in the field of refugee and migration rights in South Africa. In this role, I conducted numerous studies of policy-making, provided expert consultation to INTERPOL, the European Union (EU), the United Nations High Commissioner for Refugees (UNHCR), and the International Organization for Migration (IOM) on trafficking issues, assisted in the development of training materials on trafficking for the South African National Prosecuting Authority, and helped prepare numerous advocacy and rights-oriented inputs to South African government agencies, such as the Department of Home Affairs and the police.[4] In these and other roles, I have had the opportunity to engage in a wide array of discursive encounters with policy-makers, international NGO workers, and anti-trafficking advocates, including public debates, formal private consultations, and (often more important and useful) informal discussions and gossip. These engagements gave me several opportunities to map out the various ways in which public (as opposed to academic) truths and myths about trafficking are generated, disseminated, and sustained. In this section, I use these experiences to interpret the consistent disagreements between anti-trafficking scholars and anti-trafficking campaigners in South Africa.

A Tide of Funding, a Trickle of Victims

The issue of human trafficking emerged on the South African policy agenda in a very specific historical and political context. A conjuncture of factors following the end of the National Party rule in 1995 meant that a variety of migration rights issues would receive unprecedented levels of attention. After passing a new and progressive constitution, the African National Congress (ANC) government began to ratify a raft of international human rights conventions and treaties that the apartheid government had judiciously refused to sign. The government then sought to position itself as a global leader in international human rights law. Second, with the doors now open to foreign actors, a host of international donors, organizations, and NGOs sought to set up shop in South Africa. They intended not only to play a part in the process of democratic transition but also hoped to position themselves as key players in a virgin territory that was fast becoming a high profile case on the international human rights and humanitarian landscape.

In this context, the IOM, and to a lesser extent INTERPOL and the United Nations Office of Drugs and Crime (UNODC), emerged as the key local advocates of a human trafficking agenda that was quickly becoming a global norm. I do not have space in this chapter to consider the various factors that launched the international campaign against trafficking, but, in South Africa, the principal funders of this initiative were European countries and, to a lesser extent, the United States. The South African government has been a cooperative partner in, but not a driving force behind, this process.

In addition to this supportive context of migrant rights, the balance of institutional interests and identities among the various partners helped to launch and keep human trafficking on the agenda. Take, for example, the IOM, whose main contribution to the field has been to administer the Southern African Counter Trafficking Assistance Programme (SACTAP), which began in 2003. The IOM is a large international organization that operates largely on project funding.[5] In 2010, its operating budget stood at over US $1 billion, but only 3 percent of this was what we might call "core funding," with the remaining 97 percent consisting of voluntary contributions, mostly from member states, for projects.[6] In essence, this means that the IOM is constantly in a position of financial precarity that is common to much smaller NGOs: the majority of its operational budget comes from short-term, issue-specific funding grants like SACTAP. However, unlike small NGOs, the IOM has the problem of being a huge organization without issue area flexibility. Hence, it tends to incur a large amount of fixed costs. In South Africa alone, the IOM currently maintains offices in three cities (Pretoria, Cape Town, and Durban). These offices require money not only for staff salaries – paid at internationally competitive rates – but also for substantial contributions for infrastructure and operating expenses.

This does not mean that the IOM is a struggling organization or that it is overly dependent on trafficking for funds. However, the funding that became available for anti-trafficking work was a key factor in helping the organization establish an institutional presence in the country before it could diversify its sources of funding in subsequent years (see Table 7.1). In 2003, when the SACTAP program began, it equalled almost two-thirds (64 percent) of the South African regional office's

Table 7.1 The SACTAP's budget figures for 2003–10

	Contributors				Total SACTAP budget	Total South Africa budget	Trafficking as a percentage of total budget (%)
	Norway	South Africa	United States	United Kingdom			
2003	297,597		455,000		752,597	1,176,420	64
2004	321,373	7,403	455,000		783,776	1,689,516	46
2005	613,945	25,269			639,214	1,718,200	37
2006	1,137,093	23,534	160,000		1,320,627	4,659,326	28
2007	2,473,204		110,000		2,583,204	8,198,215	32
2008	1,185,771		205,000	103,748	1,494,519	6,574,589	23
2009	676,353		72,000		748,353	8,371,297	9
2010	– 9,589				– 9,589	11,112,303	
Total contributions 2003–10	6,695,747	56,206	1,457,000	103,748	8,312,701		

Source: IOM, *Financial Reports*, 2003–10.

annual budget expenditure. Funding for the SACTAP peaked in 2007 and then began a steady decline until 2010 when Norway, the principal funder, discontinued funding after a formal evaluation of its limited successes. However, by this stage, the IOM was far less dependent on the SACTAP. In 2009, the SACTAP only equalled about 9 percent of its South Africa budget. It had also, partly on the back of its SACTAP program, attracted funding from the governments of the United States, the United Kingdom, and South Africa and positioned itself as the key voice on trafficking in the region. Hence, in 2010, it was able to win new funding contracts for trafficking operations in South Africa, stemming from a US-funded program on the World Cup and the EU-funded training of government officials to comply with South Africa's new trafficking legislation. Given these considerations, we can see why the IOM as an organization has been institutionally committed to trafficking as a policy arena, at least in its South African "start-up" phase.

The position of the South African government is somewhat less materially determined but, nonetheless, equally constrained by issues of interest and international influence. Here, the main factors appear to be, on the one hand, South Africa's dependence on foreign aid and, on the other, South Africa's interest in maintaining its reputation as an African leader on human rights issues. A key example of the former motivating factor was the impact of the US decision to place South Africa on the "Tier 2 Watch List" in the annual trafficking in persons (TIPS) reports by the US State Department for four consecutive years from 2005 to 2008.[7] The tiered ratings in the TIPS report are less concerned with issues of prevalence and, instead, have more to do with questions of whether states can show palpable evidence that they are tackling the phenomenon through legislation, prosecution, and prevention. The US decision, which put in jeopardy elements of its US $500 million aid budget,[8] was a significant influencing factor in the South African government's decision to table trafficking legislation in 2008.

The 2010 FIFA World Cup of football is a better example of South Africa's efforts to shore up its international reputation on trafficking. Here, in the aftermath of stories of sex trafficking at the 2006 German World Cup, the US government, media, and other anti-trafficking campaigners began to raise the spectre of similar threats to the South

African event, involving the prospect of a marked increase in sex trade trafficking. Here, the government was keen to ensure that its moment in the international limelight, where it hoped to present itself as a beacon of humanitarianism and hope on the African continent, would not be sullied by the disparaging image of tourists flocking to South Africa and exploiting sex slaves.[9]

These examples do not suggest that there are no individuals within the IOM or the South African government who are personally concerned and committed to the anti-trafficking agenda or that the machinations of global development funding account entirely for their level of commitment to this issue. Rather, they suggest that structural factors provide reasons why these groups were able to successfully launch anti-trafficking initiatives onto a political landscape that was already replete with many rights (gender, HIV/AIDS, poverty, education, and so on) and non-trafficking-related criminal justice problems (rape, organized crime, human smuggling, and the like). These factors help us to understand why anti-trafficking campaigners may have been inclined to accept the initial evidence that the prevalence of trafficking in South Africa was large and growing. When preliminary research, and the IOM's own research initiatives, began to show evidence that trafficking in South Africa was widespread and particularly rife in the sex industry in Cape Town, various organizations began to use these claims as grounds to argue for a proportional response from the government.[10]

However, these basic material considerations do not help us to understand why anti-trafficking campaigners have been unwilling to accept evidence that questions the findings of these preliminary studies. Negative data first appeared in the IOM's own internal monitoring processes. Despite an extensive publicity, hotline, training, and research agenda, the SACTAP program only provided assistance to approximately 306 victims across the Southern African region between January 2004 and January 2010, and it is not clear whether these victims would classify as having been trafficked, according to their definitions or those of the Protocol to Prevent, Suppress and Punish Trafficking in Persons, especially Women and Children.[11] Despite this knowledge, IOM South Africa went on to play a lead role in the anti-trafficking campaign during the FIFA World Cup and, in so doing, continued to put forward an image of international trafficking as a large and growing problem. However, the IOM representatives had now adopted a slightly different line of argument: perhaps trafficking was a "hidden problem" that could not be revealed by research? One explanation for why the organization was not assisting as many victims as expected was that trafficking victims could not seek assistance and government officials did not know how to recognize a trafficking case.

As the anti-trafficking campaign gathered steam in South Africa, it attracted the attention of various researchers. It is important to stress at the beginning that scholars' interest in the subject was not "purely scientific" – whatever that term might mean. Rather, a broad range of scholars of gender, migration, and policing backgrounds began to become aware of this topic as the funding landscape began to shift. Scholars began to receive requests from donors to examine this topic or to incorporate analyses of trafficking into their migration and human rights research agenda. At the same time, their interest was not purely instrumental either. Scholars were genuinely curious to find out what this relatively new understanding of exploitation was and whether it was as prevalent as previous research had led them to believe.

It is against this backdrop, that Chandre Gould, a researcher at the Institute for Security Studies, formed a collaboration with Nicole Fick, from the Sex Worker Education and Advocacy Taskforce, in 2008. Gould and Fick's work began by explicitly recognizing the IOM's claims regarding the "hidden" character of the trafficking phenomenon. They argued that there were problems associated with (1) developing suitable sampling techniques to gauge the prevalence of vulnerable populations because they tended to under-report and (2) doing research on clandestine practices because everyone involved in such practices had strong reasons not to admit involvement. They developed a multi-pronged sampling method and framework to tackle these issues. They began by looking for the proverbial "easy case" to begin testing issues of prevalence: the sex work industry in Cape Town. They argued that if trafficking was prevalent across South Africa and issues of prevalence were not completely methodologically intractable, then a study of Cape

Town should reveal significant numbers of victims. The researchers then developed an elaborate and targeted research strategy to investigate the issues of prevalence in the Cape Town sex industry.

The methodology Gould and Fick adopted involved partnering with a local NGO to counter issues of access; extensive demographic and geographic mapping of the industry in order to develop a sample frame; qualitative interviews with sex workers, pimps, and brothel owners in order to gain different perspectives on the industry and the practices therein; and a quantitative survey of the sex worker industry to develop a statistical portrait of trafficking practices. The study revealed significant amounts of exploitation in the sex work industry, but few instances that resembled trafficking, and certainly nothing that resembled the claims of prevalence that had been previously put forward by organizations such as the IOM.

Gould and Fick's study is interesting for the incredible ingenuity they exhibited in developing their research strategy and approach. However, I am primarily intrigued by how practitioners responded to the findings. If the principles of scholarly research I outlined in my opening section held and knowledge about a topic proceeded, at least in some small way, in line with the idea that "the best idea will win," then we might expect some of the following responses to Gould and Fick's work:

- acceptance: efforts to tailor existing programs on human trafficking to suit the newly available evidence on prevalence
- replication/falsification: efforts to repeat Gould and Fick's method in Cape Town or across a broader sample of cases to determine whether their study was limited by contextual factors
- substantive critique: development of alternative methods to gauge issues of prevalence involving an illustration of their superiority to Gould and Fick's approach and/or their capacity in countering perceived limitations
- immanent critique: efforts to question whether Gould and Fick's normative predilections or institutional biases have in fact skewed their sample, approach, or techniques

Each of these forms of engagement might have constituted a valid means of engaging with Gould and Fick's work as a piece of scholarship. Yet none of these responses have been forthcoming. Instead, the approach has involved the following responses:

- Silence: the most common approach to Gould and Fick's work by IOM officials and trafficking campaigners has been to simply ignore it. This usually involves the reiteration of preexisting research or anecdotal evidence that was explicitly questioned by Gould and Fick but without making any reference, in passing or by implication, to Gould and Fick's substantive argument or methodology.
- Diversion: this version often builds on the previous response but adds to it through the adoption of parallel, but non-representative (or simply pseudoscientific), research that is prefigured to reveal prevalence. Here, a useful example is the recent government commissioned report on human trafficking by the Human Sciences Research Council (HSRC).[12] This report cited the Gould and Fick study but did not engage with its findings or methods. The report then adopted its own approach to issues of prevalence, which involved asking a small sample (n = 37) of public prosecutors the question: "How big do they believe the problem of human trafficking is?" It would be too painstaking and banal to point out the limits of this form of measurement.
- Insistence: this is a slightly more subtle technique, which involves recognizing Gould and Fick's findings, but refusing to engage with their explicit efforts, in terms of methodological adaptation to deal with issues of invisibility and under reporting. In this version, practitioners have acknowledged that Gould and Fick did some research, but they simply restate the fact that research will never be able to deal with prevalence because trafficking is a clandestine practice.

Anti-trafficking campaigners deployed similar rhetorical avoidance strategies in many different contexts in academic forums, closed-door policy-making sessions, individual interviews, consultancy meetings, and international intergovernmental conferences. I have repeatedly observed scholars – myself included – who are familiar with Gould and Fick's work attempting to encourage anti-trafficking practitioners to engage with the implications of their findings, including the pros and cons of the anti-trafficking agenda and why it should be guided by more sound research.

These repeated engagements have not led to a considered debate about prevalence and proportionality. However, this is not simply due to the fact that practitioners are materially vested in maintaining the image of a widespread and growing problem. Nor can it be reduced to the practitioners' unwillingness to accept the credibility of social scientific methods. Their continued avoidance of the terms of scholarly debate stems from the fact that they find themselves fundamentally conflicted on the issue of prevalence. This is revealed in the most common endpoint to these sorts of engagements between scholars and practitioners in conferences, workshops, and seminars. When repeatedly confronted with evidence to the contrary, anti-trafficking practitioners fall back on an abolitionist commitment – that "one victim is too many." At this point, practitioners and scholars tend to look at one another blankly as if they each came from different planets.

This statement is not a rejection of science but, rather, a recognition of the inherent incompatibility between an abolitionist position and a consistent approach to questions of proportionality. We can read this tension in a recent editorial in the SACTAP's *Eye on Trafficking* bulletin, where the IOM's SACTAP program manager offered a version of the abolitionist claim:

> What is the magic number then that will make us stand up and care? Somebody let us know – because that number is out there, it's just a matter of caring enough to combat it. The more partnerships we develop, the stronger the fight against trafficking will be. Let us put aside counting numbers for now – and focus on what is really happening, in our very midst![13]

This imperviousness of anti-trafficking campaigners to Gould and Fick's findings is not an isolated case. I have encountered similar resistance to research findings that strike at different numerical planks of the claim that trafficking is prevalent, including (1) that the 2010 FIFA World Cup did not, in fact, generate significant amounts of international sex trafficking or, indeed, changes in the nature of the sex trade;[14] (2) that most human smugglers working across the South Africa/Zimbabwe border are not involved in trafficking migrants for the purposes of exploitation in South Africa;[15] and (3) that insofar as trafficking is a problem in South Africa, it is more prevalent in sectors like domestic work and farm labour than in the sex industry.[16] As is implied in the quote from the SACTAP program manager, questions of prevalence draw more defensive responses from anti-trafficking campaigners, not simply because these types of critiques put their material interests in jeopardy but also because they find it difficult to accept that proportional responses will abolish modern slavery.

It is understandable why South African scholars have not seen through to this inherent tension in the abolitionist campaign. The main scholars that have taken an interest in trafficking – and here I include myself – are not scholars of slavery and abolitionism but, rather, scholars of migration, gender, and policing. We have been surprised to encounter practitioners' abolitionism, particularly given that the problem of trafficking has been presented to us in such raw numerical terms – as being tied to the funding upon which we rely to do our work. Nonetheless, if both scholars and practitioners are genuinely committed to the cause of human emancipation, it is incumbent upon both groups to find answers to the question of how to evaluate proportionality in an abolitionist campaign.

Making up the Numbers

The problems with this fraught debate on proportionality are multiple. On the one hand, it weakens the anti-trafficking campaign. When scholars and advocacy campaigners quibble over data in public settings, government representatives are generally perplexed. Lacking sound advice, they are inclined to make decisions that reflect their own commitments instead of decisions that reflect their reading of the terms of "debate." Thus, after South Africa was taken off the TIPS watch list in 2009, its trafficking bill was shelved as the ANC government moved back to its core legislative agenda: market liberalization, poverty alleviation, and crime reduction. This development could be seen as a "victory" for the scholarly side of the debate in that it appeared to bring response levels back towards what they felt was more likely to constitute a proportional response. However, it would only be by some perverse logic that anyone genuinely interested in the problem of trafficking could regard this as a positive outcome.

The struggle over questions of prevalence and proportionality has had other negative effects on the course of the campaign. However, in order to examine this result, we need to pay more attention to policy implementation. Here I draw on a three-year, comparative ethnographic study of the implementation of immigration control policies in the Department of Home Affairs and in the South African police force. Our researchers observed officials' everyday work practices in government offices, accompanied police and immigration officials on patrol, and held informal conversations and more formal interviews with local officials. This research focused on three types of research sites: (1) the Beitbridge Border Post and its surrounding areas, where the majority of Zimbabweans enter South Africa; (2) the Johannesburg Offices of the Department of Home Affairs (Harrison Street and Crown Street); and (3) six police stations spread across the greater Johannesburg metropolitan area. As part of this study, we initiated a project, albeit, as we shall see, with mixed success, to specifically analyze the manner in which the human trafficking policies of South Africa were being implemented by ordinary officials in South Africa's migration and policing regimes. This research provided us with a unique set of insights into the manner in which street-level bureaucrats confront trafficking-related problems and the set of tools (cognitive, procedural, legal, and material) that they use to develop effective interventions.

One of the ways in which anti-trafficking campaigners have sought to address the issue of prevalence has been to change the way in which government agencies and ancillary organizations conceptualize criminal activity. This approach begins with the argument that the reason why law enforcers do not uncover more cases of trafficking is not due to the fact that trafficking is not widespread. The problem instead has to do with the fact that criminal justice officials are routinely diagnosing cases of trafficking as mere instances of its component crimes (kidnapping, rape, forced labour, illegal migration, human smuggling, and so on). The key element that might transform a set of criminal activities into a trafficking offence, of course, to radically simplify, is that the victim was moved for the purpose of exploitation. Many ordinary officials simply do not ask themselves whether this element of criminal activity has occurred and, hence, do not collect evidence that might allow prosecutors to convict on this basis. So, for example, the HSRC's study of the South African criminal justice system found that "there is no 'flagging' system in place that alerts the prosecution at an early stage (prior to an arrest) that a particular investigation may be a human trafficking case."[17]

This gap, which is evident in most criminal justice systems, has several potentially problematic outcomes for the way criminal justice officials do their job. Here I want to focus on just two: policing and protection. The first issue refers to the fact that international trafficking instruments and their domestic counterparts represent a key means by which police agencies can shift their posture towards transnational criminal activity. Rather than merely responding to isolated criminal instances *in situ*, trafficking and the other two protocols within the UN Convention against Transnational Organized Crime encourage officials to think more broadly about criminal enterprise and to inquire into the expanding networks and associations that increasingly support and encourage contemporary crime.[18] While the linkages between trafficking and other forms of organized crime and transnational activity have often been overblown, there can be little doubt that trafficking, almost by definition, is heavily dependent on the existence of a broader criminal conspiracy. In countries like South Africa, there is a significant demand for a raft of measures to ensure that, in particular, detectives and prosecutors are encouraged to detect transnational criminal networks and associations rather than respond in piecemeal and isolated fashion to criminal acts as they arise or are encountered. Yet, when knowledge of, and familiarity with, international protocols are low, we cannot expect these changes to occur of their own accord.

The second issue relates to the remedies that most trafficking legislation provides to victims of trafficking. Most trafficking legislation encourages criminal justice officials to approach migrant workers as potential victims and not merely as potential lawbreakers. Here, the provisions offering victims of trafficking relief from deportation and access to a variety of victim support mechanisms in the host country create the potential for a radically different administrative response to the one suggested by immigration control laws, which often result in the mere issuance of deportation proceedings, often without complimentary sanctions against employers.

In the South African criminal justice system, anti-trafficking campaigners confront a range of policies, incentive structures, and institutional cultures that act against these international policing and protection mandates. In the case of the former, the detective work of the local police force is usually driven by the need to produce convincing and often isolated convictions of criminals, as opposed to the longer and potentially more fruitful investigations required to define, detect, and prosecute a transnational criminal conspiracy.[19] In the case of the latter, policies that encourage officials throughout the government bureaucracy to enforce immigration law[20] and the habit of typecasting foreign nationals as potential criminals limit the potential for trafficking laws to substantially alter the disposition of officials towards potential victims.

One of the potential ways in which organizations like INTERPOL have sought to encourage these sorts of broader changes in the policing and regulative posture of government officials has been by funding pilot transnational policing operations that focus on areas where good evidence exists of a transnational criminal enterprise and then by using the resources of international agencies to exhibit how they can be tackled.[21] Anti-trafficking campaigners have yet to opt for this sort of intervention. Instead, they have opted for a series of measures that – somewhat tautologically – assume prevalence and then seek to demonstrate it. These include:

- advertising campaigns that seek to reach a broad audience of potential victims or potential informants so that they can begin to conceptualize practices that they already know about as trafficking
- hotlines that provide what is assumed to be a broad audience of victims and potential informants with opportunities to ensure that this information is channelled to central data management systems

- the establishment of intra-governmental coordinating agencies that are responsible for the analysis of existing government criminal databases to check which cases of criminal activity might have involved trafficking elements and the establishment of governmental information-reporting systems that encourage officials to channel information on trafficking to the centre
- the training of government officials that encourages officials to re-classify a range of criminal activities that they ordinarily encounter as trafficking.

The latter approach has been particularly important. As part of the SACTAP program, the IOM has trained over 10,000 officials across Southern Africa in the dimensions of trafficking, its laws, and the appropriate case management procedures. Yet these training sessions rarely have sought to address the deeper structural realities that prevent officials in the South African criminal justice system from (1) investigating transnational criminal activity and (2) seeking to provide protection for foreign nationals. In part, this has to do with the fact that it is very hard to tackle these issues. One other potential reason may be that the campaign's main concern has not been with the transformation of criminal justice but, rather, with the redefinition of existing criminal activity as trafficking, so that sufficient information on suspected trafficking cases begins to filter towards the centre and, thereby, begins to deal with the problem of prevalence.

According to our research with police detectives in inner-city Johannesburg, the outcomes of this sort of approach to trafficking are likely to be at best ambivalent and at worst counterproductive and damaging. The first point to note here is that, in the absence of a broad awareness of trafficking legislation or instruments, officials often intervene in trafficking cases in ways that protect the human rights of the victim. So, for example, despite the fact that a police detective working in the Missing Persons unit in Johannesburg did not know what trafficking was, he was quite capable of locating and taking custody of a South African child sex worker and transferring custody to the Child Protection Agency. If he had felt it was necessary, he was also capable of determining whether to make a referral to the Organized Crime Unit.

The second point to note is that the way trafficking is being taught within South Africa, wherein such a broad range of activities can potentially count as trafficking, many officials are beginning to include a much broader range of crimes within their definition of trafficking. For example, one group of police officers we spoke to included cases of hijacked buildings, unpaid mineworkers, or blind migrants working in a begging "syndicate" as cases of trafficking.

The third point to note is that all criminal justice institutions, and particularly the police, depend on an array of largely unwritten case management procedures that are difficult to transform. In South Africa, these include insider understandings of the division of labour between operational police and detective services or between the police as a whole and the Departments of Social Services, Immigration, and Labour. They also include a set of often personal relationships across these divides that help to ensure that cases are appropriately handled and passed on to the organizations and individuals with the appropriate expertise. In South Africa, in part due to its apartheid history, the strongest set of relationships of this sort are between the police and the Department of Home Affairs, regarding the referral of cases of suspected illegal foreigners. The first question that police officers will ask any civilian suspect is to see their documents, and, from that point on, police officials are schooled in a set of procedures to handle a suspect leading towards deportation. In this respect, it is doubtful that the training trickling down from the human trafficking initiatives will fundamentally transform the disposition of police officers towards migrants from one of prosecution to one of protection.

Concluding Remarks

This chapter has provided some reasons why academics struggle to have critical findings about trafficking taken seriously in the policy sphere. While the structural reasons for myths about human trafficking and the fraught character of this debate have been gaining prominence in recent discussions (see the chapter by Joel Quirk in this volume), there remains a set of more fundamental reasons why scholars struggle to translate their research into palpable policy changes; words into action. In part, this difficulty has to do with the sheer material resources that anti-trafficking campaigners use to keep the issue alive, as pointed out in the discussion of the response to Gould and Fick. However, in part, it also has to do with the unpredictable responses of rescue campaigns to research-based critiques. Indeed, if the discussion in the final section of this chapter is accurate, the efforts of the campaigners to fend off criticisms by increasing their case numbers has produced a largely counter-productive training process, where the objective of proving prevalence takes precedence over improving overall performance. In this respect, the chapter concludes with the suggestion that scholars engaging critically with practitioners on questions of human trafficking would do well to first engage in, at least, a preliminary analysis of some of the epistemological assumptions and material motivations of their interlocutors. There may be room for dialogue and progress, but common ground will also be hard to find.

The upshot of this argument is not that scholars should throw their hands up in despair and return to "pure science" but, rather, that they should aim to improve the outcomes of their engagement in public debates by mapping out the contextual factors that have led various public actors to adopt specific positions and then thinking through how these factors might shape the impacts of their research. This is not to suggest that scholars can ever transform contemporary society into a classroom, where they retain the power to dictate terms, but, instead, that it may head off the development of unproductive engagements between scholars and practitioners, like the one that seems to have emerged in South Africa's human trafficking debate.

Notes

1 Jürgen Habermas, *The Theory of Communicative Action: Volume 1: Reason and the Rationalization of Society.* (Beacon Press: Boston, 1985).

2 Thomas Kuhn, *The Structure of Scientific Revolutions: 50th Anniversary Edition.* Chicago: University of Chicago Press, 2012.

3 For a thorough application of Ludwig Wittgenstein's theory to the study of the history of political thought, see Quentin Skinner, *The Foundations of Modern*

Political Thought: Volume 1 The Renaissance (Cambridge, UK: Cambridge University Press, 1978).

4 These engagements include: (2009–10) "Southern African Police Service Gauteng Management Services," Presentation to Senior Management on Corruption and Immigration Policing, Johannesburg; (2009) "Policing and Migration: Documentation, Integrity and Policy," Presentation to INTERPOL and SARPCCO Working Group Meeting, Dar es Salaam; (2009) South African National Prosecuting Authority Task Team on Human Trafficking, which provided input on training manuals for government officials; (2007) EuropeAid Training Workshop on Migration and Trafficking in Human Beings in EC External Assistance: Opportunities and Challenges in the SADC Region, Pretoria; (2006) Department of Home Affairs, Public Hearings in Preparation for the United Nations High Level Dialogue on Migration, "Workshop 1 on the Effects of International Migration on Social and Economic Development."

5 The activities of the International Organization on Migration (IOM) are sorely under-researched and under-theorized in the study of the politics of migration. For a refreshing and compelling exception, see Rutvica Andrijasevic and William Walters, "The International Organization for Migration and the International Government of Borders," *Envionment and Planning D: Society and Space* 28, 6 (2010): 977–99. More generally, the politics of anti-trafficking funding is under-researched. While a recent special issue of the *Anti-Trafficking Review* promised to "follow the money," the focus here was on the practical question of how effectively trafficking funds were being spent rather than on the political question of how funding priorities shaped organizational goals. See Mike Dottridge, "Editorial: How Is the Money to Combat Human Trafficking Spent?, *Anti-Trafficking Review* 3 (2014): 3–14.

6 International Organization for Migration, http://www.iom.int/jahia/Jahia/about-iom/organizational-structure/lang/en (accessed 23 June 2011).

7 US Department of State, *Trafficking in Persons Report*, 2005–08.

8 USAID, *South Africa Budget Fact Sheet*, Docs. FY2007–FY2009, 2007–09.

9 Joel Quirk and Darshan Vigneswaran, *Slavery, Migration and Contemporary Bondage in Africa*, Harriet Tubman Series on the African Diaspora (Trenton, NJ: Africa World Press, 2013).

10 Molo Songololo, *The Trafficking of Children for the Purposes of Sexual Exploitation* (Cape Town: Molo Songololo, 2000); Molo Songololo, *The Trafficking of Women into the South African Sex Industry* (Cape Town: Molo Songololo, 2000); J. Martens, M. Pieczkowski, and B. van Vuuren-Smyth, *Seduction, Sale and Slavery: Trafficking in Women and Children for Sexual Exploitation in Southern Africa* (Pretoria: International Organization for Migration Regional Office for Southern Africa, 2003).

11 International Organization for Migration and Norwegian Agency for Development Cooperation, *Southern African Counter Trafficking Programme (SACTAP): Review report* (Oslo, Norway: Centurion, 2010). Protocol to Prevent, Suppress and Punish

Trafficking in Persons, especially Women and Children, 15 November 2000, 40 ILM 335 (2001).

12 Human Sciences Research Council, *Tsireledzani: Understanding the Dimensions of Human Trafficking in Southern Africa* (Human Sciences Research Council, 2010).

13 M. Khokhar, "Editorial: The Numbers Game," *Global Eye on Human Trafficking* 23 (2010): 2.

14 E. Harper, D. Massawe, and M. Richter, *Report on the 2010 Soccer World Cup and Sex Work: Documenting Successes and Failures* (Johannesburg: n.p., 2010).

15 D. Vigneswaran et al., "Criminality or Monopoly? Informal Immigration Enforcement in South Africa," *Journal of Southern African Studies* 36, 2 (2010): 465–81.

16 Human Rights Watch, *Prohibited Persons: Abuse of Undocumented Migrants, Asylum-Seekers, and Refugees in South Africa* (New York: Human Rights Watch, 1998).

17 Human Sciences Research Council, *Tsireledzani*, 58

18 Convention against Transnational Organized Crime, 15 November 2000, 40 ILM 335 (2001).

19 R. Matshedisho, "Nothing Succeeds Like Success: The Manipulation of Crime Statistics," in D. Vigneswaran and J. Hornberger, eds., *Beyond "Good Cop" / "Bad Cop": Understanding Informality and Police Corruption* (Johannesburg: Forced Migration Studies Program, 2009), 33–38.

20 D. Vigneswaran, "Enduring Territoriality: South African Immigration Control," *Political Geography* 27 (2008): 783–801.

21 INTERPOL and SARPCCO Working Group Meeting, Dar es Salaam, 2009.

Reparative Justice and the Post-Conflict Phase of Modern Slavery

8

Roy L. Brooks

In 1952, the global community was still staggering with intense fear, dismay, and disgust from its discovery of the Holocaust at the end of the Second World War. It was at this time that Konrad Hermann Joseph Adenauer, who was elected the first chancellor of the Federal Republic of Germany, declared to the world: "In our name, unspeakable crimes have been committed and demand compensation and restitution, both moral and material, for the persons and properties of the Jews who have been so seriously harmed."[1] By assuming responsibility for the previous government's actions and moral failure, Adenauer helped reshape the mood and mindset of the community of nations coming out of a period of such blatant disregard for human life. His words of redress imbued the community of nations with a post-Holocaust vision of heightened morality, egalitarianism, identity, and justice. If there is a beast in all societies waiting to be unleashed, then redress – "both moral and material" – may be our only hope of ever taming it.

Two broad strategies of redress have emerged since the end of the Holocaust. These strategies – one involving the criminal process and the other the civil process – pursue various forms of post-conflict justice. Together, they cover the full gamut of justice in the reparative framework: retributive, compensatory, restorative, and redistributive. In the following chapter, I ask how models of post-conflict redress can be applied to a more contemporary issue no less serious than the Holocaust itself: modern slavery.

Various international,[2] domestic,[3] and scholarly definitions[4] of "modern slavery" can be synthesized into a working definition: human exploitation effectuated over a period of time through violence, intimidation, fraud, and trickery. Today, the enslaved are not owned, as they were in the chattel slavery of old, but, rather, are controlled by others. The services forcibly extracted most often involve sex, debt bondage (often "paid off" through sexual services), involuntary servitude or forced labour, and peonage.[5] These injustices are so pervasive as to strain credulity. According to the International Labor Organization (ILO), 12.3 million people are estimated to be held in forced labour, bonded labour, forced child labour, and sexual servitude at any given time. In addition, the US Department of State calculates that about 600,000 to 800,000 people are annually trafficked across national borders, as distinguished from the millions trafficked within their own countries. Females and children bear the brunt of this atrocity: approximately 80 percent of trafficking victims worldwide are women or girls and approximately 50 percent are minors.[6] There is little doubt that modern slavery can be found in every nook and cranny of the world; even in a progressive state like California. According to the Spring Valley Citizens Association, "9 out of 10 products eaten in Southern California [are] picked by someone who was trafficked."[7]

The "process" of modern slavery has three interconnected phases.[8] The first phase involves the recruitment and transportation of the victim to the place of exploitation, often referred to as "trafficking."[9] The victim may be transported by one of the perpetrators or she might travel on her own accord, but, in both cases, violence, the threat of violence, intimidation, fraud, or trickery are used to induce departure.[10] The second phase relates to the exploitation of the victim for profit, which may include compelled sexual or pornographic services, forced labour, and organ removal. The third and final phase occurs when the victims are no longer under the thumb of the perpetrator. Either the perpetrator has been put out of business, the victims have escaped, or they have been allowed to leave. This begins the post-conflict phase of modern slavery.

Most of the scholarly attention given to modern slavery has focused on the first two stages, while relatively little attention has been given to the end stage.[11] Indeed, the Protocol to Prevent, Suppress and Punish Trafficking in Persons, especially Women and Children (Trafficking Protocol) and similar laws give but skeletal treatment to the post-conflict stage.[12] Article 6 of the Trafficking Protocol, entitled, "Assistance to and Protection of Victims of Trafficking in Persons," holds that:

> 3. Each State Party shall consider implementing measures to provide for the physical, psychological and social recovery of victims of trafficking in persons, including, in appropriate cases, in cooperation with non-governmental organizations, other relevant organizations and other elements of civil society, and, in particular, the provision of:
>   (a) Appropriate housing;
>   (b) Counseling and information, in particular as regards their legal rights, in a language that the victims of trafficking in persons can understand;
>   (c) Medical, psychological and material assistance; and
>   (d) Employment, educational and training opportunities ...
> 6. Each State Party shall ensure that its domestic legal system contains measures that offer victims of trafficking in persons the possibility of obtaining compensation for damage suffered.

The Trafficking Protocol is right to draw our attention to the post-conflict stage, for modern slavery will end someday. In this chapter, I suggest that the lens of reparative justice offers one way to theorize and, hence, further our understanding of the post-conflict phase. I argue that modern slavery's end stage should centre on the question of redress; specifically, how can post-conflict redress be provided to the victims of modern slavery in a way that serves the ends of justice? Scholars in the international redress movement have given considerable thought to the question of post-conflict, or reparative, justice outside the context of modern slavery.[13] My ambition here is to consider the extent to which this framework can illuminate our understanding of post-conflict justice in the context of modern slavery.

To that end, I have divided this chapter into several parts. I begin by examining criminal redress within the context of modern slavery, the prime method through which the state – rather than the victims – metes out retribution and punishment. I then look at the forms of reparative justice available within the civil redress system, arguing that the twin mechanisms of apology/forgiveness and tangible reparation better serve the interests of victims in terms of compensation, restoration, and redistribution. These can be achieved, in principle, through both the tort model and the atonement model of civil redress. However, as I show through an examination of a class action lawsuit against Japan for forced labour during the Second World War, it is extremely difficult to achieve restitution for crimes that happened in the more distant past through litigation. I thus find that the atonement model offers perhaps the best chance of moving society forward in the post-conflict stage of modern slavery and endeavour to demonstrate its hypothetical application to the former child soldiers in Africa and sexual exploitation in Thailand.

Criminal Redress: Retributive Justice

Criminal redress is the government's prosecution of individual wrongdoers under international or domestic criminal law. Although there are several international criminal tribunals, domestic prosecution is the primary means of effectuating criminal redress of human rights violations. It mainly serves the ends of retributive (or punitive) justice since its objective is to punish wrongdoing through fines, imprisonment, or execution. Criminal prosecution is certainly a possible form of redress for many of the individual harms arising out of the first and second stages of modern slavery. Retributive punishment can serve as a palliative atonement for victims since the punishment meted out to their former tormentors may slake their desire for justice or give them the feeling that justice has been served.

However, there are drawbacks to criminal redress that should be considered. For example, the victims have to be able to identify their perpetrators. This kind of face-to-face encounter can be traumatic or, for many reasons, practically difficult. It is also often easier to prosecute low-level perpetrators than those higher up the food chain, a fact that often allows those causing the most damage to escape punishment. For example, the kidnappers, brothel owners, and perhaps even the customers of trafficked individuals are more identifiable than the "brains" of the operation or the governmental officials who give aid and comfort to the enterprise.[14]

More importantly, retributive justice may not be the best form of redress even where the perpetrators can be identified. This is particularly the case in transitional states. In the context of transitional justice, criminal redress can be too adversarial and backward looking to aid in the forward-looking process of heightened morality, egalitarianism, identity, and nation building. In South Africa, for example, the restorative justice of the Truth and Reconciliation Commission was allowed to trump individual cries for retribution in order to better foster racial harmony in the new, post-apartheid state. As a result, amnesty was given to those who committed criminal acts provided that they publically confessed to their crimes.[15]

The tension between retributive justice and restorative justice is a major issue in the international redress movement. Caroline Bowah, an official with the Foundation for Human Rights and Democracy in Liberia, highlights this potential conflict: "The people of this country must be reconciled, yes it's true. But again, you cannot reconcile if those who bear the greatest responsibility for this conflict ... [are not held] ... accountable."[16] Even if this conflict could be reconciled, however, criminal prosecution alone may not be a sufficient form of redress for modern slavery. Criminal prosecution primarily provides material redress for the state rather than for the victims. As such, criminal redress cannot address the victims' tangible needs. For all of these reasons, civil redress and its concomitant forms of reparative justice may be more suitable for the victims.

Civil Redress: The Full Spectrum of Justice
Civil redress works to the material benefit of the victims. It is private redress, in essence, that takes place in a public forum. Civil redress can be effectuated in a variety of ways. Some of the most common mechanisms include truth trials, truth commissions, and protests. Apologies or reparations from state or individual perpetrators are more typical forms of civil redress. While the latter are typically pursued through an adversarial process (called the tort model), both are sometimes used together in a more conciliatory process (called the atonement model). Unlike criminal redress, which can only be retributive, civil redress promotes the entire spectrum of justice – retributive, compensatory, restorative, and redistributive.

Are these reparative justice models suitable forms of redress for modern slavery? I have only enough space here to consider the suitability of apologies and reparations. My quick answers are as follows. Apologies by themselves alone do little more than lay the groundwork for restorative justice. Hence, they are not particularly useful for the post-conflict stage of modern slavery. Reparations through the tort model yield at last some semblance of compensatory justice. To that extent, they are useful. However, they may be difficult to attain through litigation and, to that extent, may have to be authorized legislatively. Reparations through the atonement model, which comes with the implicit duty of the victim to forgive, have a more limited, but important, utility. I urge creative application. The atonement model brings restorative (and potentially redistributive) justice to the post-conflict stage.

Apologies

It is no small matter when the perpetrators of an atrocity or their successors tender an apology on behalf of themselves or their government, as Adenauer did for the Federal Republic of Germany in 1952. At the very least, an expression of deep remorse allows the perpetrators to reclaim their moral character in the aftermath of a grave human injustice. So it was when Willy Brandt, who became the chancellor of West Germany six years after Adenauer left office, expressed deep remorse on a visit to the Warsaw Ghetto decades after the Second World War:

> I must express the exceptional significance of the ghetto memorial. From the bottom of the abyss of German history, under the burden of millions of victims of murder, I did what human beings do when speech fails them. Even twenty years later, I cannot say more than the reporter whose account ran: "Then he who does not need to kneel knelt, on behalf of all who do need to kneel but do not because they dare not, or cannot, or cannot dare to kneel."[17]

In an essay entitled "The Age of Apology," I noted that

> apologies [are] coming from all corners of the world – Britain's Queen Elizabeth apologizing to the Maori people; Australia to

the stolen aboriginal children; the Canadian government to the Canadian-Ukrainians; President Clinton to many groups, including native Hawaiians and African American survivors of the Tuskegee, Alabama syphilis experiment; South Africa's former President F.W. de Klerk to victims of Apartheid; and Polish, French and Czech notables for human injustices perpetrated during World War II.

I also posited that these apologies were more complex than "contrition chic" or "the canonization of sentimentality." They are "a matrix of guilt and mourning, atonement and national revival." To that extent, an apology "raises the moral threshold of a society."[18] I doubt, however, that an apology by itself is a suitable form of redress for modern slavery. Apart from the obvious question of who exactly should apologize, and to whom, for all the wrongdoing collected under the umbrella of "modern slavery," apologies simply do not have enough heft to elevate the level of humanity in the aftermath of an atrocity like modern slavery. This is especially the case with individual, low-level perpetrators, however sincere their apologies might be. From the victims' perspective, saying "I'm sorry" is not enough and may be even less satisfying than criminal redress. Apologies without reparations, and the two rarely go together, effectuate no concrete changes.[19] With criminal redress, at least someone goes to jail.

Reparations

There are two basic forms of reparations. Victim-directed reparations seek to compensate the individual or her family for their suffering; however, they can only ever be symbolic because "nothing can undo the past or truly return the victim to the status quo ante."[20] Community-directed reparations, on the other hand, respond to the lingering effects of the atrocity on the victim's social group as a whole. These are intended to rehabilitate the community, to help the community (re)build, and "to nurture the group's self-empowerment and, thus, aid in the nation's social and cultural transformation."[21] Both forms of reparations can be divided into monetary and non-monetary (or in-kind) reparations. The former is usually a direct cash transfer to the individual or to the members of the community, while the latter can take the form of medical or psychological assistance, job training or job placement, a special educational program (for example, admissions or scholarships), and so on. Monuments or other public recognitions that honour the victim(s) would also fall into this category.[22] Victim-directed reparations are typically pursued through the tort model, while community-directed reparations are more suited for the atonement model. Each model brings its own brand of justice to the table; however, both models could offer ways to redress modern slavery in the post-conflict stage.

Tort Model

Victim-directed reparations unaccompanied by an apology are meant to compensate individuals for the injuries they sustained as a result of the perpetrator's intentional acts of wrongdoing. Although most of these reparations are pursued through civil litigation under the tort model, in which the victim sues the perpetrator in court, they can also be achieved through legislation. The Rosewood Compensation Act is one example.[23] In 1994, the Florida legislature enacted the Act for the purpose of compensating blacks who had lost property as a result of a race riot that demolished the all-black town of Rosewood in 1921. No apology was issued in connection with this compensation. The Act merely sought to compensate the victims and, hence, settle the matter once and for all.[24]

The pursuit of compensation for forced labour during the Second World War is a prime example of victim-directed reparations pursued through litigation. Dozens of class action lawsuits against the governments and corporations of Japan and Germany have been filed in US courts over the years. Asserting claims under US constitutional and statutory law, state constitutional and statutory law, as well as international common law, plaintiffs in these lawsuits have sought damages for unpaid wages and the injuries they sustained while being held captive during the war. Like most civil redress litigation, these lawsuits have not been successful. They have been dismissed on numerous procedural grounds, among them the lack of subject matter jurisdiction, the violation of sovereign immunity, and the expiration of the statute of limitations.[25] The following case study illustrates this model.

The case *In re World War II Era Japanese Forced Labor Litigation*, heard in 2001 by a trial court in California, was a consolidation of several class action lawsuits brought by plaintiffs of Korean and Chinese descent against the Japanese government.[26] Plaintiffs asserted a number of claims. One set of claims was based on judge-made "common" law, while a second set of claims was based on California constitutional and statutory law. I deal with each set in turn. The first set of claims alleged false imprisonment, assault and battery, conversion, *quantum meruit* (literally, "as much as he deserves"), unjust enrichment, constructive trust, and accounting.

Quantum meruit and unjust enrichment are recurring claims in forced labour civil redress litigation and, hence, warrant further comment. Quantum meruit "requires a defendant to pay a plaintiff the reasonable value of services performed for the defendant even though there was no contract to do so."[27] In other words, "the law implies an understanding or intent to pay the value of services rendered," unless there is a specific agreement that the services will be performed gratuitously."[28] Unjust enrichment, a much more complex legal concept, is generally defined as "the unjust retention of a benefit to the loss of another, or the retention of money or property of another against the fundamental principles of justice or equity and good conscience."[29] Unjust enrichment is a necessary element or precondition of the larger claim of restitution, which seeks the return of the benefit for which it would be unconscionable for the defendant to retain.[30] The close relationship between unjust enrichment and restitution is highlighted in *Black's Law Dictionary*'s definition of the former term. Unjust enrichment is defined therein as "circumstances which give rise to the obligation of restitution, that is, the receiving and retention of property, money, or benefits which in justice and equity belong to another."[31] Thus, restitution is simply the claim that "a person who has been unjustly enriched at the expense of another is required to ... [provide redress] to the other."[32]

Typical of forced labour cases, the court ruled that these claims were barred by the statute of limitations. As such, the court disposed of the case on a procedural ground, and it never reached the merits of any of these common law claims. The judge had the possibility of applying the statute of limitations of the forum state (California) or that of the place wherein the events took place (China and Japan); however, "the statutes of limitations from all three forums are significantly shorter than the age of these claims."[33] California requires such cases to be brought within one to three years (depending on the claims), while China maintains a two-year limitation period. Japan, the most lenient of the relevant countries in this context, still requires claims to be brought within ten years under its civil code.[34]

The second set of claims brought by the plaintiffs were based on California constitutional and statutory law, specifically Article 1 of the Constitution and Penal Code, paragraph 181 (both of which prohibit involuntary servitude); the Unfair Competition Act (UCA), which is part of the California Business and Professional Code; and paragraph 354.6 of the California Code of Civil Procedure.[35] Like the common law claims, the state constitutional and statutory claims were dismissed before the judge could rule on their merits. Disposing the case on procedural grounds, the judge ruled not only that the claims were barred by the applicable statutes of limitations but also that he lacked subject matter jurisdiction (federal constitutional authority to decide the case) because the claims essentially raised political questions in violation of the political question doctrine. First announced by Chief Justice John Marshall in *Marbury v Madison* (1803), the political question doctrine basically holds that "questions, in their nature political ... can never be made in this court."[36] An enigma to constitutional scholars – the Supreme Court routinely decides political matters from discrimination in elections to the exercise of executive privilege – the political question doctrine basically gives judges the discretion to determine which cases are too controversial for the judiciary to handle.

In addition to these two sets of claims, the plaintiffs made one final claim under an ancient federal statute – the Alien Torts Claims Act (ATCA).[37] Originally enacted in the Judiciary Act of 1789 to create a right of action against nefarious nations, the ATCA gives a federal court "original jurisdiction of any civil action by an alien for a tort only, committed in violation of the law of nations or a treaty of the United States."[38] In other words, the ATCA grants federal courts subject-matter jurisdiction to entertain suits against state actors or private actors "alleging torts committed anywhere in the world against aliens in violation of the law of nations."[39] Since the ATCA has no statute of limitations, courts are instructed to "borrow" from the most suitable statute of limitations. In this case, the judge borrowed from the ten-year limitation period contained in the Torture Victim Protection Act,[40] which provides a cause of action in federal court for victims of torture wherever they might be in the world. Since plaintiffs' claims were not filed within ten years of their occurrence, their ATCA action was dismissed on statute of limitations grounds.[41]

What this case teaches us is that legislation is likely to be a more practical path to reparations for the victims of modern slavery than litigation. Even assuming a country's system of laws allows for reparative litigation, adjudication is expensive, time-consuming, cumbersome, and indeterminate. There are too many hurdles to scale and too many loops to jump through. The victims of modern slavery are, in a sense, revictimized when they pursue reparations through litigation. Equally important, low-level perpetrators are unlikely to have enough assets to make the litigation worthwhile, while high-level government perpetrators are usually immune to civil liability involving damages. Finally, judges have far less power than legislators to effectuate reparative, restorative, or redistributive justice.[42] Hence, legislation seems to be a more realistic strategy than litigation to achieve reparative justice for modern slavery.

Legislatures are authorized to create victim-directed reparations by Article 6 of the Trafficking Protocol, quoted earlier in this chapter. That and similar laws require both source and destination countries to provide housing, counselling, education, and medical services to the victims of modern slavery. Some states currently limit eligibility to victims of "severe forms of trafficking in persons,"[43] which is unfortunate as it only denies redress to victims.[44] Legislators would be better able to craft a rational and effective redress regime for modern slavery if they were guided by a theory of reparative justice that emphasized compensation or restoration rather than retribution.

Atonement Model

If reparations under the tort model are victim focused, backward looking, and compensatory or retributive, reparations under the atonement model are community focused, forward looking, and restorative, even potentially redistributive. Under the atonement model, redress is mainly about reconciliation between victims and perpetrators and moving society forward in the aftermath of an atrocity. For this to happen, the perpetrators and the victims must assume reciprocal responsibilities. The perpetrator has a moral obligation to apologize and to make that apology believable by undertaking a tangible "reparation." The victims, in response, have a civic obligation to forgive so that society as a whole can move forward. Reconciliation, then, begins with a perpetrator-issued apology, backed by reparations to solidify the rhetoric of remorse. Forgiveness, then, arrives on the victim's desk like a subpoena; a response must be given.[45]

Justice under the atonement model is primarily restorative, and, in contrast to the tort model, it never involves punishment of the perpetrators.[46] Instead, the atonement model provides perpetrators with an opportunity to restore their moral worth and to restore their broken relationship with the victims.[47] Forgiveness is the last element of the atonement model. I define forgiveness as the victims' willingness to respond affirmatively to the perpetrators' specific request for forgiveness. It is, in other words, the remission of an attitude of resentment evoked by injury and the sincere effort to restore the broken relationship. Forgiveness is essential to the forward-looking focus of the atonement model. Atonement – meaning apology plus reparations – and forgiveness are the key elements of this unique redress model. They are not, however, morally equivalent. The perpetrators' duty to atone for their heinous acts is a moral imperative, while the victims' duty to forgive can be no more than a civic responsibility. The victim of an atrocity, unlike the perpetrator, has no moral debt to pay.[48]

The key assumption underpinning the atonement model is the existence of a continuing post-conflict relationship between large numbers of victims and the perpetrators. Classic examples are blacks and whites in post-apartheid South Africa or and Japanese Americans in post-war America. This relationship can be manifested in transitional states (for example, South Africa moving to end apartheid)[49] or in stable regimes (for example, the United States when redress was given to Japanese Americans in 1988).[50] The restorative objective of the atonement model is twofold: restore the broken relationship between perpetrators and victims and restore the moral character of the perpetrators. To illustrate the application of the atonement model to modern slavery, I shall apply the model to former child soldiers in Africa and sexually exploited women and girls in Thailand.

Child soldiers have been used extensively in several recent conflicts, most notably the wars in Liberia and Sierra Leone. Liberia's civil wars (1989–2003)[51] displaced an estimated 1.5 million civilians from their homes, killed a quarter of a million people, and left thousands more viciously mutilated, tortured, and sexually abused. Many (if not most) of these grotesque and nauseating crimes were committed by the estimated 20,000–25,000 children – some as young as eight – that were conscripted into the fighting.[52] The post-conflict treatment of former child soldiers is one situation in which the atonement model and its spirit of restorative justice can be quite useful.

Retributive justice seems most inappropriate (most unjust) when, as here, the perpetrators and victims are one and the same. At a very impressionable age, these children were pressed into service through abduction carried out in a climate of extraordinary violence. Adult soldiers typically entered the children's villages and then proceeded to rape, murder, and terrorize the villagers. Some children were forced to have sex with a parent or sibling, while others were forced to watch as their parents were sexually assaulted or murdered by the adult soldiers. The induction notice to the children was indeed an abduction: join up and do what you are told or be killed.[53] Such horrendous practices served to destroy the concept of family, community, and connection. The children continued to be stripped of their innocence as they performed their military service in the bush. Child soldiers were compelled to fight, fornicate, and kill. Some soldiers, especially girl soldiers, were forced to serve an additional role as sex slaves for the militants. Many child soldiers were constantly assaulted, starved, drugged, and victimized by their own military commanders.[54] Hence, despite the violence they committed, these children were undoubtedly also victims of modern slavery.

The physical effects of being a child soldier or child sex slave are heavy and lasting. While many child soldiers died in battle, those who survived have debilitating wounds, such as missing limbs. Girl soldiers used as sex slaves became impregnated, contracted sexually transmitted diseases such as HIV/AIDS, or now have damaged reproductive systems and cannot bear children. When the Sierra Leone Civil War ended in

2002, it was estimated that over 16,000 children had HIV or AIDS and that because of AIDS-related deaths more than 40,000 children were parentless.[55] Equally devastating are the psychological scars these children now bear. Ripped from a loving familial setting, torn from a comfortable community, and abruptly thrown into a world of terror and violence, they have little sense of what constitutes appropriate social behaviour. They are fearful, anxious, and aggressive. Abandoned by their military "families," they are often shunned by their natural families because of their crimes. Sex slaves, who are no less stigmatized, are also looked down upon or disowned by their families. The offspring of these damaged children, conceived out of rape and violence, are degraded as "rebel babies." Without doubt, these children are now fighting an internal war long after the external war has ended.

A picture of revictimization is revealed in the words of one former child soldier:

> When I came to Freetown, I tried to stay with my father ... He rejected me and now I am staying in the streets. He said that he is no longer my father because I was a rebel ... I tried to explain to him that it was not my fault ... but he could not listen to me. I am now a chain smoker. I smoke cigarettes, cannabis sativa, and have sex with prostitutes everyday ... I even drink alcohol.[56]

Human rights would seem to dictate a post-conflict resolution largely informed by a theory of restorative justice rather than retributive justice. As perpetrators, the children should be given opportunities to restore their moral character. As victims, their broken relationships with their families and communities should be restored. The atonement model provides the best post-conflict structure for generating restorative justice. But because the perpetrators and victims are one and the same, it must be applied in a creative fashion.

Under the atonement model, character rebuilding begins with the issuance of an apology. Although the perpetrators were children at the time, they need to understand that they committed morally reprehensible wrongs even though they were not totally responsible. The apologies could be issued in a forum similar to South Africa's Truth and

Reconciliation Commission. These statements of remorse must be followed by a tangible act of redemption that is age and situation appropriate, such as community service. In return, the government should grant amnesty to these atoning perpetrators, and the community should cease to ostracize them. Amnesty for perpetrators is sometimes offered on the theory that it can help a community move beyond the atrocity. This certainly was the calculation in South Africa. To that extent, amnesty arguably benefits the victims as well, who in this case are also the perpetrators.[57]

As victims, the former child soldiers should receive reparations from those who exploited them, or from their governments. This is a creative, rather than a strict, application of the atonement model because the government may not, in all cases, have been an actual perpetrator. The most effective reparations would appear to be victim-directed (compensatory) reparations, which might include education, housing, jobs and job training, and medical and psychological treatment. Finally, there should be forgiveness all around. The former child soldiers should forgive their perpetrators and be forgiven by their own victims as well as their communities.

Thailand presents a very different case. The primary manifestation of modern slavery in Thailand is the sexual exploitation of women and girls, who are thrown into prostitution by force, deceit, and cultural and religious pressure. In some instances, girls as young as five years old are sold to brothels by their poverty-stricken parents to cover family debt, even though both brothels and prostitution have been illegal in the country since 1960.[58] Prostitution has endured in Thailand due to a combination of strong cultural values and deep religious convictions. There is a strong cultural imperative in the country that holds girls responsible for the care of their elderly parents.[59] Imbibing this cultural imperative, girls often seek work at a young age. Many are lured into the world of commercial sex by false promises of legitimate jobs, and once they discover the truth they are not allowed to leave. Hence, the deception nullifies the putative consent.[60]

Another contributing cultural factor is the sexual double standard that exists in Thailand: "Thai society believes that boys are mischievous, men are naturally promiscuous. Men need sex, but good women (this usually means the well-to-do) are expected to remain virgins until marriage."[61] It is therefore only "good" women who must remain chaste until marriage. "Bad" women are needed so that men can slake their sexual needs. Nine out of ten men in Thailand have reported losing their virginity to a prostitute.[62] For many men, it is a rite of passage, a moment to mark their coming of age.[63] Thus, while men are encouraged to visit prostitutes, women who meet these needs are labelled "bad" for not remaining chaste until marriage.[64]

This sexual double standard is sanctioned not only by secular custom but also by religious dogma. Like Thai culture, Thai Buddhism permits men to use prostitutes. According to the *Vihays*, the rules governing monks, wives are ranked at ten different levels. Among the ten levels of wives are "those bought for money" and "those to be enjoyed or used occasionally." Prostitutes, thus, are the "wives" that are bought for money or that are used or enjoyed occasionally.[65]

Thai Buddhism also drives the sexual exploitation of women and girls by placing them at the bottom of the social order. Women and girls are not given the same access to Thai educational institutions as are men and boys.[66] Furthermore, "in Thai (*Theravada*) Buddhism, females cannot even reach the highest levels of spiritual enlightenment. The best they can hope for in this lifetime is to build up enough good karma to be born male in their next life."[67] Thai religion teaches that if one is born female, it means that she did something wrong in a previous life.[68] More generally, a person must accept life's pain and suffering because he or she is responsible for the bad things that befall him or her. Anything bad that happens to one is a direct result of the person's actions in a previous life. Thus, sexual slavery is the karma of a female with a bad past life. Since this punishment is her own fault, she must not fight against it but accept it and try to build up good karma for the next life. If all goes well, she will be reborn a man.

When sexual exploitation ends in Thailand, and we must suppose this is possible otherwise we resign ourselves to the status quo in perpetuity, the victims and perpetrators will have to live together. One way to manage this post-conflict stage is through restorative justice. Under the atonement model, the perpetrators – the government (National Assembly and monarchy) and religious leaders – will have to not only issue a strong apology, including a request for forgiveness, but will also have to solidify this apology with a tangible act (a reparation). The latter should speak to the needs of the victims by moving Thai society away from a culture of gender subordination. Given the scale of the problem, the reparative regime must necessarily include both victim-directed (compensatory) reparations and community-directed (rehabilitative) reparations. The former might include cash payments, services such as education, vocational training, jobs, housing, and medical attention for sexually transmitted diseases or other injuries to a victim's reproductive system. Psychological counselling to deal with the stigma attached to being viewed by the public as a former prostitute might also have to be included.

Community-directed (rehabilitative) reparations of a non-monetary nature are likely to be effective as well. These measures should be designed to prevent future sexual exploitation and to affirmatively elevate the status of women and girls in Thai society. Limited only by the imagination – and, of course, the country's economic condition – such measures might include units on women's rights in educational curricula, new gender equality laws, and a stricter enforcement of laws banning prostitution. Affirmative action programs that bring females into the mainstream of Thai society and, at the same time, change the public's perception of females will also have to be implemented. Television, radio, and other social institutions that inform the public's view of women will have to be called into service to reshape the female image in Thai society.

The emphasis of religious education will also have to shift towards Buddhism's transcendent precepts of human dignity and away from rules reinforcing gender-based inequalities. As one scholar has noted, the success of Christianity and Buddhism "is to be found in certain characteristics that they hold in common. One ... was their *egalitarianism*; their brotherhood was open to all who sought admittance – women as well as men, rich and poor alike, slave and free."[69] The success of all religions is based on their embrace of such life-affirming precepts.[70] Community-directed (rehabilitative) reparations can and should be used to counter gender subordination.

It may be necessary to combine the atonement model with other redress models to help the reconciliation process. The victims' sense of justice, for example, may demand criminal prosecution of the brothel owners and sex traffickers who violated Thai law. The atonement model is ill-suited for such individual-level grievances because the victims and perpetrators are not locked into a future relationship. In contrast, atonement from, and forgiveness for, the government, monarchy, and religious leaders is essential to a forward-looking, conciliatory process of redress. Once these high-level perpetrators have atoned, the victims have a civic duty to respond affirmatively – forgive but not forget. This will take some time since the victims and their high-level perpetrators will have to negotiate the preconditions for forgiveness – the nature and extent of the reparations – before the civic duty to forgive can be executed. Forgiveness can be manifested in several ways – for example, by the victims signing a "forgiveness book" in public. Forgiveness serves another important purpose: it psychologically releases the victims from the perpetrator's control. Freed from the perpetrator and the past, the victims can move forward with their lives.

Conclusion

The post-conflict stage of modern slavery is under-theorized. We can, however, deepen our thinking about the end stage of modern slavery by applying the reparative framework developed in the aftermath of the Holocaust. Informed by a post-Holocaust spirit of heightened morality, egalitarianism, identity, and justice, three reparative justice models – criminal redress and civil redress under the tort and atonement models – have potential application. Together, they raise questions about the proper theory of justice – retributive, compensatory, restorative, and re-distributive – that should govern the post-conflict stage of modern slavery.

Applying this reparative framework to modern slavery reveals no dearth of tensions in our thinking about justice during the end stage of this atrocity. For example, although retributive and compensatory justice can provide a level of redress for the state as well as for the victims, these theories can collide with the higher mission of restorative justice to reconcile social groups and reaffirm human ideals. This conflict can arise when the victims and community wish to pursue a forward-looking, conciliatory approach to redress rather than the backward-looking, punitive approach favoured by government prosecutors.

Furthermore, while the atonement model gives the victims rights, it also imposes correlative duties upon them. The duty to forgive is not an easy duty to accept. There is also a tension between victim-directed (compensatory) and community-directed (rehabilitative) reparations. Why should members of the victims' group who are not direct victims of modern slavery receive reparations? One answer might be that, unlike victim-directed reparations, these community-directed reparations are not intended to make direct victims whole. Their purpose, instead, is to dismantle the lingering effects of modern slavery and to prevent it from ever happening again.[71] Thus, as I suggested in my discussion of Thailand, community-directed reparations can attack both the supply and demand sides of modern slavery. Since the victims of sexual slavery are typically pulled from poor communities with minimal education and job opportunities, the government should provide programs to keep women and girls in school. The opportunities for sex exploitation greatly diminish by giving women and girls in these communities real opportunities for a better life. At the same time, instilling greater respect for women – all women – in communities will shake up, and hopefully lessen, the demand side of the equation. International funding for non-governmental organizations that provide educational services and job training in these countries can play an important role in achieving these objectives.

Finally, I have had little time here to say more than a few words about redistributive justice. There are a dearth of questions that come with the pursuit of this theory of reparative justice. At what point should community-directed reparations pursue redistributive justice rather than restorative justice? What justifies the pursuit of redistributive justice in non-transitional, liberal democratic states, such as the United Kingdom and the United States? Is modern slavery a large enough event to warrant a redistribution of social benefits? Considering these and other questions of reparative justice will add some heft to our thinking about modern slavery, especially its post-conflict stage.

Notes

1 This quotation is taken from a report by the US Department of Justice Foreign Claims Settlement Commission, "German Compensation for National Socialist Crimes," in Roy L. Brooks, *When Sorry Isn't Enough: The Controversy over Apologies and Reparations for Human Injustice* (New York: New York University Press, 1999), 61.

2 Article 3(a) of the Protocol to Prevent, Suppress and Punish Trafficking in Persons, Especially Women and Children, Supplementing the United Nations Convention Against Transnational Organized Crime, G.A. Res. 55/25, U.N. Doc. A/RES/55/25, Annex II, at 32–33 (15 November 2000) (Trafficking Protocol), for example, defines "trafficking in persons" to mean "the recruitment, transportation, transfer, harboring or receipt of persons, by means of the threat or use of force or other forms of coercion, of abduction, of fraud, of deception, of the abuse of power or of a position of vulnerability or of the giving or receiving of payments or benefits to achieve the consent of a person having control over another person, for the purpose of exploitation. Exploitation shall include, at a minimum, the exploitation of the prostitution of others or other forms of sexual exploitation, forced labor or services, slavery or practices similar to slavery, servitude or the removal of organs." Article 3(b) provides that

> [t]he consent of a victim of trafficking in persons to the intended exploitation set forth in subparagraph (a) of this article shall be irrelevant where any of the means set forth in subparagraph (a) have been used. Article 3 (c) and (d) specifically deal with children, the former stating that "[t]he recruitment, transportation, transfer, harboring or receipt of a child for the purpose of exploitation shall be considered 'trafficking in persons' even if this does not involve any of the means set forth in subparagraph (a) of this article"; and the latter defining "child" to "mean any person under eighteen years of age."

The international community has, in fact, recognized the injustice of such acts a long time ago. As early as 1930, for example, the International Labor Organization (ILO) provided in Article 1.1 of the 1930 Forced Labor Convention, 28 June 1930, 39 UNTS 55, that "each Member of the International Labour Organization which ratifies this Convention undertakes to suppress the use of forced or compulsory labour in all its forms within the shortest possible period." The ILO has returned to the matter in follow-up reports. See, *inter alia*, ILO, "A Global Alliance against Forced Labour," 2005, available at http://www.ilo.org/public/english/standards/relm/ilc/ilc93/pdf/rep-i-b.pdf (accessed 9 October 2016).

As for non-governmental organizations (NGOs), see, *inter alia*, *Anti-Slavery International*, http://www.antislavery.org/english/slavery_today/what_is_modern_slavery.aspx (accessed 9 October 2016); UN Gift, "Human Trafficking: The Facts," *UN Global Contract*, https://www.unglobalcompact.org/docs/issues_doc/labour/Forced_labour/HUMAN_TRAFFICKING_-_THE_FACTS_-_final.pdf (accessed 11 April 2011). See generally "The Cost of Coercion: Executive Summary of 2009 Global Report on Forced Labour," *International Labour Organization*, http://www.ilo.

org/wcmsp5/groups/public/@dgreports/@dcomm/documents/genericdocument/
wcms_106200.pdf (accessed 11 May 2009), 3.

3 For example, consistent with the definition provided by the Trafficking Protocol,
   the US government lists a number of acts that constitute modern slavery, including
   "involuntary servitude," "commercial sex," "debt bondage," and "forced labor." See
   Victims of Trafficking and Violence Protection Act, 2000, PL 106-386 (Victims of
   Trafficking Act). Within the United States, some states have passed laws to deal with
   modern slavery within state borders. These laws employ essentially the same definition as federal law. See, for example, Jessica E. Ozalp, "Halting Modern Slavery in the
   Midwest: The Potential of Wisconsin Act 116 to Improve the State and Federal
   Response to Human Trafficking," *Wisconsin Law Review* 2009 (2009): 1391. A pleth-
   ora of laws (conventions, resolutions, and agreements) have been enacted in Europe
   to combat modern slavery so defined. Two of the most important are the Convention
   on Action against Trafficking in Human Beings, 16 May 2005, ETS 197, and Protocol
   no. 8 for the Protection of Human Rights and Fundamental Freedoms, 19 March
   1985, 1604 UNTS 271. For a discussion of other countries, see, for example, Roza
   Pati, "State's Positive Obligations with Respect to Human Trafficking: The European
   Court of Human Rights Breaks New Ground in Rantsev v. Cyprus and Russia,"
   Buffalo University International Law Journal 29 (2011): 79; Virginia Mantouvalou,
   "Modern Slavery: The UK Response," *Industrial Law Journal* 39, 4 (2010): 425; Anna
   Gekht, "Shared but Differentiated Responsibility: Integration of International
   Obligations in Fight against Trafficking in Human Beings," *Denver Journal of
   International Law and Policy* 37 (2008): 29.

4 Kevin Bales defines modern slavery as "a relationship in which one person is controlled by another through violence, the threat of violence, or psychological coercion, has lost free will and free movement, is exploited economically [for other
   people's profit], and is paid nothing beyond subsistence." Kevin Bales, *Modern
   Slavery: The Secret World of 27 Million People* (Oxford: Oneworld Publications,
   2009), 31. See, for example, Kathleen Kim, "The Coercion of Trafficked Workers,"
   Iowa Law Review 96 (2011): 409; Lukas Knott, "Unocal Revisited: On the Difference
   Between Slavery and Forced Labor in International Law," *Wisconsin International
   Law Journal* 28 (2010): 201. For a general discussion, see Silvia Scarpa, *Trafficking in
   Human Beings: Modern Slavery* (New York: Oxford University Press, 2008).

5 See Trafficking Protocol, Article 3.

6 See US Department of State, *Trafficking in Persons Report*, June 2006, http://www.
   state.gov/documents/organization/66086.pdf (accessed 9 October 2016). Regarding
   cross-border trafficking, see Bales, *Modern Slavery* 35.

7 Spring Valley Citizens Association, Human Trafficking Forum, 16 June 2011,
   Spring Valley, CA.

8 For a similar discussion, see Anna Gekht, "Shared but Differentiated Responsibility:
   Integration of International Obligations in Fight against Trafficking in Human
   Beings," *Denver Journal of International Law and Policy* 37 (2008): 29.

9 For example, the Trafficking Protocol defines "trafficking in persons" as "recruit-ment, transportation, transfer, harboring or receipt ... for the purpose of exploita-tion." Trafficking Protocol, Article 3.

10 See, for example, Moira C. Heiges, "From the Inside Out: Reforming State and Local Prostitution Enforcement to More Effectively Combat Sex Trafficking in the U.S. and Abroad," *Minnesota Law Review* 94 (2009): 428. This discusses the plight of "Leisa B.," a US citizen, "who was trafficked at the age of seventeen, when a boy-friend she met through a chat service persuaded her to move to Washington, D.C. Instead of the promised cars, clothes, and freedom, her boyfriend introduced her to a violent world of street prostitution."

11 See, for example, Heiges, "From the Inside Out"; Kathleen Kim, "The Coercion of Trafficked Workers," *Iowa Law Review* 96 (2011): 409; Barbara R. Barreno, "In Search of Guidance: An Examination of Past, Present, and Future Adjudications of Domestic Violence Asylum Claims," *Vanderbilt Law Review* 64 (2011): 225; Arthur Rizer and Sheri R. Glaser, "Breach: The National Security Implications of Human Trafficking," *Widener Law Review* 69, 17 (2011): 69; Geneva Brown, "Women and Children Last: The Prosecution of Sex Traffickers as Sex Offenders and the Need for a Sex Trafficker Registry," *Boston College Third World Law Journal* 31 (2011): 1; Virginia Mantouvalou, "Modern Slavery: The UK Response," *Industrial Law Journal* 39 (2010): 425; Gekht, "Shared but Differentiated Responsibility," 29.

12 Trafficking Protocol; Victims of Trafficking Act.

13 For a collection of these works, see generally Roy Brooks, *When Sorry Isn't Enough: Atonement and Forgiveness: A New Model for Black Reparations* (Berkeley, CA: University of California Press, 2004).

14 See, *inter alia*, Siriporn Skrobanek, Nattaya Boonpakdi, and Chutima Janthakeero, *The Traffic in Women: Human Realities of the International Sex Trade* (New York: Zed Books, 1997), 23. See generally Asia Watch and the Women's Rights Project, *A Modern Form of Slavery: Trafficking of Burmese Women and Girls into Brothels in Thailand* (New York: Human Rights Watch, 1993).

15 See "Summary of Anti-Amnesty Case: *Azanian Peoples Organization (AZAPO) and Others v. The People of South Africa*," in Brooks, *When Sorry Isn't Enough*, 477. For a more detailed discussion of the Truth and Reconciliation Commission, see gener-ally Brooks, *When Sorry Isn't Enough*, part 8 (sources collected therein).

16 Quoted in Karen Campbell-Nelson, "Liberia Is Not Just a Man Thing: Transitional Justice Lessons for Women, Peace and Security," International Center for Transitional Justice, September 2008, 11.

17 Willy Brandt, *My Life in Politics* (London: Hamish Hamilton, 1992), 200.

18 Roy Brooks, "The Age of Apology," in Brooks, *When Sorry Isn't Enough*, 3.

19 See, for example, Joint Resolution to Acknowledge the 100th Anniversary of the Overthrow of the Kingdom of Hawaii, 1993, PL 103–150; "Hawaiian Sovereignty," http://www.instanthawaii.com/cgi-bin/hawaii?Sovereignty (accessed 19 April 2011). As Hannah Reeves, a full-blooded native Hawaiian, stated in response to the

United States' formal apology for the overthrow of Hawaii: "Apology is not enough ... You must help our people." "Native Hawaiians Seek Redress for U.S. Role in Ousting Queen," *New York Times*, 11 December 1999, http://www.nytimes.com/1999/12/11/us/native-hawaiians-seek-redress-for-us-role-in-ousting-queen.html (accessed 15 April 2011).

20 Brooks, *Atonement and Forgiveness*, 156.

21 Ibid.

22 Ibid.

23 Rosewood Compensation Act, Fla. Sess. Law Serv. 94-359 (West).

24 Kenneth B. Nunn, "Rosewood," in Brooks, *When Sorry Isn't Enough*, 436.

25 See, for example, *In re Nazi Era Cases against German Defendants Litigation*, 198 FRD 429 (DNJ 2000); *Princz v Federal Republic of Germany*, 26 F.3d 1166 (DC Cir. 1994); *Burger-Fischer v Degussa AG*, 65 F. Supp. 2d 248 (DNJ 1999); *Fishel v BASF Group*, 175 FRD 525 (SD Ia. 1997); *In re Joo v Japan*, 172 F. Supp. 2d 52 (DDC 2001).

26 *In re World War II Era Japanese Forced Labor Litigation*, 164 F. Supp. 2d 1160 (ND Cal. 2001).

27 *United States v Snider*, 779 F.2d 1151, 1159 (6th Cir. 1985)

28 *Tustin Elevator & Lumber Co. v. Ryno*, 129 N.W.2d 409, 414 (Mich. 1964). Most jurisdictions require that circumstances must show that "the recipient of the benefit [was put] on notice that she (plaintiff) expected to be paid for her services." *Bellanca Corp. v Bellanca*, 169 A.2d 620, 623 (Del. 1961); *Iwanowa v Ford Motor Co.*, 67 F. Supp. 2d 424, at 471 (DNJ 1999).

29 "Restitution of Implied Contracts," in *American Jurisprudence*, vol. 66, 2nd edition (St Paul, MN: West, 1973), 945. See, for example, *Iwanowa*, 471 (cases cited therein).

30 See, for example, *Fleer Corp. v Topps Chewing Gum, Inc.*, 539 A.2d 1060, 1063 (Del. 1988).

31 William S. Anderson, ed., *Black's Law Dictionary*, 3rd edition (San Francisco: Bancroft-Whitney, 1969), 1320.

32 *Kammer Asphalt Paving Inc. v East China Township Schools*, 504 N.W.2d 635, 640 (Mich. 1993).

33 *Japanese Forced Labor Litigation*, 164 F. Supp. 2d 1153, 1182 (2001).

34 Ibid.

35 Cal. Const. art 1 (1994); Cal, Pen. Code § 181 (1977); Unfair Competition Act (UCA), Cal Bus & Prof Code §§ 17200 et seq. (1992); Cal. Code of Civ. P. § 354.6 (1999).

36 *Marbury v Madison*, 5 U.S. 137, 170 (1803).

37 Alien Torts Claims Act, 28 USC § 1350 (ATCA).

38 Ibid.

39 *Kadic v Karadzic*, 70 F.3d 232, 236 (2d Cir. 1995).

40 Torture Victim Protection Act, 28 USC § 1350 (TVPA). The TVPA was enacted in 1991 as a statutory note to the ATCA.

41 See *Japanese Forced Labor Litigation*, 1179–82. For a more detailed discussion of the ATCA, see George P. Fletcher, *Tort Liability for Human Rights Abuses* (Oxford: Hart Publishing, 2008); Julian G. Ku, "The Curious Case of Corporate Liability under the Alien Tort Statute: A Flawed System of Judicial Lawmaking," *Virginia Journal of International Law* 51 (2011): 353.

42 See Brooks, "The Age of Apology," 6.

43 Victims of Trafficking Act, s. 107(b)(1)(A), (B).

44 Ibid., s. 107(b)(1)(C)(ii)(1), which defines "severe forms of trafficking" to mean, among other things, a person "who has not attained 18 years of age."

45 Brooks, *Atonement and Forgiveness*, 141–48, 163–69.

46 Ibid., 142.

47 Ibid., 141.

48 Ibid., 168–69.

49 For a discussion of South Africa's redress process, see "South Africa," in Brooks, *When Sorry Isn't Enough*, part 8. Transitional justice is a planned response to widespread violations of human rights. It is a concerted effort to vindicate the human dignity of the victims and to promote a systemic push towards peace, reconciliation, and democracy. Transitional justice is not a special form of justice; it can be any form of justice adapted to the special circumstances of a society that seeks to transform itself after a period of pervasive human rights abuse. The transformation can take weeks or decades. See "What Is Transitional Justice," *International Center for Transitional Justice*, http://www.ictj.org/about/transitional-justice (accessed 19 August 2011). See generally Ruti G. Teitel, *Transitional Justice* (New York: Oxford University Press, 2000).

50 For a discussion of the redress legislation, see Roger Daniels, "Redress Achieved, 1983–1990," in Brooks, *When Sorry Isn't Enough*, 189.

51 There were actually two Liberian Civil Wars: 1989–1997, after which Charles Taylor was elected president in 1997, and 1997–2003, which was ignited when Liberian dissidents supported by the Guinean government attacked from Guinea. Forces loyal to Charles Taylor counterattacked from Liberia and Sierra Leone. Child soldiers were used in the Liberian armed forces as early as 1989. See, for example, Dulce Foster et al., *A House with Two Rooms: Final Report of the Truth and Reconciliation Commission of Liberia Diaspora Project* (St Paul, MN: DRI Press, 2009), 3–9, 203. See generally Alcinda Honwana, Child Soldiers in Africa (Philadelphia: University of Pennsylvania Press, 2005).

52 "[Child soldiers in Sierra Leone] suffered abduction, forced recruitment, sexual slavery and rape, amputation, mutilation, displacement, and torture. They were also forced to become perpetrators and carry out aberrations violating the rights of other civilians." See, for example, Sierra Leona Truth and Reconciliation Commission, *Witness to Truth: Report of the Sierra Leone Truth and Reconciliation Commission*, vol. 3B (2004): 234–35, 258. "During 19 years of struggle, it is estimated that between 20,000 and 25,000 children have been abducted – 12,000

since 2002." Ibid.; Euan Denholm "Uganda: Former Child Soldiers Excluded in Adulthood," http://www.assatashakur.org/forum/afrikan-world-news/11153-uganda-former-child-soldiers-excluded-adulthood.html (accessed 26 October 2016). "Boys as young as 12 years old were used as soldiers." Ibid.

53 See Sierra Leona Truth and Reconciliation Commission, *Witness to Truth*, 258–64.

54 Ibid.

55 Ibid., 318–20.

56 Ibid., 320.

57 See Roy L. Brooks, "What Price Reconciliation?," in Brooks, *When Sorry Isn't Enough*, 443.

58 See generally Asia Watch and the Women's Rights Project, *A Modern Form of Slavery: Trafficking of Burmese Women and Girls into Brothels in Thailand* (New York: Human Rights Watch, 1993).

59 See, for example, Siriporn Skrobanek, Nattaya Boonpakdi, and Chutima Janthakeero, *The Traffic in Women: Human Realities of the International Sex Trade* (New York: Zed Books, 1997), 23.

60 See Asia Watch and Women's Rights Project, *A Modern Form of Slavery*, 46. See also Skrobanek, Boonpakdi, and Janthakeero, *The Traffic in Women*, 35; Sally Cameron, "Trafficking of Women for Prostitution," in Sally Cameron and Edward Newman, eds., *Trafficking in Human$: Social, Cultural and Political Dimenstions* (New York: United Nations University Press, 2008), 81.

61 Jeremy Seabrook, *Travels in the Skin Trade: Tourism and the Sex Industry* (Sterling, VA: Pluto Press, 1996), 79.

62 Bales, *Disposable People*, 45.

63 Susan Clark, "The Impact of Prostitution and Trafficking on the Daughters of Thailand," an unpublished paper presented at Biola University, 10 December 2010, 23.

64 Seabrook, *Travels in the Skin Trade*, 79.

65 Bales, *Disposable People*, 38.

66 Cameron, "Trafficking of Women for Prostitution," 87–88.

67 David Batstone, *Not For Sale: The Return of the Global Slave Trade – and How We Can Fight It* (New York: HarperCollins Publishers, 2010), 24. See Thomas M. Steinfatt, *Working at the Bar: Sex Work and Health Communication in Thailand* (Westport, CT: Ablex Publishing, 2002), 88.

68 Batstone, *Not For Sale*, 24.

69 Leften Stavros Stavrianos, *The World to 1500: A Global History*, 6th edition (New York: Simon and Schuster, 1995), 80. I am indebted to Terry Moorhead for helping me formulate this point.

70 Ibid.

71 This is the thinking behind voluntary affirmative programs under US law. See Brooks, *Atonement and Forgiveness*, 178.

PART 3
Practice

Modern Slavery from a Management Perspective: The Role of Industry Context and Organizational Capabilities 9

Andrew Crane

The practice of modern slavery remains something of a black box. Although our understanding of the legal and institutional structures around slavery is growing,[1] and greater knowledge about the broader social, economic and political causes of slavery (such as conflict, poverty, migration, discrimination, and corruption) is emerging,[2] the deployment of slavery on the ground is, with a few notable exceptions, little understood. Nowhere is this more true than with respect to the management issues surrounding modern slavery. The adoption of slavery is, after all, an economic decision about how to manage a labour force. Why, we might ask, would an organization use an illegal practice such as slavery – with its relatively high costs of implementation and significant risks of legal and moral sanction – when other forms of labour management, with lower levels of exploitation, are available? Or if we look at it from a different angle – why do more organizations not use slavery if it is actually an economically attractive way of managing the workforce?

As has been documented elsewhere in this book, slavery remains far from just a historical artifact – contemporary forms of slavery are actively deployed across the globe in a wide range of contexts. This includes recent well-publicized cases in the West African cocoa industry,[3] the agriculture industry in Spain,[4] Uzbek cotton farming,[5] and New Zealand fishing.[6] In fact, the US Department of Labor has identified some fifty products involving significant use of forced labour across twenty-nine countries.[7] The question arises, however, as to why some industries, and some enterprises in these industries, would choose to engage in such extreme forms of labour exploitation and, perhaps more critically, how they do so given that slavery is illegal under national and international law. Although the enforcement of anti-slavery regulation remains poor in some jurisdictions, there are still numerous difficulties to overcome for any enterprise looking to utilize a slavery-based business model. In this sense, while slavery clearly represents a social and ethical challenge for contemporary society, it can also be understood as a management problem for slavery organizations. Understanding this management problem can help us move towards better ways of preventing or otherwise intervening in modern slavery practices.

To date, the embryonic literature on modern slavery has made little attempt to address these sorts of questions. Where attempts have been made to explore slavery as a business or management phenomenon, researchers have typically provided illuminating case studies of common practices but have fallen short of detailed analysis of the specific management tools and techniques used to implement slavery.[8] In fact, more attention has been paid to the tools of recruiters and traffickers rather than to the organizations at the business end that are actually practising modern slavery.

This chapter, however, is about understanding the deployment of modern slavery specifically as a management practice. The goal is to demonstrate a little of what the modern slavery literature can learn from the relevant management literature. To understand slavery through a management lens, this chapter examines the use of slavery through the two most common frames of reference in the business strategy literature. That is, slavery is examined both in terms of its strategic fit with the business environment and with the resources and capabilities necessary to institute it successfully as a business practice. The chapter starts by defining modern slavery and summarizing the business and management perspective on modern slavery thus far. Then the persistence of slavery in certain industries is explained according to how well it strategically fits with the practice of particular industry conditions. Attention is then turned to the internal capabilities and other organizational resources necessary to sustain slavery as a viable management practice in these industrial contexts. The chapter concludes with suggestions for how the insights developed in the chapter can be brought to bear on political and managerial efforts to combat slavery.

Slavery and Management

Following the abolition of slavery in most developed nations in the nineteenth and twentieth centuries, the practice of slavery has gradually transformed from an officially approved system based on legal title and ethnic distinction to a modern form of extreme labour exploitation that has been criminalized and relocated to the informal economy. This shift has made slavery more ambiguous and dynamic in the forms that it takes.[9] Although such developments pose many difficulties for any definition of slavery in the modern era, the legal designation enshrined in the 1926 League of Nations Slavery Convention is the critical reference point for contemporary interpretations of slavery. This convention defines slavery as "the status or condition of a person over whom any or all of the powers attaching to the right of ownership are exercised."[10]

The acknowledgment in the 1926 definition that modern slavery is premised on the exercise of specific powers rather than solely on formal legal title has formed the basis for most subsequent definitions of modern slavery. It is significant because slavery based on legal ownership (or chattel slavery, as it is typically referred to) is relatively rare among modern forms of slavery, given the illegality of slavery almost everywhere. Debates around modern slavery therefore typically encapsulate a range of practices involving the exercise of "powers attaching to the right of ownership." This includes forms of forced, bonded, and child labour as well as human trafficking and forced marriage.[11]

In this chapter, this conception of modern slavery is followed but with some important caveats. Specifically, given the concern with slavery as a management practice – that is, the deployment of slavery in the workplace – forced marriage is not included (since it is not strictly workplace related), and only those forms of child labour that specifically involve economic activity (for example, not child soldiers) are included. One final important distinction is the use of slavery in private versus public organizations. Given that the former accounts for approximately

80 percent of all forced labour,[12] and that the latter, such as forced labour in the military or in prisons, clearly represents a different organization of powers attached to the right of ownership, we will limit our analysis to privately imposed slavery.

Having established some important boundaries, we are still left with the task of distinguishing modern slavery from other types of labour malpractice or human rights abuse in the workplace. How, we might ask, do we identify the exercise of "powers attaching to the right of ownership"? According to the non-government organization (NG) Anti Slavery International, we need to consider four features, namely that under modern slavery people are: (1) forced to work through threat; (2) owned or controlled by an "employer," typically through mental, physical, or threatened abuse; (3) dehumanized and treated as a commodity; and (4) physically constrained or restricted in freedom of movement.

While each of these conditions must be present for us to consider an arrangement to be representative of modern slavery, they involve degrees of variability (that is, they are not strictly categorical). Indeed, in the absence of a hard legal definition, modern slavery is effectively a "multi-faceted continuum" along these dimensions.[13] In the workplace, we also need to consider an additional dimension that also needs to be present to constitute slavery, namely economic exploitation. This is typically expressed in terms of the absence of remuneration. For instance, it has been estimated that the financial costs of slavery to forced labourers in terms of the underpayment of wages amounts to something like US $19.6 billion.[14] While Yasmine Rassam states that slavery is "for purposes of extracting unpaid labor," not all modern slavery is strictly unpaid.[15] Slavery might accommodate limited financial or non-financial remuneration, but only where this is discretionary, below "living wage" levels, and subject to withholding and/or arbitrary deductions.[16] Thus, rather than unpaid labour, it is more accurate to specify an additional dimension of slavery as being (5) subject to economic exploitation through the underpayment of remuneration.

A common theme in much of the modern slavery literature is that it is in many respects a departure from "old" slavery based on race. Instead, in the "new" slavery, "the hunger for money overrides other concerns. Most slaveholders feel no need to explain or defend their chosen method of labor recruitment and management. Slavery is a very profitable business, and a good bottom line is justification enough."[17] This attention to the bottom-line benefits of modern slavery, and its positioning as a "labor recruitment and management" practice (as opposed to, say, a social or political process) might be expected to have brought to the fore a detailed analysis of the relevant management tools and techniques. However, scholarly analysis of the management of modern slavery, or modern slavery as a business practice, has to date been relatively scant. Nonetheless, there is growing interest in such phenomena, with key figures in the field such as Kevin Bales and Siddharth Kara providing some important early contributions.[18]

Bales's analysis, for example, provides critical insights into the mechanics of slavery in different regional contexts, such as in Pakistani brick kilns or Brazilian charcoal-making camps.[19] This helps to explain how debt can be accumulated and transferred in slavery operations and how recruitment and retention of slaves is carried out. Kara's analysis is more narrowly focused on the sex industry, where he provides new insight into the revenues and profits associated with slaveholding and the forces of supply and demand that sustain the practice in the global sex industry.[20]

Despite these advances, there are considerable shortcomings to some of these early analyses, and they tend to address management phenomena in rather sweeping and general terms. This is understandable given the broader set of aims of these studies and the broad-based general public audience to which they seek to appeal. However, there is clearly a case for a more sustained and sophisticated analysis of modern slavery from the perspective of management theory. Perhaps unbeknownst to modern slavery researchers, there is an entire field of research dedicated to understanding in fine-grained detail the way in which organizations are managed, why they choose particular methods of labour management, how this is embedded into their business strategy, and the impacts these decisions might have for broader society. Although the field of management studies has tended to focus on large corporations in the formal sector and effectively ignored the phenomenon of slavery, there is now growing interest in less visible and formal forms of organization.[21] For example, the theme of the 2012 meeting of the world's largest and best-known management conference, the Academy of Management Annual Conference was "the informal economy." Notwithstanding these developments, the management literature has considerable theoretical resources that can be brought to bear on the study of modern slavery that to date have been under-explored and under-used. This chapter represents one of the first fully developed attempts to do so, drawing as it does on the two principal ways of understanding organizational strategy – strategic fit and the resource-based view of organizational capabilities – in combination with a wide range of literature from a diverse set of fields – including law, economics, development studies, and slavery studies – in order to tailor insights from management to make sense of modern slavery.

Slavery and Industry Context

The proportion of the global workforce currently enslaved is estimated to be anywhere from the International Labour Organization's (ILO) relatively conservative estimate of 0.6 percent of the global workforce (based on twenty-one million slaves and a global workforce of 3.4 billion) to the Global Slavery Index's more expansive estimate of around 1.4 percent (based on forty-six million slaves). This means that despite the shock of the headline numbers, approximately 99 percent of global employment takes place without recourse to slavery. As such, slavery is a relatively unpopular form of labour practice, especially compared with other lesser forms of exploitation such as low wage labour and forced overtime. This is not to deny the severity of the problem and the impacts of modern slavery, but it does raise a number of questions about why some organizations might choose to adopt slavery, while most others do not.

From a management studies point of view, we might examine this by exploring the issue of strategic fit. Defining the appropriateness of a firm's strategy (such as the decision to utilize a slavery-based business model) in terms of its congruence or "fit" with environmental conditions is "one of the most widely shared and enduring assumptions in the strategy formulation literature."[22] Put simply, an ability to develop and deploy slavery will fit some industry contexts and not others.

The extant modern slavery literature is to some extent useful in examining these industry conditions – for example, by identifying the supply side conditions that give rise to slavery in the first place (such as poverty and migration). However, these broader social, economic, and political factors tell us little about the specifics of the industry conditions that might provide a more or less fertile context for slavery to develop. According to existing research, slavery is most prevalent in agriculture, mining and extraction, construction, and some forms of manufacturing such as brick making and carpet weaving as well as in unregulated or poorly regulated service industries, in particular, domestic work and sex work.[23] From an economic and management perspective, there are several factors that determine the attractiveness of these industries for slavery practices, namely labour intensity, value distribution, elasticity of demand, legitimacy, and regional clustering.

The decision to adopt slavery practices needs to be understood in terms of economic rationality. Most modern slavery (as with traditional slavery) will occur where labour intensity is high, especially in those industries facing a limited supply of on-site labour such as agriculture.[24] Basic industries such as agriculture, forestry, and mining are location specific, and where this location is isolated from the main sources of labour (cities, towns, villages, and so on), a high demand/low supply market for labour is created. This will tend to raise labour prices and can render small-scale operations uneconomic. Retreat to the informal sector and institutionalizing slavery through forced migration, however, can effectively lock-in low price labour. This can obviate the need for technology development, economies of scale, and other forms of cost reduction that might take place in the formal economy. A similar argument has typically been made in the context of new world slavery, where "free labour" was generally unavailable in sufficient quantities and priced at such a rate that plantation economies could only be competitively staffed through slavery.[25]

Basic industries with low technological development as well as personal service industries where labour is largely unskilled provide fertile contexts because slavery practices represent an opportunity to reduce the main costs driving profitability. Slavery will also often be associated with small-scale businesses with limited potential for capturing value. It is most likely to enter the stages of the supply chain where margins are narrow and where value is captured further downstream, often by larger and more powerful interests. One problem here is that the chain of custody for many products may be very long and often untraceable, which means that those at the beginning of the chain may not only be left with little value to claim but may also be invisible to companies further along the chain. Coffee beans, for example, may go through a multitude of organizations before ending up in a cup of brewed coffee in a café, making traceability extremely challenging. Moreover, the nature of some industries is that there are a relatively few, very large companies that effectively govern the distribution of value throughout the supply chain.[26] Big brand processed food companies, for instance, manage to capture a large amount of the value created in the supply chain of their products because there are many growers and many purchasers of their products but only a handful of competitors.[27] Slavery practices in industries such as cocoa- and cotton-growing can therefore partly be explained by industry structure and the low prices imposed on producers.

In this sense, we might conceive of "value trap slavery," whereby primary industries that have become uncompetitive due to low market prices and the high costs of existing technologies might face the necessity of coerced labour brought as close as possible to zero cost in order to survive. As such, the prevailing value distribution along the supply chain, insofar as a particular stage is associated with very low value capture, can provide significant pressure towards slavery practices. Value trap slavery is a critical phenomenon for modern slavery researchers to understand and incorporate into their analyses because, to date, there has tended to be an assumption in the literature that modern slavery in the global economy is only about high profitability. As Bales contends, "people get rich by using slaves ... This is the new slavery which focuses on big profits and cheap lives."[28] Or as Kara puts it, "slave labor makes profits soar."[29] This may be true somewhere in the supply chain, but it is most certainly not always the case for those actually deploying slavery. It is only by clearly understanding where value is captured in the supply chains where slavery is used that we can identify with any certainty where those profits are being reaped. As Raphael Kaplinsky argues, the analysis of value in the supply chain (or "value chain analysis") can help us understand why some gain and some lose from the globalization of production and exchange.[30]

In contrast, some industries using slave labour might have the potential for high profitability but face a context of high elasticity of demand coupled with a lower elasticity of supply for labour. That is, in unpleasant or illegal industries such as sex work, slavery is prompted not by limited potential for value capture but, rather, by an opportunity to substantially grow the market by lowering the price to levels at which voluntary labour leaves the market.[31] In these contexts, slavery might be viewed as an "innovation" in human resource practices that enables the opening up of new (albeit illicit) market opportunities in environments where slavery was not previously used. As Justin Webb and colleagues argue, "because formal institutions condemn the exploitation of a set of opportunities by deeming them illegal, a realm of opportunities exists for entrepreneurs willing to operate outside formal institutional boundaries."[32]

This suggests that we also need to go beyond economic rationality in explaining the influence of the industry context on the adoption of slavery practices. For instance, the legitimacy of an industry is also an important factor prompting the use of slave labour. Legitimacy is "a generalized perception or assumption that the actions of an entity are desirable, proper, or appropriate within some socially constructed system of norms, values, beliefs, and definitions."[33] Illegitimate practices (such as slavery) are more likely to persist in low legitimacy industries (such as sex work or unauthorized mining or logging) because organizations in these industries already typically seek to operate beyond the oversight of regulators and other formal institutional forces. Moreover, industries in the "renegade economy" that are judged as socially unacceptable by both formal and informal institutions (that is, as illegitimate as well as illegal) have little opportunity for gaining social legitimacy by their means of operation.[34] Their standards of conduct are governed by the institutional norms of their fellow renegades, suggesting that slavery is more likely to be perceived as appropriate.

In the same way, to the extent that we can conceive of slavery as a process "innovation," such practices are likely to become more diffuse in industries where slave operators are part of strong geographic social networks. The lack of observability of an illegal innovation such as slavery (because it remains hidden), the difficulties in trialing (because it requires an established supply network), as well as its incompatibility with existing social norms are likely to hamper its diffusion.[35] This means that "those who engage in illegal activities tend to learn about the benefits, justification, and techniques of such activities from those with whom they have more intimate, personal relationships" and with whom they share geographic proximity.[36] Thus, slavery is likely to be driven by, and in turn reflect, some level of regional clustering, as is evident, for example, in the charcoal-making industry in Brazil and in the operation of brick kilns in parts of China, Pakistan, and India. A good case in point are the brick kilns of Shanxi and Henan provinces in China, where hundreds of slave labourers were freed from illegal brickyards after police raids in 2007.[37]

Regional clustering also needs to be considered in the context of the broader geographical context in which slavery takes place. That is, slavery is more likely to take place in a physical space that is geographically isolated (such as mines, farms, or forests) and/or one that is physically, politically, or psychologically distant from the victims' normal domicile (such as recruiting a sex worker from a rural village to the city). According to the ILO, "much forced labor today is in the informal economy, in remote or hidden locations in developing and industrialized countries alike."[38]

Slavery Management Capabilities

Given the range of external industry conditions outlined above, slavery can take a range of forms and may be deployed in a number of different business models.[39] However, to develop a deeper understanding of how slavery is enabled within organizations, we need to identify the unique set of organizational capabilities that explain how enterprises successfully deploy slavery as a management practice despite a context characterized by widespread illegality and public opprobrium. An organizational capability is defined as "a firm's ability to perform repeatedly a productive task which relates either directly or indirectly to a firm's capacity for creating value through effecting the transformation of inputs into outputs."[40] Capabilities have primarily been used to explain how organizations develop and maintain a competitive advantage through access to unique resources. Here, we are concerned with the activity-related capabilities that together will form an integrated architecture of knowledge about how to successfully make slavery "work" despite its highly unethical and illegal character.

Labour Supply Chain Management

Accessing a suitable supply of labour is critical for the success of enterprises that employ slavery practices. Given that recruitment into slavery is clandestine and that, by definition, workers will not voluntarily enter the market for slave labour, enterprises need to access a suitable slave labour supply. Much like the supply chain of physical products, the supply of the "commodity" of slave labour typically comprises a multi-tier chain that involves distinct stages. In the broadest sense, these stages comprise: recruitment (where individuals are coerced or deceived into entering the supply chain); trafficking (where individuals are transferred to, and prepared for, the workplace); and deployment (where they are actually put to work). The trafficking stage may in itself involve multiple stages of buying and reselling, and various intermediaries including agents and brokers, especially in international trafficking.[41]

The supply of slaves is therefore often characterized by a network or syndicate form of organization sustained by an ordered system of relationships among the actors concerned.[42] This "oligopoly of well-organized and profitable networks of intermediaries"[43] may be more or less coupled with the enterprises actually involved in the deployment of slaves.[44] Hence, the success of these enterprises will be heavily dependent on their ability to access or build a network that can provide a suitable supply of labour (without attracting undue external scrutiny) and is efficient in terms of minimizing costs despite the complexity of the network. A competence in labour supply chain management is therefore critical to providing an affordable supply of labour. This is particularly important in the case of "value trap slavery" since businesses are already operating with very narrow margins.

Supply networks for slaves not only require substantial coordination but also cooperation and trust: "Illegal exchanges tend to take place within preexisting networks of information and exchange capable of guaranteeing the trustworthiness of the parties and of creating favorable conditions to the successful conclusion of criminal transactions."[45]

Raab and Milward take this further and suggest that "every illegal activity that needs continuing coordination is based on ties of trust that were often formed long before the illegal activity started."[46] These networks therefore routinely rely on some form of collective identity, such as shared ethnicity.[47] Many trafficking rings, for example, are based around ethnic bonds.[48] This can substitute for formal institutions in enforcing the rules and norms that facilitate the supply of slave labour.

Shared ethnicity and other forms of collective identity can also help to reduce the substantial transaction and coordination costs that are involved in accessing a suitable supply of slaves. Extant studies of the business of slavery that highlight its high profitability tend to focus primarily on the low labour costs associated with slavery. However, this is often accompanied by an under-estimation of the high costs of acquisition that can be embedded in the supply network. Hence, Kara acknowledges that the "the level of complexity and coordination among these crime groups [dealing in sex trafficking] is astounding," and he points out that "acquisition costs are low" because "slaves are easy to procure, easy to transport."[49] The point is that such high levels of coordination lead to high costs. Put simply, "transaction costs in covert networks are higher than those in overt networks."[50] This is why alternative forms of organization – such as trust networks based on shared identity – need to be developed and why a slave operator's ability to access this low cost resource will be dependent on his or her ability to exploit or substitute for a shared identity with the labour supply network. A shared ethnic identity can also act as a "defense mechanism" in that it makes the network as a whole more cohesive and difficult to penetrate by law enforcers.[51] Thus, a capability for labour supply chain management involves the creation or exploitation of collective identity that builds trust with network members, reduces costs, and increases opacity to outsiders.

Debt Management

Most slavery, whether entered into by force, subterfuge, sale, or inherited debt bondage, is enabled through a process of debt management. By definition, workers do not willingly enter into slavery-type relationships but will frequently be corralled into such arrangements through indebtedness. By indebting potential workers, enterprises are able to create debt/labour "contracts" that are enforceable by coercion.[52] This is most obviously the case with bonded labour (or debt bondage), whereby labour is directly exchanged to repay a loan, but other forms of slavery also typically make use of some degree of debt management. Research by the ILO has consistently shown that the manipulation of debt is a critical factor in trapping vulnerable workers into forced labour situations.[53] An organizational capability for debt management in a slavery business essentially facilitates two main activities – rapid debt accrual and debt transferral.

Rapid debt accrual refers to the way in which slavery-based enterprises typically establish, in a short space of time, substantial financial liability on the part of their workers in order to reinforce control. This can occur both at the level of the individual organization and through the network of organizations involved in the slavery supply chain. Ordinarily, slavery begins with a financial advance or loan, which then swiftly escalates to levels that the slave cannot hope to repay except through a long period of indenture. This rapid escalation may be achieved in four main ways: (1) high and often opaque personal relocation costs associated with trafficking or other movement from the slave's home to the labour site; (2) frequent resale and/or debt trading through the slavery network to inflate the value of the debt; (3) high-priced, monopoly-supplied subsistence (food and shelter) at the labour site; and (4) super-premium rates of interest on the original loan plus the costs of transfer and subsistence. These debt escalation techniques have been widely identified in case studies of slavery. For example, Bales recounts the story of Siri, a fifteen-year-old Thai girl sold into prostitution by her parents for 50,000 baht (about US $1,630):

> Siri's debt of 50,000 baht rapidly escalated.[54] Taken south by the broker, Siri was sold for 100,000 baht to the brothel where she now works. After her rape and beating Siri was informed that the debt she must repay, now to the brothel, equaled 200,000 baht. In addition, Siri learned of other payments she would be required to make, including rent for her room at 30,000 baht per month as well as charges for food and drink, fees for medicine and fines if she did not work hard enough or displeased a customer.

Debt transferral ensures that the rapidly accrued debts of slaves have liquidity throughout the slavery supply chain (so that slaves can be easily bought and sold) and do not disappear if the original debtor falls ill, dies, or disappears. Slave operators usually establish clear (though commonly unwritten) protocols on debt transferral (for example, to the slave's family members) as a way of prohibiting default and departure. This enables the exercise of control over the slave on an ongoing basis and, in the case of debt bondage, inter-generationally.

Accounting Opacity

In historical studies of new world slavery, accounting practices have been revealed to have played a significant role in the institutionalization of slavery and in the commodification, dehumanization, and social control of slaves.[55] That is, accounts were used to value slaves in financial terms (without any concern for their innate human worth), to facilitate transactions, secure bank loans, and measure efficiency. In modern slavery, accounting has some similar effects, but its critical roles are in establishing control over the workforce and insulating slave operators from the scrutiny of more legitimate value chain members. This securing of control and avoidance of meaningful oversight is facilitated by developing a capability for opaque accounting.

Opaque accounting is the ability to deliberately distort accounting records in ways that are obscure or unclear to users. Usually, it refers to accounts presented to investors and auditors, such as in the case of the Enron collapse.[56] However, in the slavery context, we are primarily concerned with opaque accounting to workers and other companies. Slave operators can inflate workers' debts by constructing false accounts of debts and deductions and may even compel workers to sign account books verifying debts that they have not seen or do not fully understand.[57] This opacity prevents labourers from knowing what their debt obligations are or even how much they are being charged for expenses and interest payments. Thus, the size of the debt and the termination of the labour/debt contract can remain entirely in the hands of employers, further cementing their control over the labourers.

A capability in accounting opacity can also prevent legitimate up or downstream value chain members from knowing about, exercising responsibility for, or acting upon illegal slavery practices. Companies may seek to enhance, or substitute, public governance with private action, such as monitoring supply chain conformance with core labour standards. False accounts of labour costs and relationships and sham labour contracts may be deployed to provide a sheen of legitimacy and avoid scrutiny.[58]

Access and Deployment of Violence

Perhaps the most essential capability for effecting slavery is the ability to access, and at least potentially deploy, physical and/or psychological violence. As stated earlier, the threat of violence is a definitional condition of modern slavery. Without it, labour practices may be inhumane and exploitative but would not constitute slavery because the victim would have the opportunity to exercise their freedom and walk away. Access to violence is even more important in modern slavery compared with more traditional types of slavery because it enables slave operators to enforce contracts. In "old" slavery, the enforcement of slavery "contracts" could also rely on legal means. The illegality of modern slavery means that slave operators lack the security of legal title and thus rely almost exclusively on the threat of violence to enforce working arrangements and debt/labour contracts. Moreover, in illegal markets such as prostitution or the trafficking of illegal immigrants, organizations with ready access to violence have a comparative advantage because the victims of violence have no legal recourse.[59]

Modern slave operators, however, do not necessarily have to deploy violence. In demonstrating an effective capability for accessing violence over a period of time, they can build "reputational capital" that prevents opportunistic behaviour from slaves seeking liberation or workload reductions.[60] This reputational capital might be built through plant-level acts of violence or, in the case of syndicate or organized crime networks, may be accumulated at the level of the labour supply network. Indeed, as economic analyses of organized crime have shown, provided the threat of violence is credible, contracts in the world of organized crime are typically self-enforced.[61] However, violence is not a zero-cost, or, necessarily, an easily accessible, resource. Organizations need to balance the deployment of violence against slaves (to enforce contracts and build reputational capital) with the costs in terms of injuries to labourers, remuneration to enforcement personnel, and the potential for heightened attention from law enforcers.

Moral Legitimization

Modern slavery is an extreme and, to most, an unconscionable form of human exploitation. However, those deploying slavery need to ensure that it is at least minimally accepted within and around the organization, including among the leadership, any non-slave employees (such as supervisors and security personnel), enslaved workers (so that they do not rebel), and any clients of the organization with whom it does business that are necessarily exposed to the practice (such as delivery staff). A capability for moral legitimization of slavery among these constituencies is therefore critical.

A capability for legitimizing unethical acts in organizations involves the creation of an amoral landscape within a particular microcommunity. This "amoralization" process is effective[62] when it provides rationalizations that justify the unethical practice and enables the socialization of new members into the practice.[63] According to Vikas Anand and colleagues, rationalizations are mental strategies that "individuals use to neutralize their negative feelings or regrets about their behavior."[64] Slavery operators may legitimize the practice by rationalizations such as the "denial of victim" (for example, arguing that the violated party deserved it), "social weighting" (for example, claiming that others are worse perpetrators), or "appeal to higher loyalties" (for example, by asserting that it is what the boss wants). The repetition of these rationalizations within a context of moral muteness helps to normalize slavery and reframe it as a less morally significant practice.[65]

The socialization of members into the amoral universe of the organization may take a variety of forms from cooption using rewards to an incremental escalation of involvement in unethical behaviour.[66] For example, evidence suggests that slave operators often "reward" former slaves with positions as supervisors and recruiters, thereby coopting victims into perpetrators.[67] Moreover, the stigma of slavery as "dirty work" may in itself foster group cohesion and cultural bonds among those involved in the practice.[68] This action can in turn prompt and sustain an internalization of the amoral universe of the organization among members.

Domain Maintenance

Slave operators employ illegal methods for achieving their goals (whether the goals are illegal or legal). Therefore, it is essential to develop a capability not only to manage internal audiences but also to sustain "domain maintenance," defined by Barry Baysinger as management practices designed to "challenge threats to the methods by which organizational goals and purposes are pursued, especially those posed by government."[69]

Threats to slave operators' methods come from a variety of sources but most critical are local law enforcement officials and politicians. National slavery laws and international agreements on human rights prohibit slavery. However, there is considerable variation in the extent to which these are manifested into effective coercive sanctions because of heterogeneity in the strength of governance in different contexts. Governance here refers to government effectiveness, regulatory quality, rule of law, political stability, control of corruption, and voice and accountability to citizens.[70] Where these are lacking, there is a greater propensity for slavery to thrive. Hence, given that the regulatory context is an important condition enabling slavery, the ability to secure support within the non-market environment by undermining governance is a critical success factor for enterprises using slavery.

According to David Baron, the non-market environment consists of "the social, political, and legal arrangements that structure the firm's interactions outside of, and in conjunction with, markets."[71] He argues that to be effective a firm's non-market strategy needs to complement its market strategy. In the context of a labour market strategy of forced slavery, a complementary strategy within the non-market environment is likely to involve the securing of support through bribes and other forms of inducement, which are important tactics for managing certain political risks.[72] More broadly, ongoing domain maintenance also helps sustain an institutional logic around the acceptability and legitimacy of slavery within the local environment, especially those rooted in collective identity and shared ethnicity.[73]

A capability for domain maintenance is important not only as a way of buying favour among key stakeholders within the non-market environment but also of raising interdependence and sharing risk with non-market actors. This arises from the extension of the use of illegitimate methods. That is, by using inducements to bribe public officials, slave operators can enlist officials in methods that are themselves illegal. This creates a degree of shared risk in facing exposure and a common interest in protecting the enterprise and its activities from third party scrutiny. In this way, interdependence between slave operators and law enforcement is fostered, creating what Kathy Richards terms a "symbiotic relationship" between corruption and slavery.[74] In fact, some operators succeed in enlisting non-market actors in more direct forms of participation in their illegitimate methods, such as employing police officers to act as security guards. For instance, Bales documents examples of local police acting as "slave catchers and brutal enforcers" in countries such as Thailand and Pakistan.[75] Thus, a capability for domain maintenance might involve both "transactional" strategies (for example, paying bribes) and "relational" strategies (for example, employing public servants) in managing the non-market environment.[76]

Conclusion

Modern slavery represents an emerging stream of interdisciplinary literature, yet, to date, it has afforded relatively little detailed or systematic attention to the business and management issues involved. This chapter has sought to begin to redress this lacuna in the literature by providing an analysis of industry context factors (to specify the conditions that give rise to the deployment of modern slavery), along with an exploration of micro-level factors (that reveal the specific capabilities that enterprises need in order to make this deployment work). A combination of an accommodating industry context, coupled with appropriate micro-level capabilities, can explain why and how slavery might be adopted as a management practice even though it is ethically and legally proscribed.

For governments (at various levels), NGOs, and companies, there are a number of policy and practice implications that emerge from this analysis, assuming that such actors might wish to reduce the incidence of modern slavery. Beyond the obvious need for enhanced enforcement of slavery regulation, governmental regional and industrial policy can clearly also play a role – for example, by providing assistance and access to technological development for industries and regions likely to be slavery-risk areas. As the empirical research of Peter Lund-Thomsen and colleagues demonstrates, "economic, technological and social upgrading" generates "sustained improvements in real wages and workers conditions" among low-skilled workers in developing countries.[77] This is often associated with a shift to factory-based production and other forms of larger-scale industrial organization that may help to limit some forms of slavery but would be unsuitable for addressing slavery in industries less suited to technological development, such as personal services. Incentives and sanctions of other kinds can also be used to encourage operations in at-risk industries to enter the formal sector, such as entrepreneurship outreach and support, subsidies, tax incentives, and relocation incentives.

Industrial upgrading can also be incentivized with low-cost loans and other forms of micro-credit for small businesses in at-risk sectors. The availability of affordable and accessible micro-credit has been identified as a potentially important factor in the supply side of slavery in that it dampens the causal relationship between poverty and slavery.[78] That is, access to credit on reasonable terms can obviate the risk/opportunity equation for those targeted by slavery recruiters and can offer a buffer from engaging in debt bondage. For example, international organizations have encouraged micro-credit schemes in countries with persistent debt bondage problems.[79] However, micro-credit also has a potential role to play in the business of slavery in that, to the extent that it enables greater investment in production technology, it can help shift micro-enterprises towards lower cost production through means other than labour cost minimization.

The problem of value-trap slavery is one that various actors can also seek to address. Governments can focus industrial policy on building the infrastructure for higher value-added work in at-risk regions, such as processing and refining, rather than simply growing and extraction. Similarly companies and NGOs can also help foster new higher value-added businesses. A good example is the charity Not for Sale, which in 2012 announced the development of a new business producing a beverage, REBBL, based on ingredients sourced from at-risk communities in the Peruvian Amazon.[80]

Companies further along the supply chain can also target their corporate social responsibility programs on ensuring that more value is realized by vulnerable actors in the supply chain. One way of achieving this is through "fair trade" arrangements where guaranteed prices are paid to growers. Supplier codes of conduct and other forms of labour rights enforcement can also be used by companies to ensure that basic labour standards are adhered to, thereby supplementing public governance with private action.[81] Increasing attention is also being afforded to "shared value" arrangements that focus on expanding the total pool of value that is created by supply chain members.[82] For example, a shared value perspective in basic agriculture "focuses on improving growing techniques and strengthening the local cluster of supporting suppliers and other institutions in order to increase farmers' efficiency, yields, product quality, and sustainability. This leads to a bigger pie of revenue and profits that benefits both farmers and the companies that buy from them."[83] Some cocoa companies have taken this approach in West Africa, where assistance to growers from branded confectionary companies such as Kraft and Mars – in the form of new technologies, crop yield techniques, and fairer trading arrangements – has been aimed at tackling industry conditions that create a fertile context for slavery.[84]

The analysis presented in this chapter also suggests that directly tackling slavery operators will require a concerted effort to erode the foundations of their strength, namely labour supply chain management, debt management, access and deployment of violence, accounting opacity, moral legitimization, and domain maintenance. For instance, a capability for debt management can be undermined with better education for those at risk about the types of practices used by slave recruiters and operators as well as the instigation of communication channels so that those targeted can seek advice and support. Accounting opacity can be partially tackled with better and more comprehensive financial oversight, while a capability for domain maintenance can be undermined with more vigorous anti-corruption measures and better salaries and training for law enforcement personnel. None of these actions by themselves will eradicate slavery, but without developing a more thorough understanding of how the worst forms of human exploitation are made possible, we cannot hope to avert them. Targeting the slavery management capabilities of slavery enterprises represents a critical piece of this puzzle.

Clearly, however, even from the perspective of understanding the business and management issues surrounding modern slavery, a great deal of further work remains to be done. While this chapter has focused attention on the enterprise level, and on the contexts and capabilities associated with the deployment of modern slavery, further insight is especially necessary with respect to the various supply chain issues, both in terms of the labour supply chain and the product supply chains in which slave labour is implicated. It is hoped that the theoretical analysis presented in this chapter can inform future research on modern slavery as well as other forms of labour abuse and illegal business practices. The chapter includes the identification of a number of empirically testable relationships – for instance, between industry context factors and the incidence of slavery in those industries. However as Roger Plant suggests, rigorous statistical work on modern slavery "is barely beginning,"[85] not least because of the difficulties in collecting high quality and comparable data among "hidden populations."[86] Nonetheless, case studies of bonded labour[87] and human trafficking[88] have demonstrated the potential, and the challenges, in developing more empirically grounded insights into the business of slavery, and it is hoped that this volume will inspire further work in this vein.

Notes

Acknowledgment: This chapter draws from and adapts material previously published in A. Crane, "Modern Slavery as a Management Practice: Exploring the Conditions and Capabilities of Human Explitation," *Academy of Management Review* 38, 1 (2013): 49-69.

1 See, for example, J. Allain, "The Definition of Slavery in International Law," *Howard Law Journal* 52, 2 (2009): 239–76; B. Azmy, "Unshackling the Thirteenth Amendment: Modern Slavery and a Reconstructed Civil Rights Agenda," *Fordham Law Review* 71 (2002): 981–1062; J.F. Quirk, "The Anti-Slavery Project: Linking the Historical and Contemporary," *Human Rights Quarterly* 28, 3 (2006): 565–98; A.Y. Rassam, "Contemporary Forms of Slavery and the Evolution of the Prohibition of Slavery and the Slave Trade under Customary International Law," *Virginia Journal of International Law* 39 (1998): 303–52.

2 See, for example, F. Laczko and E. Gozdziak, eds., *Data and Research on Human Trafficking: A Global Survey* (Geneva: International Organization for Migration, 2005); R. Plant, "Forced Labour, Slavery and Poverty Reduction: Challenges for Development Agencies," presentation to UK High-Level Conference to Examine the Links between Poverty, Slavery and Social Exclusion, Foreign and Commonwealth Office and Department for International Development, London, 2007; K. Richards, "The Trafficking of Migrant Workers: What Are the Links between Labour Trafficking and Corruption?" *International Migration* 42, 5 (2004): 147–68.

3 British Broadcasting Corporation, "Tracing the Bitter Truth of Chocolate and Child Labour," *Panorama*, 2010, http://news.bbc.co.uk/panorama/hi/front_page/newsid_8584000/8584847.stm (accessed 25 January 2011).

4 F. Lawrence, "Spain's Salad Growers are Modern-Day Slaves, Say Charities," *The Guardian*, 7 February 2011, http://www.theguardian.com/business/2011/feb/2007/spain-salad-growers-slaves-charities (accessed 25 January 2011).

5 A. Kelley, "Uzbekistan Ban on Child Labour Forces More Adults into Cotton Workforce" *The Guardian*, 14 November 2014, https://www.theguardian.com/global-development/2014/nov/14/uzbekistan-ban-child-labour-forces-adults-cotton-work (accessed 28 October 2016).

6 E.B. Skinner, "Slaves Put Squid on US Dining Tables from South Pacific Catch," *Bloomberg Businessweek*, 2012, http://www.bloomberg.com/news/articles/2012-02-23/slaves-put-squid-on-u-s-dining-tables-from-south-pacific-catch (accessed 25 March 2012).

7 US Department of Labor, *The Department of Labor's List of Goods Produced by Child Labor or Forced Labor* (Washington, DC: US Department of Labor, 2009).

8 For example see, S. Kara, *Sex Trafficking: Inside the Business of Modern Slavery* (New York: Columbia University Press, 2009).

9 Quirk, "The Anti-Slavery Project."

10 Cited in D. Weissbrodt and Anti-Slavery International, *Abolishing Slavery and Its Contemporary Forms* (New York: United Nations, 2002), 4.

11 For example see Azmy, "Unshackling the Thirteenth Amendment"; Weissbrodt and Anti-Slavery International, *Abolishing Slavery and Its Contemporary Forms*.

12 P. Belser, M.D. Cock, and F. Mehra, *ILO Minimum Estimate of Forced Labour in the World* (Geneva: International Labour Office, 2005).

13 Quirk, "The Anti-Slavery Project," 577.

14 International Labour Organization (ILO). *The Cost of Coercion: International Labour Conference*, Report I(B) (Geneva: ILO, 2009).

15 A.Y. Rassam, "International Law and Contemporary Forms of Slavery: An Economic and Social Rights-Based Approach," *Penn State International Law Review* 23, 4 (2004): 817.

16 See B. Andrees, *Forced Labour and Trafficking in Europe: How People Are Trapped In, Live Through and Come Out* (Geneva: International Labour Office, 2008), 25.

17 K. Bales, *Disposable People: New Slavery in the Global Economy*, revised edition (Berkeley, CA: University of California Press, 2004), 10.

18 Ibid.; Kara, *Sex Trafficking*.

19 Bales, *Disposable People*.

20 Kara, *Sex Trafficking*.

21 B. Cooke, "The Denial of Slavery in Management Studies," *Journal of Management Studies* 40, 8 (2003): 1895–1918.

22 E.J. Zajac, M.S. Kraatz, and R.K.F. Bresser, "Modeling the Dynamics of Strategic Fit: A Normative Approach to Strategic Change." *Strategic Management Journal* 21, 4 (2000): 429.

23 Bales, *Disposable People*; ILO, *The Cost of Coercion*; Richards, "Trafficking of Migrant Workers."

24 E.D. Domar, "The Causes of Slavery or Serfdom: A Hypothesis," *Journal of Economic History* 30, 1 (1970): 18–32.

25 G. Wright, *Slavery and American Economic Development* (Baton Rouge, LA: Louisiana State University Press, 2006).

26 R. Kaplinsky, "Spreading the Gains from Globalization: What Can Be Learned from Value-Chain Analysis?" *Problems of Economic Transition* 47, 2 (2004): 74–115.

27 R. Patel, *Stuffed and Starved: The Hidden Battle for the World's Food System* (Toronto: HarperCollins, 2007).

28 Bales, *Disposable People*, 4.

29 Kara, *Sex Trafficking*, 22.

30 Kaplinsky, "Spreading the Gains from Globalization."

31 See, for example, Kara, *Sex Trafficking*.

32 J.W. Webb et al., "You Say Illegal, I Say Legitimate: Entrepreneurship in the Informal Economy," *Academy of Management Review* 34, 3 (2009): 493.

33 M.C. Suchman, "Managing Legitimacy: Strategic and Institutional Approaches," *Academy of Management Review* 20, 3 (1995): 574.

34 See Webb et al., "You Say Illegal, I Say Legitimate."

35 E.M. Rogers, *Diffusion of Innovations*, 5th edition (New York: Free Press, 2003); J. Salt and J. Stein, "Migration as a Business: The Case of Trafficking," *International Migration* 35, 4 (1997): 467–94.

36 P.J. Snyder, R.L. Priem, and E. Levitas, "The Diffusion of Illegal Innovations among Management Elites," paper presented at the Academy of Management Annual Conference, Chicago, 2009.

37 A. Lorenz, "Combing the Brickyards for the Disappeared," *Spiegel Online*, 2007, http://www.spiegel.de/international/world/a-499877.html (accessed 25 March 2012).

38 Plant, "Forced Labour, Slavery and Poverty Reduction," 7.

39 L. Shelley, "Trafficking in Women: The Business Model Approach," *Brown Journal of World Affairs* 10, 1 (2003): 119–31.

40 R.M. Grant, "Toward a Knowledge-Based Theory of the Firm," *Strategic Management Journal* 17, 10 (1996): 377.

41 Andrees, *Forced Labour and Trafficking in Europe*; Kara, *Sex Trafficking*; Shelley, "Trafficking in Women."

42 Salt and Stein, "Migration as a Business."

43 G. Friebel and S. Guriev, "Smuggling Humans: A Theory of Debt-Financed Migration," *Journal of the European Economic Association* 4, 6 (2006): 1096.

44 Shelley, "Trafficking in Women."

45 L. Paoli, "The Paradoxes of Organized Crime," *Crime, Law and Social Change* 37, 1 (2002): 85.

46 J. Raab and H.B. Milward, "Dark Networks as Problems," *Journal of Public Administration Research and Theory* 13, 4 2003): 430.

47 Webb et al., "You Say Illegal, I Say Legitimate."

48 Shelley, "Trafficking in Women."

49 Kara, *Sex Trafficking*.

50 Raab and Milward, "Dark Networks as Problems," 432.

51 A. Schloenhardt, "Organized Crime and the Business of Migrant Trafficking," *Crime, Law and Social Change* 32, 3 (1999): 203–33.

52 Friebel and Guriev, "Smuggling Humans."

53 ILO, *The Cost of Coercion*.

54 Bales, *Disposable People*, 41.

55 R.K. Fleischman and T.N. Tyson, "Accounting in Service to Racism: Monetizing Slave Property in the Antebellum South," *Critical Perspectives on Accounting* 15, 3 (2004): 376–99.

56 J. Sarra, "Rose-Colored Glasses, Opaque Financial Reporting, and Investor Blues: Enron as Con and the Vulnerability of Canadian Corporate Law," *St John's Law Review* 76 (2002): 715–66.

57 D.K. Androff, "The Problem of Contemporary Slavery: An International Human Rights Challenge for Social Work," *International Social Work* 54, 2 (2011): 209–22.

58 Bales, *Disposable People*.

59 G.S. Becker, "Crime and Punishment: An Economic Approach," *Journal of Political Economy* 76 (1968): 169–217.

60 See A.R. Dick, "When Does Organized Crime Pay? A Transaction Cost Analysis," *International Review of Law and Economics* 15 (1995): 25–45.

61 Ibid.; N. Garoupa, "The Economics of Organized Crime and Optimal Law Enforcement," *Economic Inquiry* 38, 2 (2000): 278–88.

62 See A. Crane, "Corporate Greening as Amoralization," *Organization Studies* 21, 4 (2000): 673–96.

63 V. Anand, B.E. Ashforth, and M. Joshi, "Business as Usual: The Acceptance and Perpetuation of Corruption in Organizations," *Academy of Management Executive* 18, 2 (2004): 39–53.

64 Ibid., 40.

65 F.B. Bird and J.A. Waters, "The Moral Muteness of Managers," *California Management Review* 32, 1 (1989): 73–88.

66 Anand, Ashforth, and Joshi, "Business as Usual."

67 Bales, *Disposable People.*

68 B.E. Ashforth and G.E. Kreiner, "'How Can You Do It?': Dirty Work and the Challenge of Constructing a Positive Identity," *Academy of Management Review* 24, 3 (1999): 413–34.

69 B.D. Baysinger, "Domain Maintenance as an Objective of Business Political Activity: An Expanded Typology," *Academy of Management Review* 9, 2 (1984): 249.

70 D. Kaufmann, A. Kraay, and M. Mastruzzi, *The Worldwide Governance Indicators: Methodology and Analytical Issues,* Policy Research Working Paper 5430 (Washington, DC: World Bank, 2010).

71 D.P. Baron, "Integrated Strategy: Market and Nonmarket Components," *California Management Review* 37, 2 (1995): 48.

72 B.D. Keillor, T.J. Wilkinson, and D. Owens, "Threats to International Operations: Dealing with Political Risk at the Firm Level," *Journal of Business Research* 58, 5 (2005): 629–35.

73 V.F. Misangyi, G. Weaver, and H. Elms, "Ending Corruption: The Interplay among Institutional Logics, Resources, and Institutional Entrepreneurs," *Academy of Management Review* 33 (2008): 750–70.

74 Richards, "The Trafficking of Migrant Workers," 147.

75 Bales, *Disposable People,* 245.

76 A.J. Hillman and M.A. Hitt, "Corporate Political Strategy Formulation: A Model of Approach, Participation, and Strategy Decisions," *Academy of Management Review* 24, 4 (1999): 825–42.

77 P. Lund-Thomsen et al., *Labour in Global Production Networks: A Comparative Study of Workers Conditions in Football Manufacturing in China, India and Pakistan* (Frederiksberg, Denmark: Center for Corporate Social Responsibility, Copenhagen Business School, 2011): 1.

78 M.J. Iqbal, "Bonded Labor in the Brick Kiln Industry of Pakistan," *Lahore Journal of Economics* 11, 1 (2006): 99–119.

79 H. Cullen, *The Role of International Law in the Elimination of Child Labor* (Leiden: Martinus Nijhoff, 2007), 18.

80 *REBBL,* http://rebbl.co/rebbl-not-for-sale/ (accessed 28 October 2016).

81 M. Valente and A. Crane, "Private Enterprise and Public Responsibility in Developing Countries," *California Management Review* 52, 3 (2010): 52–78.

82 M.E. Porter and M.R. Kramer, "Creating Shared Value," *Harvard Business Review* 89 (2011): 62–77.

83 Ibid., 65.

84 O. Balch, "Cocoa: Ghana's Glass and a Half of Sustainability," *Ethical Corporation,* 2010, http://www.ethicalcorp.com/communications-reporting/cocoa-ghanas-glass-and-half-sustainability (accessed 28 October 2016).

85   Plant, "Forced Labour, Slavery and Poverty Reduction," 8.
86   G. Tyldum and A. Brunovskis, "Describing the Unobserved: Methodological Challenges in Empirical Studies on Human Trafficking," in Laczko and Gozdziak, *Data and Research on Human Trafficking*, 17–34.
87   T. Brass, *Towards a Comparative Political Economy of Unfree Labour: Case Studies and Debates* (London: Frank Cass, 1999).
88   Laczko and Gozdziak, *Data and Research on Human Trafficking*.

State Enslavement in North Korea **10**

Rhoda E. Howard-Hassmann

State Slavery

Much of the literature about contemporary slavery focuses on enslavement by private actors such as human traffickers or those who use bonded labour. Kevin Bales, for example, discusses the new slavery of the late twentieth and early twenty-first centuries, a slavery rooted in profit making, in which governments are often complicit but which they formally recognize as illegal.[1] However, the crime of enslavement is not only committed by private criminals, but it is also a state practice that benefits elites and sometimes the entire economy of a country. This chapter discusses state slavery, defined as enslavement of citizens by the state. State slavers are those individuals in charge of the state who instigate, direct, and often profit from state slavery. North Korea (officially known as the Democratic People's Republic of Korea) is an example of a wider problem of state slavery in contemporary dictatorial states.

Two kinds of state slavery exist in the twenty-first century; North Korea is an amalgam of both. The first is the remnant of the communist system that in the twentieth century enslaved large numbers of people in prison camps now collectively known as the gulag, originally an acronym for slave labour camps in the Soviet Union.[2] Such enslavement was also widely used in China after the revolution of 1949 and was still practised in the early twenty-first century despite China's transformation after 1979 from a totalitarian Communist system to an authoritarian state-capitalist system.[3] Conditions in China's slave labour prison camps, collectively known as the Laogai, remained abysmal. There were about 1,000 Laogai camps in 2005, which practised "reform through labour," in which, for example, prisoners mined asbestos with their bare hands.[4] Products from slave labour were integral to China's growing export economy.[5] Slave labour was also practised on an enormous scale during the genocidal regime of the Khmer Rouge in Cambodia (1975–79), where almost the entire population, including children, was enslaved in gigantic prison camps. An estimated 885,000 overworked and underfed people died from starvation or disease in these camps.[6]

The second kind of state slavery is enslavement of citizens for the financial benefit of the government and the individual slavers who control it. In Uzbekistan, the ruling elite forced school children to harvest cotton, a staple of that country's economy. Adults were also forced to participate in the harvest, even when they were teachers or physicians. The farms on which cotton was produced were privately owned, but farmers were forced to sell the harvest to the government at prices below their actual costs; thus, they agreed to use forced child labour to minimize the costs of production.[7] The children worked excessively long hours in very hot weather, were not provided with food, and often drank water from polluted canals.[8]

Eritrea, a small state on the east coast of Africa that obtained its independence from Ethiopia in 1993 after a long civil war, was another example of state slavery for the benefit of the government and those who controlled it. What was originally designed to be an eighteen-month period of obligatory military service was extended after 1998 to include the indefinite forced labour of anyone – male or female – unfortunate enough to be drafted into the army, officially until the age of fifty but sometimes even longer.[9] Members of the government and the ruling party and senior military officers used those conscripted into indefinite military servitude to build their houses, act as their personal servants, and work on farms, building sites, and enterprises owned by the state or army.[10]

The countries mentioned above are not the only ones to engage in state slavery. But their number is sufficient to show that state slavery should be considered as a separate category from enslavement by private individuals. This chapter discusses the case of North Korea to show that it is necessary for international law to acknowledge state slavery separately from both the traditional definitions of slavery and the legal definition of forced labour. The chapter presents a brief historical background of North Korea, followed by a discussion of conditions in the North Korean gulag and an explanation of who is imprisoned in its slave labour camps. It then turns to a conceptual discussion of whether North Korea's camp system should be considered forced labour or slavery. It ends with a discussion of what can be done to end state slavery in North Korea.

The chapter relies on secondary sources, news reports, and reports from two international human rights non-governmental organizations, Amnesty International and Human Rights Watch (HRW), as well as the US Department of State's (USDS) annual human rights reports. These sources, in turn, rely heavily on interviews with North Korean refugees in northern China and South Korea; in the former location, many of these interviews are clandestine. Satellite imagery of North Korean prison camps, which helps to verify the testimony of refugees, also exists.[11] It is almost impossible for foreigners to enter North Korea, and those who do enter are very carefully watched, risking incarceration or worse if they are caught investigating prison conditions. Nevertheless, the testimony that the various researchers have accrued over the years, especially from the large numbers of people who started to illegally enter China during the famine of the mid-1990s, is remarkably consistent and can be considered reliable. These are not sensationalist accounts: researchers are very careful to cross-check accounts when they can and, if possible, to conduct methodologically sound surveys of refugees.[12]

Historical Background
North Korea is severely isolated and cut off from the international community. It is officially a communist state, but it is better thought of as a state under a one-man dynastic rule: first by Kim Il-Sung from 1948 to 1994; from 1994 to late 2011 by his son, Kim Jong-Il; and since then by Kim Jong-Il's son, Kim Jong-Un. The government is characterized by deep paranoia, massive corruption, and fascistic racism as well as by almost complete control over a devastated and severely inefficient economy. Citizens enjoy absolutely no human rights, no civil or political

rights, no rule of law or right to due process, no right to property, and no economic human rights.

North Korea is a creation of the Cold War. From 1910 to 1945, the Korean peninsula was colonized by the Japanese. At the end of the Second World War, the Americans and Soviets came to an agreement that Korea would be split at the 38th parallel, a line arbitrarily chosen as it roughly divided this ancient kingdom into two equal parts. Kim Il-Sung, reputed to have been a guerilla leader against the Japanese, was chosen by the Soviets to rule North Korea. In 1950, anticipating an easy victory, he attacked the South. The United Nations and the United States came to the defence of the South, leading newly Communist China to enter the war on the side of the North. An extremely brutal three-year war ensued, at the end of which the two parties signed a truce and retreated to their respective sides of the 38th parallel. There is no peace treaty, and the two Koreas are still technically at war, although they maintain a heavily armed "demilitarized zone" between the two countries.

North Korea's official ideology, introduced in 1970, is called *Juche*, comprising "self-control, independence, and self-sufficiency."[13] It is a form of self-reliance that is, in effect, extreme autarky.[14] No one (except the extremely corrupt elite) is legally permitted access to foreign goods, thought, or media. In practice, Juche means that North Koreans rely completely on the whims of the state for the fulfillment of their basic needs.

Forced Labour

The North Korean government maintains a large system of slave labour camps – in effect a gulag. Pierre Rigoulot, publishing originally in 1997, estimated that 1.5 million people had died in these camps since 1948.[15] Jasper Becker's lower estimate suggests that as of 2005 a million people had died in the camps, assuming an annual death rate of 10 percent of the 200,000–300,000 people imprisoned at any time.[16] HRW estimates that in 2010 there were still 200,000 prisoners in labour camps,[17] but by 2014, the estimated number of prisoners had dropped to 80,000–120,000. It is not known whether this means that fewer people were imprisoned or, alternately, whether large numbers of prisoners were executed[18] or left to starve to death when one of the largest prison camps was (apparently) closed in 2013.[19]

A major reason for the high death rates in the labour camps is that prisoners are supplied with "deliberate starvation-level rations," and this has been the practice even before the food shortages and famine of the 1990s.[20] Food is allocated on the basis of productivity; the less a prisoner produces, the less he eats, resulting in a spiral downward as those deprived of even more food produce less and less. There are no health facilities to speak of, and prisoners often die of malnutrition-related diseases. A former prison guard described his shock on first entering a prison: he saw walking skeletons, many without ears or with only one eye as a result of beatings, and many covered with scars.[21]

The gulag is a major contributor to the North Korean economy.[22] Some of the prisons' products are for export – for example, prisoners have produced hardwoods for export to Japan.[23] Other prisoners perform corvée labour, repairing roads or "substitut[ing] for the lack of other forms of energy and transport ... for example, by pushing train cars."[24] Yet others produce goods for the use of the party élite and the military, such as meat, textiles, and rabbit fur to line soldiers' winter jackets.[25] Prisoners also work excavating mines and quarries and in nuclear facilities.[26] Working days for adults can reach as long as 16.5 hours, followed by grueling "ideology struggle sessions" where weak and starving prisoners are criticized and beaten for not fulfilling their production quotas.[27] Children as young as five are also subjected to forced labour in these camps.[28]

Moreover, to earn foreign currency during the Soviet era, the regime sent prisoners to work in Siberian slave labour camps, although conditions in the Siberian camps improved after the end of Soviet rule.[29] HRW reports that in 2009 there were still 1,500 North Koreans working in Russian logging camps; they had only two rest days per year, they were punished if they did not meet their production quotas, and the North Korean government appropriated the major part of their salaries.[30] It appears, however, that these workers were not prisoners; rather, they were "volunteers" lured to Siberia in the false hopes of earning money and were on contracts of several years that they were expected to honour, regardless of the working conditions.[31] HRW also reported that North Koreans worked in Bulgaria, China, Iraq, Kuwait, and Mongolia. Large portions of their salaries were allegedly to be paid directly to the government.[32] In 2012, it was estimated that 60,000–65,000 North

Koreans were working abroad in forty or more countries.[33] In 2014, it was reported that North Korean workers were being employed to construct facilities for the 2022 FIFA World Cup in Qatar – most, or all, of their pay was appropriated by the state, and they worked extremely long hours seven days a week. Nevertheless, some workers were glad they had volunteered for this assignment since they were able to eat meat and rice in Qatar, unlike in North Korea itself.[34]

In 2004, North Korea created the Kaesong industrial park, which is an hour's drive from Seoul, to attract South Korean investment. South Korean corporations employ North Korean workers, who appear to be subjected to "indirect payment" – that is, their salaries are paid to the government, raising concerns that the workers may in fact be enslaved.[35] By 2010, about 44,000 people worked in this complex under conditions that in all respects fell far short of international labour standards.[36] Moreover, North Koreans are not free to choose their type or place of employment; the Workers' Party of Korea (the state political party) "has full and exclusive control over all job assignments."[37] The government often mobilizes the general population for farm labour and other projects without pay, sometimes kidnapping people from the streets, suggesting that in effect the entire population is subjected to forced labour.[38] In mid-2011, it was reported that the government was drafting students from universities to perform manual construction and agricultural jobs until April 2012. These young people were drafted in order to complete ambitious construction projects in time to celebrate the 100th anniversary of the birth of Kim Il-Sung.[39] All of these practices violate the right to freely choose one's employment, which is enshrined in Article 12 of the International Covenant on Civil and Political Rights (ICCPR).[40]

Who Is in the Gulag?

Two types of people are most likely to be imprisoned: famine-induced criminals and those who fall into one of several disgraced classifications of North Koreans.

Famine-Induced Criminals

Famine-induced criminals are those people whose actions in search of food ensure that they are branded as criminals, resulting in their imprisonment. The discussion below of food shortages and famine provides a necessary background to understand why so many North Korean prisoners commit "crimes" as a result of famine. Their crimes consist of the following activities: fleeing to China, travelling to find food, engaging in petty trade, cultivating private plots of land, foraging for food, and cannibalism.

From 1994 to 2000, North Korea experienced a major famine.[41] A conservative scholarly estimate based on known demographic and statistical data suggests that between 630,000 and 1.1 million people lost their lives or between 3 and 5 percent of the entire population of about twenty-two million people.[42] The causes of the famine included poor harvests and flooding, exacerbated by both Russia's and China's decisions to cut off cheap food exports and food aid to North Korea.[43] The famine was also a consequence of extreme mismanagement of the economy, especially the agricultural sector, by the central government in the 1980s and early 1990s.[44] During the worst of the 1990s famine, the government also cut off rations to four provinces, where citizens were suspected of being disloyal to the regime.[45]

While food shortages are chronic in North Korea, severe shortages causing malnutrition and death have reoccurred from 2010 to 2015. In September 2011, estimates were that six million people, about a quarter of the population, were at severe risk of starvation.[46] Diplomats reported that food rations had been halved in 2010–11.[47] Foreigners observed women and children in the fields eating roots and weeds, while "feral children" ate dead dogs and rotted food in the markets.[48] Even members of the military, normally favoured by the regime, were suffering malnutrition.[49] In March 2013, over two-thirds of the population was judged to be food insecure.[50]

These famines have created conditions that result in citizens' committing "crimes" that are punished by incarceration in slave labour camps. One such crime is to go to China; one estimate is that 200,000–300,000 people fled to China during the 1990s famine.[51] China does not protect these refugees; it returns them to North Korea, where some are executed, while others are tortured and/or incarcerated.[52]

Another famine crime is to engage in private production of food or petty trade in order to find money to buy food. Since the mid-1990s, the state has inconsistently introduced reforms that have permitted private cultivation and then reneged on them. It has also inconsistently turned a blind eye to private food markets that have sprung up in urban areas, even legalizing them in 2002 only to declare them illegal again in 2005.[53] Having allowed more private cultivation and trade, however, the state also cut off the meager food rations that North Koreans had been used to receiving under the public distribution system. Thus, many North Koreans were again at risk of entering the gulag because they had cultivated their own food and sometimes sold it in the market. Yet they could also be imprisoned merely because they foraged for food.

Finally, famine in North Korea has resulted in some known cases of cannibalism. Homeless children in North Korea are reputed to run the risk of being cannibalized.[54] One refugee reported witnessing the public execution of a twenty-eight-year-old man accused of eating a four-year-old child.[55] An official North Korean document leaked in mid-2011 reported five cases of cannibalism, including one in which a guard killed one of his colleagues, ate some of his flesh, and sold the rest on the market disguised as mutton.[56]

During the 1990s, famine criminals constituted a large, although unknown and unverifiable, percentage of the slave labourers in the North Korean gulag. It is not yet known whether people who foraged, traded, or privately produced food during the 2010–15 food shortage were treated as severely as those who did so in the 1990s.

Classification of Citizens and Likelihood of Being Imprisoned

Aside from the famine, there are many other factors that might cause a North Korean to be imprisoned and enslaved. Some prisoners are "common" criminals, although it is difficult to determine what might be considered a common crime in North Korea. In addition, there are frequent political purges. Party purges began in 1953 to rid North Korea of any former guerillas not content with Kim Il-Sung's rule, and continued until at least 1997.[57] About 15,000 "anti-revolutionaries," along with 70,000 family members, were sent to camps in purges from 1966 to 1970.[58]

Even an individual never considered to have committed a political crime could face imprisonment because of his so-called class category. The North Korean state classifies its population on the basis of perceived loyalty, or lack thereof, to the regime. The three major classes are the core, or loyal, class; the wavering class; and the hostile class.[59] There also appear to be various sub-classes, perhaps as many as fifty-one, though no one seems to know exactly how many categories the regime currently uses. Membership in the three core classes is hereditary; an individual might be deemed a member of the hostile class because his great-grandfather was considered a reactionary. Members of the hostile class are most likely to be sent to the gulag.

Not content with sending individuals perceived to be hostile to the regime to the gulag, the state also sentences family members, up to three generations, to go to the gulag with them.[60] This rule is in accordance with Kim Il-Sung's 1958 directive that "[prison] inmates are class enemies and must be actively exterminated to three generations."[61] Thus, for example, Kang Chol-hwan, the author of a rare memoir of the camps, was incarcerated at the age of nine because his grandfather was suspected of a crime.[62] Members of the hostile class were also the first to have their rations cut during the famine of the 1990s.[63]

North Korea is also explicitly racist. Basing his analysis on the regime's propaganda, B.R. Myers argues that far from being a Communist state, North Korea is actually a fascist, racist state along the lines of Hitler's Germany and that it derives what little legitimacy it has in part from convincing the populace that they are a superior race.[64] Thus, people who are of mixed "racial" background are likely to be incarcerated.

Some women refugees repatriated from China are imprisoned, many after severe torture, because in addition to fleeing they committed the crime of racial pollution by having had sexual relations with Chinese men. Some of these women voluntarily marry Korean-Chinese or ethnic Chinese men. Others are trafficked to Chinese husbands since China's one-child policy has caused a surplus of men over women, and many men therefore resort to purchasing wives.[65] If these women are pregnant when they are returned to North Korea, they are forcibly aborted. If they are in the late stages of pregnancy, delivery is induced and the infants are murdered or tossed alive into garbage cans before their mothers' eyes.[66]

The regime's racist ideology stresses the perfection, as well as the purity, of the Korean people. It appears that until the late 1980s, individuals with disabilities were banned from major urban areas, special concentration camps were set up for them, and they were routinely sterilized. Kim Jong-Il had a particular aversion to "dwarfs," who did not fit his vision of a perfect North Korean race. After the 1980s, the regime apparently became more lenient towards the disabled, and in 2003, it passed a law for their protection, although discrimination against the disabled was still very common.[67] Thus, it may be safe to assume that there are now fewer disabled individuals among the prison population.

Finally, minority groups suspected of disloyalty are imprisoned. One such group is North Korean Christians, some of whom are executed, while others are sent to the gulag.[68] Another group at risk is returnees from Japan. During the period of Japanese colonialism, many ethnic Koreans lived in Japan, where they were badly treated, and some voluntarily returned to North Korea during the early post-war period. It is estimated that 93,000 Koreans, some with Japanese wives, emigrated to North Korea in the 1950s and 1960s, and many were imprisoned.[69].

Thus, the gulag population consists of many different social categories. In effect, there is only one individual in North Korea who does not fear imprisonment and enslavement, namely Kim Jong-Un himself. In this sense, it is perhaps correct to think of the entire country as a prison.

Slavery or Forced Labour?

Slavery is prohibited under international law. The 1926 Slavery Convention defines slavery as "the status or condition of a person over whom any or all of the powers attaching to the right of ownership are exercised" and further defines the slave trade, *inter alia*, as "all acts involved in the capture, acquisition or disposal of a person with intent to reduce him to slavery" and "all acts involved in the acquisition of a slave with a view to selling or exchanging him."[70] North Korea is not guilty of engaging in the slave trade; it does not sell its prisoners, who are nominally its citizens. However, as noted above, some are "rented" to other countries in return for payment to the North Korean government. Moreover, other aspects of how prisoners are treated fit the definitions of both forced labour and slavery.

The 1956 Supplementary Convention on the Abolition of Slavery, the Slave Trade, and Institutions and Practices Similar to Slavery refers in its preamble to the Forced Labour Convention of 1930.[71] The 1930 convention defines forced labour as "all work or service which is exacted from any person under the menace of any penalty and for which the said person has not offered himself voluntarily." However, it then lists several exceptions, including

> any work or service exacted from any person as a consequence of a conviction in a court of law, provided that the said work or service is carried out under the supervision and control of a public authority and that the said person is not hired to or placed at the disposal of private individuals, companies or associations.[72]

The 1930 Forced Labour Convention appears to apply to North Korea, although as of 2015 the country is not party to it.[73] Many prisoners enter North Korea's gulag without conviction in a court of law, merely being arbitrarily apprehended by the authorities. However, some do appear in court, although hardly in a manner that would conform to international norms of due process, as elaborated, *inter alia*, in the Universal Declaration of Human Rights (1948) and the ICCPR (1976).[74]

North Korea did institute constitutional reforms in 2004 that regularized sentences for economic crimes, but in 2007, it lengthened its list of crimes and the sentences for them.[75] Even if the conviction of those North Korean prisoners who went through the court system were considered legitimate, however, the incarceration of family members not tried for, or convicted of, any crime yet obliged to accompany their convicted family member to the gulag would be illegal. These imprisoned elderly people and children also endure forced labour. Moreover, although forced labour in North Korea is carried out "under the supervision and control of a public authority," as the 1930 Forced Labour Convention requires, some North Koreans are rented to private companies either inside or outside their own country, as in the Keogang industrial zone and various foreign countries. Although they appear to originally volunteer as free labour, their conditions of work resemble servitude, especially since their wages are often paid, in whole or in part, to the state.

The 1959 Convention Concerning the Abolition of Forced Labour directly addresses the type of forced labour found in North Korea. Its Article 1 is worth quoting in full:

Each Member of the International Labour Organisation which ratifies this Convention undertakes to suppress and not to make use of
any form of forced or compulsory labour –

a) as a means of political coercion or education or as a punishment
   for holding or expressing political views or views ideologically
   opposed to the established political, social or economic system;
b) as a method of mobilising and using labour for purposes of
   economic development;
c) as a means of labour discipline;
d) as a punishment for having participated in strikes;
e) as a means of racial, social, national or religious discrimination.[76]

Aside from the question of strikes, which may never have occurred
in North Korea (although prison rebellions have occurred),[77] there
is plenty of evidence that the state uses forced labour as punishment
for political views, as a means of economic development, as a means
of labour discipline, and as a means of discrimination, as the section
above on who is likely to be imprisoned has shown. However, as of
2015, North Korea was not party to this convention, which is binding
only upon its members.[78]

Yet until very recently, reports on North Korea prison labourers did
not describe them as slaves. Human rights reports by the USDS from
1996 to 2014 referred to "reform through labour," "reeducation through
labour," and, latterly, "forced or compulsory labour" in the prison camps.
Amnesty International has reported on child labour and forced labour,
but through 2014–15, it has not referred to slavery.[79] In its annual reports on North Korea from 2005 to 2011, HRW made no mention of
slavery, confining itself to sections on the treatment of workers, except
in its 2011 report, which contained a separate section on forced labour
camps.[80] In 2012 and 2013, however, HRW stated that "North Korea ...
practices collective punishment for various anti-state offenses, for which
it enslaves hundreds of thousands of citizens," and in 2014, it referred to
"effective enslavement."[81]

The question remains, therefore, whether under international law it
is advisable to redefine as slavery what seems undoubtedly to be forced

labour in North Korea. Joel Quirk notes the tendency to inflate the definition of slavery, especially by the United Nations Working Group on Contemporary Forms of Slavery. This gradual redefinition of slavery, according to Quirk, includes "forced labour for the state," including in North Korea.[82] Nevertheless, recent attempts by scholars, including Quirk himself as well as several others who are included in this volume, to define what exactly constitutes slavery suggests that the case can be made for state slavery in North Korea.

The 2012 *Bellagio-Harvard Guidelines on the Legal Parameters of Slavery* suggest that several aspects of the treatment of those imprisoned in North Korea's gulag constitute slavery.[83] These guidelines are based in the first instance on the 1926 definition of slavery, cited above. Guideline 2 refers to the exercise of the powers attached to the right of ownership, usually through force or coercion, and including "control over a person in such a way as to significantly deprive that person of his or her individual liberty, with the intent of exploitation through the use, management, profit, transfer, or disposal of that person." North Korea prisoners are forcefully and often violently deprived of their liberty and then exploited as prison labour for the profit of the North Korean elite and the "development" of the devastated economy. Those people, such as students, who are rounded up for forced labour are similarly exploited for "development" purposes or to gratify the elite, as in the case of the construction projects meant to help commemorate Kim Il-Sung's 100th anniversary. Most prisoners and forced labourers are not transferred, although the situation of North Koreans "voluntarily" working abroad or in the Keosang industrial park is problematic, as they are rented for profit to their employers, which is an aspect of possession described in Guideline 4(d).

Guideline 3 states that "possession is foundational to an understanding of the legal definition of slavery" and characterizes possession as "control over a person by another such as a person might control a thing." North Korean prisoners, worked to the bone without any pay and deprived of even a minimal diet are certainly treated like things by the state. Guideline 4(f) refers to the "disposal, mistreatment, or neglect of a person," in such a way as to result in "the physical or psychological exhaustion of a person, and ultimately to his or her destruction." This certainly occurs in North Korea's gulag. Overwork, in particular, constitutes the "imposition of physical demands that severely curtail the capacity of the human body to sustain itself," which is noted as a characteristic of slavery in Guideline 4(f). All of these prisoners are also disposed of, in the sense that their deaths from starvation, disease, violence, and cruelty are foreseeable and preventable, yet encouraged by the state. Aborted or murdered half-Chinese infants, imprisoned Christians, returnees from Japan, disabled people, and others are similarly disposed of.

Importantly, these guidelines do not mandate that all aspects of enslavement have to be present for a system to be considered slavery. Guideline 5 states that "the exercise of *any* or all of the powers attaching to the right of ownership ... shall provide evidence of slavery" (emphasis added). Thus, the evolving opinion of scholars and jurists is that prison and forced labour of the kind exercised by North Korea does constitute slavery. The guidelines are not law; they are the effort of a group of scholars and jurists to refine and clarify the legal definition of slavery. However, such guidelines are often incorporated into judicial opinions and later into international law itself.

Whether or not what I call state slavery is indeed currently slavery under international law, the question remains what can be done to stop it in North Korea. The answer, sadly, is very little. State slavers operate with an impunity not granted to private slavers.

Possible Interventions to Punish and Prevent Slavery in North Korea

In their introduction to this volume, Annie Bunting and Joel Quirk note that despite much legislative activity to outlaw modern slavery, states' commitment to eliminate it has in fact been rather shallow.[84] One would think that the conditions in North Korea, including state slavery, would make it a country of immediate concern to the international community; however, the human rights of its population take second place to various geostrategic concerns. Bunting and Quirk argue that the reason for the international community's preoccupation with slavery in "backward" areas of the world is that the focus on such "exceptional" cases frequently consolidates dominant economic and political interests in the Global North that actually benefit from slavery. But no one in the Global North supports the North Korean regime and its policies of enslavement. The enslavement of North Korean prisoners does benefit the North Korean elite and some economic actors who rent North Koreans from their government, such as Qatar, but it is only marginally, if at all, implicated in the "global supply chain."[85] While, as I discuss below, both humanitarian intervention and referral to the International Criminal Court (ICC) to try those North Korean leaders responsible for state slavery are extremely unlikely, the major reason for this is serious concern with North Korea's nuclear threat, not the economic and political interests of the Global North.

Humanitarian Intervention

The principal concern of the international community with regard to North Korea is not the way it treats its citizens but, rather, the threat its nuclear program poses to the world. It is also thought to possess illegal chemical and biological weapons. A further international concern is North Korean participation in international drug trafficking, which is one of the key ways it earns foreign currency.[86] Slave labourers in the gulag have cultivated opium poppies to supply the drug trade.[87]

Several key state actors have focused primarily on North Korea's threats to international security rather than on the right of its citizens not to be enslaved. The United States fears both North Korea's nuclear and conventional weapons; indeed, it appears that North Korea has already developed ballistic missiles that could hit the US West Coast.[88] The North Korean regime also counterfeits US currency.[89] Despite this, many Americans are concerned about North Korea's human rights record. In 2004, the US Congress passed a North Korea Human Rights Act,[90] and the United States has had sanctions on North Korea for many years. One purpose of these sanctions is to stem the flow of luxury goods to North Korea, which allows the elite to live in luxury – and especially to eat very well – at the same time as the population starves.

China, on the other hand, protects North Korea, which it has viewed in the past as a buffer state between itself and South Korea, Japan, and Taiwan.[91] It appears, however, that China has had less need of such a buffer since it became a major capitalist power. But China also fears the development of nuclear weapons, especially since the North Korean tests of such weapons in 2006, 2009, 2013, and 2016.[92] China also fears a refugee overflow from North Korea into its northern region should the regime fall. China has been investing in North Korean mines and is also interested in building a dock in the city of Rajin-Sonbong, which would give it access to the Sea of Japan, off North Korea's east coast.[93]

South Korea is interested in North Korean political stability. According to South Korea's Constitution, all North Koreans are its citizens, yet like China it fears a refugee overflow,[94] although only about 25,000 North Koreans had actually managed to reach South Korea by 2015. South Korea is also interested in the return of an estimated 500 of its citizens whom North Korea appears to have abducted, along with some elderly South Korean prisoners of war still held in North Korea,[95] and it has a short-term interest in the reunification of families that were split after the 1953 truce. Finally, South Korea has a very real fear of attack by North Korea, which already possesses conventional weapons that could wipe out its capital, Seoul, even if nuclear weapons were not used.[96]

For the international community, the United States, China, and South Korea, the first strategic priority is a stable North Korea that does not develop or use its nuclear capacity. This interest overshadows concern for the victims of state slavery. Yet we must be careful not to confer impunity on states that are so closed and dangerous that it is easy to neglect their citizens' suffering. One means that has been used elsewhere to undermine impunity is referral of state criminals to the ICC.

ICC

Grace Kang, a legal scholar, has suggested that the late Kim Jong-il should have been referred to the ICC on suspicion of crimes against humanity, including slavery.[97] The ICC defines enslavement as "the exercise of any or all of the powers attaching to the right of ownership over a person."[98] According to Kang, in the case of *Prosecutor v Kunarac et al.* at the International Criminal Tribunal for the Former Yugoslavia, factors further clarifying the meaning of the crime of enslavement were elucidated and included

> the control of someone's movement, control of physical environment, psychological control, measures taken to prevent or deter escape, force, threat of force or coercion, duration, assertion of exclusivity, subjection to cruel treatment and abuse, control of sexuality and forced labour.[99]

These criteria of enslavement are reflected in the *Bellagio-Harvard Guidelines*, which have been shown above to apply to North Korea.

Kang argued that the forced labour in North Korean prison camps met all of these conditions. She also noted that as of 2006 North Korea owned factories in several countries, including the Czech Republic, Russia, Libya, Bulgaria, Saudi Arabia, and Angola, where its workers were exploited. For example, in the Czech Republic, North Korean women workers worked under "extremely harsh conditions," and their wages were deposited to a North Korean government account. Kang argued that the treatment of these workers could be considered enslavement, even though it appeared that they were working voluntarily.[100]

Against Kang's claims, the North Korean government could argue that it does not engage in enslavement since it exercises no rights of ownership over prison labourers, who are merely convicts engaged in labour as part of their sentence. However, as Kang suggested this so-called prison labour meets many of the conditions now defined legally as enslavement. The North Korean government could also argue that it does not sell these labourers or traffic in them. Indeed, those who traffic in North Koreans are those who enslave women refugees in China and sell them to brothels or prospective husbands. Since North Korea prohibits migration to China, the government could argue that it is not implicated in such enslavement. Kang, however, was skeptical about this claim and argued that there should be an investigation to ascertain whether, in fact, the North Korean government and Kim Jong-Il himself were connected to such trafficking.[101] Such a connection is not inconceivable, given the number of other international crimes in which the regime engages, such as illegal arms exports and the sale of illegal narcotics. In any case, engagement in the slave trade or human trafficking is not a necessary aspect of enslavement itself.

Kim Jong-Il could also have been indicted for crimes against humanity. A strong case can be made that he was guilty of all crimes against humanity except apartheid, including murder, extermination, torture, rape, deportations, enslavement, forced disappearances, and persecution.[102] Kim Jong-Il was personally responsible for the gulag prisons; they were run by the National Security Service, which reported directly to him.[103] Since North Korea is not a party to the ICC, however, any indictment of Kim Jong-il would have had to be referred by the United Nations Security Council (UNSC). Furthermore, any such indictments could refer only to crimes committed since the ICC came into existence on 1 July 2002.

Kim Jong-Il's son and successor, Kim Jong-Un, could be referred to the ICC. In 2013, the Human Rights Council of the United Nations established a Commission of Inquiry (COI) into North Korea, and on 7 February 2014 the United Nations General Assembly (UNGA) released the commission's report). The COI listed numerous ways that North Korea had committed crimes against humanity, including enslavement, arguing that it occurred not only in North Korea's political prisons but also in its prisons for "ordinary" criminals.[104] It asserted specifically that in the worst of North Korea's political prison camps, prisoners were "subject to gradual extermination through starvation and slave labour" and that the existence of the political prison camps was a crime against humanity.[105]

The COI called on the UNSC to refer the responsible North Korean officials – government, military, and security officials – to the ICC for trial. On 18 December 2014, the UNGA voted to submit the COI report to the UNSC, asking it in turn to consider "referral of the situation in the Democratic People's Republic of Korea to the International Criminal Court."[106] This referral was unusual in that its justification was not North Korea's nuclear program but, rather, its possible crimes against humanity. Debating an earlier report on North Korea by the UNGA's Third Committee, China and Russia had backed a defeated amendment proposed by Cuba to remove the suggestion that the UNGA accept the commission's view that crimes against humanity were being committed in North Korea and also to remove the call to refer North Korea to the ICC. North Korea, in its turn, had angrily threatened to resume nuclear tests in response to the Third Committee's resolution.[107]

This case shows the difficulty of relying only on the ICC to punish crimes against humanity, including enslavement. It was unlikely that the UNSC would vote to refer North Korea to the ICC, as China and Russia would probably exercise their veto. The international human rights regime does not make strong demands on the international system as a whole. Few mechanisms exist that can actually check even the most severe human rights abuses, such as in North Korea's prison camps. As long as the geostrategic concern to contain North Korea's nuclear ambitions tops the international community's agenda, it is unlikely that Kim Jong-Un and other leaders of North Korea will be referred for trial to the ICC.

Conclusion

North Korea exemplifies both the "old" Communist use of forced labour/enslavement and the "new" use of forced labour and enslavement for a country's "development" or the personal profit of its rulers. Guideline 6 of the *Bellagio-Harvard Guidelines* incorrectly maintains that "as the State generally does not support a property right in persons, a negative obligation against the state [to desist from enslavement] generally no longer exists."[108] Several states are known to enslave labourers in the twenty-first century. Given that North Korea is not the only state to enslave its own citizens, the guidelines should have included a definite obligation on the state not to engage in slavery, reinforcing international law as in Article 8(1) of the ICCPR, which states that "no one shall be held in slavery: slavery and the slave trade in all their forms shall be prohibited." In the absence of a term for this type of slavery in the guidelines, I have coined the term state slavery to describe North Korea and analogous cases, referring to Kim-Jong-il, Kim Jong-Un, and other such dictators as state slavers. Scholars and others concerned with human rights and with countering slavery need to pay more attention to the role of the state in instigating and perpetuating it.

Notes

Acknowledgments: I am most grateful to Kwan-Sen Wen, Elizabeth Baisley, and Jinelle Piereder for research assistance for this chapter. I also thank the Canada Research Chairs program for the time and funds necessary for the research, and Wilfrid Laurier University for nominating me for my Canada Research Chair.

1 Kevin Bales, *Disposable People: New Slavery in the Global Economy* (Berkeley, CA: University of California Press, 1999).
2 Anne Applebaum, *Gulag: A History* (New York: Random House, 2003); Adam Hochschild, *The Unquiet Ghost: Russians Remember Stalin* (New York: Houghton Mifflin, 2003).

3   Jean-Louis Margolin, "China: A Long March into Night," in S. Courtois et al., eds., *The Black Book of Communism: Crimes, Terror, Repression* (Cambridge, MA: Harvard University Press, 1999), 497–513.

4   Harry Wu, *Appendix to Forced Labour in China*, ed. Congressional-Executive Commission on China (Washington, DC: US Government Printing Office, 2005), 25, 30.

5   Ibid., 33–34; Gregory Xu, *Appendix to Forced Labour in China*, ed. Congressional-Executive Commission on China. Washington, DC: US Government Printing Office, 2005), 42–43.

6   Helen Fein, *Human Rights and Wrongs: Slavery, Terror, Genocide* (Boulder: Paradigm, 2007), 26.

7   European Center for Constitutional and Human Rights, *Child Labour in Uzbek Cotton Production and the Responsibility of European Corporations* (Berlin: European Center for Constitutional and Human Rights, 2011).

8   International Labour Rights Forum and Human Rights Defenders in Uzbekistan, *Forced Child Labour in Uzbekistan's 2008 Spring Agricultural Season*. Washington, DC: International Labour Rights Forum (2008): 6.

9   Human Rights Watch, *Service for Life: State Repression and Indefinite Conscription in Eritrea* (New York: Human Rights Watch, 2009).

10   Gaim Kibreab, "Forced Labour in Eritrea," *Journal of Modern African Studies* 47, 1 (2009): 59–63.

11   David Hawk, *The Hidden Gulag: Exposing North Korea's Prison Camps* (Washington, DC: US Committee for Human Rights in North Korea, 2003).

12   Stephan Haggard and Marcus Noland, *Repression and Punishment in North Korea: Survey Evidence of Prison Camp Experiences* (Honolulu: East-West Center, 2009).

13   Pierre Rigoulot, "Crimes, Terror, and Secrecy in North Korea," in Courtois et al., *Black Book of Communism*, 548.

14   Bruce Cumings, *Korea's Place in the Sun: A Modern History* (New York: W.W. Norton, 2005), 429.

15   Rigoulot, "Crimes, Terror, and Secrecy in North Korea," 564.

16   Jasper Becker, *Rogue Regime: Kim Jong Il and the Looming Threat of North Korea* (New York: Oxford University Press, 2005), 87.

17   Human Rights Watch, *World Report: Events of 2011* (New York: Human Rights Watch, 2011), 345.

18   Alex J. Bellamy, "A Chronic Protection Problem: The DPRK and the Responsibility to Protect," *International Affairs* 91, 2 (2015): 231.

19   US Department of State, *Country Report on Human Rights Practices: Korea, Democratic People's Republic of* (Washington, DC: US Department of State, 2012 and 2013).

20   Hawk, *The Hidden Gulag*, 15.

21   Becker, *Rogue Regime*, 85.

22 Commission of Inquiry, *Report of the Detailed Findings of the Commission of Inquiry on Human Rights in the Democratic People's Republic of North Korea* (New York: UN Human Rights Council, 2014), para. 775.

23 Hawk, *The Hidden Gulag*, 31.

24 Haggard and Noland, *Repression and Punishment in North Korea*, 11.

25 Becker, *Rogue Regime*, 85.

26 Rigoulot, "Crimes, Terror, and Secrecy in North Korea," 555.

27 Amnesty International, *North Korea: Political Prison Camps* (London: Amnesty International, 2011).

28 Commission of Inquiry, *Report of the Detailed Findings*, para. 779.

29 Rigoulot, "Crimes, Terror, and Secrecy in North Korea," 557.

30 Human Rights Watch, *World Report: Events of 2009*. New York: Human Rights Watch, 2010), 328–29.

31 Alain Devalpo, "North Korean Slaves," *Le Monde Diplomatique* 8 April 2006.

32 Human Rights Watch, *World Report: Events of 2008* (New York: Human Rights Watch, 2009), 282.

33 Choe Sang-Hun. "North Korea Exports Forced Laborers for Profit, Rights Groups Say," *New York Times*, 20 February 2015, A9.

34 Human Rights without Frontiers International. "North Korea: Qatar's Ambitious Future Driven on by North Korean 'forced labour,'" *North Korea: Democracy, Rule of Law and Human Rights*, 12 November 2014.

35 Human Rights Watch, *North Korea: Workers' Rights at the Kaesong Industrial Complex* (New York: Human Rights Watch, 2006), 1.

36 Human Rights Watch, *World Report 2011*, 346.

37 Commission of Inquiry, *Report of the Detailed Findings*, para. 359.

38 US Department of State, *2009 Human Rights Report: Democratic People's Republic of Korea* (Washington, DC: US Department of State, 2010). See also Ralph Hassig and Kongdan Oh, *The Hidden People of North Korea: Everyday Life in the Hermit Kingdom* (New York: Rowman and Littlefield, 2009), 79.

39 Yojana Sharma, "North Korea: Learning Stops as Students Must Work," *University World News*, 30 June 2011; Julian Ryall, "North Korea Shuts Down Universities for 10 Months," *The Telegraph*, 28 June 2011.

40 Commission of Inquiry, *Report of the Detailed Findings*, para. 366. International Covenant on Civil and Political Rights, 16 December 1966, 999 UNTS 171.

41 Rhoda E. Howard-Hassmann, "State-Induced Famine and Penal Starvation in North Korea," *Genocide Studies and Prevention* 7, 2/3 (2012), 147–65.

42 Suk Lee, *The DPRK Famine of 1994–2000: Existence and Impact* (Seoul: Korea Institute for National Unification, 2005), 47.

43 Barbara Demick, *Nothing to Envy: Ordinary Lives in North Korea* (New York: Spiegel and Grau, 2009), 67; B.R. Myers, *The Cleanest Race: How North Koreans See Themselves – and Why It Matters* (Brooklyn, NY: Melville House, 2010), 50.

44 Marcus Noland, "North Korea as a 'New' Famine," in S. Devereux, ed., *The New Famines: Why Famines Persist in an Era of Globalization* (New York: Routledge, 2007), 197–221.

45 Ibid.

46 Daniel Ten Kate, "North Korea's Food Shortages Worsening, U.N. Says," *Bloomberg News*, 16 September 2011.

47 Gerald Bourke, "North Korea Slashes Food Rations: Aid Worker," *Agence France-Presse*, 28 June 2011.

48 "Deprive and Rule," *Economist*, 17 September 2011, 42.

49 Julian Ryall, "Half of North Korea's Army 'Starving,'" *The Telegraph*, 13 September 2011.

50 "External Aid Essential for Subsistence of Millions in DPR Korea-Official," *United Nations News Centre*, 15 March 2013.

51 Hawk, *The Hidden Gulag*, 56

52 Rhoda E. Howard-Hassmann, "North Korea: A Case for a New International Treaty on the Right to Food," *Asia-Pacific Journal on Human Rights and the Law* 15, 1 and 2 (2014): 42–43.

53 Christian Caryl, "The Other North Korea," *New York Review of Books* 55, 13 (2008): 25–27.

54 Demick, *Nothing to Envy*, 168.

55 Mike Kim, *Escaping North Korea: Defiance and Hope in the World's Most Repressive Country* (New York: Rowman and Littlefield, 2008), 50.

56 Emily Lodish, "Cannibalism in North Korea," *Minnpost.com*, 24 June 2011.

57 Rigoulot, "Crimes, Terror, and Secrecy in North Korea," 551–52.

58 Hassig and Oh, *The Hidden People of North Korea*, 208.

59 Ibid., 195–215.

60 Hawk, *The Hidden Gulag*, 24.

61 Becker, *Rogue Regime*, 90.

62 Kang Chol-hwan, "The Aquariums of Pyongyang," in P. Hollander, ed., *From the Gulag to the Killing Fields: Personal Accounts of Political Violence and Repression in Communist States* (Wilmington, DE: ISI Books, 2006), 688.

63 Hassig and Oh, *The Hidden People of North Korea*, 203

64 Myers, *The Cleanest Race*.

65 Norma Kang Muico, *An Absence of Choice: The Sexual Exploitation of North Korean Women in China* (London: Anti-Slavery International, 2005).

66 Hawk, *The Hidden Gulag*, 61–62; Stephen Haggard and Marcus Noland, *Witness to Transformation: Refugee Insights into North Korea* (Washington, DC: Peterson Institute for International Economics, 2011), 97.

67 Park Young-ho et al., *White Paper on Human Rights in North Korea* (Seoul: Korea Institute for National Unification, 2010), 249–60.

68 Patricia Goedde, "Legal Mobilization for Human Rights Protection in North Korea: Furthering Discourse or Discord?" *Human Rights Quarterly* 32, 3 (2010): 554; Hawk, *The Hidden Gulag*, 67.

69 Hassig and Oh, *The Hidden People of North Korea*, 208.

70 Slavery Convention, 25 September 1926, 60 LNTS 253, Article 1(1) and (2)

71 Supplementary Convention on the Abolition of Slavery, the Slave Trade, and Institutions and Practices Similar to Slavery, 7 September 1956, 226 UNTS 3, preamble, para. 5. Forced Labour Convention, 28 June 1930, 39 UNTS 55.

72 Forced Labour Convention, 28 June 1930, 39 UNTS 55, Article 2, 1.

73 Ibid.

74 Universal Declaration of Human Rights, 10 December 1948, UN Doc. A/810 (1948).

75 Haggard and Noland, *Witness to Transformation*, 82

76 Convention Concerning the Abolition of Forced Labour, 17 January 1959, 320 UNTS 291.

77 Becker, *Rogue Regime*, 91

78 Convention Concerning the Abolition of Forced Labour, Article 4.

79 Amnesty International, *Reports: North Korea*, 2011, 2012, 2013, 2014/2015.

80 Human Rights Watch, *World Report 2011*, 345

81 Human Rights Watch, *World Reports: Events of 2012, 2013, 2014* (New York: Human Rights Watch, 2012, 2013, 2014).

82 Joel Quirk, *Unfinished Business: A Comparative Survey of Historical and Contemporary Slavery* (Paris: United Nations Educational, Scientific and Cultural Organization, 2009), 29, 98.

83 Research Network on the Legal Parameters of Slavery, *Bellagio-Harvard Guidelines on the Legal Parameters of Slavery*, 2010–11. The guidelines are reprinted in the appendix at the end of this volume.

84 Bunting and Quirk, "Contemporary Slavery and Its Definition in Law," in this volume.

85 Ibid.

86 Richard Bernstein, "How Not to Deal with North Korea," *New York Review of Books* 54, 3 (2007): 37–39.

87 Hawk, *The Hidden Gulag*, 99.

88 Bernstein, "How Not to Deal with North Korea."

89 Ibid.

90 Goedde, "Legal Mobilization for Human Rights Protection in North Korea," 560.

91 "Lips, Teeth, and Spitting the Dummy," *Economist*, 4 December 2010, 56.

92 "Not Waving. Perhaps Drowning," *Economist*, 29 May 2010), 23, 23–25.

93 Ibid., 25.

94 Bernstein, "How Not to Deal with North Korea," 39.

95 Human Rights Watch, *World Report 2009*, 329.

96 Bernstein, "How Not to Deal with North Korea," 38.

97 Grace M. Kang, "A Case for the Prosecution of Kim Jong Il for Crimes against Humanity, Genocide, and War Crimes," *Columbia Human Rights Law Review* 38 (2006): 86.

98   Rome Statute of the International Criminal Court, 17 July 1998, 2187 UNTS 90, Article 7(2)(c).

99   Kang, "A Case for the Prosecution of Kim Jong Il," 89. ICTY, *Prosecutor v Kunarac et al.*, Case nos. IT-96–23 and IT-96–23/1-A, 12 June 2002.

100   Kang, "A Case for the Prosecution of Kim Jong Il," 87.

101   Ibid., 88.

102   Goedde, "Legal Mobilization for Human Rights Protection in North Korea," 554.

103   Hawk, *The Hidden Gulag*, 26.

104   Commission of Inquiry, *Report of the Detailed Findings*, para. 1078.

105   Ibid., paras. 767 and 1067.

106   United Nations General Assembly, *Situation of Human Rights in the Democratic People's Republic of Korea* (New York: United Nations, 18 December 2014).

107   Miriam Donath, "UN Panel Calls for North Korea Referral to International Court," *Reuters*, 18 November 2014; "UN Committee Urges Court Action against N. Korea," *VOA News*, 18 November 2014.

108   Research Network on the Legal Parameters of Slavery, *Bellagio-Harvard Guidelines on the Legal Parameters of Slavery*.

Letting Go: How Elites Manage Challenges to Contemporary Slavery   **11**

Austin Choi-Fitzpatrick

The English-speaking world has entered a fourth wave of the abolitionist movement. While each of the four waves has had different defining features, a shared utilization of social movement tactics to end slavery ties them all together. The first wave led Britain to outlaw slavery in the early nineteenth century. The second wave saw the United States adopt a uniform approach to slavery in the Emancipation Proclamation. Both set out to end chattel slavery and set a baseline for legal emancipation, if not actual political and economic citizenship.

The third abolitionist wave centred around the "white slave trade" in the early twentieth century, while the fourth, and most recent, wave has focused on trafficking for sexual and labour exploitation within an increasingly global system. It is in the third and fourth waves that the explicit focus on ownership – and the deep social, legal, and cultural rituals that ownership underwrote – was replaced by new struggles around rights and dignity.

Scholarly and popular attention to this issue has flourished to such an extent that it is no longer clear if it is slavery itself or attention to slavery that is on the increase. Simplistic assessments of the issue have fuelled this flame. Previous studies have focused on the problem (that it is exclusively or primarily related to sexual exploitation) and the solution (that "rescuing" victims will end the practice). The present moment is driven by a narrow notion of the Other, and it is disconnected from politics, supply chains, systems of inequality, and everyday life.[1] This Othering has been so successful that consumers and corporations profess a commitment to eradication without a hint of irony; it is rare to find one's self implicated in the horrors of slavery.

A broader perspective, however, suggests that a broader set of actors are required to produce what we call slavery and trafficking: the brokers and recruiters who secure the victims; the intermediaries, traffickers, and enforcers responsible for solidifying control over individuals; and the direct beneficiaries of the victim's labour (or service). The story usually ends here. Trafficking and slavery, however, rely on a much larger network of indirect economic beneficiaries that spans the globe in ways that trafficking networks never will. The web of accountability maps onto routes of exploitation but extends far beyond, riding shotgun with the products produced under exploitative conditions.

The focus is rarely on these broader implications but more narrowly on villains with criminal intent. My interviews with contemporary slaveholders in rural India suggest that the logic of everyday offenders might stand us in better stead than the current vernacular and scholarly approaches. This observation has a direct bearing on our understanding of emancipation. Dominant logics of emancipation relegate perpetrators to a singular status – criminal – with a single mode of intervention – arrest. This is a limited perspective, and it may be improved upon with more sophisticated modes of inquiry, as this special volume hopes to demonstrate. Unfortunately, for those enthused about the anti-slavery movement, a broader assessment of accountability may implicate far more of us – as consumers, investors, and voters – than we are comfortable with.

In this chapter, I want to address slaveholders and emancipation. Almost nothing is known about life at their intersection, and little is known about them independently. What happens to slaveholders after emancipation? Of what use is the power that had so recently secured control over a vulnerable person's total economic capacity? Slavery is the most prevalent in those places where it is woven into the social fabric of everyday life, where it is a way of life rather than a crime. The best example is South Asia, where an estimated half of the world's enslaved individuals are trafficked or bonded into slavery.[2] Many are vulnerable to exploitative schemes promising a better life in another city, while others are born with debts they struggle for a lifetime to repay. Whether trafficked or held *in situ*, it is the enslaved individual that has captured the attention of policy-makers, donors, and the general public.

Programs to rescue and rehabilitate enslaved victims abound, as laws like the Victims of Trafficking and Violence Protection Act in the United States are passed to ensure that trafficked individuals are treated as victims rather than as criminals.[3] These same laws ensure that perpetrators are framed as criminals and that a combination of sentencing guidelines and political pressure ensure that rights violation is met with long sentences. Investigations, trials, and convictions free from corruption are hard to come by, but they are the hallmark of law enforcement and deterrence-centric approaches to anti-trafficking, which cast trafficked individuals as victims and perpetrators as criminals.[4]

This issue framing – trafficked individuals as victims – is the location of intense debate between second-wave and third-wave feminists. The former organize against prostitution under the conviction that prostitution and the purchase of sex is a fundamental violation of human rights. Sex cannot be sold, as it is an inseparable component of the human spirit. A contrary position is held by those focused on the biological fact of the sex act and, therefore, part of the bodily repertoire of labour. The problem, therefore, is not necessarily the exchange of sex for money but, instead, the lack of legal, economic, and political protection around this exchange. The resulting policy recommendations could not be more stark. While one community promotes the "rescue and rehabilitation" of the "victim," the other suggests "labor organizing" of "sex workers." Much of the energy driving this conversation has spilled over from earlier debates about pornography and is fuelled by new legislation in Scandinavia and new studies on the same issue. A resolution to this debate does not appear on the horizon.

It is time for a robust discussion about perpetrators. Much scholarship and practice has been built on a particular set of understandings about the trafficker. This understanding is narrow and often has more to do with overarching frameworks than actual empirical evidence. I have argued elsewhere that there are several broadly popular ways of conceptualizing trafficking and slavery.[5] These frameworks directly shape and shade each community's concept of who the rights violator is and, by extension, what sorts of approaches will be best suited to engaging their behaviour. From here, we can sketch several ideal-type relationships between dominant conceptualizations of the problem and hypothesized notions of the perpetrator.

Those arguing that trafficking and slavery are primarily rooted in prostitution tend to focus their energy exclusively on trafficking for sexual exploitation (alternately dubbed "sex slavery," "sex trafficking," or "sex work"). This emphasis directs attention to a particular range of perpetrators: a combination of end-users ("johns") and intermediaries (recruiters, traffickers, enforcers, and pimps). For the abolitionist camp, solutions include the arrest of intermediaries and the reeducation of users (through "johns schools," for example). In areas where prostitution is regulated, the recommended solution is the passage of laws that curtail the sale of sex or sexual services. Such an approach frames both the individual users and the intermediaries as abusers and as criminals.

The criminal justice approach to trafficking and slavery has the clearest vision of the perpetrator. Two decades of advocacy have pushed law enforcement and border security officials to recognize the fact that many trafficked individuals are victims, rather than criminals, and that traffickers are perpetrators of a particular sort. Here we find perhaps the most consistent perspective of the perpetrator – as a criminal – and of the solution – imprisonment or deportation.

The migration approach – whose unit of analysis is the flow of individuals across borders – focuses attention on human smugglers, diaspora networks, and sundry brokers. The International Organization for Migration's approach to the issue is rooted in the United Nations' (UN) Protocol to Prevent, Suppress and Punish Trafficking in Persons, especially Women and Children, which is itself rooted in the UN's Convention against Transnational Organized Crime.[6] As a result, much of this thinking circles back around to a "law and enforcement" focus on the role of, and response to, traffickers, whether they be individual actors or organized networks.

These three approaches – prostitution, criminal justice, and migration – are the most typical ways of conceptualizing contemporary slavery.

Four more approaches, or frameworks, are persistent and deserve some attention, especially since they provide an opportunity to ask new sets of questions about perpetrators. The forced labour approach, exemplified by the International Labour Organization (ILO), has traditionally recognized a wider range of perpetrators. Attention to the state-sponsored corporate slavery projects that drove some economies during the Second World War was followed by a focus on sustained slave labour in the Soviet Union, China, Burma, and North Korea. The ILO's experience in these areas suggests a much wider array of actors – what we may think of as direct and indirect beneficiaries. Direct beneficiaries include corporations, while indirect beneficiaries include other stakeholders, such as stockholders. While some promising theoretical work is being done in this area, and advocacy groups like Walk Free are quite willing to name and shame corporations and nation-states, there is a poverty of empirical work on the role of institutional perpetrators.[7]

The contemporary slavery approach sees the perpetrator as a slaveholder or a slave master.[8] This framing is in keeping with the broader comparative-historical commitments of Kevin Bales and his fellow travellers.[9] Here, the emphasis is on the socio-economic process of total control, rather than on the legal reality of ownership present in chattel slavery. This approach has room for a greater number of roles for the slaveholder – they might be international criminal syndicates, well-respected community members, otherwise God-fearing businessmen, local entrepreneurs, recidivist sadists, or some combination thereof.[10] Recent empirical assessments suggest there is much to learn from this comparative historical assessment.[11]

The human rights framework locates the individual as the core unit of analysis in the trafficking and enslavement (and emancipation!) process. In this way, the human rights approach displaces a state-centric emphasis on the law, borders, and commerce. Most work within the human rights approach has been done by the "labor-organizing" wing of the prostitution debate, a group that has long argued that the structural marginalization of women in prostitution leads to abuse, rather than the act of exchanging sex for money. Groups using community-organizing techniques to combat labour exploitation have also employed such a human rights framework.

Yet the real potential in such a taxonomic exegesis lies in extending the human rights approach to both the victim and the perpetrator. The ramifications of this extension are barely understood since most attention has gone to the rescue and rehabilitation of the enslaved, rather than to the redirection and rehabilitation of perpetrators. The incarceration of perpetrators, as advocated by many of the approaches listed above, should certainly be part of this toolbox; however, to stop there would overestimate criminality and underestimate the roles of economics, politics, and culture as mobilizing factors in the perpetration of human trafficking and slavery.

What might a human rights approach to the perpetrator look like? There is much to be learned from the scholarly literature and communities of practice focused on truth and reconciliation processes. Especially designed for contexts in which catastrophic events preclude the routine dispensation of justice, truth and reconciliation approaches are meant to address the past in a way that lays a firm foundation for the future. What would truth and reconciliation processes look like in India, Pakistan, and Bangladesh, where countless millions are held against their will in bonded labour, even in the face of each country's democratic heritage? Certainly, the path is perilous, especially in the absence of shared notions of moral respect.[12] Exploitation persists in South Asia because of a lack of such shared notions, something no amount of legislative wrangling or international cajoling appear to have changed.

A human rights approach recognizes the individuality and inherent worth of the perpetrator. If slavery is a fundamentally social act, then so too is emancipation.[13] Failure to address the root causes of slavery may result in some perpetrators simply pivoting to new forms of exploitation. For example, shifts from slavery to sharecropping may be found in the agricultural sectors of the post-bellum American South[14] and in contemporary India.[15]

At this point, several things bear mentioning. The first is that while every approach has a host of sophisticated solutions when it comes to the problem (reduce inequality, increase respect for women, secure borders more effectively) and the victims (holistic aftercare with wraparound services, taskforce-level responses, job training), far less imaginative effort goes into explaining the perpetrator and his or her world. This is unfortunate since there is every reason to believe that traffickers and their victims hail from very similar backgrounds[16] and are possibly even the same person in different roles at different points in time.[17] We now know that rights violators are as likely to be women as men and are far more likely to be small-time operators working independently or in a loosely organized fashion than they are to be members of organized crime.[18] Furthermore, they are often vulnerable to the exact same tectonic forces – poverty and inequality, lack of mobility, entrenched sexism, and lack of education – as the victims.

We have mistaken humans breaking laws for villains, an observation made by Bales more than a decade ago, but one largely overlooked in the past decade.[19] This issue has been overlooked by scholars as well as practitioners. A brief tour of several competing perspectives on slavery provides a sense of how much is lost by not keeping the humanity of slaveholders in mind. Perhaps these six ideal-type camps may be a useful heuristic, but even more is to be gained by focusing on how anti-trafficking groups conceptualize traffickers.

What Activists Talk about When They Talk about Traffickers

Recently, I worked with Marija Stojanovska to make an empirical assessment of the websites of several leading advocacy groups in the English-speaking world.[20] Qualitative analysis of the data suggests that a limited view of the perpetrator prevails. While virtually every organization recognizes the reality of a perpetrator, virtually none have a fully formed notion of the perpetrator as an actual social actor. In some cases, rights violations are described as if they emerge on their own. Victims are "subjected to intense cruelty" or are "held against their will." Left unspoken is who exactly is doing the subjecting and the holding. One might expect these sentences to end with a direct object: "Held against their will *by local landlords* [or brothel owners, or labor brokers, etc]" (emphasis added).

The end result is an erasure of the social nature of the relationship that lies at the heart of every case of enslavement. At its core, slavery is a fundamentally relational affair, in which one individual exercises control over another through various forms of power and with a particular purpose. The relationship may be abusive in the extreme, but it is fundamentally rooted in the intersection of two or more lives, often/ predominantly as one uses and manipulates another to maximize profits in a socially embedded niche in the market.

The implications for our understanding of both slavery and emancipation should be clear. If slavery is relational, then so too is emancipation. New scholarship has demonstrated that victims and perpetrators know one another through prior ties, whether regional, linguistic, ethnic, or otherwise.[21] Emancipation, therefore, cannot mean simply returning to one's original conditions no longer enslaved (is "free" truly the correct term?)! We know that many vulnerable individuals are fleeing even more desperate conditions in their places of origin. Structural inequality, individual poverty, and domestic vulnerability often combine to push entrepreneurial residents out in search of better options. The uncritical reintegration of individuals back into these conditions is unacceptable.

If emancipation is relational, then it must be so for both victim as well as perpetrator. The implications for this are only beginning to emerge, as advocacy groups experiment with a wider variety of intervention strategies. Groups supported by the US–based human rights group Free the Slaves work with community mobilization models based on the assumption that empowered communities know best how to identify and pursue their own anti-slavery objectives. This experience suggests that the pursuit of these objectives always challenges the status quo. These challenges lead to emancipation, first of the mind and later of the community. This is the stuff of which sustainable emancipation is made.

Others, such as the International Justice Mission (IJM), a US–based group founded by a human rights lawyer, have their sights set on the law as a critical component of the social change process. Basic rule of law is seen as the fulcrum for a number of key issues, including land reform (especially for widows and orphans), trafficking for sexual exploitation, and bonded labour. Here, the perpetrator plays a vital role in the social change model. However, this model is rooted more directly in the deterrence effect that is produced by high profile arrests than it is in the lived experience of individual survivors of exploitation. Emancipation becomes more a matter of public relations (ensuring that other rights violators know about a high profile sentencing, for example) than it is about interpersonal relations.

The Coalition of Immokalee Workers (CIW), a US–based group that blends collective action with corporate shaming, approaches perpetrators from yet another perspective. The CIW's "name and shame" model of corporate accountability relies on public outrage over rights-violating behaviour. Corporations, for their part, are extremely sensitive to dips in the value of their stocks and declines in the public's opinion of their brand and products. While the CIW's model appears adversarial at first blush, it is rooted in a model of change that uses public opinion to pressure corporate managers to cut rights-violating middlemen from the supply chain. In 2007, I joined a CIW march on the headquarters of Yum! Brands in Irvine, California, along with thousands of other everyday citizens. The demand was that the major corporation clean up shop and not go out of business. In the end, that is exactly what Yum! Brands did, promising to pay more per pound for the tomatoes they purchased for Taco Bell. This decision had the effect of driving wages up in the field.

This assessment of contemporary online anti-slavery discourse reveals a variety of opinions about the perpetrator. What is missing, however, are the actual references to this population. Free the Slaves mentions traffickers and slaveholders, but IJM and CIW do not. While experience with each of these groups over the past fifteen years allows me to draw together a certain analysis of each group's theory of the perpetrator in the emancipation process, none of these three organizations deliver a fully formed view of who exactly is doing the enslaving.

What Scholars Talk about When They Talk about Traffickers

The lack of attention to perpetrators in advocacy materials is mirrored in academic discourse in scholarly journals.[22] Pioneering work in India sheds light on the reality that perpetrators were as likely to be lower-caste, middle-aged women than a member of an organized crime syndicate.[23] Interviews with individuals arrested for human trafficking in Cambodia support these findings. Those most likely to be incarcerated on trafficking-related charges were members of traditionally marginalized communities, whether for reasons of class, gender, or geography.[24] Unpublished work by Ami Carpenter and her colleagues suggests that, while a significant number of gang members interviewed in San Diego county jails were involved in some aspect of "domestic human trafficking," they very rarely did so in a way that would be considered "organized crime."[25] In an analysis of seventy-two trafficking cases in the United States, Erin Denton found that the majority of perpetrators were of the same ethnicity as those whom they had trafficked.[26] Anqi Shen's interviews with females involved in the sale and trafficking of children in China suggest that those individuals were very rarely in a position of social power and were often unable to negotiate their compensation with slightly stronger or better networked individuals in the exploitation process.[27] Most thought of themselves as good mothers. This work has made substantial contributions to what we know about exploitation. Future work should draw on a human rights approach to the issue because doing so will shed important light on the complex motivations of traffickers. It is often said that they are "motivated by greed." In fact, they may be as motivated by desperation or a lack of other options. This does not make trafficking less of a crime, but it does suggest alternate avenues for eradication and emancipation.

What All of This Means for Emancipation

Traffickers and slaveholders are criminals. That is a simple empirical fact in light of legislation the world over. However, this perceived black-and-white distinction erases important distinctions regarding individuals' willingness and ability to engage in trafficking. In particular, interpretation assumes a certain set of relationships related to an individual's willingness to disregard social norms around life (bodily integrity) and property (private). This perception is rooted in the accurate observation made by popular anti-trafficking groups that "slavery is illegal everywhere." This was true for chattel slavery in the 1990s, and laws around the world have been updated to reflect newer modalities, such as human trafficking, largely in response to political pressure from the United States. Slavery may be illegal everywhere, but it is not considered to be unethical everywhere. As subsequent data from India will show, slavery is most widespread, deeply rooted, and difficult to eradicate in those places where economic exploitation is complemented by cultural inequality.

Such inequality is exacerbated by particular social practices that lend cultural legitimacy to unequal socio-economic relations. I am thinking specifically of the caste system, with its cosmological assessment of particular human relations and the idea that each person is born to a particular social station that they should not – cannot – rise above. When this assessment is shared by both the perpetrator and the victim, emancipation involves far more than offering the exploited individual a "chance for a better life," as many reformers suggest. Individual freedom flourishes when it is buttressed by cultural, economic, and political rights. Perpetrators working outside the law, but within cultural norms, know this all too well and frequently turn this shared perception of slavery's alternatives to their advantage, such as when they remind workers of their duties and obligations as members of a lower caste.

When thinking about emancipation, there may be some merit in differentiating between an individual's willingness and ability to violate norms and laws. In India, a deeply patterned set of social practices combine to produce individuals who are willing and able to violate laws protecting fellow citizens against the threats of trafficking and slavery. When challenged by social movements, which are focused on arresting lawbreakers or mobilizing collective action efforts against them, these individuals face a choice between persisting in their behaviour or quitting. Some are able to persist. Some choose to persist. Some of those who choose to persist are not able. Others who are able to persist choose to quit. Why they quit exploiting others is complicated by the fact that they may not see themselves as criminals but, instead, as important seams in the social fabric. The decision to quit may therefore be a decision between doing "what's right by the community" and "what's required by the law."

The fact that emancipation may be an ethical dilemma for the slaveholder is seldom considered, but it is not impossible to imagine. What are we to make of perpetrators who told me of their concern for workers after bonded labour ends? "Who will care for the workers?" one skepticism landowner asked me, after expressing his skepticism about the anti-trafficking group that worked in the area. He was convinced that the Delhi-based non-profit organization was engaged in anti-slavery work in order to siphon funds from international donors and that once the funds dried up the community organizers would decamp to the city and take up a different cause. The unspoken punchline of his story seemed to be that, when the advocates eventually abandoned their cause, he would remain. In his worldview, it is slaveholding that is sustainable, not emancipation.

The cost/benefit calculation made by slaveholders, together with the radical variation in how willing they are to persist exploiting in the face of adversity, have implications for assessing the effectiveness of the various anti-trafficking modalities being funded by donors in the United States and the United Kingdom. Is it better to raise financial and opportunity costs on perpetrators, change public opinion about caste, or increase resources and perceived opportunities for the enslaved? Or is the best intervention perhaps some combination of the three? The answer has a whole lot to do with what we know, or what we think we know, about perpetrators. It is important that policy-makers, donors, and activists on the ground get this right. Interviews with traffickers are few and far between, but they have consistently found that imprisoned traffickers are poor and powerless. Whether this is because they fit the profile of all traffickers or because they fit society's profile of a catchable criminal remains to be seen.

A focus on perpetrators may also help us to make better sense out of the ways enslaved individuals exit slavery. There are many paths out of slavery. Some emerge as a result of an intervention, including rescue, community mobilization, rebellion, and voluntary manumission. While these interventions have been the primary response to instances of slavery, none of these preclude the possibility that the survivor and the perpetrator remain within the same community after slavery's end. As suggested earlier, rescues may result in reintegration responses from sympathetic organizations, which then place survivors back in the context from which they originally fled or were trafficked.

Non-intervention–based emancipation includes escape and self-emancipation, discharging a debt, being discarded by the slaveholder, and death. With the exception of death, none of these are guaranteed to result in a break of contact between perpetrator and victim. Conversely, discharging a debt is a common strategy among individuals engaged in bonded labour. There is little reason to believe individuals who discharge their debt subsequently leave the community in which they worked. Of course, this may happen, but it is not guaranteed.

What Slaveholders Say about Slaveholding and Emancipation

"We should not harass the poor ... As far as possible, I try to not tell lies. But this is business, so you have to lie a little," Aanan told me, as we surveyed his mining operation.[28] Aanan may represent the new face of labour exploitation.[29] His labourers mine stones and crush them into silica sand for one of India's largest industrial conglomerates. He has built this operation from the ground up, pointing out that though he is upper caste, he was born without money, with nothing but his name. Aanan is one of a million minor players in the gradual emergence of India as a regional and global power. He is also one of the tiny links in the expansive web of exploitation that continues to hold millions in slavery the world over.

Aanan, like others in his region, said he was concerned by a host of issues. These issues ranged from farmers' concerns over a drought that resulted in fewer crops, new laws guaranteeing employment for labourers, new roads paved straight into nearby urban labour markets, and outside community-organizing groups training labourers to demand their rights. These sweeping changes impacted perpetrators differently, but when it came to the labourers themselves, the theme was consistent: things have changed in such a way that masters suffer while their servants excel. This situation is complicated and painful for slaveholders, who must find ways to survive.

Times Have Changed

> Earlier, the *harijans* (untouchables) would come running for work ... Now, times have changed. It's the opposite now. I am the one who goes to them with folded hands. I request that they farm my land on whatever terms they want.
>
> Karmjit (Pseudonym), small landholder

Broad economic shifts have combined with local advocacy efforts to undermine the traditional authority of local landowners, who were always of a higher caste than those who were bonded to them. What had changed, respondents told me time and time again, was something cultural and relational. Many complaints were about politics and economics until my conversations with these men turned to their labourers. Their responses were often sad, as if they had lost something more important than simple economic inputs – they had lost the respect of their labourers. This is not to say economics were not important but, rather, that the loss was simultaneously financial, relational, and cultural.

Masters Suffer

> People who have invested in business don't have a problem. They are doing very well financially. But all the landowners, who are dependent only on agriculture and don't have any income from a job or a business, are suffering. The situation is reversed now.
>
> Karmjit (Pseudonym), small landholder

Some respondents were at pains to emphasize that their ability to cope with these changes was contingent on their ability to transition into new sectors of the economy. Those who had caste-based power, but were unable to shift this intangible asset into something with market value – a mining operation, for example – were simply unable to continue business as usual. Some were unwilling to make this change and insisted on further repressing their workers. Whether this repression was ultimately successful had everything to do with their economic standing, which proved to be far more durable than their cultural status, especially in an era of transition.

While Servants Excel

> If the things don't change then the [lower caste] people who have got the jobs and have the money will form a new class ... In the last ten years, everyone is trying to be independent.
>
> Karmjit (Pseudonym), small landholder

The perception that these losses occurred at the very moment the poor began securing benefits served to make things worse. This transition was frequently seen as a zero-sum game. Increased rates of education, access to employment programs, and an increased willingness and ability to engage in elections by lower caste labourers were issues that were marked as a full-frontal assault to elites. Again, this assault could be withstood by ramparts built of capital, but efforts to appeal to caste status were crumbling quickly under the weight of practical emancipation. It is hard to hem people in when they have other options for employment.

This Is Complicated and Painful

> Sometimes we feel bad but there is no choice. We have to bear all this ... So the times are not good now. Everybody has surrendered.
>
> Karmjit (Pseudonym), small landholder

Full-frontal assaults on slaveholder power are economic and political, but they are also social and relational. Many respondents expressed their concern that labourers would not be able to cope without the protection that the bonded labour relationship had offered. "Who will care for the workers now [that they free]?" one erstwhile employer asked me. Here again, a human rights perspective on the lived experience of the slaveholder suggests that a much more nuanced view of their attitudes and behaviour is in order.

But Responses Vary on Willingness and Ability

> The big farmers, even if they face these same problems [with insurgent laborers], they're not affected, because they have money. Either a good amount of money, or another source of income. But we only have this here [gesturing to his modest holdings].
>
> Rajdeep (Pseudonym), large landowner

Emancipation poses a significant challenge to perpetrators. This challenge is economic, political, and relational. How perpetrators respond to social movement efforts depends on a combination of their attitude (whether they want to persist) and their resources (whether they are able to persist). Interviews with human rights violators show that when vulnerable communities gain resources, political opportunities, and useful ways of framing their experience as injustice, the paternalism used to justify exploitation loses its power. Former oppressors, therefore, must find a way to respond. Sometimes the response is active counter-mobilization, repression, or persistence, but often it is more sanguine. Adaptation and quitting explain the bulk of post-movement outcomes in my own work and may describe many post-intervention outcomes in other situations.

Discussion and Conclusion

In interview after interview, rights violators, especially farmers and plantation owners, reported a sense of loss when their paternalistic authority was undermined by a combination of resources, political opportunities, framing from social movements, and structural challenges from the broader political and economic context. These new forms of collective interpretation and action have created cognitive liberation for the oppressed, catalyzing new opportunities that call into question the caste-based paternalism that the perpetrators have used to justify their domination and exploitation. When confronted by the power of the formerly powerless, many movement adversaries simply have resigned themselves to this new state of affairs. They have done so because they are either unwilling or unable to persist in their newly stigmatized behaviour. This resignation tells us that sometimes adversaries simply quit. But it also tells us something about the durability of inequality at the societal level.

In this case, movement efforts do not appear to change underlying attitudes. The reason for this may be that slaveholders face local movement efforts and broader political and economic transformations altogether, and their assessments of bonded labour perhaps resemble popular opinion. Instead, the dominant groups' paternalism evolves into new sets of concerns related to affirmative action and education policies that are thought to produce arrogant and demanding claimants. Paternalism has long served as the deep substrate upon which all manner of discrimination blossoms, something observed quite some time ago by Mary Jackson.[30] Dominant perspectives persist, demonstrating the tremendous elasticity of ideas about inequality and the ability of these ideas to extend into new circumstances and articulate around the cognitive liberation of the oppressed. This has profound implications for post-emancipation social relations since it suggests that oppressor consciousness is quite durable. Stronger stuff is needed than rescue and rehabilitation if we are going to end slavery in our lifetime. The articulation and evolution of inequality is not the only movement outcome. Advocacy efforts not only have helped lead to a new state of affairs for the oppressed but have also generated a new set of grievances for elite adversaries. It remains to be seen whether these new grievances – local challenges from labourers together with broader economic and cultural displacement – will generate new forms of collective action.

A Note on Intention and Ability

The emphasis on criminality and criminal intent introduced earlier is built on the assumption that deterrence works. The jailing of perpetrators has a direct effect on both the future behaviour of the incarcerated individual as well as the current behaviour of bystanders who are actively, or might be considering, engaging in the same illegal behaviour. It bears mentioning that the previous data comes directly from slaveholders targeted for community mobilization efforts, rather than from traffickers who have been arrested and incarcerated. Community organizing represents an altogether different set of assumptions about how social change occurs. The redistribution of power, rather than the enforcement of the law, drives lasting change. Organizing modalities include securing cash wages for the first time, securing access to federal benefits, and empowering the marginalized to participate in local elections.

As I have argued, rights-violating behaviour is predicated on a combination of intention and ability and is supported by a combination of mindset and money. Empirical evidence suggests that human rights violations emerge at the intersection of individual willingness to exploit an economic incentive to do so.[31] Emancipation strategies strike at this unique combination of interest and ability in various ways. All approaches increase costs, but these costs are experienced differently by actors with different combinations of resources.

The reason for this is simple and straightforward. Some rights violators abuse because they perceive this behaviour to be in their rational self-interest and to not violate any overriding social norm. The intersection of interest and ability is underwritten by particular social economic and political conditions that are amenable to change. Change may come from macro-factors and macro-forces (for example, economic collapse), from meso-factors and meso-forces (for example, new cultural norms), and from micro-factors and micro-forces (for example, a change of heart). Macro-factors are relatively obvious in cases of large wars, new laws, and economic collapse. Here, large-scale forces affect society at all levels, including the ability of rights violators to actually violate rights, which may increase, decrease, or otherwise change. At the other end of the spectrum are situations in which large-scale forces are stable and micro-factors come to the fore. These factors include varying levels of commitment to inequality as some individuals violate rights with a pang in their conscience, while others do it with a perverse sense of fulfillment.

It should be clear, based on this simple observation about ability and intent, that a simple typology is sufficient to explain a range of responses to such change. Perpetrators may be relieved to find that changes in the means of production eliminate the need for the physical labour of enslaved workers, for example. When faced with challenges to their power and authority, perpetrator responses vary along these two axes. The admittedly anecdotal evidence in the previous sentence provides us with a potentially useful way of differentiating between the truly villainous actors portrayed by anti-trafficking campaigners and the more complex reality faced by advocates on the ground.

Emancipation represents a cultural affront because it recalibrates the power dynamic between the powerful (slaveholders or traffickers) and the powerless (the trafficked individual, the landless labourer, and undocumented migrants). Cultural threats, especially in India, interrupt expectations around class, ethnicity, status, and other culturally, economically, and politically specified ways differentiating individuals. In India, the caste system is the most obvious of these hierarchies, but such differentiations exist the world round.[32]

Emancipation simultaneously represents an affront to the financial status quo. While we are accustomed to thinking of slaveholders as powerful and weaponized transnational actors who penetrate borders, break bones, and enter bodies at will, the reality is often times more sanguine. The net beneficiaries of slavery are almost always wealthier by orders of magnitude than the enslaved.[33] Facilitators of slavery, however, are usually much closer to their victims in social and economic status. India's configuration here is unique and worth noting. There, the cultural acceptability of inequality is rooted in the caste system, meaning many economically marginalized, but high caste, landowners occupy positions of enormous power, authority, and control over their lower caste labourers.

Inserting human rights advocacy groups into this equation, especially with the emancipatory ideas and additional resources they bring, has the effect of illuminating differences and similarities between upper and lower caste villagers, where untouchability had previously enforced the gap between the castes. Emancipation represents an economic and cultural affront. The financial affront varies based on the exposure of the perpetrator to the economic inputs of their victims. Indirect net beneficiaries, like those purchasing a discounted taco at Taco Bell, are not bothered in any way by the negligible fluctuation in price that a wage hike represents. For a farmer whose livelihood relies on bonded labour, however, the impact may be devastating. Powerful perpetrators may continue to exploit, or they may quit, especially if they have financial interests and abilities that lie elsewhere. Emancipation is difficult and chaotic. However, for those possessing the right resources, chaos may be a ladder used to climb from the old world into the new. In some instances, it is the newly emancipated individuals who perceive more options than their oppressors. Slavery ensnares the slaveholders as well.

Conclusion

In this chapter, I have emphasized the importance of two opportunities for further scholarship and advocacy in the area I will stubbornly continue to call "contemporary slavery studies."[34] The first is related to perpetrators, a pivotal actor in the exploitation process, yet one that has been viewed simplistically through a law and enforcement lens. The second is related to emancipation, which is often imagined as a return to a prior state of freedom, rather than a critical engagement of the complicated social and economic conditions that usually place survivors into unchallenged systems of exploitation, often alongside their erstwhile abuser.

I have set out to demonstrate how contemporary perpetrators feel about being challenged, and I hope the reader filters this qualitative evidence through the notion of a more comprehensive human rights approach to contemporary slavery. Such a framework prioritizes individual rights over a host of other factors: national security, immigration regimes, exploitative cultural and gender norms, criminal codes, economic prerogatives, and demands from the state. A human rights approach privileges all forms of contemporary slavery and recognizes the complex social relations and cultural conditions in which both perpetrators and enslaved persons are embedded. I hope this approach provides an improved way to understand both perpetrators and emancipation.

Doing so illuminates the ways in which contemporary slavery is connected to larger cultural systems – for example, caste in India. This line of thinking allows us to theorize slavery as a culturally acceptable practice and invites the reader to extend these theoretical observations to other instances in which oppressors violate human rights but not local norms. Seen in this light, the case of bonded labour in India has much in common with a wide variety of rights violations, including servile marriage, female circumcision, and child labour worldwide. In each instance, the simple cessation of the rights violating act does not guarantee that rights will be respected in the future. Speaking directly with human rights violators provides an opportunity to explore how they experience these changes and perhaps how more sustainable emancipation projects may be undertaken. In the final analysis, emancipation is not a fixed and static point that lies somewhere in the past (for example, in the United States in 1865) or at a particular moment in the future (slave-free textiles made by free women bent over new looms for Western consumption). Emancipation – for slaves, slaveholders, and scholars alike – is as difficult to seize as it is to explain. Nevertheless, we try our best.

Notes

1 See Bunting and Quirk, "Contemporary Slavery as More Than Rhetorical Strategy?," in this volume.
2 Kevin Bales, *Disposable People: New Slavery in the Global Economy* (Berkeley, CA: University of California Press, 2012).
3 Victims of Trafficking and Violence Protection Act, 2000, PL 106-386.

4 Austin Choi-Fitzpatrick, "In Plain Sight? Human Trafficking and Research Challenges," in *Human Rights and Human Welfare* 6 (2006): 63–73.

5 Austin Choi-Fitzpatrick, "From Rescue to Representation: A Human Rights Approach to the Contemporary Anti-Slavery Movement," *Journal of Human Rights* 14, 4 (2015): 486–503.

6 Rebecca Surtees, *Traffickers and Trafficking: Challenges in Researching Human Traffickers and Trafficking Operations* (Geneva: United Nations International Organization for Migration, 2014). Protocol to Prevent, Suppress and Punish Trafficking in Persons, especially Women and Children, 15 November 2000, 40 ILM 335 (2001); Convention against Transnational Organized Crime, 15 November 2000, 40 ILM 335 (2001).

7 Ashley Feasley, "Eliminating Consumer Exploitation: Examining Accountability Regimes to Eradicate Forced Labor from Global Supply Chains," *Journal of Human Trafficking* (forthcoming).

8 Bales, *Disposable People.*

9 See Joel Quirk, "When Human Trafficking Means Everything and Nothing," in this volume.

10 Kevin Bales, "Slavery and the Human Right to Evil," *Journal of Human Rights* 3, 1 (2004): 55–65.

11 Austin Choi-Fitzpatrick, *What Slaveholders Think: How Contemporary Perpetrators Rationalize What They Do* (New York: Columbia University Press, 2017); C. Keo et al., "Human Trafficking and Moral Panic in Cambodia," *The Annals* 653, 1 (2014): 202–24.

12 Ernesto Verdeja, *Unchopping a Tree: Reconciliation in the Aftermath of Political Violence* (Philadelphia: Temple University Press, 2009).

13 Bales, *Disposable People.*

14 Edward Royce, "The Origins of Southern Sharecropping: Explaining Social Change," *Current Perspectives in Social Theory* 6 (1985): 279–99; Edward Royce, *The Origins of Southern Sharecropping* (Philadelphia: Temple University Press, 1993).

15 Choi-Fitzpatrick, "As if We Are Equals."

16 Erin Denton, "Anatomy of Offending: Human Trafficking in the United States, 2006–2011," *Journal of Human Trafficking* 2, 1 (2016): 32–62.

17 Sankar Sen and P.M. Nair, *A Report on Trafficking in Women and Children in India: 2002–2003* (New Delhi: National Human Rights Commission, UN Women, and Institute on Security Studies, 2005).

18 Anqi Shen, "Female Perpetrators in Internal Child Trafficking in China: An empirical study," *Journal of Human Trafficking* 2, 1 (2016): 63–77; Denton, "Anatomy of Offending."

19 Bales, "Slavery and the Human Right to Evil."

20 This exploratory research involved content analysis of fourteen organizations' websites. The organizations were: Anti-Slavery International, Freedom Network, Global Alliance against Traffic in Women, Coalition against Trafficking in Women,

Verite, Safe Horizon, Polaris Project, Coalition of Immokalee Workers, LaStrada, International Justice Mission, Free the Slaves, Not 4 Sale, Solidarity Center, Coalition to Abolish Slavery and Trafficking, Vital Voices, World Vision (United States), and Walk Free. A constrained Google keyword search was employed to determine the density of usage. See Austin Choi-Fitzpatrick, "The Good, the Bad, the Ugly: Human Rights Violators in Comparative Perspective," introductory essay to guest-edited special issue, *Journal of Human Trafficking* 2, 1 (2016): 1-14.

21 Shen, "Female Perpetrators in Internal Child Trafficking in China; and Denton, "Anatomy of Offending."

22 Choi-Fitzpatrick, "The Good, the Bad, the Ugly."

23 Sen, *Report on Trafficking in Women and Children in India*.

24 Keo, "Human Trafficking and Moral Panic in Cambodia."

25 Unpublished work on file with author.

26 Denton, "Anatomy of Offending."

27 Anqi Shen, *Offending Women in Contemporary China: Gender and Pathways into Crime* (London: Palgrave Macmillan, 2015); Shen, "Female Perpetrators in Internal Child Trafficking in China."

28 A brief methodological note is in order. This section draws on fieldwork in Uttar Pradesh, Bihar, and Karnataka, India. I worked alongside local advocacy groups that were implementing community-organizing activities in areas considered to have high rates of bonded labour and human trafficking. My study took me to sixteen intervention sites and generated 150 key informant interviews with perpetrators, victims, and survivors, community members, community leaders, representatives from the local advocacy groups, and representatives of the international donors that supported their work. This study generated an enormous amount of data; however, here I have focused more narrowly on the reported experiences of current and former slaveholders.

29 All names are pseudonyms.

30 Mary Jackson, *The Velvet Glove: Paternalism and Conflict in Gender, Class, and Race Relations* (Berkeley, CA: University of California Press, 1994).

31 Choi-Fitzpatrick, "The Good, the Bad, the Ugly."

32 Jackson, *The Velvet Glove*; Jim Sidanius and Felicia Pratto, *Social Domination: An Intergroup Theory of Social Hierarchy and Oppression* (Cambridge: Cambridge University Press, 1999).

33 See Choi-Fitzpatrick, "The Good, the Bad, the Ugly."

34 Austin Choi-Fitzpatrick, "Rethinking Trafficking: Contemporary Slavery," in Alison Brysk and Austin Choi-Fitzpatrick, eds., *From Human Trafficking to Human Rights: Rethinking Contemporary Slavery* (Philadelphia: University of Pennsylvania Press, 2012), 13–24.

Child Domestic Labour: Work Like Any Other, Work Like No Other

12

Jonathan Blagbrough

> Child Domestic Workers (CDWs) are amongst the most numerous, vulnerable and exploited of the world's child labourers. They are hard to reach not only because they work behind the closed doors of their employers' homes, but also because society sees the practice as normal and – in relation to girls – important training for later life.
>
> – Maggie Black, *Child Domestic Workers –*
> *Finding a Voice: A Handbook on Advocacy*

Child Domestic Workers (CDWs) are persons under eighteen years of age who work in households other than their own, doing domestic chores, caring for children, tending the garden, taking care of animals, running errands, and helping their employers run their small businesses, among other tasks. They include children who "live in" and those who live separately from their employers as well as those who are paid for their work, those who are not paid, and those who receive "in-kind" benefits, such as food and shelter.[1] Estimates from the International Labour Organization (ILO) in 2012 indicate that there are at over seventeen million child domestic workers and that there are more girls aged below the age of sixteen in domestic service than in any other type of work.[2] More than half of these children are considered to be in hazardous situations (work that by its nature or the circumstances in which it is carried out is likely to harm the health, safety, or morals of children.)[3]

Child domestic work warrants particular attention because of the conditions under which CDWs – the majority of whom live with their employers – are working. Time and again, child domestic workers report that their daily experience of discrimination and isolation in the household is the most difficult part of their burden. Their live-in situation also makes them highly dependent on their employers for their basic needs. This seclusion and dependency makes CDWs particularly vulnerable to exploitation and abuse and routinely results in physical, psychological, and sexual violence.[4] However, child domestic workers are vulnerable to abuse and exploitation not only because they are children and predominantly female but also because they are workers in people's homes. Domestic work continues to be "undervalued and invisible," with domestic workers "particularly vulnerable to discrimination in respect of conditions of employment and of work, and to other abuses of human rights."[5]

A key concern relating to domestic work in general is that it is "often perceived to be something other than employment."[6] The paternalistic notions that frequently accompany domestic work – that domestic workers are "like one of the family" – serve to conceal the existence of an employment relationship. These notions, the vestiges of the master-servant nexus, "wherein domestic work is a "status" that attaches to the person performing the work," defines the worker and limits her future options as a result.[7] These notions and the resulting impacts are amplified when it comes to children working as domestics, with further ambiguity created because they are as likely to be working for relatives as for strangers. The blurred relationship with the employing family is characterized in the following terms: the child is working but is not considered to be a worker, and she lives as part of the family but is not treated like a family member. Consequently, at the heart of the concern about the situation of a child in domestic service is that, as a result of her ambiguous relationship to others in the household, the child is ultimately no one's responsibility. The familial and legal "care vacuum" that this situation produces, coupled with the child's physical and emotional isolation in the household, creates a particular vulnerability to exploitation and abuse.[8]

The premise of this chapter is that, despite widespread recognition of child domestic work as a cause for concern, the narrow labour-oriented focus on their situation hinders a broader understanding of their circumstances as well as the consideration of the varied triggers and motivations pushing and pulling them into domestic service. Indeed, there is growing recognition that "child labour" is only one of many lenses with which to view the practice.[9] A more rounded conceptual understanding will, it is argued, not only provide greater insight into the lives of CDWs but will also benefit our analysis of how best to protect them from exploitation, abuse, and violence and minimize the vulnerability of future generations to a similar fate.

However, the lenses we use to view the situation and perspectives of CDWs are only part of the picture. The data collection methods that we use to inform our understanding are no less critical. Indeed, research methods that emphasize the importance of talking to CDWs directly are central to our increasing comprehension of their circumstances and of how to conceptualize the issue. For this reason, this chapter also offers an insight into some of the lessons learned from much of the multi-country research with child domestic workers reported in this chapter as well as several key of the ethical and practical issues that have arisen.

Key Features of Child Domestic Work

Despite the many and varied manifestations of the practice in different contexts, there are a number of important similarities in the circumstances and experiences of CDWs across countries and continents as well as close parallels between the basic triggers and motivations for entering domestic service.

Pushed and Pulled

Poverty invariably underlies a child's vulnerability to this form of exploitation. The majority of CDWs come from poor families and are sent to work to supplement their family's income or simply to lessen the financial strain at home.[10] However, other so-called push factors such as gender and ethnic discrimination, social exclusion, lack of educational opportunities, domestic violence, rural-to-urban migration, displacement, and the loss of close family members as a result of conflict and disease are also important triggers.[11] In some locations, particularly in South Asia, it is not uncommon to find children working as domestics to repay family debts. Children, particularly in some African countries, have recounted that they were forced into domestic work upon the death of family members to HIV/AIDS since they had no reliable relatives to take care of them.[12]

While much of the literature continues to present poverty as a key driver, it has been argued that the catch-all use of the term masks more complex and fundamental push factors, such as the cultural motivations of parents to send their girls into "safe" and suitable situations in advance of married life.[13] For example, the movement of large numbers of children in Liberia from rural areas to live with relatives or friends of relatives in urban settings mirrors the long-established tradition of child fostering across much of West Africa.[14] Initial results from a recent study of the psychosocial impact of domestic work on children has found that the level of cultural and social acceptability of child domestic work in a society impacts upon the age at which children enter the sector and how they are subsequently treated – with children in societies where the practice is widely accepted found to be starting work at a younger age and subject to greater exploitation than those in places where the practice is less tolerated.[15]

The practice of child fostering invokes notions of benign kinship relations and community support for raising children but, in reality, conceals their large-scale exploitation and abuse:[16]

> My aunt made me sell cold water and after selling I had to do housework in the evening. I spent a year and a half, but I was not going to school. I sent a message to my mother, but no response. So, I decided to leave the house. I spent two months with friends until a truck driver helped me and took me back to Zwedru. My mother was not happy to see me because I had run away from my aunty.[17]

Child-fostering arrangements are perceived as being benign by parents and foster families alike, with powerful and enduring myths surrounding the practice that encourages its continuance. Parents and most of the other adults in studies of this kind are reported to strongly believe that sending their children away to be brought up by other "better off" families will afford their children far greater opportunities than they could offer them at home. It is also believed that living with a foster family offers a more protective environment for their children and that whatever work is asked of the child by his or her foster family will be less arduous than other kinds of labour. Compounding this, foster families, far from seeing themselves as exploiters, consider that they are helping out by taking the child in. Their perception of themselves is as benefactors who treat the child in their care as "one of their own."[18]

Discrimination and Isolation

Children often report that the daily experience of discrimination and isolation in the employer's household are the most difficult part of their burden. A recent study in Bangladesh found that it was "neither the verbal or physical punishments, nor the possible lack of material goods or even food, that upset [the CDWs] most; it was the discrimination, exclusion, disrespect, ingratitude, and other assaults on their emotional needs that truly hurt them."[19] Even if their relationship with members of the household is good, these relationships are not on equal terms. A typical manifestation of this discrimination is that the employer's children go to school, while the CDW cannot. The child often has to eat separately from the employing family, may have to eat food of inferior quality, and often receives second-rate treatment in times of ill health. While she may sleep in the same room as the employer's children, she may equally end up in the kitchen or on the veranda.[20] "Once, I had tea with my employers. They told me to go in the corner and drink."[21]

CDWs have limited freedom of movement, living in their employers' houses and being subject to their rules. Commonly, these children are told not to leave the house by their employers, who frighten them with stories of what they will face on the outside. Even if they are paid, they may not handle their wages or have enough money to escape. While most employers do not take on CDWs with the express intention of perpetuating violence against them, research from many regions indicates that children are preferred to adults by some employers because they perceive them to be more "submissive" and "easier to control."[22]

Violence and Abuse

The child's isolated situation and her indistinct role in the employer's household makes her particularly vulnerable to physical, verbal, and sexual abuse. The negative social connotations attached to domestic work in many settings compounds the ambiguity of the CDW's relationships to the employing family members. Even though they know that their child will be working as a domestic, parents will place them with a new family, not as a "worker" but, rather, as a "daughter."[23] The informality of this arrangement suits both the parents and the employers, in that it allows for the continuation of the parental pretense that their child is being cared for in a family environment, while encouraging employers to believe that they are assisting the child and her family back home. However, it often works against the interests of the child herself by disguising an exploitative arrangement and masking violence and abuse. If violence does occur, the child's dependency on her employer for basic needs and her acceptance of violence as an occupational hazard makes her far less likely to report it.[24]

There are broad similarities with regard to the incidence and range of violence against CDWs, although differences exist in local manifestations of violent behaviour towards these children. For example, in some countries, research has indicated that girls tend to suffer more from verbal bullying and boys more from physical violence. In a 2006 study of 500 CDWs in West Bengal, for example, it was found that 68 percent had faced physical abuse, with almost half suffering severe abuse that had led to injuries. In addition, 86 percent of CDWs had experienced emotional abuse. The study also found that nearly a third of families had no idea where their daughters were working, and 27 percent admitted they knew that they were being beaten and harassed.[25]

An Impediment to Education

Much research has shown how child domestic work directly impedes the child's right to education. Most CDWs themselves attach great importance to becoming educated and, in some cases, consider that being a domestic worker is a way of continuing their studies. In reality, more often than not, their situation is a serious obstacle to studying. Commonly, this is simply because employers do not allow them to go to school or renege on an initial agreement to do so.[26] As one child confides: "I was going to study this year but my employer said it wasn't possible: we couldn't leave the children alone. Both he and his wife go out to work."[27]

However, even when CDWs are given the opportunity, the long working hours and requirements of their job often make it impossible to take up education. In Lima, for example, some children persevere with night schools but report that they have little time for homework and are frequently tired at school, which has made it difficult to progress. Similar issues are commonly reported among CDWs elsewhere.[28] Preliminary results from a multi-country study on the impact of child domestic work has found that while many CDWs, particularly in middle-income countries, manage to combine their work with school attendance, these children tend not to perform as well as non-working children at school. They have higher dropout rates, a poorer perception of their own achievement, and are more likely to have to repeat school years.[29]

The inflexibility of the formal education system is seen as another obstacle to continuing their education, as is the poor teaching quality in some schools and the difficulty in affording school books, equipment, uniforms and in paying school fees. Many CDWs also end up dropping out during the school year because of these problems and are discouraged from returning to formal education because of the need to earn money for their families.[30] In addition to seeing education as a tool for advancement, a 2008 study indicates that education is a key factor in protecting CDWs "because it denotes the support of their parents, community and teachers and allows them to participate, grow and have aspirations."[31] A 2010 study has found that CDWs who are unable to attend school are more likely to suffer from poor psychosocial health, particularly low self-esteem, than those who do.[32]

Child Domestic Work as Slavery
A number of the features of domestic work described so far, such as the discrimination faced particularly by CDWs and the ambiguity of their relationship to their employers, are intrinsic to both the nature of the

work and the circumstances in which it is carried out and are more than reminiscent of the master-servant relationship that many consider to have long since died out. At the same time, the myriad manifestations of child domestic work, and the variety of outcomes that result, makes it inadvisable and impractical to suggest that all child domestic work is analogous to slavery when it comes to considering realistic policy and practice responses to ending their vulnerability to exploitation and abuse.

Thus, while it is clear that by no means all CDWs are in slavery-like situations, experts have been concerned about these children for some time, particularly those who "live in" with their employers. In 1925, for instance, the Temporary Slavery Commission of the League of Nations condemned the transfer of children for domestic service under the pretext of adoption as slave dealing.[33] Article 1(d) of the 1956 Supplementary Convention on the Abolition of Slavery, the Slave Trade, and Institutions and Practices Similar to Slavery (Supplementary Convention) considers as "servitude" situations of children living away from home to work, whether or not they are paid.[34] Discussions during the drafting process of the Supplementary Convention provide strong indications of the practices that it was intended to prohibit, including versions of the *Mui Tsai* (literally meaning "Little Sister") system that was prevalent in China earlier in the century, which involved the transfer of young children (mainly girls) by parents or guardians, under the guise of adoption, to be used by their new family as domestic servants.

In practice, there are many parallels between the *Mui Tsai* system that was of concern to slavery specialists in the twentieth century and the situation faced by many live-in CDWs today. First, control of the child has been handed over to another person, whether the child has been sold, given up to be "looked after," or used as collateral for a debt. The child is therefore under the control of adults whose first concern is not her well-being. Second, the child is living as well as working away from family and home, limiting the ability of parents to monitor the child's welfare and increasing the child's dependence on her employer for her well-being and basic needs. Third, the child is often not directly compensated for her work (if she is paid at all). Wages may be transferred to her parents, deducted in repayment of a debt, or withheld on any number of pretexts. This not only denies the child access to her own money but also has the effect of tying her to her employer.

There is evidence that considerable numbers of CDWs are in debt bondage (compelled to work against a debt where the terms and conditions of the loan are either unspecified or not followed or the lending agreement is highly exploitative), often as a side effect of traditional feudal relationships between landlords and tenants as well as on an individual basis.[35] For example, families in agricultural bonded labour in Pakistan and Nepal have for centuries been required to send a daughter to the landlord's house to work as a domestic, and sometimes such children are sent away from the rural estate to work at the landlord's city home or another urban household connected to the landlord's family. There are also reports of parents pledging children into individual bondage as domestics (outside of any landlord-tenant relationship) due to the need to obtain money for survival or for some exceptional expense.[36]

A further example of the close relationship between aspects of child domestic work and slavery was picked up by the ILO in 1993, when its Committee of Experts on the Application of the Conventions and Recommendations discussed the situation of young children working as domestic servants as a forced labour issue, drawing on information that they had received about restavèk ("stay with") children in Haiti. The committee recognized and noted the child's separation from her home and family, the threat of physical and sexual abuse, the long hours, the exploitative conditions, and the humiliation she must endure. The committee also took note of the restavèk child's total dependence upon her employing family for her welfare as well as her complete lack of freedom of movement. They further noted that the child was not consulted regarding her work as a domestic and was often so young upon her departure from her natural family that if she were able to return home at some point she would not know where to go. The committee commented that restavèk children were found "to work as domestics in conditions which are not unlike servitude. The children were forced to work long hours, with little chance for bettering their conditions; many children were reported to have been physically or sexually abused."[37]

More recently, with the development of international standards on trafficking, child domestic work has also been identified as a trafficking issue. At its simplest, child trafficking can be described as the process of recruiting and moving a child for the purpose of exploitation.[38] While prospective employers may approach the child or her family directly, more often than not it is intermediaries who broker the deals between parents and employers and who transport the children to their employing families. Commonly, intermediaries deceive or coerce the child or her parents/guardians, who are fed false promises about the working conditions, the opportunities for education, and what life for the child will be like. This means that the way in which significant numbers of children (but by no means all) enter domestic service can legitimately be described as trafficking. Sometimes it is the children themselves or their families who take the initiative to migrate and who themselves approach recruiters. Although these children may be more aware of what they will be doing, they are generally unaware of the hardships that they are likely to face.[39] Invariably, the trafficked child is totally dependent on the trafficker for her well-being, particularly during the transportation process. Additional vulnerabilities arise when national borders are crossed illegally – for example, in situations where the child is undocumented or located in a place where she does not speak the local language.

Not Just a Labour Issue

Over the last twenty years, there has been a transformation of perceptions among international actors, in particular, from understanding child domestic work as a benign practice to the widespread acknowledgment of the many ways in which it undermines children's rights. While the dominant view remains that the practice is predominantly a "child labour" issue, a growing number of studies have been looking beyond this analysis to examine the issue as a gender-based social phenomenon with links to a range of other child rights concerns, including the growing commercialization of traditional upbringing practices, sexual abuse, child marriage, and the movement of children.[40] Understanding has also been shifting beyond consideration of CDWs simply as passive victims of exploitation and abuse towards recognition of them as agents of change in their own lives and the lives of others.

This broader understanding is all the more important given the current focus of international attention on an expansive definition of what constitutes hazardous child labour. In particular, the trend towards defining all child domestic work as hazardous (and, therefore, to be banned for all individuals under the age of eighteen, as per the terms of the Convention Concerning the Prohibition and Immediate Action for the Elimination of the Worst Forms of Child Labour (Child Labour Convention) requires careful consideration.[41] A number of studies have shown that, while aspects of their situation and the work they do make CDWs vulnerable to hazard, it is also possible to reduce these risks to an extent that would allow CDWs who are above the legal minimum working age (usually fourteen or fifteen years) to work. It is neither acceptable nor practical to deny the opportunity of work to an adolescent who is entitled to do so.[42]

Child Domestic Work through a Gender Lens

Understanding child domestic work as a child labour issue alone is only a partial analysis. CDWs are linked to wider patterns of exploitation and abuse, not only because they are children but also because they are girls. Evidence shows that the practice is hugely gender biased, in large part due to entrenched societal notions of domestic work as fundamentally the domain of women and girls.[43] Across the world, domestic work is an important source of employment for adults as well as children. In Asia, for example, it has been estimated that employment in households accounts approximately for a third of female employment.[44] At the same time, domestic work, including childcare, is seen as economically unproductive and is consequently given little or no value.

Typically, because domestic work is the assumed role of women, it is not recognized as "work" and therefore lies outside the ambit of labour legislation in many countries.[45] Despite widespread acknowledgment of the numbers and needs of CDWs, international and national policies and programs for adolescent girls still largely fail to recognize CDWs as a specific target.[46] In spite of the importance of domestic work to the functioning of economies and society, its sheer commonness and ordinariness conspire to maintain its continued invisibility. However, there is evidence of a growing concern about the situation of domestic workers. After years of campaigning and discussion, 16 June 2011 saw the ILO adopt the Convention Concerning Decent Work for Domestic

Workers, the purpose of which was to bring the rights of domestic workers into line with protections afforded to other workers.

Two-thirds of the more than 750 million people in the world who cannot read and write are female, an indication of the continuing lack of relative value placed on girls' education in certain settings. When it comes to adolescent girls – many of whom work as domestics – the prevailing view among parents is that schools are unsafe places because of the exposure to sexual harassment both in school and on the journey to and from school, compounding the widespread belief that schooling is an irrelevance for their girls' future roles as wives and mothers.[47] In many cases, their lack of education and the ability to develop other skills leaves young domestic workers with few options other than to continue in domestic service. In addition, their experiences in domestic labour often stay with them and may serve to strengthen their low self-esteem and inertia.

CDWs as Children "on the Move"

The large majority of CDWs move large distances, often hundreds of miles, away from their own families and into employers' households. This mostly rural-to-urban (and sometimes cross-border) migration is part of a wider pattern of population movements taking place in many settings – a trend that is set to continue as a result of economic imperatives, conflict, state failure, natural disasters, and environmental and resource pressures.[48] However, analysis of the movement of CDWs and other children on the move has largely been linked to highly emotive discussions around child trafficking and equally highly politicized debates around adult migration. As a result, neither of these frameworks has adequately aided our understanding of CDWs' actual experiences of movement, of what kinds of support they require, or of how protection systems might best be adapted to suit their needs.[49]

In particular, a loose understanding of "trafficking" to describe the movement of all children into domestic service has largely obscured an understanding of the variety of triggers and motivations for such movement as well as how these CDWs travel and what situations they end up in.[50] The trafficking label also remains an obstacle to the development of child-centred responses that keep the best interests of CDWs as their uppermost concern.[51] Evidence from West Africa, in particular, has shown that community-based structures such as "anti-trafficking committees," set up to intercept trafficked children, have been intercepting all children who are on the move. By failing to focus exclusively on children being trafficked, these committees, along with other measures to stop young people migrating, have become a source of abuse rather than protection.[52]

Furthermore, the restricted trafficking focus has led governments to prioritize the punishment of traffickers above the protection of victims' rights. Many efforts to end trafficking have also focused on preventing children from moving into situations in which they would be exploited, rather than on ending the exploitative element of the movement or creating an alternative to an exploitative outcome. While this approach may well protect children from exploitation, it may also deny children access to other rights, including their right to freedom of movement as well as education, health, and other services. A more holistic rights-based view – and one that does not assume that movement is necessarily negative for children – is therefore likely to be a more appropriate framework for understanding the full implications of children's movement.[53]

Child Domestic Workers as Agents of Change

The right of children to participate has come to the fore since the almost universal adoption of the 1989 Convention on the Rights of the Child (UNCRC).[54] Article 12(1) of the UNCRC asserts that "States Parties shall assure to the child who is capable of forming his or her own views the right to express those views freely in all matters affecting the child, the views of the child being given due weight in accordance with the age and maturity of the child." This means shifting adult perceptions of children as passive victims of abuse, exploitation, and violence towards understanding them as citizens and individuals capable of analyzing and responding to their situations and problems. They have a right to voice their views, to be heard, and to be taken seriously on decisions affecting their lives.[55] In numerous studies, CDWs have demonstrated themselves to be central agents of change in their own lives and in the lives of children in similar situations.[56]

Invariably, soliciting the views of CDWs, including the very youngest, provides an essential perspective on their situation and needs and results in information with which to target assistance more effectively. Findings resulting from consultations by Anti-Slavery International and its partners with more than 400 current and former CDWs have exemplified the importance of service providers and adult decision makers recognizing the competence and agency of CDWs. The research also highlights that the most effective interventions are those that systematically involve CDWs in their planning and implementation.[57]

CDWs' right to free association, which is listed in Article 15 of the UNCRC, is also a key aspect of their participation as well as representing a very tangible way of supporting their protection from workplace abuses. Self-help groups and associations of CDWs are actively engaged in advocacy and mutual support to protect their interests. A pioneer in this regard has been Sumapi – a self-help group for child and adult domestic workers in the Philippines. The group has grown considerably since its inception in 1995 to become a national movement of domestic workers, with formal links to national trade union bodies. Sumapi's collective approaches have had a major impact on its members and on those they have reached. In addition to reducing CDWs' isolation through mutual support and providing national and local advocacy platforms for domestic worker concerns, Sumapi members continue to provide CDWs with information and assistance – increasingly via social networking sites such as Facebook and through mobile phone texting – that protects them from abuse and has offered opportunities for education, training, and counselling.[58]

Implications for Policy and Practice

Current conceptions of CDWs have created a number of policy and practice gaps, the identification of which may assist practitioners and policy-makers to better understand and target actions to improve the protection of CDWs. More broadly, despite a number of similarities in CDWs' situations, the differences and nuances in manifestations of the practice in different contexts requires that programs aimed at reaching and supporting CDWs must be based on a detailed understanding of the setting in question, not on generalized perceptions. Comic Relief, a key UK funder on street and working children's issues, has further noted that, since the vast majority of CDWs are girls (typically over 90 percent), and the most common working girls' occupation is domestic service, the failure to reach and support CDWs indicates a bias against girls within child labour programs generally.[59]

Measures to improve the visibility of, and access to, CDWs are crucial to protecting CDWs from harm. This requires the development of systems to identify where child domestic workers are (for example, through local registration schemes) as well as the systematic monitoring of their well-being, such as through house visits and dialogue with employing families. Daily and weekly time off for CDWs, as well as banning the confinement of children in their employer's house, would ensure opportunities for them to make contact with peers and family and decrease dependency on the employing family.[60]

Measures are needed to curb violence, abuse, and harassment (and their threat), including the development of accessible complaints mechanisms; the prompt investigation and prosecution of perpetrators; and the training of law enforcement officials on how to respond appropriately to complaints from CDWs, including how to investigate and collect evidence and provide referrals for assistance.[61] Removal and recovery programs are needed to protect CDWs from immediate danger, such as those that can provide temporary accommodation, immediate physical and psychological health care, legal assistance, and education-related support.[62]

In the absence of adequate legal protection for CDWs in many countries, international standards such as ILO's Child Labour Convention have been instrumental in putting child domestic labour on various national agendas. National and local legal provision for CDWs remains a policy priority both because it establishes minimum standards of protection and makes it easier to bring the issue out into the open. The ILO's recent adoption of standards specific to domestic workers (Domestic Workers Convention and Recommendation no. 201 on Domestic Workers) is likely to be a further step towards highlighting the inherent vulnerability of domestic workers and protecting them from exploitation and abuse.[63] The new standards require states to protect young children from domestic work, while ensuring that adolescents who are entitled to work do so without impinging on their education. States are further recommended to provide special protection for adolescents entitled to work by strictly limiting their working hours and banning night work as well as carefully controlling and monitoring their working conditions.

However, legislation and its interpretation in some countries actively work against the protection of CDWs, serving to create and maintain their vulnerability to exploitation – for example, the systemic denial of the minimum wage to domestic workers, the inability of those above the minimum working age but under eighteen years to negotiate or sign a contract, or their inability to officially organize. Extending these labour protections to those who are entitled to work would make them more visible and decrease their dependency and, as a result, their vulnerability.[64] A step that could play a significant part in reducing the exploitation and abuse of adolescent CDWs (who have reached the legal working age) is the introduction of standard agreements or contracts that regulate their employment and formalize their protection. This would be a natural extension to the progress made by the introduction of "codes of conduct" in many countries to improve the situation of CDWs. Such agreements would assist the worker in understanding her rights, make clear to employers their responsibilities to the child (such as the right to education), and would help in "visiblizing" CDWs vis-à-vis the authorities and service providers. CDWs who are entitled to work should be allowed to enter into such fair and reasonable employment contracts with free and informed consent.[65]

Experience in some regions of the world has already shown that improving a child's working conditions or developing a contract can often be an effective response to a working situation that is harmful in some way. In regions such as West Africa, this response is more realistic and feasible than a policy of taking children out of employment and leaving them stranded (as they often see it) or in residential care situations that may result in their further abuse and exploitation. Further, the practice of withdrawing abused child workers routinely confers impunity on their employer, who simply replaces them and continues with the same harsh treatment as before.[66]

A 2008 study of the views of more than 400 CDWs and former CDWs in over twenty locations in Africa, Asia, and Central and Latin America also provides crucial insight into these children's perspectives on the kinds of support and help they need from practitioners and on what affords them the best protection from abuse and exploitation.[67] Broadly, the findings indicate that the interventions that are having the most positive impact for CDWs are those that seek to: (1) maintain or reestablish contact between the child and her or his close relatives; (2) intervene directly with their employers in a non-confrontational way; (3) establish and support groups of domestic workers to enable them to help themselves; and (4) encourage CDWs back to education and to retain them in education by, for example, making schooling more girl friendly.

CDWs in the 2008 study also spoke of the need for service providers and adult decision makers to recognize their competence and agency and to develop responses that build the capacities of CDWs to help themselves. This is particularly important since there are still far too few service providers in existence to be able to reach the very large numbers of CDWs around the world. Another clear message to emerge from the consultations was the importance of practitioners and policy-makers talking directly to CDWs about what they need. Evidence from the consultations indicate that the most effective interventions were those that systematically involved CDWs themselves in the planning and implementation of their projects and programs.[68]

A number of researchers have reported the need for practitioners and policy-makers to tackle the chronic lack of self-esteem in CDWs, which disempowers many of them from self-improvement and increases their vulnerability.[69] A recent study of CDWs in Bangladesh noted that they run a high risk of long-term mental health problems, regardless of their material and physical security,[70] with an Ethiopian study concluding that "childhood mental and behavioural disorders were more common in the domestic child labourers [than among other working and non-working children]."[71]

Preliminary results from a recent multi-country study to assess the health and psychosocial impact of child domestic work found that migrant CDWs commonly suffer from poorer psychosocial health than other CDWs as a result of separation from their family networks and being subject to unfamiliar environments and cultures.[72] This research further shows that there are several determining factors that look to have protective or negative effects on a CDW's well-being, including (1) that education contributes to well-being and, conversely, that CDWs who do not attend school have worse psychosocial outcomes (particularly low self-esteem) than those who do; (2) that available support networks, including those provided by non-governmental organizations (NGOs) and employers, can make a significant difference to the way working and living conditions impact on CDWs' psychosocial health – that is, those who do not have strong social networks or close family, friends, or support organizations to rely on have worse psychosocial outcomes; (3) that children with poor psychosocial outcomes are also more likely to suffer from poor physical health; (4) that the nature of the tasks performed impacts on CDWs' well-being; and (5) that children who are proud of their work are less likely to have poor psychosocial outcomes. For many children, pride comes from being able to help their families.[73]

Building a Better Understanding

The methods used to collect many of the findings reported earlier in this chapter also offer the researcher material insight into understanding the situation of CDWs. The past twenty years has seen growing numbers of studies examining child domestic work issues as well as the increasing use of participatory methods and tools to solicit the perspectives of CDWs directly. With a great deal still to understand about child domestic work and the perspectives and concerns of these uniquely isolated and vulnerable children, this trend is to be welcomed in enhancing future research methods. So, which study methods have been proven to work? What are the ethical issues and practical concerns that confront researchers in this field of study? And how have these challenges been overcome?

Numerous studies have shown that CDWs are often extremely isolated inside their employer's households. Talking to them in their workplaces is likely to make them feel constrained and fearful of the consequences of upsetting their employers. It has been shown that in-depth interviews with children are therefore best conducted in a setting outside their place of work, preferably a place where the child feels safe and comfortable. Unless the interviewer is experienced in interviewing children, it is necessary to build up the child's confidence in her or him. Thus, it has been found that interviewing children in depth is best done over a period of time in a relatively unstructured and informal way. The ideal setting is an existing project in which CDWs are participating – for example, a drop-in centre or an education program. The fieldwork for Nanna Baum's research in Bangladesh, for instance, took place in a secure semi-public space, outside of the employer's apartment, with local NGOs facilitating access to CDWs through education centres in a middle-class neighbourhood in Dhaka. In this way, contact was made with approximately eighty CDWs, with interviews spread over five months.[74]

Interviewing can often be highly stressful for CDWs. Some researchers have found that an interview can make a child depressed or cause her to run away subsequently. As a result, experience has shown that in-depth interviewing should only be considered if the researcher is prepared to provide help for the child concerned – either from a service provider with whom the researcher has links or from another source. Recent research with CDWs has centred on locations where there are a range of good quality and accessible services for them and, in particular, the availability of trained personnel who are able to assist participants in dealing sensitively with their recall of distressing experiences. In a number of cases, it was necessary for members of the research teams to speak to employers and guardians about the purpose of the research and to seek consent from them to allow the children to participate. This process presented an opportunity to identify and reach out to a number of children who were subsequently able to benefit from the services provided by the NGOs. Several participants reported abuse by their current employers, and the service providers were able to take immediate action in consultation with the children concerned.[75]

In-depth techniques that elicit information from the children without subjecting them to the rigours of questioning, such as drawing, painting, acting out, and storytelling, have proven to be effective methods of eliciting information. They have been found to be especially useful in cultural settings where people are not used to being bombarded with questions. Informed consent is vital in cases where images (including photographs and drawings) are taken for use. Explaining to children how images will be used is important, with the images themselves anonymized unless express permission is otherwise given. Informing all research participants beforehand of the purpose of the process and of the intended uses of the information they have provided is also essential. Children should be able to opt out of discussions and request that their input be kept off the record.

Research with CDWs very often involves talking to former workers with experience of the issue. Apart from the obvious difficulties of verifying the age of children under eighteen, the principal reason for involving those no longer working as CDWs is to include the perspectives of individuals who can put their experience into a wider context. In particular, these individuals are often well placed to analyze what interventions have been of most benefit to them and which provide them with the best protection from abuse and exploitation. At the same time, however, discussions involving older and younger CDWs can often be dominated by the older group members, which oftentimes constrains younger discussants from sharing information. As a result, experience has shown that debates and focus group discussions are often more productive and less intimidating for younger members if the participants are divided up by age groups. In this way, younger children are more prepared to raise intimate concerns.[76]

Data Collection: Lessons Learned

The purpose of Anti-Slavery International's 2008 action-oriented research (discussed earlier) was to consult with current and former CDWs in order to identify what forms of assistance (interventions) were most useful to them and which offered them the best protection from abuse and exploitation. Participants were selected to represent the diverse experiences of CDWs more generally, taking into account, among other things, their age, gender, religion, socio-economic and ethnic backgrounds, place of origin, education levels, and levels of pay (including those who are unpaid).[77] In keeping with the ethical principles outlined in Anti-Slavery International's 1997 handbook, most of those current or former CDWs who were consulted were already in contact with a service provider in order to ensure that they were in a position to seek support, if necessary, as a result of any issues raised in the discussions.[78] In cases where individuals were not already linked to a service provider, information was provided to them about where they could go to receive help.

In Anti-Slavery International's 2008 research, a variety of methods were used to find out about the situation of current and former CDWs and to gather their views. The basic methods of information capture were individually structured and semi-structured interviews and group discussions, although the expression of these varied widely between contexts. In many cases, the CDWs who were involved (particularly the younger children) expressed themselves through drawings. In addition, some discussions took place with key informants such as employers, guardians, and community leaders. Several lessons have emerged from the research, which have implications for future data collection practice.[79]

Identifying and Accessing CDWs

In three Peruvian cities where the interviews took place, contact with current and former CDWs was made easier as a result of the interviewers' previous working experience with this population. In Lima and Cajamarca, the interviewers belonged to NGOs already providing services to CDWs. In Pucallpa, one of the interviewers had a great deal of experience working in schools and ground-level organizations in the region. Collaboration with school authorities, community leaders, and agents (as a result of contacts developed by the NGO service providers) also facilitated contact with current and former CDWs. Even so, identifying children in domestic service of different ages and diverse ethnic and educational backgrounds (for the purposes of comparison) was difficult. In Tanzania, the involvement of local community leaders (street leaders) in the process proved important in assisting in the identification of, and access to, CDWs. Their involvement also served to allay the fears of employers, who were happy to allow the children to participate because of the street leaders' presence.

Choosing the Right Time and Place

In Benin and Togo, selecting the right kind of venue and location took careful consideration. Venues were chosen with a view to removing children as much as possible from their everyday environment in order to avoid interruptions. In one location, the setting hindered the discussion because it took place within walking distance of the homes in which the participants worked. While this meant that the venue was easy to get to, it also made it easy for them to be disturbed, as was the case when a local leader became curious about what was taking place. In Costa Rica, considerable effort and imagination was needed to overcome the difficulties involved in generating spaces for interaction and discussion in pairs among a group of young people, most of whom were juggling work and school. In Tanzania, it was important to get the timing right for interviews and group discussions with CDWs since many were only in a position to participate when their employers were at home. It was found that the best time for the CDWs was on weekends, particularly after church on Sunday.

Tools and Testing

Pilot testing of information-gathering tools emerged as a crucial issue in Peru. More dynamic instruments were needed for the adolescent participants. At the same time, it was difficult to keep the younger children focused and motivated to the end of the interview schedule. Icebreaking games, songs, and dances were important features of the consultations in Benin and Togo, helping to keep the participants alert and interested. Consultation dynamics were particularly enhanced as a result of activities that sought to include all of the participants, rather than presentations performed by only some of the participants. This in turn was said to have had a positive impact on the quality of the output of the consultation.

In Benin and Togo, drawing was used extensively as a method for putting interviewees at their ease, with CDWs using the drawings as props, giving them the confidence to speak up. In Tamil Nadu, India, group discussions were considered to be particularly helpful in drawing out the experiences of those who were less talkative, as the participants supported and encouraged each other. In Benin, a fictitious case study was developed to lead the discussion on interventions. The story of Cica and Tété, which combined common elements from real situations faced by CDWs, proved to be an effective way of helping the participants think about concrete ways of assisting the characters and led to lively discussion.

Confidentiality
In Nepal, confidentiality was emphasized in order to ensure that participants felt secure in being able to express their thoughts and feelings without fear of retribution. In particular, some children were concerned about commenting on their employers and the consequences of criticizing the local service provider and other NGO programs. It was found that children who had only just begun participating in the local service providers' programs were more open about speaking their minds. In the Philippines, participants were assured that their comments about the actions of the service providers would be raised with relevant members of the staff, without divulging who said it.

Verifying and Validating the Findings
In the Philippines, most participants had worked with various employers (both good and bad) prior to the consultations. This made it challenging to verify and sort out the various perceptions and experiences that the CDWs shared. Care and sensitivity was required in putting into context the various responses elicited during one-on-one interviews, and it was important to consult with the interviewer/enumerator to verify the responses gathered. When consulting children, considerable care was taken to avoid "putting words into their mouths." Facilitators verified children's answers with follow-up questions such as "Did you say that ... ?" or "What did you mean about ... ?"

Conclusion
Child domestic work is both work like any other and work like no other. Defying simple categorization, it is the intersection of pervasive cultural norms surrounding labour, the role of family, as well as the place of children and girls in society. The resulting ambiguity for children in these situations, compounded by their isolation and dependency on those for whom these children's best interests is not of paramount

concern, creates excessive vulnerability and can, in certain contexts, be considered analogous to slavery.

In various studies, CDWs themselves have clearly articulated that their vulnerability to exploitation is directly due to the isolation and discrimination they face in their employers' households. Maintaining contact with their origin families, and socializing with children of their own age (other than their employer's children), is vital to countering potential exploitation and abuse, as is creating opportunities for domestic workers, young and old, to meet, support each other, and fight collectively for improvements in their working conditions and treatment.

A broader and more rounded conception of the situation and needs of CDWs – beyond child work and slavery perspectives – not only offers an opportunity for greater insight into their lives, motivations, and perspectives but also brings benefits to the efficiency and effectiveness of efforts to improve their situation. Therefore, a priority must be made to ensure that the realities of CDWs are considered in other relevant policy fields, including debates relating to women, migration, and the protection of workers in the private sphere.

Research methods that emphasize the importance of talking to the children themselves have been central to augmenting our understanding, and research of this type plays a key role in ensuring that CDWs are placed (and remain) on relevant policy agendas. Without more evidence and greater clarity on the perspectives and needs of these children, there is a real danger that child domestic work will remain a "niche" children's issue that never results in an airing of the big questions that it raises about societal attitudes to girls.

Notes

1   It is also recognized that many children, particularly girls, carry significant domestic workloads in their own homes and face similar issues to child domestic workers (CDWs). However, their situation is different from CDWs in at least one major respect: these children are under the control of adults, for whom the child's best interests is, in the main, their primary concern. The situation of children, particularly of girls, expected to work long and hard and often denied an education also warrants attention but is not the subject of this chapter.

2   International Labour Organization (ILO), *Child Domestic Workers: Global Estimates 2012* (Geneva: ILO, 2012); ILO and International Programme on the Elimination of Child Labour (IPEC), *Helping Hands or Shackled Lives? Understanding Child Domestic Labour and Responses to It* (Geneva: ILO, 2004).

3   Convention Concerning the Prohibition and Immediate Action for the Elimination of the Worst Forms of Child Labour, 17 June 1999, 2133 UNTS 161 (Child Labour Convention), Article 3(d).

4   J. Blagbrough, *They Respect Their Animals More: Voices of Child Domestic Workers* (London: Anti-Slavery International/WISE, 2008).

5   Convention Concerning Decent Work for Domestic Workers, 16 June 2011, ILO Convention no. 189, preamble.

6   ILO, *Decent Work for Domestic Workers*, Report IV(1), International Labour Conference, 99th Session (Geneva: ILO, 2010), para. 45.

7   "Her" should equally be taken to mean "his." Ibid., para. 45.

8   J. Blagbrough, "Child Domestic Labour: A Global Concern," in G. Craig, ed., *Child Slavery Now: A Contemporary Reader* (Bristol: Policy Press, 2010), 81-98.

9   M. Black, *Comic Relief Review: What Are the Best Ways to Develop Effective Strategies and Approaches to Reach and Support Child Domestic Workers?* (London: Comic Relief, 2011).

10 UN Children's Fund (UNICEF) and International Child Defence Centre (ICDC), *Child Domestic Work*, Innocenti Digest no. 5 (Florence: UNICEF and International Child Development Centre, 1999).

11 Blagbrough, "Child Domestic Labour."

12 Blagbrough, *They Respect Their Animals More.*

13 Black, *Comic Relief Review.*

14 J. Blagbrough, *Blind Hope: Children on the Move in Liberia* (London: Save the Children UK, 2008).

15 Anti-Slavery International, *Interim Research Report on the Psychosocial Impact of Child Domestic Work* (London: Anti-Slavery International, 2010).

16 M. Dottridge and O. Feneyrol, *Action to Strengthen Indigenous Child Protection Mechanisms in West Africa to Prevent Migrant Children from Being Subjected to Abuse* (Lausanne: Terre des Hommes Foundation, 2007).

17 CDW, Liberia, quoted in Blagbrough, *Blind Hope*, 12.

18 Ibid.

19 N. Baum, "Girl Domestic Labour in Dhaka: Betrayal of Trust," in G.K. Lieten, ed., *Working Boys and Girls at Risk: Child Labour in Urban Bangladesh* (Dhaka: University Press, 2011).

20 UNICEF and ICDC, "Child Domestic Work."

21 CDW, India, quoted in Anti-Slavery International and Children Unite, *Stand with Us: Decent Work for Domestic Workers –Recommendations on Domestic Work* (London: Anti-Slavery International and Children Unite, 2010).

22 J. Blagbrough, "Violence against Child Domestic Workers," paper presented at Workshop "Towards a Strategy to Address Corporal Punishment of Children in Southeast Asia Pacific," Save the Children Alliance, Bangkok, 6–9 October 2003.

23 Baum, "Girl Domestic Labour in Dhaka."

24 Blagbrough, *Child Domestic Labour.*

25 Save the Children UK, *Abuse among Child Domestic Workers: A Research Study in West Bengal* (West Bengal: Save the Children UK, 2006).

26 Blagbrough, *Child Domestic Labour.*

27 CDW, Peru, quoted in Blagbrough, *They Respect Their Animals More*, 18.

28 Ibid.

29 Anti-Slavery International, *Interim Research Report.*

30 Blagbrough, *Child Domestic Labour.*

31 A. Meyers, "Psychosocial Impacts of Domestic Child Labour in India: Through the Lens of a Save the Children Development Education Resource," MA dissertation, Institute of Education, University of London, 2008, 74 (unpublished).

32 Anti-Slavery International, *Interim Research Report.*

33 S. Miers, *Slavery in the Twentieth Century: The Evolution of a Global Problem* (Walnut Creek, CA: AltaMira Press, 2003).

34 Supplementary Convention on the Abolition of Slavery, the Slave Trade, and Institutions and Practices Similar to Slavery, 7 September 1956, 226 UNTS 3 (Supplementary Convention).

35 Debt bondage is defined in the 1956 Supplementary Convention as "the status or condition arising from a pledge by a debtor of his personal services or of those of a person under his control as security for a debt, if the value of those services as reasonably assessed is not applied towards the liquidation of the debt or the length and nature of those services are not respectively limited and defined." Supplementary Convention, Article 1(a).

36 Harris Gazdar and Ayesha Khan, "A Rapid Assessment of Bonded Labour in Domestic Work and Begging in Pakistan," Working Paper 22, Collective for Social Science Research, Karachi (Geneva: International Labour Office, March 2004).

37 ILO, Summary of Reports (Articles 19, 22 and 35 of the Constitution), International Labour Conference, 80th Session 1993, Report III (Parts 1, 2 and 3), Third Item on the Agenda: Information and Reports on the Application of Conventions and Recommendations (Geneva: International Labour Office), 101. http://www.ilo. org/public/libdoc/ilo/P/09661/09661(1993-80).pdf.

38 This paraphrases the Protocol to Prevent, Suppress and Punish Trafficking in Persons, especially Women and Children, 15 November 2000, 40 ILM 335 (2001) (supplementing the Convention against Transnational Organized Crime, 15 November 2000, 40 ILM 335 [2001]), which defines child trafficking as "the action of recruitment, transportation, transfer, harbouring, or receipt [of a child] for the purposes of exploitation, which includes exploiting the prostitution of others, sexual exploitation, forced labour, slavery or similar practices, and the removal of organs."

39 ILO and IPEC, *Unbearable to the Human Heart: Child Trafficking and Action to Eliminate It* (Geneva: ILO, 2002).

40 Black, *Comic Relief Review.*

41 Child Labour Convention.

42 Author's correspondence with ILO and IPEC on child domestic labour guidelines, 29 January 2010.

43 Plan UK, *Because I Am A Girl (the State of the World's Girls 2009): Girls in the Global Economy: Adding It All Up* (London: Plan UK, 2009).

44 Blagbrough, *They Respect Their Animals More.*

45 J.M. Ramirez-Machado, *Domestic Work, Conditions of Work and Employment: A Legal Perspective*, Conditions of Work and Employment Series no. 7 (Geneva: ILO, 2003).

46 Plan UK, *Because I Am A Girl.*

47 Black, *Comic Relief Review.*

48 D. Reale, *Away from Home: Protecting and Supporting Children on the Move* (London: Save the Children UK, 2008).

49 Ibid.

50 Blagbrough, *Blind Hope.*

51 M. Dottridge, *A Handbook on Planning Projects to Prevent Child Trafficking* (Lausanne: Terre des Hommes Foundation, 2007).

52 M. Dottridge and O. Feneyrol, *Action to Strengthen Indigenous Child Protection Mechanisms in West Africa to Prevent Migrant Children from Being Subjected to Abuse* (Lausanne: Terre des Hommes Foundation, 2007).

53 Blagbrough, *Blind Hope.*

54 Convention on the Rights of the Child, 20 November 1989, 1577 UNTS 3.

55 M. Bourdillon, *A Place for Work in Children's Lives?* (Toronto: Plan Canada, 2010).

56 Blagbrough, *They Respect Their Animals More.*

57 Ibid.

58 ILO and IPEC, *Child Domestic Labour in South East and East Asia: Emerging Good Practices to Combat It* (Bangkok: ILO, 2010); author's communication with Sumapi.

59 Black, *Comic Relief Review.*

60 Based on recommendations made in 2010 by more than 150 current and former CDWs from Africa, Asia, and Central and South America who were consulted by Anti-Slavery International and Children Unite about the ILO's proposed standards on domestic work as well as the author's correspondence with the ILO and IPEC on child domestic labour guidelines, 29 January 2010.

61 Ibid.

62 Ibid.

63 Blagbrough, *Child Domestic Labour.* Domestic Workers Convention; Recommendation no. 201 on Domestic Workers, 16 June 2011.

64 Author's correspondence with the ILO and IPEC on child domestic labour guidelines, 29 January 2010.

65 Ibid.

66 Ibid.

67 Blagbrough, *They Respect Their Animals More.*

68 Ibid.

69 Black, *Comic Relief Review.*

70 Baum, "Girl Domestic Labour in Dhaka."

71 Cited in A. Meyers, "Psychosocial Impacts of Domestic Child Labour in India."

72 Anti-Slavery International, *Interim Research Report.*

73 Ibid.

74 Baum, "Girl Domestic Labour in Dhaka."

75 Blagbrough, *They Respect Their Animals More.*

76 M. Black, *Child Domestic Workers: A Handbook for Research and Action* (London: Anti Slavery International, 1997).

77 Blagbrough, *They Respect Their Animals More.*

78 Black, *Child Domestic Workers.*

79 For more information on the research processes used and the lessons learned by Anti-Slavery International and its local partners, see the handbooks developed by Maggie Black, *They Respect Their Animals More.*

Appendix
Bellagio-Harvard Guidelines on the Legal Parameters of Slavery

We, the Members of the Research Network on the Legal Parameters of Slavery,

Recognizing that there has been a lack of legal clarity with regard to the interpretation of the definition of slavery in international law;

Conscious that the starting point for understanding that definition is Article 1(1) of the 1926 Slavery Convention which reads: "*Slavery is the status or condition of a person over whom any or all of the powers attaching to the right of ownership are exercised*";

Recalling that this definition is reproduced in substance in Article 7(a) of the 1956 Supplementary Convention on the Abolition of Slavery, the Slave Trade, and Institutions and Practices Similar to Slavery;

Also noting that the 1926 definition of slavery is once again reproduced in substance in the definition of enslavement found in Article 7(2)(c) of the 1998 Statute of the International Criminal Court and developed in more detail in the secondary legislation of the Court, in its Elements of Crimes;

Bearing in mind the provisions in international human rights law regarding slavery within the 1948 Universal Declaration and 1966 International Covenant on Civil and Political Rights; as well as the provisions regarding slavery in regional human rights conventions of the African, European, and Inter-American systems;

Considering the inclusion of slavery as an enumerated type of human exploitation in both the 2000 United Nations Palermo Protocol on Trafficking in Persons and the 2005 Council of Europe Convention on Action against Trafficking in Human Beings;

Mindful of the pronouncements and case-law related to slavery of international, regional and domestic courts;

Having met to consider the issue at the 2010 symposium entitled: "The Parameters of Slavery" at the Rockefeller Foundation's Bellagio Conference Centre in Bellagio, Italy; having further deliberated in 2011 at a meeting under the auspices of the Harriet Tubman Institute for Research on the Global Migrations of African Peoples, York University, Canada; and came together once more at a 2011 symposium entitled: "The Legal Parameters of Slavery: Historical to the Contemporary" at Harvard University, under the auspices of the Charles Hamilton Houston Institute for Race and Justice, Harvard Law School; the Harvard Sociology Department; the W.E.B. DuBois Institute;

Recommend the following Guidelines related to the legal parameters of slavery:

Guideline 1 – The Legal Definition

The legal definition of slavery in international law is found at Article 1(1) of the 1926 Slavery Convention, which reads: "Slavery is the status or condition of a person over whom any or all of the powers attaching to the right of ownership are exercised."

Guideline 2 – The Exercise of the Powers Attaching to the Right of Ownership

In cases of slavery, the exercise of "the powers attaching to the right of ownership" should be understood as constituting control over a person in such a way as to significantly deprive that person of his or her individual liberty, with the intent of exploitation through the use, management, profit, transfer or disposal of that person. Usually this exercise will be supported by and obtained through means such as violent force, deception and/or coercion.

Guideline 3 – Possession is Foundational to Slavery

Where there is a right of ownership in respect of a thing, ownership implies a background relation of control. That control is the power attaching to the right of ownership known as possession.

Possession is foundational to an understanding of the legal definition of slavery, even when the State does not support a property right in respect of persons. To determine, in law, a case of slavery, one must look for possession.

While the exact form of possession might vary, in essence it supposes control over a person by another such as a person might control a thing. Such control may be physical, but physical constraints will not always be necessary to the maintenance of effective control over a person. More abstract manifestations of control of a person may be evident in attempts to withhold identity documents; or to otherwise restrict free movement or access to state authorities or legal processes; or equally in attempts to forge a new identity through compelling a new religion, language, place of residence, or forcing marriage.

Fundamentally, where such control operates, it will significantly deprive that person of his or her individual liberty for a period of time which is, for that person, indeterminate.

Cases of slavery are to be distinguished from those where, though there has been control exercised, it does not constitute control tantamount to possession, such as where employers make legitimate decisions about the management of workers.

Possession is foundational in that, not only is it a power attaching to the right of ownership, it also creates the factual conditions for the exercise of any or all of other powers attaching to the right of ownership, such as those set out in *Guideline 4*.

Guideline 4 – Further Examples of Powers Attaching to the Right of Ownership

Where a person controls another such as he or she would control a thing owned, such possession makes possible the exercise of any or all of the powers attaching to the right of ownership.

Correlatively, the exercise of any or all of the powers attaching to the right of ownership may serve to indicate the presence of control of a person tantamount to possession, and so provide evidence of slavery.

The following are further examples of powers attaching to the right of ownership:

(a) Buying, Selling or Transferring a Person

Buying, selling or otherwise transferring a person may provide evidence of slavery. Having established control tantamount to possession; the act of buying, selling or transferring that person will be an act of slavery.

Evidence of slavery may also be found in similar transactions, such as bartering, exchanging, or giving or receiving a person as a gift, where control tantamount to possession has been established.

(b) Using a Person

Using a person may provide evidence of slavery. Having established control tantamount to possession; the act of using that person will be an act of slavery.

Evidence of such use of a person may include the derived benefit from the services or labour of that person. In such cases, a person might be used by working for little or no pay, utilised for sexual gratification, or used by providing a service.

(c) Managing the Use of a Person

Managing the use of a person may provide evidence of slavery. Having established control tantamount to possession; the act of managing that person will be an act of slavery.

Evidence of such management of the use of a person may include indirect management such as a brothel owner delegating power to a day manager in a situation of slavery in the context of sex work.

(d) Profiting from the Use of a Person

Profiting from the use of a person may provide evidence of slavery. Having established control tantamount to possession; the act of profiting from the use of that person will be an act of slavery.

Evidence of profiting from the use of a person may include cases where a person is mortgaged, lent for profit, or used as collateral.

Evidence of profiting from the use of a person may also include making money or deriving any other kind of income or benefit from the use of the person. Such as the use of an agricultural worker in a

situation of slavery, where the profit from the picking of a crop is taken or received by another whether in the form of wages or of the harvest.
(e) Transferring a Person to an Heir or Successor

Transferring a person to an heir or successor may provide evidence of slavery. Having established control over a person tantamount to possession; the act of willing that person to a child or other heir or successor will be an act of slavery.

Evidence of such transferring of a person may include a case of inheritance where a woman, on the death of her husband, is deemed to be inherited by another person.

Evidence of such a transferring of a person may also include the conveying of a status or condition of a person to that of a successive generation, such as from mother to daughter.
(f) Disposal, Mistreatment or Neglect of a Person

Disposing of a person following his or her exploitation may provide evidence of slavery. Having established control over a person tantamount to possession; the act of disposing of a person will be an act of slavery.

Mistreatment or neglect of a person may provide evidence of slavery. Having established control tantamount to possession, such disregard may lead to the physical or psychological exhaustion of a person, and ultimately to his or her destruction; accordingly the act of bringing about such exhaustion will be an act of slavery.

Evidence of such mistreatment or neglect may include sustained physical and psychological abuse, whether calculated or indiscriminate; or the imposition of physical demands that severely curtail the capacity of the human body to sustain itself or function effectively.

Guideline 5 – Making a Determination as to Whether Slavery Exists
The exercise of any or all of the powers attaching to the right of ownership just considered shall provide evidence of slavery, insofar as they demonstrate control over a person tantamount to possession.

Accordingly, in determining whether slavery exists in a given case, it is necessary to examine the particular circumstances, asking whether *"powers attaching to the right of ownership"* are being exercised, so as to demonstrate control of a person tantamount to their possession.

In evaluating the particular circumstances to determine whether slavery exists, reference should be made to the substance and not simply to the form of the relationship in question.

The substance of the relationship should be determined by investigating whether in fact there has been an exercise of one or more of the powers attaching to the right of ownership. This will include a determination as to whether control tantamount to possession is present.

Guideline 6 – Expropriation

Ordinarily exclusion from expropriation or "security of holding" would be deemed a power attaching to the right of ownership. However, as the State generally does not support a property right in persons, a negative obligation against the State generally no longer exists.

However, the State has *at minimum* the positive obligation to bring about the end of either the status or condition of a person over whom any or all of the powers attaching to the right of ownership are exercised.

The State may have further positive obligations with regard to the prohibition against slavery on the basis of domestic law as well as regional or international instruments.

Guideline 7 – Terminology

The term "slavery" has often been utilised to describe circumstances that go beyond the legal definition as established by the 1926 Slavery Convention.

In law, only "slavery" and "institutions and practices similar to slavery," which is often abbreviated to "practices similar to slavery" have standing and are defined in international law via the 1926 Slavery Convention and the 1956 Supplementary Convention.

Guideline 8 – Distinction between Slavery and Forced Labour

The 1926 Slavery Convention recognises that forced labour can develop "into conditions analogous to slavery."

Although forced or compulsory labour is defined by the 1930 Forced Labour Convention as "all work or service which is exacted from any person under the menace of any penalty and for which the said person has not offered himself voluntarily"; forced labour will only amount to slavery when, in substance, there is the exercise of the powers attaching to the right of ownership.

Slavery will not be present in cases of forced labour where the control over a person tantamount to possession is not present.

Guideline 9 – Distinction between Slavery and "Institutions and Practices Similar to Slavery"

Article 1 of the 1956 Supplementary Convention recognises that the "institutions and practices similar to slavery," that is: debt bondage, serfdom, servile marriages, or child exploitation; may be "covered by the definition of slavery contained in article 1 of the Slavery Convention of 1926."

The distinction between these servile statuses as defined by the 1956 Supplementary Convention in the following terms and slavery is that slavery is present where in substance there is the exercise of the powers attaching to the right of ownership.

It should be emphasised that slavery will only be present in cases of such "institutions and practices similar to slavery" where control over a person tantamount to possession is present.

The following are the conventional servitudes set out in the 1956 Supplementary Convention on the Abolition of Slavery, the Slave Trade, and Institutions and Practices Similar to Slavery:

(a) Debt bondage, that is to say, the status or condition arising from a pledge by a debtor of his personal services or of those of a person under his control as security for a debt, if the value of those services as reasonably assessed is not applied towards the liquidation of the debt or the length and nature of those services are not respectively limited and defined;

(b) Serfdom, that is to say, the condition or status of a tenant who is by law, custom or agreement bound to live and labour on land belonging to another person and to render some determinate service to such other person, whether for reward or not, and is not free to change his status;

(c) Any institution or practice whereby:

  (i) A woman, without the right to refuse, is promised or given in marriage on payment of a consideration in money or in kind to her parents, guardian, family or any other person or group; or

  (ii) The husband of a woman, his family, or his clan, has the right to transfer her to another person for value received or otherwise; or

  (iii) A woman on the death of her husband is liable to be inherited by another person;

(d) Any institution or practice whereby a child or young person under the age of 18 years is delivered by either or both of his natural parents or by his guardian to another person, whether for reward or not, with a view to the exploitation of the child or young person or of his labour.

Guideline 10 – When Slavery and Lesser Servitudes Are Present
Accepting that both slavery and lesser servitudes such as forced labour or "institutions and practices similar to slavery" may be found in substance in a particular circumstance; the manner to proceed is by making reference to that substance and not simply to the form, and first ask whether there has been an exercise of the powers attaching to the right of ownership. If so, then the more serious offence of slavery is present.

If not, reference should be made to the legal definition of the lesser servitude which corresponds in substance to the particular circumstance in question.

Adopted on this day, 3 March 2012, by the Members of the Research Network on the Legal Parameters of Slavery.

Jean Allain, Queen's University, Belfast
Kevin Bales, Free the Slaves
Annie Bunting, York University
John Cairns, University of Edinburgh
William M. Carter, Jr., Temple University
Holly Cullen, University of Western Australia
Seymour Drescher, University of Pittsburgh
Stanley Engerman, University of Rochester

Paul Finkelman, Albany Law School
Bernard Freamon, Seton Hall University
Allison Gorsuch, Yale University
Robin Hickey, Durham University
Richard Helmholz, University of Chicago
Anthony Honoré, University of Oxford
Aidan McQuade, Anti-Slavery International
Orlando Patterson, Harvard University
James Penner, University College, London
Joel Quirk, University of Witwatersrand
Jody Sarich, Free the Slaves
Rebecca Scott, University of Michigan

Selected Bibliography

Adams, Niki. "Anti-Trafficking Legislation: Protection or Deportation?" *Feminist Review* 73, 1 (2003): 135–39. http://dx.doi.org/10.1057/palgrave.fr.9400084.

African Rights. *Rwanda: Death, Despair and Defiance*. London: African Rights, 1994.

–. *Rwanda: Killing the Evidence: Murder, Attack, Arrests and Intimidation of Survivors and Witnesses*. London: African Rights, 1996.

Alexander, Jeffrey C. *The Meanings of Social Life: A Cultural Sociology*. Oxford: Oxford University Press, 2003.

Allain, Jean. "The Definition of Slavery in International Law." *Howard Law Journal* 52, 2 (2009): 239–76.

Amnesty International. *North Korea: Political Prison Camps*. 2011.

–. *Reports: North Korea*. 2011, 2012, 2013, 2014–15.

Anand, Vikas, Blake E. Ashforth, and Mahendra Joshi. "Business as Usual: The Acceptance and Perpetuation of Corruption in Organizations." *Academy of Management Executive* 18, 2 (2004): 39–53. http://dx.doi.org/10.5465/AME.2004.13837437.

Andrees, Beate. *Forced Labour and Trafficking in Europe: How People Are Trapped In, Live Through and Come Out*. Geneva: International Labour Office, 2008.

Androff, David K. "The Problem of Contemporary Slavery: An International Human Rights Challenge for Social Work." *International Social Work* 54, 2 (2011): 209–22. http://dx.doi.org/10.1177/0020872810368395.

Ansett, Sean. Uzbek Cotton and Forced Child Labour: Is The Government Serious? Ethical Corporation. 2009. http://www.ethicalcorp.com/content.asp?ContentID=6093 (accessed 25 January 2011).

Anti-Slavery International. *Interim Research Report on the Psychosocial Impact of Child Domestic Work*. London: Anti-Slavery International, 2010 (unpublished).

Anti-Slavery International and Children Unite. *Stand with Us: Decent Work for Domestic Workers: Recommendations to the ILO from Young Domestic Workers*. London: Anti-Slavery International and Children Unite, 2010.

–. *Stand With Us: Protecting Young Workers through the ILO Convention and Recommendation on Domestic Work*. London: Anti-Slavery International and Children Unite, 2011.

Applebaum, Anne. *Gulag: A History*. New York: Ramdom House, 2003.

Ashforth, Blake E., and Glen E. Kreiner. ""How Can You Do It?": Dirty Work and the Challenge of Constructing a Positive Identity." *Academy of Management Review* 24, 3 (1999): 413–34.

Azmy, Baher. "Unshackling the Thirteenth Amendment: Modern Slavery and a Reconstructed Civil Rights Agenda." *Fordham Law Review* 71 (2002): 981–1062.

Baaz, Maria Eriksson, and Maria Stern. *A Critical Analysis of Sexual Violence in the Democratic Republic of Congo (DRC)*. Working Paper on Gender-based Violence. Stockholm: Swedish International Development Cooperation Agency, 2010.

Balch, Oliver. *Cocoa: Ghana's Glass and a Half of Sustainability*. 2010. Ethical Corporation. http://www.ethicalcorp.com/communications-reporting/cocoa-ghana's-glass-and-half-sustainability (accessed 28 October 2016).

Bales, Kevin. *Disposable People: New Slavery in the Global Economy*. Berkeley, CA: University of California Press, 1999.

–. *Ending Slavery: How We Free Today's Slaves*. Berkeley, CA: University of California Press, 2012.

–. "Slavery and the Human Right to Evil." *Journal of Human Rights* 3, 1 (2004): 55–65.

–. *Understanding Global Slavery: A Reader*. Berkeley, CA: University of California Press, 2005.

Baron, David. P. "Integrated Strategy: Market and Nonmarket Components." *California Management Review* 37, 2 (1995): 47–65.

Baum, Nanna. "Girl Domestic Labour in Dhaka: A Betrayal of Trust." In *Working Boys and Girls at Risk: Child Labour in Urban Bangladesh*, ed. G.K. Lieten. Dhaka, Bangladesh: The University Press, 2011.

Baysinger, Barry D. "Domain Maintenance as an Objective of Business Political Activity: An Expanded Typology." *Academy of Management Review* 9, 2 (1984): 248–58.

British Broadcasting Corporation. *Tracing the Bitter Truth of Chocolate and Child Labour*. 2010. Panorama. http://news.bbc.co.uk/panorama/hi/front_page/newsid_8584000/8584847.stm (accessed 25 January 2011).

Beah, Ishmael. "Foreword." In *Kamara M. and Susan McClelland's Bite of the Mango*. Richmond Hill: Annick Press, 2008.

Becker, Gary S. "Crime and Punishment: An Economic Approach." *Journal of Political Economy* 76, 2 (1968): 169–217. http://dx.doi.org/10.1086/259394.

Becker, Jasper. *Rogue Regime: Kim Jong Il and the Looming Threat of North Korea.* New York: Oxford University Press, 2005.

Bellamy, Alex J. "A Chronic Protection Problem: The DPRK and the Responsibility to Protect." *International Affairs* 91, 2 (2015): 225–44. http://dx.doi.org/10.1111/1468-2346.12232.

Belser, Patrick, Michaëlle de Cock, and Farhad Mehra. *ILO Minimum Estimate of Forced Labour in the World.* Geneva: International Labour Office, 2005.

Bernstein, Elizabeth. "The Sexual Politics of the "New Abolitionism." *Differences: A Journal of Feminist Cultural Studies* 18, 3 (2007): 128–51. http://dx.doi.org/10.1215/10407391-2007-013.

Bernstein, Richard. "How Not to Deal with North Korea." *New York Review of Books* 54, 3 (2007): 37–39.

Bernstein, Richard J. "Militarized Humanitarianism Meets Carceral Feminism: The Politics of Sex, Rights, and Freedom in Contemporary Anti-Trafficking." *Signs* 36, 1 (2010): 45–71. http://dx.doi.org/10.1086/652918.

–. J. *Praxis and Action.* Philadelphia: University of Pennsylvania Press, 1971.

Bird, Frederick B., and James A. Waters. "The Moral Muteness of Managers." *California Management Review* 32, 1 (1989): 73–88. http://dx.doi.org/10.2307/41166735.

Black, Maggie. *Child Domestic Workers: Finding a Voice: A Handbook on Advocacy.* London: Anti-Slavery International, 2002.

–. *Child Domestic Workers: A Handbook on Good Practice in Program Interventions.* London: Anti-Slavery International, 2005.

–. *Child Domestic Workers: A Handbook for Research and Action.* London: Anti Slavery International, 1997.

–. *Comic Relief Review: What Are the Best Ways to Develop Effective Strategies and Approaches to Reach and Support Child Domestic Workers?* London: Comic Relief, 2011.

Blagbrough, Jonathan. *Blind Hope: Children on the Move in Liberia.* London: Save the Children UK, 2008 (unpublished).

–. "Child Domestic Labour: A Global Concern." In *Child Slavery Now: A Contemporary Reader*, ed. G. Craig, 81–98. Bristol, UK: Policy Press, 2010.

–. *Child Domestic Work in Indonesia: A Preliminary Situation Analysis.* Geneva: International Labour Organization and International Programme on the Elimination of Child Labour, 1995 (unpublished).

–. *They Respect Their Animals More: Voices of Child Domestic Workers.* London: Anti-Slavery International, 2008.

–. *Violence against Child Domestic Workers.* Paper presented at the Workshop entitled Towards a Strategy to Address Corporal Punishment of Children in Southeast Asia Pacific, 6–9 October 2003. Bangkok: Save the Children Alliance, 2003.

Bouhours, Thierry, Roderic Broadhurst, Chenda Keo, and Brigitte Bouhours. "Human Trafficking and Moral Panic in Cambodia." *The Annals* 653, 1 (2014): 202–24.

Bourdillon, M. *A Place for Work in Children's Lives?* Toronto: Plan Canada, 2010.

Bourke, Gerald. "North Korea Slashes Food Rations: Aid Worker." *Agence France-Presse*, 28 June 2011.

Brass, Tom. *Towards a Comparative Political Economy of Unfree Labour: Case Studies and Debates*. London: Frank Cass, 1999.

Brysk, Alyson, and Austin Choi-Fitzpatrick, eds. *From Human Trafficking to Human Rights*. Philadelphia: University of Pennsylvania Press, 2012. http://dx.doi.org/10.9783/9780812205732.

Bunting, Annie. "Forced Marriage in Conflict Situations: Researching and Prosecuting Old Harms and New Crimes." *Canadian Journal of Human Rights* 1, 1 (2012): 165–85.

Buss, Doris. "Rethinking 'Rape as a Weapon of War.'" *Feminist Legal Studies* 17, 2 (2009): 145–63. http://dx.doi.org/10.1007/s10691-009-9118-5.

Bwibo, Nimrod O., and Philista Onyango. *Final Report of the Child Labour and Health Research*. Nairobi: University of Nairobi, 1987.

Cadet, Jean-Robert. *Restavec: From Haitian Slave Child to Middle-Class American*. Austin, TX: University of Texas Press, 1998.

Camacho, Anges Z.V., Maria C. Flores-Oebanda, Virgilio Montano, Rolando R. Pacis, and Roserillan Robidillo. *The Phenomenon of Child Domestic Work: Issues, Responses and Research Findings*. Paper presented at the Asian Regional Consultation on Child Domestic Workers, Manila, 19–23 November 1997.

Capous-Desyllas, Moshoula. "A Critique of the Global Trafficking Discourse and U.S. Policy." *Journal of Sociology and Social Welfare* 34, 4 (2007): 57–79.

Carlson, Khristopher, and Dyan Mazurana. *Forced Marriage within the Lord's Resistance Army, Uganda: Strengthening the Humanity and Dignity of People in Crisis through Knowledge and Practice*. Somerville, MA: Feinstein International Center, May 2008.

Caryl, Christian. "The Other North Korea." *New York Review of Books* 55, 13 (2008): 25–27.

Choe, Sang-Hun. "North Korea Exports Forced Laborers for Profit, Rights Groups Say." *New York Times*, 20 February 2015.

Choi-Fitzpatrick, Austin. "The Good, the Bad, the Ugly: Human Rights Violators in Comparative Perspective," Introductory essay to guest edited special issue. *Journal of Human Trafficking* 1, 2 (2016): 1–14.

–. "In Plain Sight? Human Trafficking and Research Challenges." *Human Rights and Human Welfare* 6 (2006): 63–73.

–. "From Rescue to Representation: A Human Rights Approach to the Contemporary Anti-Slavery Movement." *Journal of Human Rights* (2015): 486–503. http://dx.doi.org/10.1080/14754835.2015.1032222.

–. "Rethinking Trafficking: Contemporary Slavery." In *Human Trafficking and Human Rights: Rethinking Contemporary Slavery*, ed. Alison Brysk and Austin Choi-Fitzpatrick, 13–24 Philadelphia, PA: University of Pennsylvania Press, 2012.

–. *What Slaveholders Think: How Contemporary Perpetrators Rationalize What They Do.* New York: Columbia University Press, 2017.

Chol-hwan, Kang. "The Aquariums of Pyongyang." In *From the Gulag to the Killing Fields: Personal Accounts of Political Violence and Repression in Communist States,* ed. P. Hollander, 683–97. Wilmington, DE: ISI Books, 2006.

Clarke, Kamari Maxine. *Fictions of Justice: The International Criminal Court and the Challenge of Legal Pluralism in Sub-Saharan Africa.* Cambridge: Cambridge University Press, 2009. http://dx.doi.org/10.1017/CBO9780511626869.

Commission of Inquiry. *Report of the Detailed Findings of the Commission of Inquiry into on Human Rights in the Democratic People's Republic of North Korea.* United Nations Human Rights Council, 2014.

Cooke, Bill. "The Denial of Slavery in Management Studies." *Journal of Management Studies* 40, 8 (2003): 1895–1918. http://dx.doi.org/10.1046/j.1467-6486.2003.00405.x.

Copelon, Rhonda. "Gender Crimes as War Crimes: Integrating Crimes against Women into International Criminal Law." *McGill Law Journal* 46, 3 (2000): 217–40.

–. "Gender Violence as Torture: The Contribution of CAT General Comment no. 2." *New York City Law Review* 11 (2009): 229–63.

Coulter, Chris. *Bush Wives and Girl Soldiers: Women's Lives through War and Peace in Sierra Leone.* Ithaca, NY: Cornell University Press, 2009.

Crane, Andrew. "Corporate Greening as Amoralization." *Organization Studies* 21, 4 (2000): 673–96. http://dx.doi.org/10.1177/0170840600214001.

Crosby, Alison, and M. Brinton Lykes. "Mayan Women Survivors Speak: The Gendered Relations of Truth Telling in Postwar Guatemala." *International Journal of Transitional Justice* 5 (2011): 456–76.

Cubilié, Anne. *Women Witnessing Terror: Testimony and the Cultural Politics of Human Rights.* New York: Fordham University Press, 2005.

Cullen, Holly. *The Role of International Law in the Elimination of Child Labor.* Leiden: Martinus Nijhoff, 2007. http://dx.doi.org/10.1163/ej.9789004162853.i-303.

Cumings, Bruce. *Korea's Place in the Sun: A Modern History.* New York: W.W. Norton, 2005.

da Silva, Ana Paula, Thaddeus Gregory Blanchette, and Andressa Raylane Bento. "Cinderella Deceived: Analyzing a Brazilian Myth Regarding Trafficking in Persons." *Vibrant: Virtual Brazilian Anthropology* 10, 2 (2013): 377–419.

Delgado, Richard. "Storytelling for Oppositionists and Others: A Plea for Narrative." *Michigan Law Review* 87, 2411 (1989): 2436–37.

Demick, Barbara. *Nothing to Envy: Ordinary Lives in North Korea.* New York: Spiegel and Grau, 2009.

Denton, Erin. "Anatomy of Offending: Human Trafficking in the United States, 2006–2011." *Journal of Human Trafficking* 2, 1 (2016): 32–62. http://dx.doi.org/10.1080/23322705.2016.1136540.

"Deprive and Rule." *Economist,* 17 September 2011.

Devalpo, Alain. "North Korean Slaves." *Le Monde Diplomatique*, 4 August 2006.

Dick, Andrew R. "When Does Organized Crime Pay? A Transaction Cost Analysis." *International Review of Law and Economics* 15, 1 (1995): 25–45. http://dx.doi.org/10.1016/0144-8188(94)00010-R.

Domar, Evsey. "The Causes of Slavery or Serfdom: A Hypothesis." *Journal of Economic History* 30, 1 (1970): 18–32. http://dx.doi.org/10.1017/S0022050700078566.

Donath, Miriam. "U.N. Panel Calls for North Korea Referral to International Court." *Reuters*, 18 November 2014.

Dottridge, Mike. *A Handbook on Planning Projects to Prevent Child Trafficking*. Lausanne, Switzerland: Terre des Hommes Foundation, 2007.

—, ed. "Special Issue: Following the Money: Spending on Anti-Trafficking." *Anti-Trafficking Review* 3 (2014): 3–175.

Dottridge, Mike, and Olivier Feneyrol. *Action to Strengthen Indigenous Child Protection Mechanisms in West Africa to Prevent Migrant Children from Being Subjected to Abuse*. Lausanne, Switzerland: Terre des Hommes Foundation, 2007.

European Center for Constitutional and Human Rights. *Child Labour in Uzbek Cotton Production and the Responsibility of European Corporations*. European Center for Constitutional and Human Rights, 2011.

Feasley, Ashley. "Eliminating Corporate Exploitation: Examining Accountability Regimes as Means to Eradicate Forced Labor from Supply Chains." *Journal of Human Trafficking* 2, 1 (2016): 15–31.

Fein, Helen. *Human Rights and Wrongs: Slavery, Terror, Genocide*. Boulder, CO: Paradigm, 2007.

Fleischman, Richard K., and Thomas N. Tyson. "Accounting in Service to Racism: Monetizing Slave Property in the Antebellum South." *Critical Perspectives on Accounting* 15, 3 (2004): 376–99. http://dx.doi.org/10.1016/S1045-2354(03)00102-3.

Flores-Oebanda, Ma. Cecilia, Roland Romeo R. Pacis, and Virgilio P. Montano. *The Kasambahay: Child Domestic Work in the Philippines: A Living Experience*. Manila: ILO and Visayan Forum Foundation, 2001.

Friebel, Guido, and Sergel Guriev. "Smuggling Humans: A Theory of Debt-Financed Migration." *Journal of the European Economic Association* 4, 6 (2006): 1085–1111. http://dx.doi.org/10.1162/JEEA.2006.4.6.1085.

Garoupa, Nuno. "The Economics of Organized Crime and Optimal Law Enforcement." *Economic Inquiry* 38, 2 (2000): 278–88. http://dx.doi.org/10.1111/j.1465-7295.2000.tb00017.x.

Gazdar, Harris, and Ayesha Khan. "A Rapid Assessment of Bonded Labour in Domestic Labour and Begging in Pakistan." Working Paper 22, Collective for Social Science Research, Karachi. Geneva: International Labour Office, March 2004.

Global Alliance Against Traffic in Women. *Collateral Damage: The Impact of Anti-Trafficking Measures on Human Rights Around the World*. Bangkok: Global Alliance against Traffic in Women, 2007.

Godoy, Oscar. *El Salvador. Trabajo infantil doméstico: Una evaluación rápida*. Geneva: International Labour Organization and International Programme for the Elimination of Child Labour, 2002.

Goedde, Patricia. "Legal Mobilization for Human Rights Protection in North Korea: Furthering Discourse or Discord?" *Human Rights Quarterly* 32, 3 (2010): 530–74. http://dx.doi.org/10.1353/hrq.2010.0008.

Goodale, Mark, and Sally Engle Merry, eds. *The Practice of Human Rights: Tracking Law between the Global and the Local*. Cambridge: Cambridge University Press, 2007. http://dx.doi.org/10.1017/CBO9780511819193.

Gould, Chandre, and Nicole Fick. *Selling Sex in Cape Town: Sex Work and Human Trafficking in a South African City*. Pretoria, South Africa: Institute for Security Studies, 2008.

Grant, Robert M. "Toward a Knowledge-Based Theory of the Firm." *Strategic Management Journal* 17, 2 (1996): 109–22. http://dx.doi.org/10.1002/smj.4250171110.

Habermas, Jürgen. *Communication and the Evolution of Society*. Boston: Beacon Press, 1979.

Haggard, Stephan, and Marcus Noland. *Repression and Punishment in North Korea: Survey Evidence of Prison Camp Experiences*. Honolulu: East-West Center, 2009.

–. *Witness to Transformation: Refugee Insights into North Korea*. Washington, DC: Peterson Institute for International Economics, 2011.

Harper, Eric, Diane Massawe, and Marlise Richter. *Report on the 2010 Soccer World Cup and Sex Work: Documenting Successes and Failures*. Johannesburg: n.p., 2010.

Hassig, Ralph, and Kongdan Oh. *The Hidden People of North Korea: Everyday Life in the Hermit Kingdom*. New York: Rowman and Littlefield, 2009.

Hawk, David. *The Hidden Gulag: Exposing North Korea's Prison Camps*. Washington, DC: US Committee for Human Rights in North Korea, 2003.

Heyman, Josiah. "Putting Power in the Anthropology of Bureaucracy: The Immigration and Naturalization Service at the Mexico-United States Border." *Current Anthropology* 36, 2 (1995): 261–87. http://dx.doi.org/10.1086/204354.

Hillman, Amy J., and Micheal A. Hitt. "Corporate Political Strategy Formulation: A Model of Approach, Participation, and Strategy Decisions." *Academy of Management Review* 24, 4 (1999): 825–42.

Hirsch, Marianne, and Leo Spitzer. "'We Would Not Have Come without You': Generations of Nostalgia, by *American Imago*." *Studies in Psychoanalysis and Culture* 59, 3 (2002): 253–76.

Hochschild, Adam. *The Unquiet Ghost: Russians Remember Stalin*. New York: Houghton Mifflin, 2003.

Howard-Hassmann, Rhoda E. "North Korea: A Case for a New International Treaty on the Right to Food." *Asia-Pacific Journal on Human Rights and the Law* 15, 1–2 (2014): 31–50.

–. "State-Induced Famine and Penal Starvation in North Korea." *Genocide Studies and Prevention* 7, 2/3 (2012): 147–65. http://dx.doi.org/10.3138/gsp.7.2/3.147.

Horowitz, Sara R. *Voicing the Void: Muteness and Memory in Holocaust Fiction*. New York: State University of New York Press, 1997.

Human Rights Watch. *North Korea: Workers' Rights at the Kaesong Industrial Complex*. New York: Human Rights Watch, 2006.

–. *"Prohibited Persons": Abuse of Undocumented Migrants*. New York: Asylum Seekers, and Refugees in South Africa, 1998.

–. *Service for Life: State Repression and Indefinite Conscription in Eritrea*. New York: Human Rights Watch, 2009.

–. *Swept under the Rug: Abuses against Domestic Workers around the World*. New York: Human Rights Watch, 2008.

–. *World Report: North Korea, Events of 2008*. New York: Human Rights Watch, 2009.

–. *World Report: North Korea, Events of 2009*. New York: Human Rights Watch, 2010.

–. *World Report: North Korea, Events of 2010*. New York: Human Rights Watch, 2011.

–. *World Report; North Korea, Events of 2011*. New York: Human Rights Watch, 2012.

–. *World Report; North Korea, Events of 2012*. New York: Human Rights Watch, 2013.

–. *World Report; North Korea, Events of 2013*. New York: Human Rights Watch, 2014.

Human Rights Without Frontiers International. "North Korea: Qatar's Ambitious Future Driven on by North Korean 'Forced Labour.'" Newsletter: North Korea: Democracy, Rule of Law and Human Rights,12 November 2014.

Human Sciences Research Council. *Tsireledzani: Understanding the Dimensions of Human Trafficking in Southern Africa*, 2010.

Hughes, Rachel. "The Abject Artefacts of Memory: Photographs from Cambodia's Genocide." *Media Culture and Society* 25, 1 (2003): 23–44. http://dx.doi.org/10.1177/0163443703025001632.

"ICC Looks into Possible War Crimes by North Korea." *International Justice Tribune*, 6 December 2010.

International Labour Organization. *Child Domestic Work: Global Estimates 2012*. Geneva: International Labour Organization, 2012.

–. *The Cost of Coercion*, Report I(B). Geneva: International Labour Organization, 2009.

–. *Decent Work for Domestic Workers*, Report IV(1). Geneva: International Labour Organization, 2010.

–. *Global Estimate of Forced Labour: Results and Methodology*. Geneva: International Labour Organization, 2012.

International Labour Organization and International Programme for the Elimination of Child Labour. *Child Domestic Labour in South East and East Asia: Emerging Good Practices to Combat It*. Bangkok: International Labour Organization, 2005.

–. *Flowers on the Rock: Phenomenon of Child Domestic Workers in Indonesia*. Jakarta: International Labour Organization, 2004.

–. *Helping Hands or Shackled Lives? Understanding Child Domestic Labour and Responses to It.* Geneva: International Labour Organization, 2004.

–. *Unbearable to the Human Heart: Child Trafficking and Action to Eliminate It.* Geneva: International Labour Organization, 2002.

International Labour Rights Forum and Human Rights Defenders in Uzbekistan. *Forced Child Labour in Uzbekistan's 2008 Spring Agricultural Season.* Washington, DC: International Labour Rights Forum, 2008.

Iqbal, Muhammad J. "Bonded Labor in the Brick Kiln Industry of Pakistan." *Lahore Journal of Economics* 11, 1 (2006): 99–119.

Jacobsen, Christine M., and May-Len Skilbrei. "'Reproachable Victims'? Representations and Self-Representations of Russian Women Involved in Transnational Prostitution." *Ethnos: Journal of Anthropology* 75, 2 (2010): 190–212. http://dx.doi.org/10.1080/00141841003764013.

Jackson, Mary. *The Velvet Glove: Paternalism and Conflict in Gender, Class, and Race Relations.* Berkeley, CA: University of California Press, 1994.

James, Erica. *Democratic Insecurities: Violence, Trauma, and Intervention in Haiti.* Berkeley, CA: University of California Press, 2001.

Jayashri, Srikantiah. "Perfect Victims and Real Survivors: The Iconic Victim in Domestic Human Trafficking Law." *Boston University Law Review* 87, 1 (2007): 157–211.

Kalra, Monika Satya. "Forced Marriage: Rwanda's Secret Revealed." *University of California Davis Journal of International Law and Policy* 7 (2001): 197.

Kamara, Mariatu, with Susan McClelland. *Bite of the Mango.* Richmond Hill: Annick Press, 2008.

Kang, Grace M. "A Case for the Prosecution of Kim Jong Il for Crimes against Humanity, Genocide, and War Crimes." *Columbia Human Rights Law Review* 38 (2006): 86.

Kaplinsky, Raphael. "Spreading the Gains from Globalization: What Can Be Learned from Value Chain Analysis?" *Problems of Economic Transition* 47, 2 (2004): 74–115.

Kara, Siddharth. *Sex Trafficking: Inside the Business of Modern Slavery.* New York: Columbia University Press, 2009.

Kaufmann, Daniel, Aart Kraay, and Massimo Mastruzzi, *The Worldwide Governance Indicators: Methodology and Analytical Issues,* Policy Research Working Paper 5430. New York: World Bank, 2010.

Keillor, Bruce D., Timothy J. Wilkinson, and Deborah Owens. "Threats to International Operations: Dealing with Political Risk at the Firm Level." *Journal of Business Research* 58, 5 (2005): 629–35. http://dx.doi.org/10.1016/j.jbusres.2003.08.006.

Khokhar, Mariam. "Editorial: The Numbers Game." *Global Eye on Human Trafficking* 23, 2 (2010).

Kibreab, Gaim. "Forced Labour in Eritrea." *Journal of Modern African Studies* 47, 1 (2009): 41–72. http://dx.doi.org/10.1017/S0022278X08003650.

Kim, Mike. *Escaping North Korea: Defiance and Hope in the World's Most Repressive Country.* New York: Rowman and Littlefield, 2008.

Kuhn, Annette, and Kirsten Emiko McAllister, eds. *Locating Memory, Photographic Acts.* New York: Berghahn Books, 2006.

Kuhn, Thomas S. *The Structure of Scientific Revolutions.* Chicago: University of Chicago Press, 1962.

Laczko, Frank, and Elzbieta Gozdziak, eds. *Data and Research on Human Trafficking: A Global Survey.* Geneva: International Organization for Migration, 2005.

Langer, Lawrence L. *Using and Abusing the Holocaust.* Bloomington, IN: Indiana University Press, 2006.

Lawrence, Felicity. "Spain's Salad Growers Are Modern-Day Slaves, Say Charities." *The Guardian*, 7 February 2011. http://www.theguardian.com/business/2011/feb/2007/spain-salad-growers-slaves-charities (accessed 25 March 2012).

Lee, Suk. *The DPRK Famine of 1994–2000: Existence and Impact.* Seoul: Korea Institute for National Unification, 2005.

Lennon, J. John, and Margaret Mitchell. "Dark Tourism: The Role of Sites of Death in Tourism." In *Remember Me: Constructing Immortality – Beliefs on Immortality, Life, and Death*, ed. Margaret Mitchell, 167–78. London, New York: Routledge, 2007.

Levy, Jay, and Pye Jakobsson. "Abolitionist Feminist as Patriarchal Control: Swedish Understandings of Prostitution and Trafficking." *Dialectical Anthropology* 37, 2 (2013): 333–40. http://dx.doi.org/10.1007/s10624-013-9309-y.

"Lips, Teeth, and Spitting the Dummy." *Economist*, 4 December 2010.

Lodish, Emily. "Cannibalism in North Korea." *Minnpost.com*, 24 June 2011.

Lorenz, Andreas. "Combing the Brickyards for the Disappeared." Spiegel Online. 2007. http://www.spiegel.de/international/world/a-499877.html (accessed 25 March 2012).

Lovejoy, Paul. "Internal Markets or an Atlantic-Sahara Divide? How Women Fit into the Slave Trade of West Africa." In *Women and Slavery*, ed. Gwyn Campbell, Suzanne Miers, and Joseph C. Miller, 259–80. Athens, OH: Ohio University Press, 2007.

Lund-Thomsen, Peter, Khalid Nadvi, Anita Chan, Navjote Khara, and Hong Xue. *Labour in Global Production Networks: A Comparative Study of Workers Conditions in Football Manufacturing in China, India and Pakistan.* Frederiksberg, Denmark: Center for Corporate Social Responsibility, Copenhagen Business School, 2011.

Lutnick, Alexandra. *Domestic Minor Sex Trafficking: Beyond Victims and Villians.* New York: Columbia University Press, 2016.

Margolin, Jean-Louis. "China: A Long March into Night." In *The Black Book of Communism: Crimes, Terror, Repression*, ed. S. Courtois, N. Werth, J.-L. Panne, A. Paczkowski, K. Bartosek, and J.-L. Margolin, 497–513. Cambridge, MA: Harvard University Press, 1999.

Martens, Jonathan, Maciej "Mac" Pieczkowski, and Bernadette van Vuuren-Smyth. *Seduction, Sale and Slavery: Trafficking in Women and Children for Sexual Exploitation in Southern Africa*. Pretoria, South Africa: International Organization for Migration Regional Office for Southern Africa, 2003.

Matshedisho, Rajohane. "Nothing Succeeds Like Success: The Manipulation of Crime Statistics." In *Beyond "Good Cop"/"Bad Cop": Understanding Informality and Police Corruption*, ed. D. Vigneswaran and J. Hornberger, 33–38. Johannesburg, South Africa: Forced Migration Studies Program, 2009.

McDougall, Gay J., Special Rapporteur on Contemporary Forms of Slavery. "Systematic Rape, Sexual Slavery and Slavery-Like Practices during Armed Conflict." Doc. E/CN.4/Sub.2/1998/13, 1998.

Merry, Sally Engle. *Human Rights and Gender Violence: Translating International Law into Local Justice*. Chicago: University of Chicago Press, 2006.

Meyers, Arti. "Psychosocial Impacts of Domestic Child Labour in India: Through the Lens of a Save the Children Development Education Resource." Master's thesis, Institute of Education, University of London, 2008 (unpublished).

Miers, Suzanne. *Slavery in the Twentieth Century: The Evolution of a Global Problem*. Walnut Creek, CA: AltaMira Press, 2003.

Misangyi, Vilmos F., Gary Weaver, and Heather Elms. "Ending Corruption: The Interplay among Institutional Logics, Resources, and Institutional Entrepreneurs." *Academy of Management Review* 33, 3 (2008): 750–70. http://dx.doi.org/10.5465/AMR.2008.32465769.

Mistrati, Miki, and U. Roberto Romano. *The Dark Side of Chocolate*. 2010. http://www.thedarksideofchocolate.org (accessed 25 January 2011).

Mountz, Allison. *Seeking Asylum: Human Smuggling and Bureaucracy at the Border*. Minneapolis, MN: University of Minnesota Press, 2010. http://dx.doi.org/10.5749/minnesota/9780816665372.001.0001.

Muico, Norma Kang. *An Absence of Choice: The Sexual Exploitation of North Korean Women in China*. London: Anti-Slavery International, 2005.

Musto, Jennifer Lynne. "Carceral Protectionism and Multi-Professional Anti-Trafficking Human Rights Work in the Netherlands." *International Feminist Journal of Politics* 12, 3–4 (2010): 381–400. http://dx.doi.org/10.1080/14616742.2010.513107.

–. *Control and Protect: Collaboration, Carceral Protection, and Domestic Sex Trafficking in the United States*. Berkeley, CA: University of California Press, 2016.

Mwakitwange, Rosemary. *Fighting Commercial Sexual Exploitation of Children: Study of Good Practices in Interventions in Tanzania*, vol. 3. Dar es Salaam: International Labour Organization, 2002.

Myers, Brian R. *The Cleanest Race: How North Koreans See Themselves – And Why It Matters*. Brooklyn, NY: Melville House, 2010.

National Coalition for Haitian Rights. *Restavèk No More: Eliminating Child Slavery in Haiti*, New York: National Coalition for Haitian Rights, 2002.

Noland, Marcus. "North Korea as a 'New' Famine." In *The New Famines: Why Famines Persist in an Era of Globalization*, ed. S. Devereux, 197–221. New York: Routledge, 2007.

"Not Waving. Perhaps Drowning." *Economist*, 29 May 2010.

Nowrojee, Binaifer. "Making the Invisible War Crimes Visible: Post-Conflict Justice for Sierra Leone's Rape Victims." *Harvard Human Rights Journal* 18 (2005): 85–105.

–. "'Your Justice Is Too Slow'; Will the ICTR Fail Rwanda's Rape Victims?" United Nations Research Institute for Social Development, Occasional Paper 10, 2005.

O'Brien, Erin. "Human Trafficking Heroes and Villains: Representing the Problem in Anti-Trafficking Awareness Campaigns." *Social and Legal Studies* 25, 2 (2016): 205–24. http://dx.doi.org/10.1177/0964663915593410.

O'Connell Davidson, Julia. "Will the Real Sex Slave Please Stand Up?" *Feminist Review* 83, 1 (2006): 4–22. http://dx.doi.org/10.1057/palgrave.fr.9400278.

Ollier, Leakthina Chau-Pech, and Tim Winter, ed. *Expressions of Cambodia: The Politics of Tradition, Identity, and Change*. New York: Routledge, 2006.

Oosterveld, Valerie. "Sexual Slavery and the International Criminal Court: Advancing International Law." *Michigan Journal of International Law* 25 (2004): 605–51.

Paoli, Letizia. "The Paradoxes of Organized Crime." *Crime, Law, and Social Change* 37, 1 (2002): 51–97. http://dx.doi.org/10.1023/A:1013355122531.

Park, Young-ho, Kim Su-am, Lee Keum-soon, and Hong woo-taek. White Paper on Human Rights in North Korea. Seoul: Korea Institute for National Unification, 2010.

Patel, Raj. *Stuffed and Starved: The Hidden Battle for the World's Food System*. Toronto: HarperCollins, 2007.

Plan UK. *Because I Am a Girl (The State of the World's Girls 2009): Girls in the Global Economy: Adding It All Up*. London: Plan UK, 2009.

Plant, Roger. *Forced Labour, Slavery and Poverty Reduction: Challenges for Development Agencies*, Presentation to UK High-Level Conference to Examine the Links between Poverty, Slavery and Social Exclusion. London: International Labour Organization, 2007.

Pollock, Griselda. "Holocaust Tourism: Being There, Looking Back and the Ethics of Spatial Memory." In *Visual Culture and Tourism*, ed. David Crouch and Nina Lubbren, 175–89. Oxford: Berg, 2003.

Porter, Michael E., and Kramer, Mark R. "Creating Shared Value." *Harvard Business Review* 89 (2011): 62–77.

Quirk, Joel, and Darshan Vigneswaran. *Slavery, Migration and Contemporary Bondage in Africa*. Part of the Harriet Tubman Series on the African Diaspora. Trenton, NJ: Africa World Press, 2013.

–. "Mobility Makes States." In *Mobility Makes States: Migration and Power in Africa*, ed. Joel Quirk and Darshan Vigneswaran, 1–34. Philadelphia: University of Pennsylvania Press, 2015.

Quirk, Joel F. "The Anti-Slavery Project: Linking the Historical and Contemporary." *Human Rights Quarterly* 28, 3 (2006): 565–98. http://dx.doi.org/10.1353/hrq.2006.0036.

–. *Unfinished Business: A Comparative Survey of Historical and Contemporary Slavery.* Paris: United Nations Educational, Scientific and Cultural Organization, 2009.

Raab, Jörg, and H. Brinton Milward. "Dark Networks as Problems." *Journal of Public Administration: Research and Theory* 13, 4 (2003): 413–39. http://dx.doi.org/10.1093/jopart/mug029.

Ramirez-Machado, José Maria. *Domestic Work, Conditions of Work and Employment: A Legal Perspective, Conditions of Work and Employment Series no. 7.* Geneva: International Labour Organization, 2003.

Rassam, Anne Y. "Contemporary Forms of Slavery and the Evolution of the Prohibition of Slavery and the Slave Trade Under Customary International Law." *Virginia Journal of International Law* 39 (1998): 303–52.

–. "International Law and Contemporary Forms of Slavery: An Economic and Social Rights-Based Approach." *Pennsylvania State International Law Review* 23, 4 (2004): 809–55.

Rawls, John. *A Theory of Justice.* Oxford: Oxford University Press, 1973.

Razack, Sherene. *Casting Out: Race and the Eviction of Muslims from Western Law and Politics.* Toronto: University of Toronto Press, 2008.

Reale, Daniela. *Away from Home: Protecting and Supporting Children on the Move.* London: Save the Children UK, 2008.

Research Network on the Legal Paramaters of Slavery. *Bellagio-Harvard Guidelines on the Legal Parameters of Slavery.* 2012.

Richards, Kathy. "The Trafficking of Migrant Workers: What Are the Links between Labour Trafficking and Corruption?" *International Migration* 42, 5 (2004): 147–68. http://dx.doi.org/10.1111/j.0020-7985.2004.00305.x.

Rogers, Everett M. *Diffusion of Innovations,* 5th edition. New York: Free Press, 2003.

Royce, Edward. "The Origins of Southern Sharecropping: Explaining Social Change." *Current Perspectives in Social Theory* 6 (1985): 279–99.

–. *The Origins of Southern Sharecropping.* Philadelphia, PA: Temple University Press, 1993.

Ryall, Julian. "North Korea Shuts Down Universities for 10 Months." *The Telegraph,* 28 June 2011.

–. "Half of North Korea's Army 'Starving.'" *The Telegraph,* 13 September 2011.

Salt, John, and Jeremy Stein. "Migration as a Business: The Case of Trafficking." *International Migration* 35, 4 (1997): 467–94. http://dx.doi.org/10.1111/1468-2435.00023.

Sarra, Janis. "Rose-Colored Glasses, Opaque Financial Reporting, and Investor Blues: Enron as Con and the Vulnerability of Canadian Corporate Law." *St John's Law Review* 76 (2002): 715–66.

Save the Children UK. *Abuse among Child Domestic Workers: A Research Study in West Bengal.* West Bengal: Save the Children UK, 2006.

Schaffer, Kay, and Sidonie Smith. *Human Rights and Narrated Lives: The Ethics of Recognition*. New York: Palgrave Macmillan, 2004. http://dx.doi.org/10.1057/9781403973665.

Schloenhardt, Andreas. "Organized Crime and the Business of Migrant Trafficking." *Crime, Law, and Social Change* 32, 3 (1999): 203–33. http://dx.doi.org/10.1023/A:1008340427104.

Sen, Sankar, and P.M. Nair. *A Report on Trafficking in Women and Children in India: 2002–2003*. New Delhi: National Human Rights Commission, UN Women, and Institute for Security Studies, 2005.

Shah, Svati P. "South Asian Border Crossings and Sex Work: Revisiting the Question of Migration in Anti-Trafficking Interventions." *Sexuality Research and Social Policy* 5, 4 (2008): 19–30. http://dx.doi.org/10.1525/srsp.2008.5.4.19.

Sharma, Yojana. North Korea: Learning Stops as Students Must Work. *University World News*, 30 June 2011.

Shelley, Louise. "Trafficking in Women: The Business Model Approach." *Brown Journal of World Affairs* 10, 1 (2003): 119–31.

Shen, Anqi. "Female Perpetrators in Internal Child Trafficking in China: An Empirical Study." *Journal of Human Trafficking* 2, 1 (2016): 63–77. http://dx.doi.org/10.1080/23322705.2016.1136537.

–. *Offending Women in Contemporary China: Gender and Pathways into Crime*. London: Palgrave Macmillan, 2015. http://dx.doi.org/10.1057/9781137441447.

Sherwin, Richard K. "Law Frames: Historical Truth and Narrative Necessity in a Criminal Case." *Stanford Law Review* 47, 1 (1994): 39–83. http://dx.doi.org/10.2307/1229221.

Sidanius, Jim, and Felicia Pratto. *Social Domination: An Intergroup Theory of Social Hierarchy and Oppression*. Cambridge: Cambridge University Press, 1999. http://dx.doi.org/10.1017/CBO9781139175043.

Skinner, E. Benjamin. "Slaves Put Squid on U.S. Dining Tables from South Pacific Catch." *Bloomberg Businessweek*, 2012. http://www.bloomberg.com/news/articles/2012-02-23/slaves-put-squid-on-u-s-dining-tables-from-south-pacific-catch (accessed 25 March 2012).

Skinner, Quentin. *The Foundations of Modern Political Thought*. Cambridge: Cambridge University Press, 1978.

Snajdr, Edward. "Beneath the Master Narrative: Human Trafficking, Myths of Sexual Slavery and Ethnographic Realities." *Dialectical Anthropology* 37, 2 (2013): 229–56. http://dx.doi.org/10.1007/s10624-013-9292-3.

Snyder, Peter J., Richard L. Priem, and E. Levitas. "The Diffusion of Illegal Innovations among Management Elites." Paper presented at the Academy of Management Annual Conference, Chicago, 2009. http://dx.doi.org/10.5465/AMBPP.2009.44264879.

Songololo, Molo. *The Trafficking of Children for the Purposes of Sexual Exploitation*. Cape Town, South Africa: Molo Songololo, 2000.

–. *The Trafficking of Women into the South African Sex Industry*. Cape Town, South Africa: Molo Songololo, 2000.

Steinfatt, Thomas M. "Sex Trafficking in Cambodia: Fabricated Numbers versus Empirical Evidence." *Crime, Law, and Social Change* 56, 5 (2011): 443–62. http://dx.doi.org/10.1007/s10611-011-9328-z.

Suchman, Mark C. "Managing Legitimacy: Strategic and Institutional Approaches." *Academy of Management Review* 20, 3 (1995): 571–610.

Surtees, Rebecca. *Traffickers and Trafficking: Challenges in Researching Human Traffickers and Trafficking Operations*. Geneva: United Nations International Organization for Migration, 2014.

Ten Kate, Daniel. "North Korea's Food Shortages Worsening, U.N. Says." *Bloomberg News*, 16 September 2011.

Tyldum, Guri, and Anette Brunovskis. "Describing the Unobserved: Methodological Challenges in Empirical Studies on Human Trafficking." In *Data and Research on Human Trafficking: A Global Survey*, ed. F. Laczko and E. Gozdziak, 17–34. Geneva: International Organization for Migration, 2005. http://dx.doi.org/10.1111/j.0020-7985.2005.00310.x.

"UN Committee Urges Court Action against N. Korea." VOA News, 18 November 2014.

UNICEF and International Child Development Centre. *Child Domestic Work: Innocenti Digest no. 5*. Florence: UNICEF and International Child Development Centre, 1999.

United Nations General Assembly. *Situation of Human Rights in the Democratic People's Republic of Korea*. New York: United Nations, 18 December 2014.

United Nations News Centre. "External Aid Essential for Subsistence of Millions in DPR Korea – Official." United Nations News, 15 March 2013.

United States Department of Labor. *The Department of Labor's List of Goods Produced by Child Labor or Forced Labor*. Washington, DC: United States Department of Labor, 2009.

US Department of State, *Country Report on Human Rights Practices: Korea, Democratic People's Republic of*. Washington, DC: US Department of State, 2010, 2012, 2013.

Valente, Mike, and Andrew Crane. "Private Enterprise and Public Responsibility in Developing Countries." *California Management Review* 52, 3 (2010): 52–78. http://dx.doi.org/10.1525/cmr.2010.52.3.52.

Vance, Carole. "Innocence and Experience: Melodramatic Narratives of Sex Trafficking and Their Consequences for Law and Policy." *History of the Present* 2, 2 (2012): 200–18. http://dx.doi.org/10.5406/historypresent.2.2.0200.

Verdeja, Ernesto. *Unchopping a Tree: Reconciliation in the Aftermath of Political Violence*. Philadelphia: Temple University Press, 2009.

Vigneswaran, Darshan. "Enduring Territoriality: South African Immigration Control." *Political Geography* 27, 7 (2008): 783–801. http://dx.doi.org/10.1016/j.polgeo.2008.10.003.

Vigneswaran, Darshan, Tesfalem Araia, and Colin Hoag. "Criminality or Monopoly? Informal Immigration Enforcement in South Africa." *Journal of Southern African Studies* 36, 2 (2010): 465–81. http://dx.doi.org/10.1080/03057070.2010.485797.

Webb, Justin W., Laszlo Tihanyi, and R. Duane Ireland. "You Say Illegal, I Say Legitimate: Entrepreneurship in the Informal Economy." *Academy of Management Review* 34, 3 (2009): 492–510. http://dx.doi.org/10.5465/AMR.2009.40632826.

Webster, Jane. "Looking for the Material Culture of the Middle Passage." *Journal for Maritime Research* 7, 1 (2005): 245–58. http://dx.doi.org/10.1080/21533369.2005.9668352.

Weissbrodt, David, and Anti-Slavery International. *Abolishing Slavery and Its Contemporary Forms*. New York: United Nations, 2002.

Weitzer, Ronald. "Flawed Theory and Method in Studies of Prostitution." *Violence Against Women* 11, 7 (2005): 934–49. http://dx.doi.org/10.1177/1077801205276986.

–. "The Growing Moral Panic over Prostitution and Sex Trafficking." *Criminologist* 30, 5 (2005): 3–5.

–. "The Mythology of Prostitution: Advocacy, Research and Public Policy." *Sexuality Research and Social Policy* 7, 1 (2010): 15–29. http://dx.doi.org/10.1007/s13178-010-0002-5.

Williams, Paul. "Witnessing Genocide: Vigilance and Remembrance at Tuol Sleng and Choeung Ek." *Holocaust and Genocide Studies* 18, 2 (2004): 234–54. http://dx.doi.org/10.1093/hgs/dch063.

Wilson, Richard A. *Writing History in International Criminal Trials*. New York: Cambridge University Press, 2011. http://dx.doi.org/10.1017/CBO9780511973505.

Wood, Marcus. *Blind Memory: Visual Representations of Slavery in England and America*. New York: Routledge, 2000.

–. "Significant Silence: Where Was Slave Agency in the Popular Imagery of 2007?" In *Imagining Transatlantic Slavery*, ed. Cora Kaplan and John Oldfield, 162–90. Basingstoke, UK: Palgrave Macmillan, 2010.

Wright, Gavin. *Slavery and American Economic Development*. Baton Rouge, LA: Louisiana State University Press, 2006.

Wu, Harry. *Appendix to Forced Labour in China*, ed. Congressional-Executive Commission on China. Washington, DC: US Government Printing Office, 2005.

Xu, Gregory. *Appendix to Forced Labour in China*, ed. Congressional-Executive Commission on China. Washington, DC: US Government Printing Office, 2005.

Zajac, Edward J., Matthew S. Kraatz, and Rudi K.F. Bresser. "Modeling the Dynamics of Strategic Fit: A Normative Approach to Strategic Change." *Strategic Management Journal* 21, 4 (2000): 429–53. http://dx.doi.org/10.1002/(SICI)1097-0266(200004)21:4<429::AID-SMJ81>3.0.CO;2-#.

Contributors

Jean Allain is Professor of Law at Monash University and holds an Extraordinary Professorship with the Centre of Human Right of the Faculty of Law, University of Pretoria. Professor Allain received his PhD from the Graduate Institute of International Studies (HEI), University of Geneva; and, while undertaking those studies, clerked for the first President of the International Criminal Tribunal for the former Yugoslavia. He is also Special Adviser to Anti-Slavery International, the world's oldest international human rights organization, and the author of the following books relating to slavery: *The Slavery Conventions* (2008, ed.), *The Legal Understanding of Slavery* (2012), *Slavery in International Law* (2013), and *The Law and Slavery* (2015).

Jonathan Blagbrough has worked on child exploitation issues for over twenty-five years as a practitioner and researcher – with a particular focus on understanding the condition, and raising the voice, of children in domestic work situations. Jonathan is Senior Visiting Research Associate, Wilberforce Institute for the study of Slavery and Emancipation (WISE), University of Hull, UK and is currently a PhD candidate in human geography at the University of Dundee, exploring relations between child domestic workers and the children they serve.

Roy L. Brooks is Warren Distinguished Professor at the University of San Diego School of Law and the author of many books and articles on civil and human rights.

Annie Bunting is an associate professor in the Law and Society program at York University in Toronto, teaching in the areas of legal pluralism and human rights. Her research expertise includes socio-legal studies of marriage and childhoods, feminist international law, and culture, religion, and law. She is currently directing an international research collaboration on conjugal slavery in conflict situations with historians of slavery and women's human rights scholars. She is the coeditor of *Marriage by Force? Contestation over Consent and Coercion in Africa* (Ohio, 2016).

Austin Choi-Fitzpatrick is an assistant professor at the Kroc School of Peace Studies at the University of San Diego and a fellow at the Center for Media, Data, and Society at Central European University. He is the author of *What Slaveholders Think* (Columbia, 2017) and coeditor of *From Human Trafficking to Human Rights* (Penn, 2013).

Andrew Crane is a professor of business and society and Director of the Centre for Business, Organisations and Society in the School of Management at the University of Bath, UK. His research focuses on issues of corporate responsibility and sustainability with a particular focus on business and modern slavery.

Rhoda Howard-Hassmann is a professor emeritus at Wilfrid Laurier University, where she was Canada Research Chair in International Human Rights from 2003 to 2016. Her most recent books include *State Food Crimes* (2016), *Can Globalization Promote Human Rights?* (2010), and *Reparations to Africa* (2008), as well as the coedited volumes *The Human Right to Citizenship* (2015) and *The Age of Apology* (2008). She is currently writing a book entitled *In Defense of Universal Human Rights*.

Fuyuki Kurasawa is an associate professor in the Department of Sociology at York University in Toronto, where he holds a York Research Chair in Global Digital Citizenship. He is the author of *The Ethnological Imagination:*

A Cross-Cultural Critique of Modernity (Minnesota, 2004) *The Work of Global Justice: Human Rights as Practices* (Cambridge, 2007), and of *Perilous Light: The Visual Economy of Humanitarianism* (Chicago, forthcoming).

Benjamin N. Lawrance is the Hon. Barber B. Conable, Jr. Endowed Professor of International Studies, and a professor of history and anthropology at the Rochester Institute of Technology. He has published ten books, including *Amistad's Orphans: An Atlantic Story of Children, Slavery, and Smuggling* (Yale, 2015) and, as coeditor, *African Asylum at a Crossroads* (Ohio, 2015), *Adjudicating Refugee and Asylum Status* (Cambridge, 2015), and *Marriage by Force?* (Ohio, 2016).

Joel Quirk is a professor in the Department of Political Studies, University of the Witwatersrand. His research focuses on slavery and abolition, social movements, and the politics of arguments, human mobility and human rights, repairing historical wrongs, and the history and politics of sub-Saharan Africa. Joel is the author or coeditor of seven books, including *The Anti-Slavery Project* (2011) and *Mobility Makes States* (2015). He is a current member of the International Scientific Committee of the UNESCO Slave Route Project, where he serves as Rapporteur, and is also an editor for openDemocracy's "Beyond Trafficking and Slavery."

Darshan Vigneswaran is the codirector of the Institute for Migration and Ethnic Studies and assistant professor at the Department of Political Science, University of Amsterdam. He is also a senior researcher at the African Centre for Migration and Society at the University of the Witwatersrand. His work is primarily interested in how the state's claim to territory has been reconfigured in response to changing patterns of human mobility. He is the author of *Territory, Migration and the Evolution of the International System* (2013) and coeditor of *Slavery, Migration and Contemporary Bondage in Africa* (2013) and *Mobility Makes States* (2015). He also edits the journal *Environment and Planning D: Society and Space.*

Index

abductions: of children, 116–17, 137; of children for military purposes, 214, 225n52; and forced conjugal association, 104, 133–34; and human trafficking, 60, 82, 85, 86, 221n1; narratives of, 130, 145, 151, 152; of women, 137, 140–41. *See also* kidnapping

abolitionism: four waves of, 279; iconography of, 172; and proportionality, 193–98

abolitionists, 10, 17, 20, 56, 160, 166, 179, 192, 193; in Britain, 59, 166, 279; feminist, 75–76

Aboriginal children, 207–8

accounting, 210; opacity in, 242–43, 248

activism: anti-slavery, 6, 11, 18, 23, 24, 28, 143, 174, 179; in Brazil, 16; in the Global South, 18; human rights, 7, 71; modern slavery, 131; political economy of, 15; Quaker, 59. *See also* anti-slavery campaigns and advocacy; anti-trafficking campaigns/initiatives

Adenauer, Konrad Hermann Joseph, 202, 207

adoption: illegal, 59; as slave dealing, 308

affirmative action, 294

Africa: child domestic workers in, 304, 317; child soldiers in, 205, 214–16; colonialism in, 54; forced labour in, 80; forced marriage in, 99; slavery in, 57; sub-Saharan, 80. *See also* African countries; Rwanda; Sierra Leone; South Africa; West Africa

Africa Rights, 136, 138, 139

African Americans, 208–9

African countries: Angola, 57, 271; Benin, 321–22; Côte d'Ivoire, 108, 117–18; Democratic Republic of Congo (DRC), 142, 144; Eritrea, 256; Ethiopia, 54; Ghana, 57, 102, 109–10, 115; Liberia, 130, 142, 151, 206, 225n51, 304; Libya, 271; Madagascar, 11; Mali, 15, 16; Mauritania, 11, 15; Mozambique, 57; Niger, 15, 16; Nigeria, 41; Portuguese Guinea

(Guinea-Bissau), 57; Rhodesia, 57; Sudan, 131, 148–49; Tanzania, 57, 322; Togo, 108–9, 113, 114, 321–22; Zimbabwe, 193, 194

African National Congress (ANC), 184, 193

agency, 8; of children, 27, 313–14

agriculture. *See* farm labour

Agustín, Laura María, 74

Ahmad, Muneer, 107

Akallo, Grace, 131

Alien Torts Claims Act (ATCA), 211

American Anti-Slavery Almanacs, 166

American Anti-Slavery Society, 175n5

amnesty, 206, 216

Amnesty International, 133, 257, 266

analogical juxtaposition: explaining, 161–64; use of, 160–61, 174

Anand, Vikas, 244

Anderson, Bridget, 75

Angola, 57, 271

anthropology of human rights, 132

anti-immigration efforts, 77

anti-poverty work, 24

anti-slavery campaigns and advocacy: analogical juxtaposition in, 161–64; arguments for state intervention, 179; classification of website images, 164; competing claims of, 158–59; global, 16; history of, 17; use of iconography in, 159–160; and the issue of accountability, 280; NGOs, 172

Anti-Slavery International (ASI), 11, 88, 169, 173, 174, 176n6, 177n14, 232, 314; study on child domestic workers, 320–21, 327n60

anti-slavery legislation and regulations, 230, 245, 268, 288

Anti-Slavery Record, 166, 168

anti-slavery rhetoric, 7, 10, 11, 13–14, 15, 17, 19, 28, 67; disaggregation of, 22–23; global vs. local approaches, 16

anti-trafficking: committees, 313; organizations, 11, 15, 74–75; scholarship, 184, 190–91, 193

anti-trafficking campaigns/initiatives, 26, 77, 89–90, 184, 188, 191–92, 196; problems inherent in, 21, 70, 71, 73, 74, 90; in South Africa, 180–81, 188–89, 189

anti-trafficking legislation, 14, 19, 59, 197; application of, 86; bipartisan support for, 19–21

apartheid, 57, 58, 208, 213

apologies, 207–8, 215–16, 218

Armed Forces Revolutionary Council (AFRC; Rwanda), 140–41

Arts and Humanities Research Council (UK), 38

Asia: child domestic workers in, 317; forced labour in, 80. *See also* China; Japan; North Korea; South Asia; Southeast Asia

Asian countries: Burma, 283; Cambodia, 256; Mongolia, 259; Nepal, 309, 323; Thailand, 205, 216–19, 246

Asian Regional Initiative against Trafficking in Women and Children, 67

asylum law: and human rights, 106; in the US, 98

asylum petitions: adjudication of, 98; and the fear of persecution, 101–3; and forced marriage, 97, 98–99, 104; and the "forced marriage paradox," 100–6; gender-based claims, 101–2; human rights claims, 102; language issues in, 105–6; and the role of translation, 107, 110–14, 118–19

asylum seekers, 17, 85, 101–2; from
  Côte d'Ivoire, 109, 117–18; and the
  "forced marriage paradox," 106–8;
  from Ghana, 109–10; and human
  trafficking/slavery, 17, 85; judicial
  reframing of narratives, 114–19;
  narratives of, 108–10, 118–19;
  from Togo, 108–9, 110, 113, 114;
  translation of narratives, 110–14,
  118–19; violence against, 101–2,
  107–8, 115
atonement model, 213, 219–20;
  for child soldiers in Africa, 214–16;
  for sexual exploitation in Thailand,
  216–19
Australia, 207–8
Australian High Court, 37, 46, 50, 120

Backward Society Education, 88
Bales, Kevin, 16, 38, 131, 132, 144,
  222*n*4, 233, 236, 246, 283
Ban Ki-Moon, 67
Bandung Conference, 57
Bangladesh, 284, 319
Bangura, Zainab, 140
Baron, David, 245
Baum, Nanna, 319
Baysinger, Barry, 245
Beah, Ishmael, 131, 145, 150
Beardsley, Brent, 137
Becker, Jasper, 258
*Bellagio-Harvard Guidelines on the
  Legal Parameters of Slavery*, 37, 39, 54,
  62, 267, 271, 273; text of, 329–36
Benin, 321–22
betrothal contracts, 98
Bhoola, Urmila, 11–12
Biard, François-Auguste, 170, 171
Bite of the Mango, The (Kamara), 131,
  146, 147–48, 150
Blake, William, 165–66, 176*n*7

Bob, Clifford, 18
Bolivia, 25
bonded labour, 11, 16, 78, 83, 203,
  231, 249, 286, 290, 294, 298, 309;
  on the Indian subcontinent, 87–88
Bonded Labour Liberation Front
  of Pakistan, 88
border protection, 8, 21, 284; and
  human trafficking, 76, 90
Bowah, Caroline, 206
Brandt, Willy, 207
Brazil: activists in, 16; charcoal-
  making camps in, 167, 233, 238;
  labour abuses in, 14; pro-gun lobby
  in, 25; UN missions to, 10, 11
brick kilns, 233, 235, 238
bride price and bride wealth, 113
Britain. *See* United Kingdom
Brookes slave ship, 169, 172, 173,
  177–78*nn*15–16
Brown, Wendy, 24
Bulgaria, 259, 271
Bunting, Annie, 268
Burma, 283
Bush, George W., 8, 13, 77
Bush Wife Phenomenon, 140–41. *See
  also* forced conjugal relations (FCA);
  forced marriage
*Bush Wives and Girl Soldiers: Women's
  Lives through War and Peace in Sierra
  Leone* (Coulter), 151
business ethics, 24. *See also*
  management issues
Buss, Doris, 137, 138, 141

Cadet, Jean-Robert, 131, 145, 150
Cambodia, 256
Cambridge School, 182
Canada, 108, 208
Canadian-Ukrainians, 208
cannibalism, 262

capitalism, 8, 161

Caple James, Erica, 151

Caribbean, 80, 170. *See also* Haiti

Carpenter, Ami, 288

caste system, 288–89, 296, 297, 298

Cecil, Robert (Viscount of Chelwood), 55

Central America, 317; Costa Rica, 322. *See also* Latin America

Central Europe, 83

charcoal-making camps, 167, 233, 238

chattel slavery, 44, 46, 120, 279. *See also* slavery

child domestic workers (CDW): abuse of, 306, 309; as agents of change, 313–14; in Benin and Togo, 321–22; in Costa Rica, 322; and debt bondage, 309; discrimination against, 305–6; education for, 306–7, 315; exploitation of, 302, 304, 316, 324; gender issues, 311–12; interviews with, 318–23; isolation of, 305–6, 318–19; issues in addressing, 318–20; in Nepal, 323; networking and support for, 314, 317; in Peru, 321–22; in the Philippines, 177*n*14, 323; protection for, 315–16; provision of help for, 319, 320–21; psychosocial health of, 317–18; research on, 27, 301–3; as slaves, 144, 307–10; in Tanzania, 322; trafficking of, 309–10, 312–13; triggers and motivations, 303–5

child fostering, 304–5

child labour: and exploitation, 22; forced labour, 83, 203; in India, 298; in North Korea, 266; as slavery, 11–12, 231; and trafficking, 70, 79. *See also* child domestic workers (CDW); children

child pornography, 59

children: abduction of, 116–17, 137; Aboriginal, 207–8; abuse of, 310–11; agency of, 27, 313–14; domestic trafficking of, 68; exploitation of, 27, 43, 336; with HIV/AIDS, 214–15; as hostages, 116–17; in labour camps, 259; as mine workers, 12; and poverty, 134, 216, 303–4; as refugees, 149; rights of 14, 310–11; sale of, 83, 288, 308, 336; as sex slaves, 214–15; and sex trafficking, 83; as sex workers, 17, 197; as soldiers, 59, 83, 87, 131–32, 149, 214–16, 225*n*52; trafficking of, 12, 54, 61, 68, 70, 203, 288, 326*n*38. *See also* child domestic workers (CDW); child labour; girls

Children Unite, 327*n*60

China: brick kilns in, 238; North Korean refugees in, 261, 270–71; relationship with North Korea, 269–70; sale and trafficking of children in, 288; slave labour in, 255–56, 259, 283

Choi-Fitzpatrick, Austin, 28

Chuang, Janie, 79

civil liberties, 25

civil redress, 206–7; atonement model, 205, 219–20; tort model of, 205, 206, 209–12, 219

civil rights movement, 24

Clark, William, 169

class action lawsuits: against Germany, 209; against Japan, 209–10

Clinton, William "Bill," 208

Coalition of Immokalee Workers (CIW), 287

Coalition to Stop the Use of Child Soldiers, 145

cocoa industry, 229, 236, 248

coercion: into conjugal unions, 101, 109; and debt/labour contracts, 241;

political, 266; and slavery, 10, 11, 39, 41, 82, 86, 99, 174, 222*n*4, 267, 270, 330; and trafficking, 60, 221*n*2
coffee industry, 236
colonialism, 170; in Africa, 54, 57, 58; European, 24; Portuguese, 57
Comic Relief, 314–15
commercial sex work: abuses in, 78–79; decriminalization of, 71, 75–77; feminist debate on, 281; global sex industry, 233; and human trafficking, 13, 71–72, 283; protection for sex workers, 75; rescue efforts, 21, 89; as slavery, 17, 20, 41, 50–51, 76, 237; in South Africa, 189–90, 193; in Thailand, 216–19; and trafficking, 84, 188, 193, 281–83. *See also* prostitution; sex trafficking; sexual exploitation
Commission on Human Rights, 58
Commission of Inquiry (UN), 272
Committee of Experts on Slavery (League of Nations), 55, 56
consent: informed, 319–20; question of, 23, 60, 76, 82, 83, 99, 103–4, 121, 216, 221, 316
constructive trust, 210
contemporary slavery: and the atonement model, 213–14; definitions of, 36–37, 58–59, 203; diverse aspects of, 9–10; fallacious claims regarding, 6; and forced labour, 78; forced marriage as, 144; gender violence as, 133; human trafficking and, 78; identifying characteristics of, 232; issues of redress, 202–3; Kevin Bales definition of, 222*n*4; management issues, 229–31; phases of, 203; as political cause, 11; post-conflict phase, 203, 219–20; shallow support for combatting, 7;

and structural violence, 175*n*2; US government definition of, 222*n*3; visual representation in, 163; ways of combatting, 12, 180, 246–49. *See also* slavery
contemporary slavery studies, 28, 132, 297
Convention Concerning the Abolition of Forced Labour (1959), 265–66
Convention Concerning Decent Work for Domestic Workers, 311–12
Convention Concerning the Prohibition and Immediate Action for the Elimination of the Worst Forms of Child Labour (Child Labour Convention), 311
Convention for the Protection of Human Rights and Fundamental Freedoms (ECHR), 45, 102
Convention Relating to the Status of Refugees (Refugee Convention), 102
Convention on the Rights of the Child (UNCRC), 313
Convention against Transnational Organized Crime, 82, 195
corporal punishments, 23–24
corporate social responsibility, 248
Costa Rica, 322
Côte d'Ivoire, 109, 117–18
cotton farming, 169, 229, 236, 256
Coulter, Chris, 151
counterstories, 131
Covenant of the League of Nations (1919), 54
Cowper, William, 167–68, 177*n*13
crimes against humanity, 130, 134, 144, 270–72; enslavement as, 60–61
criminal activity: transnational, 197
criminal intent, 295
criminal justice, 12, 17, 27, 46, 188; migration approach, 282; in South

Africa, 195, 197–98; and trafficking, 282
criminal punishments, 23–24
criminal redress, 205–6, 219
criminality, 17, 295; and human trafficking, 76
critical sociology, 159
Cubilié, Anne, 134, 138
cultural practices, 112–13, 122*n*11
"Cutting the Sugar Cane, Antigua," 169
Cyprus, 45
Czech Republic, 271

Dallaire, Roméo, 137
dark tourism, 129
Dauvergne, Catherine, 98, 104, 105
de Klerk, F.W., 57
Death, Despair and Defiance, 138
debt bondage, 12, 43, 56, 83, 144, 203, 240–42, 326*n*35, 335; and child domestic workers, 309
debt management, 248
debt slavery. *See* debt bondage
decolonization, 57
Delgado, Richard, 131
Democratic People's Republic of Korea. *See* North Korea
Democratic Republic of Congo (DRC), 142, 144
Denton, Erin, 288
Department of Home Affairs (South Africa), 184, 194, 198
deportation, 196, 198, 271
Diary of a Young Girl (Frank), 146
discrimination: based on sexuality, 103; against child domestic workers, 302; descent-based, 17, 22; ethnic, 303; gender, 303; and paternalism, 294; against women, 135
Doezema, Joe, 72
domestic minor trafficking, 16

domestic servitude, 12, 83
domestic violence, 294; and forced marriage, 103
Domestic Violence Act (Ghana), 102
domestic workers, 17, 45, 193, 311–12; abuse and exploitation of, 18, 22. *See also* child domestic workers (CDW)
dowry, 113
Drescher, Seymour, 38
drug trafficking, 6, 269

Ecuador, 11
education: for at-risk populations, 248, 293, 294; for child domestic workers, 303, 306–7, 310, 313–20; for girls, 312, 324*n*1; in Thailand, 217; of users, 282, 285; as victim reparations, 209, 212, 216, 218, 220
Elizabeth (Queen of England), 207
emancipation, 280, 283, 286, 289–90, 295–98; challenges of, 294; non-intervention-based, 290
Emancipation Proclamation, 279
Engerman, Stanley, 38
enslavement: as crime against humanity, 60–61; criteria of, 270–71; definition of, 45; of fishermen, 83; for the purposes of forced marriage, 136, 138, 151; of sex workers, 50–51; symbols of, 172; wartime, 130; of women, 133. *See also* reparations; slavery
Eritrea, 256
Ethiopia, 54
ethnographies, 151, 194
EU Directive 2011/36 on Preventing and Combating Trafficking in Human Beings and Protecting Its Victims, 67
European Court of Human Rights (ECtHR), 45, 47

European Union (EU), 184, 187

evangelicalism: Anglican, 59

exploitation: of child domestic workers, 302, 304, 316, 324; of children, 27, 43, 313, 336; and debt, 22; of domestic workers, 45; economic, 232, 288; of farm workers, 83; and human trafficking, 86; of migrants, 69–70, 193; relationship to slavery, 10, 17, 43, 55–56, 86; of sex workers, 59, 190; sexual, 11–13, 22, 60, 69–71, 82, 86, 97, 205, 216–19, 279, 282, 326*n*38; in Southern Africa, 181; and the Trafficking Protocol, 60, 82; of trafficking victims, 203; various forms of, 44. *See also* labour; exploitation

Eye on Trafficking (SACTAP bulletin), 192

fair trade practices, 248

famine, 257, 259, 260–63

farm labour, 16, 41, 169, 193, 229, 235, 248, 260–61, 284, 292, 309, 332. *See also* migrant workers

Feingold, David, 74

female genital cutting (female genital mutilation; female circumcision), 101–2, 298

feminist scholarship, 131, 281

feudalism, 309

Fick, Nicole, 189, 190, 191, 192, 199

FIFA World Cup, 187–89, 193, 260

fishing and fishermen, 83, 229

forced conjugal association (FCA): and asylum petitions, 102; effect on men, 122*n*6; and forced marriage, 99–100; as slavery, 119–21; in wartime, 104. *See also* forced marriage

forced disappearances, 271

forced genital cutting. *See* female genital cutting (female genital mutilation; female circumcision)

forced labour: of children, 326*n*38; civil redress litigation for, 210; compensation for, 209; and debt transferral, 241–42; and human trafficking, 12, 69, 78, 80, 81, 83, 86, 87, 195; in the informal economy, 238; in military, 232; in North Korea, 21, 258–60; prevalence of, 80–81, 230; in prisons, 22, 232; as punishment, 266; and rapid debt accrual, 241; as slavery, 10–12, 45, 55, 203, 231, 334–35; vs. slavery, 43; stages of, 239; state-sponsored, 16, 18, 22, 87, 88; suppression of, 54; in wartime, 130; of women, 130

Forced Labour Convention (ILO 1930), 43, 264–65

forced marriage: as basis for asylum claims, 26, 97–99, 104; as crime against humanity, 144; and domestic violence, 103; in the DRC, 144; as forced conjugal association, 99; as human rights violation, 23; in international criminal law, 144; legal representations of, 136–43; as a means of obtaining logistical support for troops, 140; as modern slavery, 11–12, 17, 22, 59, 104, 144, 231; and sexual slavery, 120; as trafficking, 87; UK legislation against, 103; in wartime, 130, 132, 136, 140, 142–43. *See also* forced conjugal association (FCA)

Forced Marriage (Protection) Act (2007–08; United Kingdom), 103

"forced marriage paradox," 26, 100, 100–6

forced marriage protection order, 103

forgiveness, 213, 216, 218, 219, 220
Foundation for Human Rights and Democracy (Liberia), 206
Fragmented (Holocaust memoir), 132
Frank, Anne, 146, 147
Free the Slaves (FTS), 11, 144, 176*n*6, 287
French Caribbean, 80, 170. *See also* Haiti

Gallagher, Anne, 81, 82
Gandhi Peace Foundation, 88
gender inequalities, 161, 218. *See also* inequality
gender issues, 193
gender subordination, 218
gender-based violence: in asylum courts, 100, 101, 119–20; as crimes against humanity, 133–36; documentation of, 131; legal representations of, 136–44, 150; in wartime, 27, 133, 151; and women's rights, 25
genocide, 18; in Rwanda, 137. *See also* Holocaust
Germany: class action lawsuits against, 209; reparations for Holocaust, 202, 207
Ghana, 57, 102, 109–10, 115
Girl Soldier (Akallo), 131
girls: as child domestic workers, 301, 304, 311–12, 315, 323–24; as domestic workers in their own homes, 324*n*1; education for, 220, 312; as sex slaves, 214–15; sexual exploitation of, 216–19
Gleeson, Murray, 50–51
Global Alliance against Forced Labour (ILO report), 80
global capitalism, 8, 161
Global North: anti-slavery efforts in, 8; financial linkages with Global

South, 15; NGOs in, 11; and North Korea, 268–69; support for activism in Global South by, 18
Global Slavery Index, 98, 234
Global South: activism in, 18; anti-slavery efforts in, 7; asylum petitions from, 98; enslaved populations in, 170, 171; financial linkages with Global North, 15
global supply chains, 22, 269. *See also* supply chains
globalization, 236
Goldstein, Daniel, 25
Gould, Chandre, 189, 190, 191, 192, 199
gulag camp prisoners: disgraced citizens, 262–64; famine-induced criminals, 260–62
gulag labour camps: in North Korea, 255, 258–60, 267–68, 271; in South Korea, 271; in the Soviet Union, 255, 259
gun ownership, 25

Habermas, Jürgen, 182
Haiti, 11, 131, 145, 151; *restavèk* children in, 309. *See also* Caribbean
Hathaway, James, 79, 81
Hausa-Fulani people, 41
Hawaiians, 208
Hayne, Kenneth Madison, 50, 52, 53, 63*n*30
hereditary bondage, 17, 22, 86
High Court of Australia, 37, 46, 50, 120
HIV prevention, 15
HIV/AIDS: children with, 214–15
Holocaust, 175*n*3, 202, 219
homophobia, 103
Honoré, Anthony, 38
honour crimes, 103, 122*n*11
housing rights, 24

human rights: abuses of, 232, 257–58, 272–73, 295; advocacy for, 297; and asylum law, 106; and asylum petitions, 102; and contemporary slavery, 9; as discourse, 23; and gender bias, 105; and human trafficking, 12, 15, 71; international agreements on, 245; interventions, 26; issues, 181, 187; and labour exploitation, 283; NGOs, 76; in North Korea, 268, 269; organizations, 76, 134; protection of, 7, 24; reporters, 151; scholarship, 181, 183; and social vulnerabilities, 23; violations of, 23, 27, 298; and women's rights, 131

Human Rights Commission of Pakistan, 88

human rights discourse: feminist critique of, 23

human rights law: international, 24, 27, 184, 272

Human Rights Watch (HRW), 88, 133, 137, 138, 257, 258, 266

Human Sciences Research Council (HSRC), 191

human smuggling. *See* human trafficking

human trafficking: agendas, 185; and anti-slavery rhetoric, 13; and border protection, 76, 90; and child domestic workers, 309–10; of children, 12, 54, 61, 68, 70, 203, 288, 326n38; classifications of, 70–73; as contemporary slavery, 17, 18, 20, 28, 68–70, 78, 82–83, 85, 87, 203, 231, 249, 280, 283; and criminality, 76, 84, 282; criticism of efforts to combat, 8; and debt bondage, 83; and domestic servitude, 83; domestic workers, 287; efforts to combat, 59–61; ethnic bonds in, 240; and exploitation, 86; and forced labour, 12, 78, 81,

83, 283; and forced marriage, 98; global awareness of, 5; human rights framework, 283–84; interventions, 27; for labour exploitation, 279; maximalist approach to, 78–89; and migration, 83–84, 85, 87; as moral panic, 21; and the "movement" requirement, 86–87; and NGOs, 134, 183; and organized crime, 69–70, 195; perpetrators of, 281–83; political reasons for expanding definition of, 87–88; problems of addressing, 5–7, 9; and prostitution, 20, 70, 75, 90; and sexual exploitation, 12–13, 144, 279, 282; studies, 199; Trafficking Protocol definition of, 81–82, 85–86; and the use of child soldiers, 83; victims of, 195–96. *See also* child labour; contemporary slavery; organ trafficking; sex trafficking; traffickers; trafficking in persons (TIPS) reports

humanism, 171

humanitarianism, 188

ICCPR (International Covenant on Civil and Political Rights), 260, 265, 273

iconographic conventions: massification, 168–69; on NGO websites, 164; personification, 165–66; rescue, 170–71

iconography, 10, 27, 175n5

identity: collective, 240, 245

Igbo people, 41

immigration: control, 196; illegal, 85; law, 196

immigration research: in South Africa, 194

imperialism, 135

impregnation, 130, 133

In re World War II Era Japanese Forced Labor Litigation, 209–10

incarceration, 73
incest, 59
indentured labour, 144. *See also* bonded labour; forced labour
India: advocacy work in, 300n28; bonded labour in, 16, 284; brick kilns in, 238; caste system in, 296, 298; child domestic workers in, 322; rescue and rehabilitation schemes in, 14; slavery in, 280, 288
Indian subcontinent: Bangladesh, 284, 319; bonded labour on, 87–88; hereditary bondage in, 86; indentured labour in, 144. *See also* India; Pakistan
inequality, 294–95, 297; cultural, 288; gender, 161, 218; racial, 161
informal economy, 231, 234, 238
Informal Sector Service Centre, 88
informed consent, 319–20. *See also* consent
Initiative pour la Résurgence du Mouvement Abolitionniste, 15
Institute for Security Studies, 189
International Covenant on Civil and Political Rights (ICCPR), 260, 265, 273
International Criminal Court (ICC), 45, 61, 133, 135, 269, 272; and North Korea, 270–71
international criminal law, 59, 135, 143; and gender crimes, 133
International Criminal Tribunal for the former Yugoslavia (ICTY), 46, 49, 60, 135, 270
International Criminal Tribunal for Rwanda (ICTR), 130, 135, 137, 141, 143
International Justice Mission (IJM), 164, 171, 176n6, 178n21, 286
International Labour Organization (ILO), 12, 43, 78, 80, 81, 88, 203,
234, 238, 241, 266, 283, 301, 309; standards for domestic work, 311–12, 315, 327n60
International Monetary Fund, 59
International Organization for Migration (IOM), 12, 88, 184, 185, 187, 188, 189, 192, 197, 200n5
INTERPOL, 184, 185, 196
Iraq, 259

Jackson, Mary, 294
Jackson, Robert, 133
Jal, Emmanuel, 131, 145, 148–49, 150
Japan: class action lawsuits against, 209–11
Japanese Americans, 213
Judiciary Act of 1789, 211
justice: compensatory, 219–20; redistributive, 220–21; restorative, 215, 217–18; retributive, 205–6, 215, 219; social, 25, 136; transitional, 225n49; vigilante, 25
juveniles: detained, 59. *See also* children

Kaesong industrial park, 260
Kalra, Monika, 139
Kamara, Mariatu, 131, 145, 146, 147, 148, 150
Kang, Grace, 270, 271
Kang Chol-hwan, 263
Kaplinsky, Raphael, 236
Kara, Siddharth, 233, 240
Kazakhstan, 11
Keosang industrial park, 267
Kerry, John, 78
kidnapping, 85, 194, 205, 269. *See also* abductions
Kim Il-Sung, 257, 258, 260, 262–63, 267
Kim Jong-Il, 257, 264, 270, 271, 272, 273
Kim Jong-Un, 257, 264, 272, 273

Korea. *See* North Korea; South Korea
Kuhn, Thomas, 182
Kupur, Ratna, 76
Kurasawa, Fuyuki, 10
Kuwait, 259

"L'abolition de l'esclavage dans les colonies françaises," 170
labour: exploitation, 8, 21, 79, 229–30, 231, 279 (*see also* exploitation); issues, 181; legislation, 161; malpractice, 232; management (*see* management issues); rights, 14, 248
land reform, 286
Langer, Lawrence, 132, 146, 147
Laogai camps, 255–56
Latin America, 80, 317. *See also* Caribbean; Central America; South America
law reform, 23, 24
League of Nations, 54, 55, 61
League of Nations Slavery Convention, 231
Lennon, John, 129
liberation theology, 25
Liberia, 130, 142, 151, 206, 225*n*51, 304
Libya, 271
logging, 159, 235, 237
Long Way Gone, A (Beah), 131
Lost Boys of Sudan, 148–49
Lugard, Frederick, 54
Lund-Thomsen, Peter, 247
Lyon Johnson, Kelli, 131

Madagascar, 11
Make Poverty History, 145
Mali, 15, 16
management issues: access and deployment of violence, 243–44, 248; accounting opacity, 242–43, 248; debt management, 240–42, 248; domain maintenance, 245–46, 248;

labour supply chain management, 239–40, 242, 248, 249; of modern slavery, 229–31; moral legitimization of slavery, 244, 248; slavery management capabilities, 238–39
management studies, 233
management theory, 233
Maori people, 207
Marbury v Madison, 211
marriage: *in absentia*, 98, 109, 117, 118; arranged, 97, 103, 104, 112; child, 58, 98; consent to, 23, 104; early, 11, 12, 17, 22, 59; servile, 12, 22, 43, 98, 133, 298; and slavery, 41; violence in, 102. *See also* forced marriage
Marshall, John, 211
Mauritania, 11, 15
McClelland, Susan, 146
Médicins Sans Frontières, 133
memoirs: of contemporary war, 131, 143–50; of Holocaust survivors, 145; of modern slavery, 131, 134, 143–50; of wartime violence, 142, 145, 151
Merry, Sally Engle, 25
micro-credit, 247
Middle East: migrant labourers in, 21; sale of women and children in, 83
Miers, Suzanne, 58
migrant workers, 21, 59, 88. *See also* farm labour
migrants: abuse and exploitation of, 69–70, 73, 79, 193; children as, 27; illegal, 161; prosecution of, 198; rights of, 14, 185. *See also* migration
migration, 8, 17, 181, 184, 193, 324; and anti-trafficking initiatives, 77; economic, 85; and exploitation, 22; forced, 235; and human trafficking, 83–84, 85, 87; illegal, 195; "open borders" approach to, 77; policing of, 71; rural-to-urban, 303, 312; "undesirable," 76. *See also* migrants

militarization, 73
Millbank, Jenni, 98, 104, 105
Milward, H.B., 240
mining, 235, 237, 291–92; artisanal, 12
Mitchell, Margaret, 129
modern slavery. *See* contemporary
  slavery
Modern Slavery Act (2015; United
  Kingdom), 103
modernity, 161, 182. *See also*
  postmodernity
Mongolia, 259
Mozambique, 57
Mugabe, Robert, 8
Mui Tsai system, 308
murder, 271
Murphy, Laura T., 131
Myers, B.R., 263

narratives. *See* rescue narratives; slave
  narratives
National Commission for Social
  Action (NaCSA), 129
National Rifle Association, 25
Nazer, Mende, 131
"Negro Hung Alive by the Ribs to
  a Gallows, A" (Blake), 165–66
"Negro's Complaint, The" (Cowper),
  168, 177*n*13
neocolonialism, 71. *See also*
  colonialism
Nepal, 309, 323
New Zealand: asylum petitions in,
  103; fishing in, 229
Niger, 15, 16
Nigeria, 41
Non-Aligned Movement, 57
non-governmental organization
  (NGOs): anti-slavery, 159, 164, 172,
  176*n*6, 232, 246–47; anti-trafficking,
  134, 183; and child domestic
  workers, 319; documenting gender

violence, 129–30, 133; for education
  and job training, 220; in the Global
  North, 11, 88; human rights, 76;
  in India, 87–88; international, 184;
  and situational violence, 158; in
  South Africa, 190; in West Africa, 15
North America: exploitation of farm
  workers in, 83. *See also* Canada;
  United States
North Korea: disposal of persons
  in, 268; drug trafficking in, 269;
  economic sanctions against, 269;
  famine in, 257, 259, 260–63; gulag
  labour camps in, 21, 258–60, 271;
  historical background, 257–58;
  humanitarian intervention in,
  269–70; as nuclear threat, 269–70,
  273; prisoners in gulag camps,
  260–64; prisoners of war in, 270;
  slave and forced labour in, 16, 283;
  state slavery in, 255–57, 267, 273
North Korea Human Rights Act
  (US, 2004), 269
Not for Sale, 164, 171, 176*n*6, 247
Nowrojee, Binaifer, 130, 137
Nuremberg Tribunal, 133

O'Connell Davidson, Julia, 75
Obama, Barack, 13, 77
organ trafficking, 12, 59, 60, 82, 203,
  326*n*38
Organization for Security and
  Co-operation in Europe, 12
organizational strategy, 234
organized crime: convention against,
  82; and trafficking, 69–70, 188, 195
Ouagadougou Action Plan to Combat
  Trafficking in Human Beings, 67
ownership: and the ability to sell,
  39–40, 43; and the aggregation
  of powers, 52; and the buying of
  persons, 62; as control, 39, 42; and

the destruction of a person, 62;
as dominion, 52–53; and profit, 41,
43, 62; and the right of the state
to expropriate, 42; and the right to
transfer ownership to an heir, 41;
and the right to use a person, 40–41,
43; and the right to use up property,
42, 43; rights of, 36, 38–39, 44, 48–49,
53, 54, 55, 56, 59, 61, 62, 121, 231,
232, 267, 271, 330–35; and the selling
of persons, 62

Pacific arena: forced labour in, 80
Pakistan, 246, 284; brick kilns in, 233,
238; child domestic workers in, 309
Pakistan Institute of Labour,
Education and Research, 88
party politics, 25
paternalism, 294, 302
patriarchy, 8
Patterson, Orlando, 38
peonage, 203
people smuggling. *See* human
trafficking
persecution, 97, 271; in asylum claims,
101–3, 105–7
personal service industries, 235
personification: and the enslaved
body, 165–67; and testimony, 167–68
Peru, 11, 321–22
Philippines: child domestic workers
in, 177*n*14, 323; domestic workers
in, 314
Plant, Roger, 249
Polaris Project, 11, 176*n*6
police violence, 25
policing, 193; transnational, 196
political question doctrine, 211
pornography, 281; child, 59
Portugal, 57; anti-slavery laws of, 14
Portuguese Guinea (Guinea-Bissau),
57

possession: as necessary to slavery,
39–42, 49, 52–53, 61, 267, 331–35.
See also ownership
post-colonialism, 135. *See also*
colonialism
postmodernity, 183. *See also* modernity
poverty: of children, 134, 216, 303–4;
as driving force of trafficking, 68,
188; efforts to combat, 24, 193; as
political cause of slavery, 229, 235,
247, 285, 286; and wartime rape,
134–35
prison labour. *See* forced labour;
gulag labour camps
prison populations. *See* gulag camp
prisoners
prisoners of war, 270
*Prosecutor v Alex Tamba Brima, Brima
Bazzy Kamara, and Satigie Borbor
Kanu*, 140
Prosecutor v Charles Ghankay Taylor,
136
*Prosecutor v Issa Hassan Sesay, Morris
Kallon, Augustine Gbao*, 140
Prosecutor v Jean-Paul Akayesu, 137, 139
Prosecutor v Kunarac et al., 46, 60, 270
*Prosecutor v Theoneste Bagosora, Gratien
Kabiligi, Aloys Ntabakuze, and Anatole
Nsengiyumva*, 137
prostitution, 8, 15, 17, 22, 46–47, 60,
68, 77, 79, 82, 241, 281, 326*n*38; and
anti-trafficking initiatives, 77; child,
326*n*38; differing views of, 20–21,
281–82; efforts to combat, 15, 77;
and exploitation, 59; and human
trafficking, 8, 20, 45, 60, 70, 75, 79–80,
82, 90, 326*n*38; legal status of, 21,
68; as slavery, 17, 18, 20, 22, 46–47;
in Thailand, 216–19, 241. *See also*
commercial sex work
Protocol to Prevent, Suppress and
Punish Trafficking in Persons,

especially Women and Children (2000; Trafficking Protocol), 12, 59, 60, 75, 188, 221n2, 282; Article 6, 204
punishments: corporal and criminal, 23–24

Qatar, 260, 269
quantum meruit, 210
The Queen v Tang, 37, 46, 47, 48, 50–51, 53, 61, 120, 121
Quirk, Joel, 266, 267, 268

Raab, J., 240
racial inequalities, 161. *See also* inequality
racism, 161; in North Korea, 257, 263
Rantsev v Cyprus and Russia, 45, 62n7
rape: as an act of genocide, 133, 137, 144; as criminal justice issue, 188; in international criminal law, 143–44; within marriage, 102; narrative of, 148; in Rwanda, 137–38, 140; spousal, 102; as torture, 144; and trafficking, 195; during wartime, 130, 133, 135; as a weapon of war, 137
Rassam, Yasmine, 232
reconciliation, 212–13, 219, 225n49, 284. *See also* Truth and Reconciliation Commissions (TRCs)
redistributive justice, 220–21
redress: civil, 205, 206–7, 209–12, 219–20; criminal, 205–6, 219; for victims, 202–6
refugees: North Korean, 261, 270–71; in South Africa, 184. *See also* asylum seekers; migrants
religious right, 59
renegade economy, 237
reparations, 22, 208–9; atonement model, 212–19; community-directed, 218, 220; for enslavement, 22;

rehabilitative, 220; tort model of, 209–12; victim-directed, 218, 220
rescue: iconography of, 170–71; politics of, 72–73; of slaves, 170–71
rescue industry, 72–73
rescue narratives, 279
Research Network on the Legal Parameters of Slavery, 62
Restavec (Cadet), 131, 145, 150
restavèk children, 309
restorative justice, 215, 217–18
retributive justice, 205–6, 215, 219
Revolutionary United Front (RUF; Rwanda), 140–41
Rhodesia, 57
Richards, Kathy, 246
rights advocacy, 23, 24
Rigoulot, Pierre, 258
Romania, 11
Rome Statute of the International Criminal Court (1998), 37, 45, 60, 61, 133
Rosewood Compensation Act (1994), 209
Russia, 255, 259, 271, 289
Rwanda, 130, 151; genocide in, 136–37; Revolutionary United Front (RUF), 140–41
Rwanda: Death, Despair and Defiance, 137

sanctuary, 85
Saudi Arabia, 271
Schaffer, Kay, 134–35, 142
Second World War: forced labour during, 205, 209; sexual enslavement of Korean women, 142. *See also* Holocaust
serfdom, 12, 43, 55, 56, 335
servitude. *See* slavery
sex tourism, 59

sex trafficking, 15, 83, 84, 188, 193, 240, 282. *See also* commercial sex work; human trafficking; prostitution; sexual exploitation; sexual slavery

sex work. *See* commercial sex work; prostitution; sex trafficking

Sex Worker Education and Advocacy Taskforce, 189

sexual abuse, 71, 214, 310–11; commercial, 78–79

sexual assault within marriage, 102

sexual exploitation: efforts to combat, 13; forced marriage as, 97; and human trafficking, 12, 60, 69–71, 82, 86, 279, 282, 286, 326n38; as slavery, 11, 22; in Thailand, 205, 216–19. *See also* sex trafficking; sexual slavery

sexual servitude, 78

sexual slavery: and forced conjugal association, 99; and forced marriage, 120; as modern slavery, 203, 220; during the Second World War, 133; and trafficking, 70, 89, 282; in wartime, 130, 133, 142. *See also* sex trafficking; sexual exploitation

sexual violence, 71, 135, 138, 139, 141, 142, 143, 302; in marriage, 102

sexuality, 8

Shahinian, Gulnara, 11

Shattered Lives (HRW), 138

Shen, Anqi, 288

Sherwin, Richard, 134

Siberia, 259. *See also* Soviet Union

Sierra Leone, 103, 130, 131, 142, 146, 150, 151; forced marriage in, 141

Sierra Leone International Court. *See* Special Court for Sierra Leone (SCSL)

Siliadin v France, 45, 47

Slaughter, Joseph, 27

Slave (Nazer), 131

slave labour: stages of, 239. *See also* forced labour

slave labour camps. *See* gulag labour camps

slave narratives, 131, 132, 144; modern, 27, 131, 149

slave trade, 55; definition of, 55; in Ethiopia, 54; and human trafficking, 85; transatlantic, 10, 27, 59, 160–61, 163, 166, 168–69, 172–74, 175n3; "white," 18, 70, 72, 279

slaveholders, 283, 287; and emancipation, 280; lived experiences of, 293; response to emancipation, 294–97; viewpoints of, 291–94. *See also* traffickers

slavery: abolition of, 10, 54, 171, 172, 231, 279; chattel, 44, 46, 120, 279; conjugal, 136; contemporary visual signifiers of, 162; as a criminal offense, 60; *de facto*, 48, 51, 62, 121; *de jure*, 44, 46, 48, 51, 62, 121; by descent, 11; determining factors, 333–34; as different from trafficking, 28; economic benefits of, 232–33; geographical context of, 238; historical systems of, 15, 16, 22; and the industry context, 234–38; in the informal economy, 231, 234, 238; involuntary servitude, 203; and management, 231–34; management capabilities, 238–39; in mines, 144; moral legitimization of, 244, 248; perpetrators of, 294–98; possession as necessary to, 39–42, 49, 52–53, 61, 267, 331–35; practices similar to, 37, 43, 57–58, 60, 65, 82, 179, 221, 334, 335–36; privately imposed, 232; property paradigm of, 36, 38–39;

reintegration from, 290; state, 267,
273; state-sponsored, 255–57; value
trap, 236, 239, 247; in the workplace,
231–32. *See also* child domestic
workers (CDWs); commercial sex
work; contemporary slavery; debt
bondage; enslavement; exploitation;
forced conjugal association (FCA);
forced marriage; human trafficking;
prostitution; sexual slavery; slave
trade; slavery definitions; slaves
Slavery Convention (1926), 36, 44, 49,
51, 54, 55, 56, 121, 264
slavery definitions: contemporary,
231; contemporary relevance of
1926 definition, 44–53; genesis of,
61; legal, 42–43, 175*n*1, 330; 1926
definition, 45, 47–48, 53–61, 55, 267;
sociological, 132; understanding,
37–44;
slaves: lived experiences of, 37, 144–45,
167–68
Smith, Sidonie, 134–35, 142
social constructivism, 183
social justice, 25, 136
social weighting, 244
socialism, 25
sorcery, 112. *See also* witchcraft
South Africa: anti-trafficking
agenda in, 185, 188; apartheid in,
57; apologies for apartheid, 208;
criminal justice in, 195, 197–98;
foreign aid to, 187; post-apartheid,
213; prevalence of trafficking in,
193–98; refugee and migration
rights in, 184; slavery in, 55;
trafficking in, 6, 180–81, 189–90,
193; transitional justice in, 225*n*49.
See also Truth and Reconciliation
Commissions (TRCs)
South African National Prosecuting
Authority, 184

South American countries: Bolivia,
25; Ecuador, 11; Peru, 11, 321–22.
See also Brazil
South Asia: child domestic workers in,
304; slavery in, 280–81. *See also* Asia;
Asian countries
South Asian Coalition on Child
Servitude, 88
South Korea: relationship with North
Korea, 270
Southeast Asia: enslavement of
fishermen in, 83
Southern African Counter Trafficking
Assistance Programme (SACTAP),
185, 187, 188, 192, 193, 197; budget
figures, 186
Soviet Union, 255, 259, 271, 283
Spain, 229
Special Court for Sierra Leone (SCSL),
99, 129, 135, 136, 140, 143
state slavery, 255–57, 267, 273
statute of limitations, 211–12
Stojanovska, Marija, 285
*Stolen Angels: The Kidnapped Girls
of Uganda*, 131
storytelling, 133, 136; by children, 319;
as commodification, 148
strategic fit, 234
sub-Saharan Africa, 80. *See also* Africa;
African countries
Sudan, 131, 148–49
Sudan People's Liberation Army
(SPLA), 149
Sumapi, 314
Supplementary Convention on
the Abolition of Slavery, the Slave
Trade, and Institutions and Practices
Similar to Slavery (1956), 37, 43, 55,
56–57, 58, 264, 335
supply chains, 12, 21, 86, 88, 236;
global, 22, 269; management of,
239–40, 242, 248, 249

surveillance, 73
survivor victims, 27–28, 142–45,
    141, 286, 290, 297, 300*n*28; asylum
    applications of 99, 104, 109, 114–15;
    narratives of, 120–21, 129–35, 138;
    protection for, 313; rescue and
    rehabilitation of, 281; trafficked
    persons as, 281
*Survivors of Slavery: Modern-Day Slave
    Narratives* (Murphy), 131–32
symbolic analogy. *See* analogical
    juxtaposition

Tanzania, 57, 322
Temedt, 15
Temporary Slavery Commission
    (League of Nations), 55, 308
testimonies: legal, 27, 151; of the
    slave's experience, 167–68; of
    survivors, 120–21, 129–35, 138;
    of wartime violence, 131
Thai Buddhism, 217
Thailand, 246; sexual exploitation in,
    205, 216–19
Timidria, 15
To Plead Our Own Cause (Bales and
    Trodd), 131, 144–45
Togo, 108–9, 113, 114; child domestic
    workers in, 321–22
torture, 112–13, 214, 271; rape as, 144;
    of slaves, 166–67
Torture Victim Protection Act,
    212
traffickers: as criminals, 288, 290;
    human rights activists' conception of,
    285–87; shaming method of dealing
    with, 287. *See also* slaveholders;
    human trafficking
trafficking. *See* human trafficking;
    sex trafficking
"Trafficking is Modern Slavery"
    campaign, 169, 173

trafficking in persons. *See* human
    trafficking; sex trafficking
trafficking in persons (TIPS) reports,
    13, 77, 78, 83, 86, 187; on South
    Africa, 193
Trafficking Protocol, 80, 81, 88, 212;
    definition of trafficking, 85–86
transitional justice, 225*n*49
trauma tourism, 129
treaties, 47
Trodd, Zoe, 131
Truth and Reconciliation
    Commissions (TRCs), 130, 135, 206,
    215–16
truth and reconciliation processes, 284
Tuskegee syphilis experiment, 208

Uganda, 131, 142
underpayment, 232
Unfair Compensation Act (UCA), 211
UNIFEM (UN Women) skills training,
    129
Union of South Africa. *See* South
    Africa
unionization, 25
United Kingdom: abolition of slavery
    in, 172, 279; asylum claims in, 103,
    115; asylum legislation in, 102–3;
    legislation against forced marriage,
    103; redistributive justice in, 220
United Nations (UN), 56, 61
United Nations Children's Fund, 12,
    145
United Nations Convention
    Concerning the Abolition of Forced
    Labour (1959), 265–66
United Nations Convention
    Concerning Decent Work for
    Domestic Workers, 311–12
United Nations Convention
    Concerning the Prohibition
    and Immediate Action for the

Elimination of the Worst Forms of Child Labour (Child Labour Convention), 311

United Nations Convention for the Protection of Human Rights and Fundamental Freedoms (ECHR), 45, 102

United Nations Convention Relating to the Status of Refugees (Refugee Convention), 102

United Nations Convention on the Rights of the Child (UNCRC), 313

United Nations Convention against Transnational Organized Crime, 82, 195

United Nations General Assembly (UNGA), 272

United Nations Global Initiative to Fight Human Trafficking (UN.GIFT), 12, 67

United Nations High Commissioner for Refugees (UNHCR), 102, 184

United Nations Human Rights Council, 272

United Nations Office of Drugs and Crime (UNODC), 12, 185

United Nations Office of the High Commissioner for Human Rights, 12

United Nations Rapporteur on Trafficking in Persons, 12, 67

United Nations Security Council (UNSC), 272

United Nations Special Rapporteur on Contemporary Forms of Slavery, 11

United Nations Working Group on Contemporary Forms of Slavery, 12, 58, 267

United States: abolition of slavery in, 279; anti-trafficking policies and legislation in, 13, 19–21, 60, 71, 77, 90, 281; asylum law in, 98; asylum petitions in, 101–2, 103; definition of modern slavery, 222n3; domestic minor trafficking in, 16; funding for anti-slavery initiatives, 14–15; human trafficking in, 288; monitoring of global anti-trafficking efforts by, 77; prison industrial complex, 77; redistributive justice in, 220; religious right in, 59

Universal Declaration of Human Rights (1948), 265

universality of rights, 105

unjust enrichment, 210

unlawful recruitment, 83

US Department of Labor, 229–30

US Department of State, 13, 77, 203

Uzbekistan, 229, 256

value chain analysis, 236, 242

value trap slavery, 236, 239, 247

victims. *See* survivor victims

Victims of Trafficking and Violence Protection Act (Victims of Trafficking Act), 19, 59, 65n52, 77, 281

Vienna Convention on the Law of Treaties (VCLT, 1969), 47, 49

vigilante justice, 25

Vigneswaran, Darshan, 6

violence: access and deployment of, 248; against asylum seekers, 107–8; against child domestic workers, 306; associated with slavery, 10; domestic, 26, 294; economic, 135; in modern slavery, 243–44; police, 25; sexual, 71, 104, 130, 135, 138, 139, 141, 142, 143, 302; situational, 158, 175n2; state, 145; structural, 135, 175n2; and trafficking, 203; wartime, 27, 147–48; against women, 130, 131, 135. *See also* gender-based violence

visual symbols, 162. *See also* analogical juxtaposition
Volunteers for Social Justice, 88

Waldron-Ramsey, Waldo, 57, 58, 64–65n46
Walk Free Foundation, 98, 283
War Child, 145
War Child (Jal), 131, 148–49
Warsaw Ghetto, 207
wartime: abuses, 22; captivity, 22; casualties, 132; violence, 27, 147–48
Webb, Justin, 237
Wei Tang, 120–21, 121
West Africa: anti-trafficking initiatives in, 15, 313; child domestic workers in, 316; child fostering in, 304; cocoa industry in, 229, 248; hereditary bondage in, 86. *See also* Africa; African countries
West Bengal, 306
"white" slavery, 18, 70, 72, 279
widows: inheritance of, 58; as property, 41. *See also* women
William Wilberforce Trafficking Victims Protection Reauthorization Act of 2008, 60, 65n52
Wilson, Richard, 135, 150
witchcraft, 112–13, 115–16

witnessing, 131, 138, 142, 145; collective, 145; ethical, 145, 156n88; national, 155n60
Wittgenstein, Ludwig, 182
women: abduction of, 137, 140, 141; agency of, 76, 89; as domestic workers, 311–12, 324; education for, 220; forced to kill, 142; inheritance of, 41, 58, 336; Korean, 135, 142, 145, 271; narratives of, 120–21, 129–35, 138; as property, 41; reluctance to testify to rape, 138; respect for, 220, 284; rights of, 25; sale of, 12, 83; sexual exploitation of, 216–19; as single mothers, 117; trafficking of, 54, 61, 203; as victims, 175; violence against, 130, 131, 135. *See also* commercial sex work; forced marriage; marriage; prostitution
workers: protection for, 324
Workers' Party of Korea, 260
World Bank, 59
World Cup of football (FIFA). *See* FIFA World Cup

Your Justice Is Too Slow (Nowrojee), 130

zero tolerance approach, 179
Zimbabwe, 193, 194